The Complete Guide to
Blender Graphics

Blender™ is a **free Open-Source 3D Computer Modeling and Animation Suite** incorporating Character Rigging, Particles, Real World Physics Simulation, Sculpting, Video Editing with Motion Tracking and 2D Animation within the 3D Environment.

Blender is **FREE** to download and use by anyone for anything.

The Complete Guide to Blender Graphics: Computer Modeling and Animation, Eighth Edition is a unified manual describing the operation of the program, updated with reference to the Graphical User Interface for **Blender Version 3.2.2**, including additional material covering **Blender Assets, Geometry Nodes, and Non-Linear Animation**.

Divided into a two-volume set, the book introduces the program's Graphical User Interface and shows how to implement tools for modeling and animating characters and created scenes with the application of color, texture, and special lighting effects.

Key Features:

- The book provides instruction for New Users starting at the very beginning.
- Instruction is presented in a series of chapters incorporating visual reference to the program's interface.
- The initial chapters are designed to instruct the user in the operation of the program while introducing and demonstrating interesting features of the program.
- Chapters are developed in a building block fashion providing forward and reverse reference to relevant material.

Both volumes are available in a discounted set, which can also be purchased together with **Blender 2D Animation: The Complete Guide to the Grease Pencil**.

Abut the author

John M. Blain has become a recognised expert in Blender having seven successful prior editions of this book to date. John became enthused with Blender on retirement from a career in Mechanical Engineering. *The Complete Guide to Blender Graphics* originated from personal notes compiled in the course of self-learning. The notes were recognized as an ideal instruction source by Neal Hirsig, Senior Lecturer (Retired) at Tufts University. Neal encouraged publication of the First Edition and in doing so is deserving of the author's gratitude. Gratitude must also be extended to the author's wife Helen for her continuing encouragement and patience as new editions of the book are compiled.

T0133703

The Complete Guide to
Blender Graphics
Computer Modeling
& Animation

EIGHTH EDITION

Volume 1

JOHN M. BLAIN

CRC Press
Taylor & Francis Group
Boca Raton London New York

CRC Press is an imprint of the
Taylor & Francis Group, an **informa** business

AN A K PETERS BOOK

Eight edition published 2024
by CRC Press
2385 Executive Center Drive, Suite 320, Boca Raton, FL 33431

and by CRC Press
4 Park Square, Milton Park, Abingdon, Oxon, OX14 4RN

CRC Press is an imprint of Taylor & Francis Group, LLC

© 2024 John M. Blain

First edition published by AK Peters 2012
Second edition published by AK Peters 2014
Third edition published by AK Peters 2016
Fourth edition published by AK Peters 2017
Fifth edition published by AK Peters 2019
Sixth edition published by AK Peters 2020
Seventh edition published by AK Peters 2022

ISBN: 978-1-032-51058-3 (hbk)
ISBN: 978-1-032-51060-6 (pbk)
ISBN: 978-1-003-40091-2 (ebk)

DOI: 10.1201/9781003400912

Publisher's note: This book has been prepared from camera-ready copy provided by the authors.

Printed in Great Britain by Bell and Bain Ltd, Glasgow

Contents

Introduction

The Complete Guide to Blender Graphics - 8th Edition provides instruction in the use of the Computer Graphics 3D Program **Blender.** The book has been compiled in two separate volumes with Volume 1 being inclusive of all material allowing a new user to obtain, install and operate the program. Volume 2 is complementary to Volume 1 encompassing some of the more advanced aspects of the program. The books are an operation manual for those who wish to undertake a learning experience and discover a wonderful creative new world of computer graphics. The books also serve as a reference for established operators.

Instructions throughout the books introduce Blender's features with examples and diagrams referenced to the **Graphical User Interface (GUI)**.

The **Graphical User Interface** is the arrangement of windows or panels displayed on the computer Screen when the program is in operation.

The Complete Guide to Blender Graphics originated when Blender's Graphical User Interface was transformed with the release of Blender version 2.50. Subsequent editions of the book have kept pace with developments to the program and have included new material.

The **8th Edition of The Complete Guide to Blender Graphics** is applicable to:
Blender Version 3.2.2

The Blender program is maintained by the **Blender Foundation** and released as **Open Source Software** which is available for download and **FREE** to be used for any purpose.

The program may be downloaded from: www.blender.org

Blender is a 3D Computer Graphics Program with tools for modeling and animating objects and characters and creating background scenes. Scenes may be made into still images. Animated sequences may be used for video production. Models and Scenes are enhanced with color and texture producing brilliant realistic effects. The still images and video may be for artistic appreciation or employed as architectural or scientific presentations. There are also tools for 2D animation production. Stand-alone models may be used for 3D Printing.

The Complete Guide to Blender Graphics provides a fantastic learning experience in **Computer Graphics** using **Blender,** by introducing the operation of the Blender program through the use of its Graphical user Interface. The book is intended to be read in conjunction with having the program in operation, with the interface displayed.

Instruction is presented using the tools displayed in the Graphical User Interface, with basic examples demonstrating results. Understanding where tools are located, their uses and how they are implemented will allow the reader to more easily follow detailed instruction in the many written and video tutorials available on the Internet.

Instruction provided on the internet in the form of written and video tutorials is integral to the compendium of Blender learning material. Although comprehensive, **The Complete Guide to Blender Graphics** is limited by the number of pages in a single volume. The internet vastly expands the knowledge base of learning material.

Important: The Blender Program is continually being developed with new features being added and improvements to the interface and operation procedures being amended. When reading instructions or viewing video tutorials the version of the Blender program for which the instruction is written should be considered.

Program Evolution

Blender is continually evolving. New versions of the program are released as additions and changes are incorporated, therefore, it is advisable to check the Blender website, from time to time for the latest version.

At each release of Blender, a different **Splash Screen Image** is displayed in the interface.

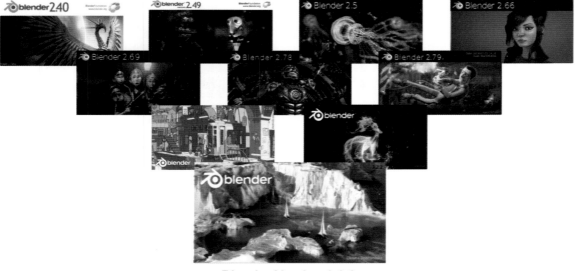

Blender Version 3.2.2

Earlier versions of the program and documentation may be obtained which provide valuable information when you are conversant with the current release of the program. Video tutorials available on the internet may not strictly adhere to the current user interface or workflow. Major transformations occurred when the program changed from version 2.49 to 2.50 and again at the change from version 2.79 to version 2.82. Since 2.82 development has continued.

Previous releases of the Blender program may be downloaded at:

https://download.blender.org/release/

Blender Features

A comprehensive display of the Blender features is available at:

www.blender.org/features/

Modeling   Animation

Blender Platforms

A **computing platform** or **digital platform** is the environment in which a piece of <u>software</u> is executed. It may be the <u>hardware</u> or the <u>operating system</u> (OS)

Blender is a cross-platform application for **Windows , Linux** and **MacOS** operating systems.

The operation of Blender in **The Complete Guide to Blender Graphics** applies to all operating platforms but operations ancillary to the program, such as saving work to the computer's hard drive, have been described exclusively using a Windows operating system.

System Requirements

The System Requirements to run Blender are usually expressed in terms of computer power alone but the hardware package employed also determines the results that can be achieved.

To try Blender you do not have to outlay thousands of dollars on expensive computers and monitors. The Blender software is free to download and use for anything you wish and may be run on a modest laptop or PC.

The equipment you employ will depend on your aspirations and at what level you wish to operate Blender. Blender is a fantastic program that is capable of producing amazing results but a new user should be aware that the fantastic displays depicted in demonstration reels will not be achieved unless a computer with sufficient power and a display screen (monitor) to match is available.

Give the program a go no matter what equipment you have. When you see what Blender can do you will be surprised, then you can go get all that super gear and expand your horizons to the limit.

As a starter the following equipment specifications are offered:

General Equipment

A Laptop or Desktop PC both with a Three Button Mouse connected. You may use the Laptop touchpad but Blender is designed for Mouse operation. A Laptop screen will suffice to start with but a reasonably large Monitor is preferable. You will discover that, as you progress, multiple monitors make life a whole heap better.

The following specifications are found on the Blender website:

Ready for Action.

Whether it's on a USB stick, sitting on a folder on your desktop, or fully installed, Blender runs out of the box.

No installation needed.
No internet connection required.

 Truly portable, take it with you wherever you go!

Runs anywhere

Blender is cross-platform, it runs on every major operating system:

 Windows 8.1, 10, and 11

 MacOS 10.13 Intel – 11.0 Apple Silicon

 Linux

All efforts to make Blender work on specific configurations are welcome, but can only officially be supported by those used by active developers.

For Windows, there is an installer available if you wish to add an icon on the desktop, associate .blend file extension, etc.

Hardware Requirements

Minimum

64-bit quad core CPU with SSE2 support
8 GB RAM
Full HD display
Mouse, trackpad or pen+tablet
Graphics card with 2 GB RAM, OpenGL 4.3
Less than 10 year old

Recommended

64-bit eight core CPU
32 GB RAM
2561440 display
Three button mouse or pen-tablet
Graphics card with 8 GB RAM

Hardware requirements are generally referring to the speed or power of your computer in terms of how many cores the CPU has (Central Processing Unit) and the amount of memory (RAM) available. To run a program, in basic terms, information is first stored (installed) on the hard drive.

When you run the program information is transferred to memory (RAM). If there is not enough RAM available only some of the information gets transferred, therefore, the computer has to swap information between the hard drive and memory as the program is run. This slows the process down. The more RAM you have the better.

With a graphics program, running the program entails processing which creates a visual display on the computer screen. This process is called **Rendering**. Again, generally speaking, you may consider the running of the program to be done by the Central Processing Unit (CPU) which will include Rendering. Rendering may be much faster if the processing is performed by the GPU which is a dedicated processing unit incorporated in the Graphics Card. A GPU has its own dedicated RAM.

Having an adequate Graphics Card with enough power and RAM is, therefore, an important consideration.

Blender Supported Graphics Cards

Always make sure to install the latest drivers from the graphics card manufacturer website. These requirements are for basic Blender operation, Cycles rendering using the GPU has higher requirements.

NVIDIA

GeForce 400 and newer, Quadro Tesla GPU architecture and newer, including RTX-based cards, with NVIDIA drivers (list of all GeForce and Quadro GPUs)

AMD

GCN 1st gen and newer. Since Blender 2.91, Terascale 2 architecture is fully deprecated, try using 2.90 (albeit not supported, it might still work) [list of all AMD GPUs]

Intel

Haswell architecture and newer. [list of all Intel GPUs]

macOS

Version **10.13** or newer for Intel processors on supported hardware. Version **11.0** for Arm-based processors (Apple Silicon).

Previous Versions of Blender

As previously stated, Blender is continually evolving with new versions being released. To fully utilise internet material you may find it advantageous to study older tutorials by installing previous Blender versions. Previous versions of the program can be obtained at:

https://download.blender.org/release/

Index of /release/

```
../
Blender1.0/                11-Jul-2020 07:17
Blender1.60/               05-Jul-2020 16:22
Blender1.73/               20-Aug-2003 11:13
Blender1.80/               20-Aug-2003 11:13
Blender2.04/               20-Aug-2003 11:13
Blender2.26/               20-Aug-2003 11:13

Blender2.93/               03-Aug-2022 08:58    -
Blender3.0/                26-Jan-2022 13:21    -
Blender3.1/                01-Apr-2022 08:23    -
Blender3.2/                03-Aug-2022 08:58    -
BlenderBenchmark1.0/       17-Aug-2018 12:31    -
BlenderBenchmark2.0/       20-Jan-2020 14:19    -
Publisher2.25/             20-Aug-2003 11:13    -
plugin/                    23-Nov-2004 12:56    -
yafray.0.0.6/              03-Feb-2004 22:31    -
yafray.0.0.7/              05-Aug-2004 10:33    -
GPL-license.txt            19-Aug-2013 11:54    17997
GPL3-license.txt           19-Aug-2013 11:54    35147
blender2.04-ipaq.zip       20-Aug-2003 11:14    2048262
```

Installation

Note: You may install multiple versions of Blender on you PC. See; **Download and Installation**.

Download & Installation

Download Blender from: **www.blender.org**

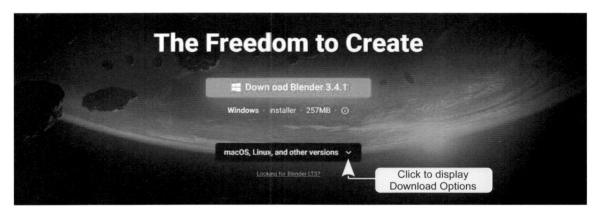

Select the current Blender version which applies to your operating system. Blender is available for **Windows**, **MacOS**, **Linux** and **Steam**.

Clicking the download button on a Windows operating system saves the **Installer Package** to the **Downloads Folder**.

Download Options ——➤

The options are available to download a **.msi installer package** or a **ZIP Archive** for **Windows** and packages for other Operating Systems.

Installation on a Windows Operating System

Installing with the Installer(.msi) Option

Double-click on the file name in the Downloads folder, follow the prompts and Blender will be automatically installed in the **Program Files** folder on your computer and an icon will be placed on your **Desktop**.

Installing with the ZIP Option

In some cases, you may download a compressed ZIP File instead of an MSI Installer.

With a ZIP file, you have to unzip the file. You first create a new folder on your computer's hard drive then use a program like 7-Zip or Win-Zip to unzip (decompress) the zip file into the new folder.

When the file is unzipped into the new folder you will see **blender.exe** as one of the entries. You double click on this to run Blender or you create a shortcut that places an icon on your desktop.

When using either installation option you double-click the **blender.exe** file to run the program. Shortcuts on the Desktop are shortcuts to the blender.exe file.

Note: By having one version of Blender installed via the Installer(.msi) option and another using the ZIP method you can have more than one Blender version installed on your computer at the same time. This is useful for version comparison or for development purposes.

Installing Blender on a Linux Operating System

macOS

https://docs.blender.org/manual/en/latest/getting_started/installing/macos.html

Linux

https://docs.blender.org/manual/en/latest/getting_started/installing/linux.html

Opening (Running) the Program

When you open Blender for the first time you will see the Screen display as shown above with the Splash Screen in the center. At this point, the Splash Screen Panel contains several buttons (Text Annotations) for **Quick Setup Options**.

Be aware that Blender may be customized to personal preferences. The diagram above shows the Blender Screen as it displays when Blender is first opened following installation. The display Theme is called **Blender Dark** which is one of several in-built Themes available.

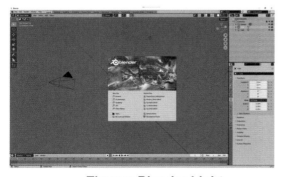

Theme: Blender Light

Theme: Blender Modo

How to select a different Theme will be explained later.

The Author

John M. Blain

John was born in Swindon, Wiltshire in England in 1942. At the time of writing this makes him a pretty old dude. He emigrated to Canada with his family in 1952 and now lives in Coffs Harbour, New South Wales in Australia.

Drawing and painting were skills John developed from an early age and while attending school on Vancouver Island he became interested in wood sculpture inspired by the work of the indigenous west coast people. Artistic pursuits were curtailed on graduating from high school when he returned to England to undertake a technical engineering apprenticeship. Following his apprenticeship, he worked for a short period in England and then made the decision to return to Vancouver, Canada. On the voyage between Southampton and Vancouver, he met his wife to be and Vancouver became a stopover for a journey to Sydney Australia. In this new country, he began work as an engineering draughtsman, married, had children and studied engineering. The magic milestone of seven years saw John with his young family move out of the city to the coastal town of Coffs Harbour, New South Wales.

Coffs Harbour was a center for sawmill machinery and John became engaged in machinery design and manufacture. He acquired a sound knowledge of this industry acting as installation engineer then progressing to sales. This work afforded travel throughout Australia, Canada, the United States and New Zealand.

On retirement, artistic pursuits returned with additional interests in writing and computing. Writing notes whilst learning computer animation using Blender resulted in **The Complete Guide to Blender Graphics**. The first edition, published in 2012, was well received and encouraged John to compile a second edition inline with the latest version of the Blender program. This afforded the opportunity to include new material. Subsequent editions have followed until this newly reformatted eighth edition.

Preamble

The **Preamble** will walk you through the method of reading this book in conjunction with operating the Blender program. Operating the Blender program entails entering commands via the computer Keyboard and Mouse. Commands are entered in the **Graphical User Interface (GUI)** which is the display on the monitor (computer Screen). Entering a command is accomplished by positioning the Mouse Cursor in the Screen on a control point (button) and clicking the Mouse Button or entering (Typing) values into specific Screen locations via the Keyboard.

The Fundamental Objective in using a computer graphics program, such as **Blender**, is to produce a display on a computer Screen that **Renders** (converts) into a digital image or series of images for an animation sequence. The display may only contain a single inanimate model or Object, such as that used for 3D printing but will usually contain multiple 3D models of animate and or inanimate Objects. The arrangement of **Objects** displayed against a background constitutes a **Scene**. Animate Objects (animated Objects) are the moving characters in animation sequences. Inanimate Objects are the components of a Scene with which the characters interact. These may be obstacles in a Scene, such as, ground planes, terrain and background objects.

In Blender the **components of a Scene** such as models of characters, models of objects, lamps and lighting providing scene illumination and cameras determining what part of a scene is captured and rendered are all said to be **Objects**.

Assumption

Before you begin to read this book it is assumed you know how to operate a computer. In the past this assumption meant you knew how to operate using a **Keyboard** and **Mouse**. Today many of you will be more familiar with touch screens or laptop touch pads, therefore, although this may appear to be a retrograde step the first instruction will be to familiarise you with Mouse and Keyboard operations.

Blender has been designed to be operated using a Keyboard and Mouse and instruction will be provided using these devices. You may of course adapt a drawing tablet and stylus.

Formats Conventions and Commands

In writing this book, the following formatting conventions have been adopted:

> Paragraphs are separated by an empty line and have not been indented.

> Keywords and phrases are printed in **bold text** with the first letter of a component name specific to Blender capitalised.

> Headings are printed in Bold Olive Green.

The following conventions are used when giving instructions.

When using a Mouse connected to a computer, the commands will be:

Click or **Click LMB** – In either case, this means make a single click with the left mouse button with the Mouse Cursor positioned over a control on the computer Screen.

In some instances, it is explicit that the left mouse button should be used.

Note: Computer Screen and Monitor are synonymous.

Mouse Over: Place the Mouse Cursor over a control.

A **Control** is a specific area of the Computer Screen.

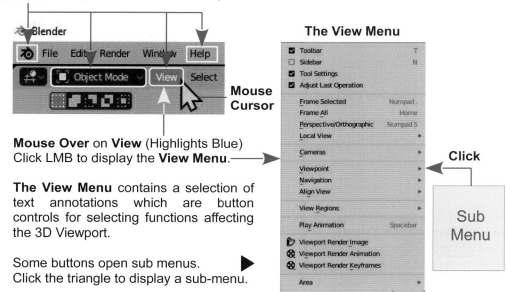

Mouse Over on **View** (Highlights Blue)
Click LMB to display the **View Menu**.

The View Menu contains a selection of text annotations which are button controls for selecting functions affecting the 3D Viewport.

Some buttons open sub menus.
Click the triangle to display a sub-menu.

A Control: A designated area on the computer Screen represented by an icon in the form of a button or bar, with or without text annotation.

Double Click – Make two clicks in quick succession with LMB (the left mouse button).

Click, Hold and Drag – Click the left mouse button, hold it depressed while moving the mouse. Release the button at the end of the movement.

Click RMB – Click the right mouse button.

Click MMB – Click the middle mouse button.
(the middle mouse button may be the scroll wheel).

Clicking is used in conjunction with placing the Mouse Cursor over a button, icon or a slider that is displayed on the Screen.

Scroll MMB – Scroll (rotate) the scroll wheel (MMB).

The Graphical User Interface (GUI)

When Blender is first opened what you see on the computer Screen is the **Graphical User Interface (GUI)** for the program. This arrangement of panels is the interface which allows you to communicate with the program by entering commands (data) using the Keyboard and Mouse previously described. The panels that you see are called **Editors** or **Headers**, with one exception, the **Splash Screen**.

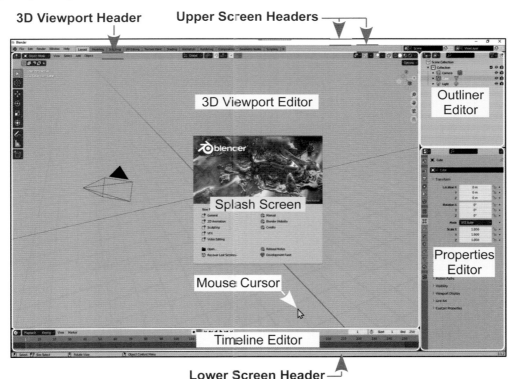

Note: In the diagram above, the different Editors have been colored to distinguish one from the other. Changing Editor background colors modifies the color scheme or Theme of the GUI. The Theme of the GUI in the diagram is different from what you see when you first run Blender.

> How to download and install the Blender program has been previously described.
> (see **Download and Installation**).

Running Blender for the First Time

To run Blender, you activate the Blender Application file ' 🔵 blender ' (blender.exe) in the folder where the program has been installed on your computer.

On a PC with a Windows operating system, you double-click the logo that has been placed on your Desktop.

The first time Blender runs the Graphical User Interface displays on the computer Screen with a default Theme or color scheme named **Blender Dark**. You will see this as one of the **Quick Setup options** in the **Splash Screen**.

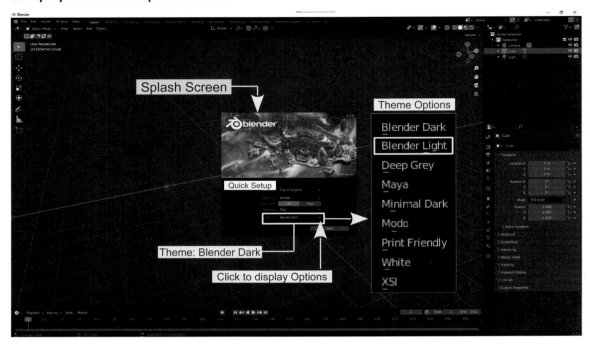

Clicking the **Theme button** displays a menu with alternative **Theme Options**. You may select any option depending on your preference. When you have made a selection, click the **Next button** to apply your Theme. The color scheme changes and the **Splash Screen** is replaced.

The Graphical User Interface with **Theme: Blender Light** selected.

Clicking the Left Mouse Button with the Mouse Cursor in the Screen causes the Splash Screen to be cancelled.

Note: The **Quick Setup** Splash Screen only displays the first time you run Blender.

What! You want to try a different Theme!

Logically, you would think, reinstating the Splash Screen would provide the **Quick Setup** controls previously employed.

To reinstate the Splash Screen click the little Blender Logo in the Screen Header and select Splash Screen in the menu that displays.

Click the Blender Logo.

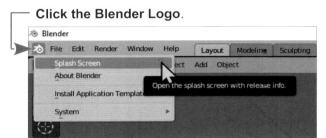

The Splash Screen is reinstated but it is different from the initial display containing the Quick Setup options.

To try a different Theme, in fact, to customise Blender to your personal choice you go to the **Preferences Editor** by clicking **Edit, Preferences** in the Screen Header..

In the **Preferences Editor**, select **Themes** in the left-hand column and click on **Presets** to display the list of color schemes.

Click Presets

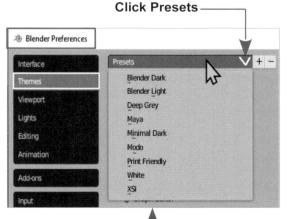

Click to display the Preferences Editor.

Note: The following diagram showing the different Editor Panels colored was previously shown and is duplicated here for convenience.

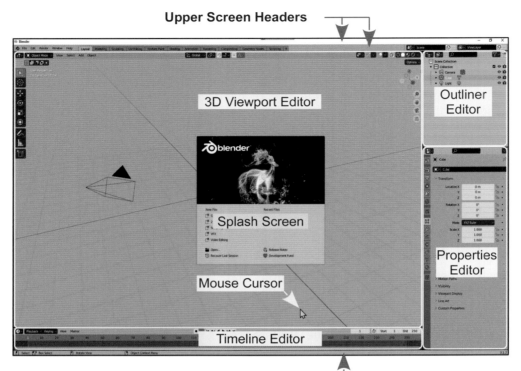

Upper Screen Headers

3D Viewport Editor

Outliner Editor

Splash Screen

Properties Editor

Mouse Cursor

Timeline Editor

Lower Screen Header

Editors

There are four **Editors** displayed when Blender is first opened. The Editors are; the **3D Viewport Editor**, the **Outliner Editor**, the **Properties Editor** and the **Timeline Editor**. In the center of the display, you see the **Splash Screen** showing you which version of Blender you have opened and containing buttons for selecting a variety of functions.

Traditionally the Splash Screen image is changed at each new release of the Blender Program.

At the top and bottom of the Screen, you see **Screen Headers**. At the top of each Editor Panel there is also an **Editor Header**. Headers contain Button Controls for selecting functions pertaining to the Screen or the Editor as the case may be.

Note: Clicking the Left Mouse Button with the Mouse Cursor in the 3D Viewport Editor cancels the display of the Splash Screen (Reinstate as previously described).

Note: In the preceding diagram, the default background colors of the different Editors have been altered to distinguish the panels. You will be shown how to do this later on.

Controls - Buttons, Icons and Sliders

Each Editor in the **GUI** is a separate panel with a **Header** at the top of the panel. The Headers contains buttons which activate functions or display sub menus with buttons for activating functions.

A button may be a text annotation which highlights blue on Mouse Over or an icon representing a function or a bar with text annotation.

Clicking a button relays data to the program to perform an action.

Example 1 : The 3D Viewport Editor (the default Screen display – **Upper LH Side**)

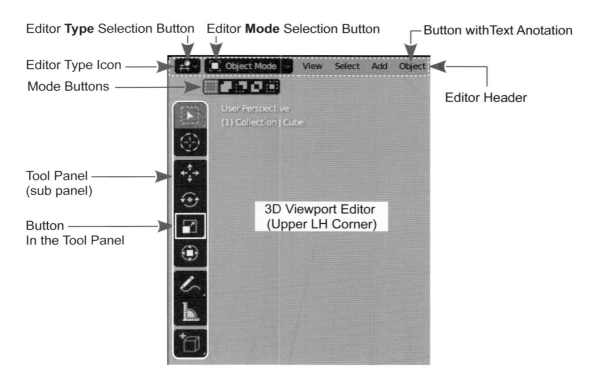

Note: The buttons shown in the diagram can be seen in the panel at the upper left hand side of the **default** Blender Screen arrangement. A detailed description of the Screen Arrangement with its Editors and panels constituting **Blender's GUI** (Graphical User Interface) is presented in **Chapter 1**.

Note: In giving instructions, **Default** means, that which is displayed on the computer Screen before any action is taken.

Example 2: The Properties Editor (the default Screen display – **Lower RH Side**)

The default display shows the content of the **Properties Editor** with the **Object Properties** active. In this state, the controls affect the default **Cube Object** in the 3D Viewport Editor.

Note: In this instance, the **Editor Header** is extended to the vertical array of buttons at the left-hand side of the Editor.)

Properties Editor Icon

Editor Display Selection buttons. The display in the Editor panel depends on which button is clicked.

Object Properties

(Content of the Editor Panel with the active Property – see Note)

Tabs >
(Click to open a Panel)

Tab Closed >

Tab Open ⌄

Panel Opened

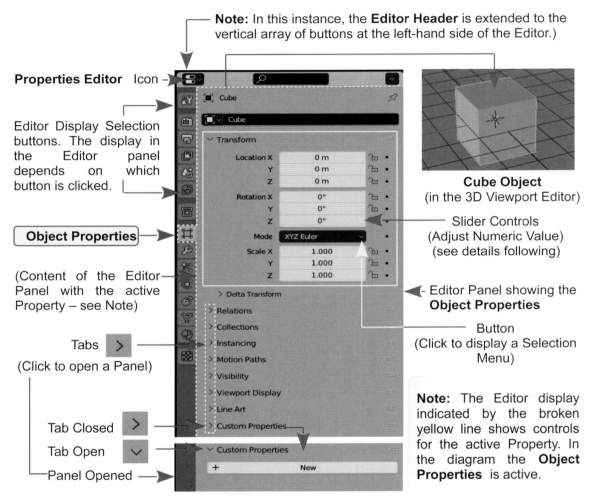

Cube Object
(in the 3D Viewport Editor)

Slider Controls
(Adjust Numeric Value)
(see details following)

- Editor Panel showing the **Object Properties**

Button
(Click to display a Selection Menu)

Note: The Editor display indicated by the broken yellow line shows controls for the active Property. In the diagram the **Object Properties** is active.

A **Button** in Blender can be a small square or rectangular area on the screen or an elongated rectangle, in which case it may be referred to as a bar. Some buttons display with icons.

An **Icon** is a pictorial representation of a function. In the diagram, the icon in the upper left-hand corner indicates that the **Properties Editor** is displayed.

A **Slider** is an elongated area, usually containing a numeric value, which is modified by clicking, deleting and retyping the value, or clicking, holding and dragging the Mouse Cursor that displays on **Mouse Over**, left or right to decrease or increase the value. Some sliders have a small arrow at either end which display when the Mouse Cursor is **positioned over the Slider** (Mouse Over).

Click on an arrow to incrementally alter the value. Some sliders directly alter the display on the computer Screen.

Slider Controls in the **TransformTab** affect the position of the Cube (the selected Object) in the 3D Viewport Editor.

Properties Editor
Object Properties Button
Transform tab

Mouse over to display double headed arrow. Click to show Typing Cursor (blue line).

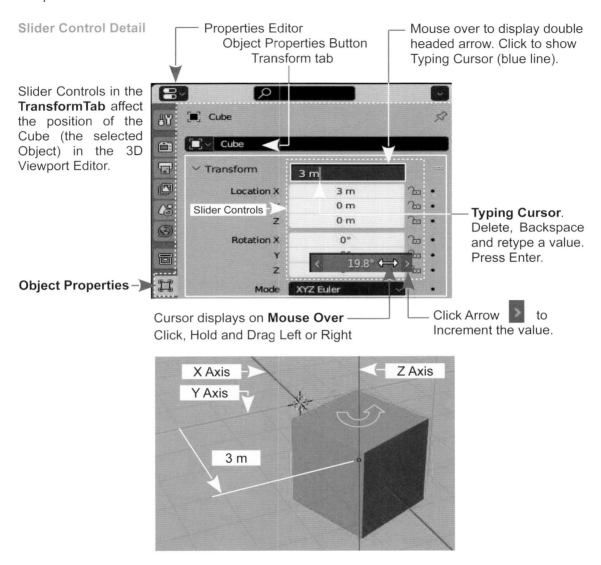

Object Properties –

Typing Cursor. Delete, Backspace and retype a value. Press Enter.

Cursor displays on **Mouse Over**
Click, Hold and Drag Left or Right

Click Arrow to Increment the value.

With the Cube Object selected in the 3D Viewport Editor, altering the **X Location Slider** value to 3m and the **Z-Axis Rotation Slider** to 19.8° moves the Cube forward along the X-Axis (Red Line) and rotates the Cube about the vertical Z-Axis.

For Keyboard input, a command is; to press a specific Key or a series of Keys. Press **Shift + Ctrl + T Key** means press and hold both the **Shift** and **Ctrl** Keys simultaneously and tap the **T Key**. **Num Pad** (Number Pad) Keys are also used in which case the command is Press **Num Pad 0** to **9** or **Plus** and **Minus**.

Command Instruction Example:

Go to the **Blender Screen Header, Render Properties,** click **Render Image:**

Remember: A control button, icon or slider which is displayed, indicates a specific location on the computer Screen. Positioning the Mouse Cursor at this location and clicking the Mouse button or depressing a keyboard button, inputs a signal to the computer. The interpretation , made by by the computer is; signal received at specific location = perform explicit computation and export result.

The example above means; in the **Blender Screen Header,** position the **Mouse Cursor** over the **Render Properties** button and click the left mouse button, clicking once. In this case the signal received by the computer with the Mouse Cursor at the position of the Render Properties button tells the computer to display the **Render Options Sub-Menu**. Positioning the Mouse Cursor over **Render Image** in the sub menu and clicking once renders an image of **Camera View** (what the camera sees). The Rendered Image is displayed in a new Editor panel, the **Image Editor**. The Image may be saved from this location but for the time being press **Esc** on the Keyboard to cancel the Render and return to the 3D Viewport Editor.

Mouse Cursor over the Render Button   **Camera View**

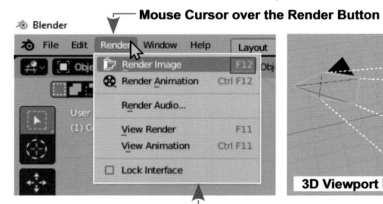

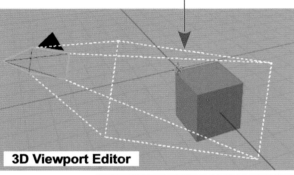

3D Viewport Editor

Render Options Sub Menu

Pressing **Num Pad 0** on the Keyboard shows a preview in the 3D Viewport Editor of what will be **Rendered** in an image (What the Camera sees).

Render Preview

Rendered Image
As seen in the Image Editor

Note: The annotation **F12** adjacent to **Render Image** is a **Keyboard Shortcut**. Pressing **F12** on the Keyboard will also Render the Camera View.

Remember: The purpose of exercises in this preamble are to familiarise you with commands and diagrams not to provide instruction an any particular task. Full instruction will be provided later.

Book Work Flow

The initial work flow in the book will introduce the Editors and panels which make up the **Graphical User Interface (GUI)** and familiarise you with basic control operations. During the initial introduction detailed explanation of the Blender processes will be limited to a need-to-know basis. To start with, you will have to blindly follow along without understanding why. Explanations will be given as you progress and are made aware of the different Blender features.

In demonstrating one of the previous **Command Examples** the command was; **Click Render Image.**

Rendering

Rendering means generating a digital Image of what the Camera sees. The Definition from the Wiki, when specifically applied to computer graphics follows. The Wiki? The Free Encyclopedia Wikipedia.

Https://en.wikipedia.org/wiki/Rendering_(computer_graphics)

Rendering or **Image Synthesis** is the automatic process of generating a photo-realistic or non-photorealistic image from a 2D or 3D model (or models in what collectively could be called a Scene file) by means of a computer program. Also, the results of displaying such a model can be called **Rendering**. A Scene file contains objects in a strictly defined language or data structure; it would contain geometry, viewpoint, texture, lighting, and shading information as a description of the virtual Scene. The data contained in the Scene File is then passed to a rendering program to be processed and output to a digital image or raster graphics Image File. The term "rendering" may be by analogy with an "artist's rendering" of a Scene.

Render Engines - GUI Versions in Blender

Render Engines are the parts of the Blender program that produce the Screen display and convert the display into an image or sequence of images. Image sequences generate animations which in turn produce movie files.

In Blender 3.0.0 there are three **Render Engine options**. With the selection of each Render Engine type the Graphical User Interface (GUI) is displayed in a slightly different manner. Which option you chose depends on the particular process, to which the engine type is suited.

The Render Engines in Blender 3.0.0 are named; Eevee Render, Cycles Render, Workbench Render.

Eevee Render

The default Render Engine presented when Blender starts is Eevee. This is an acronym for *"Extra Easy Virtual Environment Engine"*. Eevee can display a real time rendered view (depending on the Viewport Shading option selected – explanation to follow). In other words, what you see on the Screen as you make changes, is a good approximation of what you get in your final image view. Eevee quickly renders the Scene as you work but the quality of the render can incur a time disadvantage in the advanced stages of modeling.

Cycles Render

Cycles Rendering is specifically designed to produce a photo realistic high quality display of an image or frame in an animation incorporating colors, textures and special lighting. The quality of the display is adjustable since high resolution rendering comes at a cost with respect to time.

Workbench Render

Workbench Rendering uses the 3D View's drawing for quick *preview* renders. This allows you to inspect your animation (for object movements, alternate angles, etc.). This can also be used to preview your animations – in the event your Scene is too complex for your system to play back in real-time in the 3D View. You can use Workbench to render both images and animations.

> **Note: Workbench Render** was formerly **OpenGL Render**. The definition has been taken from the Blender Manual. Each Render Engine type displays the view in the computer Screen in different ways **depending on the Viewport Shading method that you selec**t. This will be explained as you progress through the book.

Workspace

A **Workspace** is the arrangement or configuration of **Editor** panels on the computer Screen. Blender includes numerous Editors for specific functions and these Editors are selected and arranged to facilitate particular operations.

Several Workspace Arrangements (Editor arrangements) are provided and may be selected in the Blender Screen Header. There is also the facility for users to build and save specialized arrangements of Editors to suit their working environment for specific tasks.

Workspace options in the Blender Screen Header
Layout displays the default **Workspace**

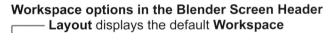

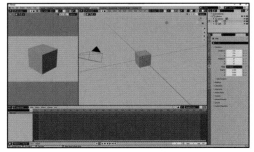

Animation Workspace

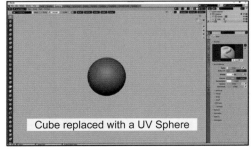

Sculpting Workspace

Although not designated as Workspaces there are five other Screen arrangements for specific tasks. In the Header at the top of the Screen, click on **File** then **New** to display the option menu.

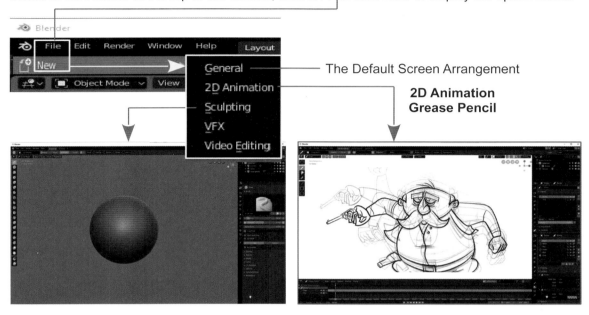

The Default Screen Arrangement

2D Animation
Grease Pencil

2D Animation – Grease Pencil

Blender incorporates a dedicated **Workspace** for creating **2D Animation** called **The Grease Pencil**.

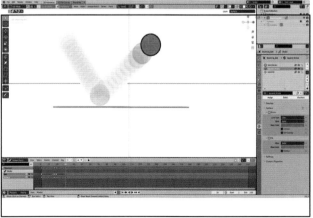

This environment provides 2D Animation tools within Blender's 3D Pipeline. 2D Animation creates characters, storyboards, and backgrounds in two-dimensional environments, which may be used in advertisements, films, television, computer games, or websites and is just a fun thing to do. As mentioned in the Introduction, the operation of the **Grease Pencil** is described in detail in a separate dedicated publication titled:

Blender 2D Animation – The Complete Guide to the Grease Pencil

Content and sample pages of the authors books may be viewed on the Author's website at:

https://www.tamarindcreativegraphics.com

Content and sample pages of the three Blender books may be viewed by: mouse over and clicking the cover images on the website.

Supplements to the Book

Blender is a comprehensive application and as such, it is impossible to include instruction for everything in a single publication. That being the case, supplements to the book are to be found on the author's website.

Summary

Remember: The Preamble is to familiarise you with Blender, in general and introduce you to the methods of entering commands in the Graphical User Interface.

Before you attempt to do anything in Blender you should become familiar with the Blender interface. In the following chapter (**CH01 Understanding the Interface**) the **Graphical User Interface (GUI)** will be studied in detail showing how the Editor Panels interrelate and how commands are executed to generate a simple animation incorporating a sample of Blender's effects. Of necessity instructions will be limited to a need-to-know basis until you become familiar with Blender.

Understanding the Interface

The Interface

When Blender opens you are presented with a Screen arrangement displaying multiple panels. This arrangement is called the **Graphical User Interface (GUI)** (Figure 1.1). The panels in **Blender** are called **Editors.**

To get you started using Blender, this chapter will show you how to interact with the interface. This introduction will familiarise you with the Editors, demonstrate entering command using the controls and give you an insight into how the different Editors interrelate. The Preamble preceding this chapter introduced controls, command instructions and presented example diagrams (**Figures**) touching on a sample of this material.

At this point, the explanation of functions available in Blender will be minimised. This is just the beginning and it is assumed you are looking at Blender for the first time. Too much information may be confusing. In following chapters the information in Chapter 1 will be repeated and expanded.

By following the instructions with reference to diagrams you will see how Blender works and experience examples. Understanding the Interface and knowing what tools are available, which buttons to press and what to expect is the key to understanding Blender.

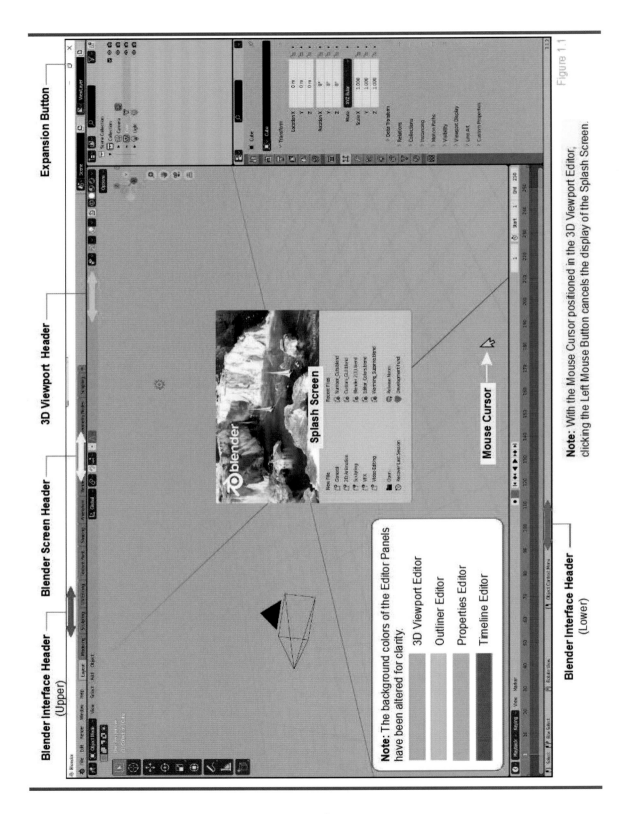

Blender Interface Header
(Upper)

Blender Screen Header

3D Viewport Header

Expansion Button

Mouse Cursor

Splash Screen

Note: The background colors of the Editor Panels have been altered for clarity.

3D Viewport Editor

Outliner Editor

Properties Editor

Timeline Editor

Blender Interface Header
(Lower)

Note: With the Mouse Cursor positioned in the 3D Viewport Editor, clicking the Left Mouse Button cancels the display of the Splash Screen.

Figure 1.1

1.1 Examining the Interface

Drag your **Mouse** to see the **Mouse Cursor** somewhere in the Screen. **Oops!** You clicked the left Mouse Button and the **Splash Screen** disappeared?

Figure 1.2

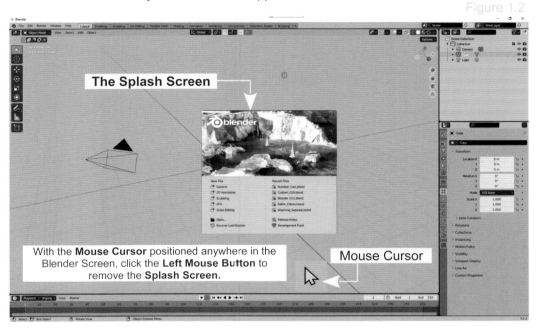

The Splash Screen

With the **Mouse Cursor** positioned anywhere in the Blender Screen, click the **Left Mouse Button** to remove the **Splash Screen.**

Mouse Cursor

The Blender Graphical User Interface (GUI)

Figure 1.3

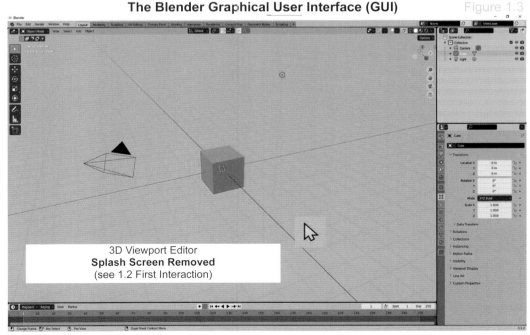

3D Viewport Editor
Splash Screen Removed
(see 1.2 First Interaction)

1.2 First Interaction

Removing the **Splash Screen** from the interface, intentional or not, will probably be your first interaction with the **Blender GUI** (Graphical User Interface).

The **Splash Screen** actually contains useful information and buttons which activate functions, therefore, you may wish to reinstate it.

To reinstate the Splash Screen, position the Mouse Cursor over the little black and white Blender logo (button) in the upper left hand corner of the Screen (Figure 1.4).

Position the Mouse Cursor over the **Blender Logo** (highlights blue on Mouse Over)

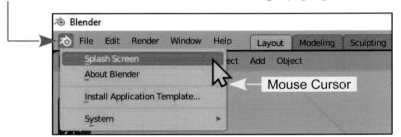

Figure 1.4

Click the Left Mouse Button (LMB), drag the mouse placing the cursor over **Splash Screen** (highlights blue on Mouse Over) and click LMB again. **The Splash Screen is reinstated**.

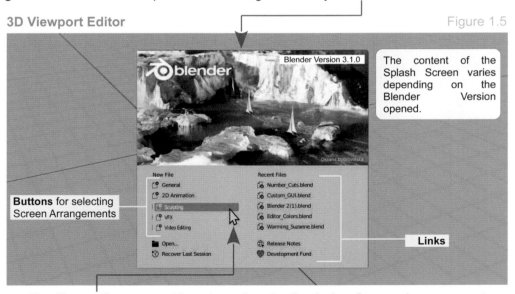

Figure 1.5

The **Mouse Cursor,** positioned to select the **Sculpting Screen Arrangement**

The **Splash Screen** panel shows which version of Blender you have opened. Text notations in the Splash Screen are buttons which you click to access Screen arrangements for working with specific aspects of the program. There are also links to access Recent Files and Release Notes.

1.3 Quit Blender

When you start something it's a good idea to know how to quit. Blender is no exception. This may be stating the obvious but inevitably things will get messed up and, at some stage, you will want to start over fresh. There are two ways of doing this. One method is to close and restart the program, a second method is restart the program without closing.

Close the Program

To close Blender click the **Cross** in the upper right hand corner of the Screen (Figure 1.6). **Click the Cross** means, place the Mouse Cursor over the Cross (Quit button) and click LMB

Blender Screen Upper Right Hand Side   Figure 1.6

Before **Blender** shuts down a panel displays with a reminder to save changes (Figure 1.7). At this point you can Save, Discharge Changes you have made (Don't Save) or Cancel quitting.

Figure 1.7

> **Note:** When you click the Quit button at the top of the Screen the warning only displays when you have performed an operation. If you haven't done anything the warning does not display.

Saving Changes

When you have Blender open and you are performing operations in the Graphical User Interface you will be creating a **Blender File**. The File will contain all the information relevant to the work that you have done. The **Save Changes Before Closing** message gives you the opportunity to save the information which will allow you to retrieve the File in the future.

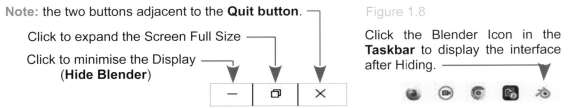

To restart Blender double click the **Blender Icon** on your Desktop or ———➤
double click the Blender Application file name in the directory where you installed Blender (see
Starting the Program in the **Introduction**).

Note: the two buttons adjacent to the **Quit button**. ———┐

Figure 1.8

Click to expand the Screen Full Size ———

Click the Blender Icon in the
Taskbar to display the interface
after Hiding. ————————➤

Click to minimise the Display ———
(**Hide Blender**)

Alternative Close and Restart

You may also close **Blender** by clicking on **File** in the upper left hand corner of the Screen and
selecting (click) **Quit** in the menu that displays. Restart as previously described.

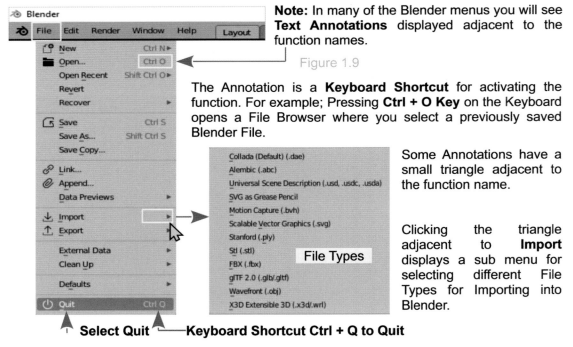

Note: In many of the Blender menus you will see
Text Annotations displayed adjacent to the
function names.

Figure 1.9

The Annotation is a **Keyboard Shortcut** for activating the
function. For example; Pressing **Ctrl + O Key** on the Keyboard
opens a File Browser where you select a previously saved
Blender File.

Some Annotations have a
small triangle adjacent to
the function name.

Clicking the triangle
adjacent to **Import**
displays a sub menu for
selecting different File
Types for Importing into
Blender.

Select Quit ———**Keyboard Shortcut Ctrl + Q to Quit**

Start Over - Restart Without Closing

Restarting Blender without closing the Program means you open a new Blender File without
closing Blender.

The following outlines the procedure for restarting which includes the **Save Changes Before
Closing** message. How to save your work and navigate the **File System** is described in detail in
Chapter 3.

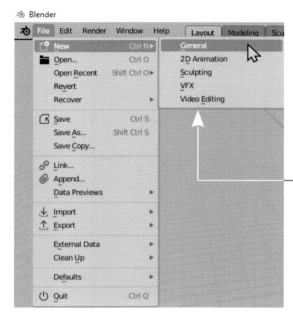

To restart **without closing** Blender, click (LMB) on **File** in the upper left hand corner of the Screen (highlights blue) (Figure 1.10), drag the Mouse Cursor over **New,** then **General** and click LMB.

This method opens a new Blender Screen Arrangement.

Figure 1.10

The other selections in this sub menu open Blender with Screen Arrangements For specific applications.

For example, **2D Animation** opens a Screen Arrangement for the **Grease Pencil** (Blender's 2D Workspace – Chapter 2 - 2.19).

When you click General, the **Save Changes Before Closing** panel displays if changes to the default arrangement have been made.

1.4 Getting Help

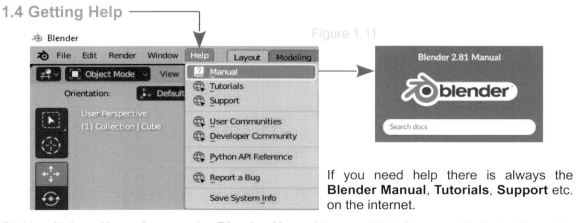

Figure 1.11

If you need help there is always the **Blender Manual**, **Tutorials**, **Support** etc. on the internet.

Clicking **Help** – **Manual** opens the **Blender Manual** in your Web Browser. Similarly, **Tutorials** and **Support** access websites with information.

1.5 The Interface – Figure 1.1

The **Blender Graphical User Interface** (GUI) as depicted in Figure 1.1 is replicated here (Figure 1.12) with additional annotation.

Figure 1.12

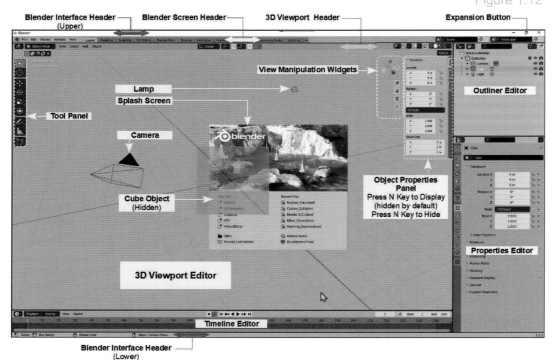

As you see, there is a lot of information in what at first appears to be a simple arrangement.

The **Blender Graphical User Interface** (GUI) is made up with four (4) Panels called **Editors** and three (3) **Headers**. In addition, each **Editor Panel** also has its own Header which is usually at the top of the Panel. Headers contain icons and text notations which are buttons for selecting or activating **functions**.

> Consider **Functions** as the computer code working behind the Scene which make things happen.

1.6 Further Examination

The default Blender interface as shown in Figure 1.3 and here in Figure 1.13 opposite, with Splash Screen removed, shows the Editors and Headers described above.

Figure 1.13

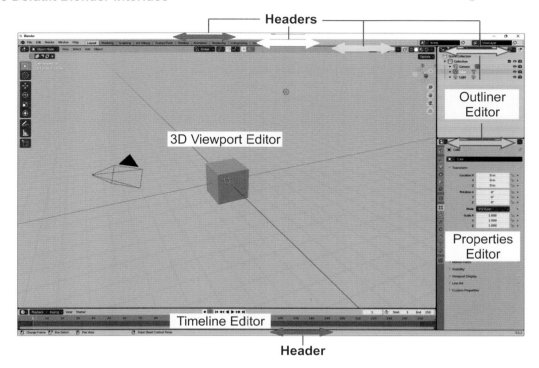

Headers

3D Viewport Editor

Outliner Editor

Properties Editor

Timeline Editor

Header

Remember: With the Mouse Cursor positioned in the 3D Viewport Editor, clicking the Left Mouse Button cancels the display of the Splash Screen.

Note: The arrangement of Editors and Headers shown in Figure 1.13 are for the default Blender Screen.

This arrangement may be reconfigured for specific operations of the program and may be fully customized for user preference.

Figure 1.14

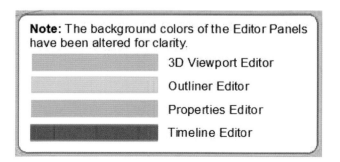

Note: The background colors of the Editor Panels have been altered for clarity.

3D Viewport Editor

Outliner Editor

Properties Editor

Timeline Editor

1.7 3D Viewport Work Modes

Some (not all) Editors display in different **Modes**. The Mode you select depends on the particular type of operation to be performed. The 3D Viewport Editor has six different **Working Modes**.

3D Viewpot Mode selection button.

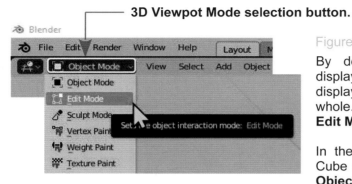

Figure 1.15

By default the 3D Viewport Editor displays in **Object Mode** which is the display for constructing a Scene as a whole. One of the alternative displays is **Edit Mode** in which you Model Objects.

In the default 3D Viewport Editor the Cube at the centre of the Scene is an **Object**.

To change from the default Object Mode to Edit Mode, click the **Mode selection button** in the 3D Viewport Editor Header and select (click) **Edit Mode** in the menu that displays.

When Modelling (Editing an Object) you will change from Object Mode to Edit Mode and back again frequently, therefore, you may toggle between the Modes by pressing the Keyboard **Tab Key**.

Figure 1.15 above   **3D Viewport Editor – Object Mode**   Figure 1.16

Object Mode Tool Panel

Press the T Key
to toggle the display
Of the Tool Panel

Press the N Key
to toggle the display
Of the Object Properties Panel

Cube Object

3D Viewport Editor – Edit Mode

Figure 1.17

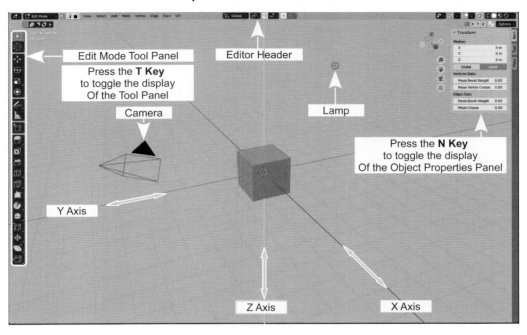

The main differences between the 3D Viewport Editor in Object Mode and Edit Mode are seen in the Tool Panels at the left of the Editor. In Edit Mode the Tool Panel is more extensive. There are also differences in the 3D Viewport Editor Header.

With the Splash Screen removed you see a gray **Cube** in the center of the 3D Viewport Editor in both Object and Edit Modes.

The Cube, is suspended in 3D Space (three dimensional space) . For reference, when positioning Objects in Space a horizontal **Mid Plane Grid is provided**. The Grid is marked with a horizontal **X Axis** (red line) and a horizontal **Y Axis** (green line). By default a vertical **Z Axis** is not displayed.

In Blender, the **Cube** is said to be an **Object**. In the default Scene there is also a **Camera** Object and a **Lamp** Object. You see the Objects listed in the **Outliner Editor** (upper RHS of the Screen).

The Cube is one of several basic building blocks from which to commence modelling (see Figure 1.21). In **Object Mode t**he orange outline indicates that the Cube is **selected** which means you can work on it to create something (Figure 1.16).

In **Edit Mode** (Tab Key to toggle between Object Mode and Edit Mode) the cube displays with a different shade of gray (brownish tinge in Figure 1.17) and with small orange dots at the corners connected by thin orange lines. The orange dots are called **Vertices**, the thin orange lines are called **Edges** and the shading surrounded by the Edges are termed **Faces**.

In **Object Mode** clicking **LMB** (left mouse button) with the **Mouse Cursor** over an empty part of the 3D Viewport Editor you will **deselect the Cube**. The orange outline disappears. To re-select the Cube or select another Object you place the Mouse Cursor over the Object and click **LMB**.

Figure 1.18

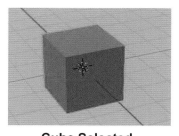

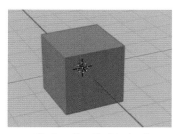

Cube Selected   **Cube De-Selected**

Note: In Figure 1.11 the background color of the 3D Viewport Editor has been changed from the default gray. With the default gray it is difficult to see the grid. You will be shown how to do this at a later stage (see Chapter 2 – 2.18).

Note: Header colors may vary, 3D Viewport and 3D View are synonymous as is Lamp and Light.

Note: Default means, that which is displayed or occurs without any action being taken.

1.8 Rotating in 3D Space

The distinction should be made between **Rotating an Object in 3D Space** and **Rotating the Scene** (Viewport) which changes how you see the Object or Objects relative to other components of the Scene.

Rotating the Object (Cube)

In the default Scene, The Cube Object is located at the center of the 3D Space. **Have the Cube selected**. Place the Mouse Cursor, in the 3D Viewport Editor to one side of the Cube. Press the **R Key** (rotate) on the Keyboard and drag the Mouse to rotate the Cube. Click LMB to set in position.

Figure 1.19

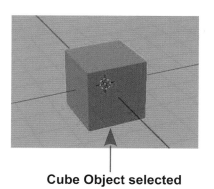

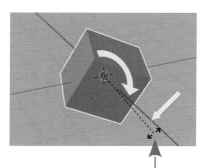

Cube Object selected   **Mouse Cursor when R Key pressed.**

With the Mouse Cursor positioned in the 3D Viewport Editor, click and hold the **Middle Mouse Button** (Scroll Wheel) and drag the Mouse. The Scene in the 3D View Editor is rotated. Release the Mouse button.

Figure 1.20

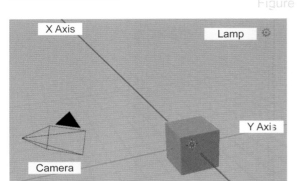

Default Scene

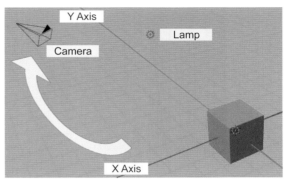

Scene (Viewport) **Rotated**

This exercise has distinguished between rotating an Object and rotating the View which is advantageous when modeling. Of course you have messed up the View and may wish to get back to square one. At this stage the options are to restart Blender or restart without closing as described in Section 1.3. There are Keystrokes for rotating the View and **Manipulation Widgets** for rotating the Object or the View (see 1.11 and Chapter 2 -2.14).

1.9 Other Objects

Besides the Cube Object, the default Scene contains a **Lamp Object** and a **Camera Object.**

The **Lamp** represents a light source which illuminates the Scene, determining how you will see the View when it is converted into an Image (see Chapter 12).

The **Camera** determines what part of the Scene is captured for Rendering (see 1.17 Figure 1.48).

The Lamp and the Camera have Properties which may be modified to produce effects. How to do this will be placed on hold for the time being.

There are several default Object called **Primitives** which you can add to the Scene (Figure 1.21 over).

With one exception the Primitives are not pre-constructed models of characters but mesh shapes from which you begin modeling. The one exception is Suzanne the pre-constructed Mesh model of a Monkey, affectionately named **Suzanne.**

To demonstrate adding an Object, **Suzanne** will be added to the default Scene.

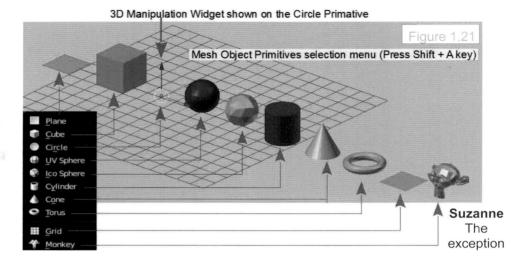

3D Manipulation Widget shown on the Circle Primative

Figure 1.21

Mesh Object Primitives selection menu (Press Shift + A key)

Plane
Cube
Circle
UV Sphere
Ico Sphere
Cylinder
Cone
Torus
Grid
Monkey

Suzanne
The
exception

The basic principle in Blender, when modeling, is to add one of the basic Mesh Objects (Primitives), then modify (model) that shape into whatever you want. You may combine several primitives if you wish.

To Add a Primitive you either click the **Add button** in the 3D Viewport Editor Header or with the Mouse Cursor in the 3D Viewport Editor, press the **Shift Key + the A Key** (keyboard) to display the **Add Menu**.

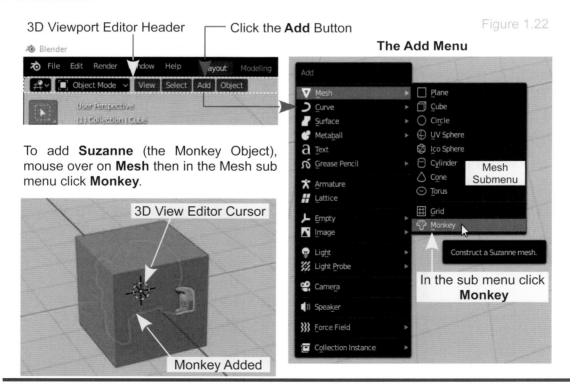

3D Viewport Editor Header

Click the **Add** Button

Figure 1.22

The Add Menu

To add **Suzanne** (the Monkey Object), mouse over on **Mesh** then in the Mesh sub menu click **Monkey**.

3D View Editor Cursor

Monkey Added

Add

Mesh   Plane
Curve   Cube
Surface   Circle
Metaball   UV Sphere
Text   Ico Sphere
Grease Pencil Cylinder   Mesh
Armature   Cone   Submenu
Lattice   Torus
Empty   Grid
Image   Monkey
Light
Light Probe   Construct a Suzanne mesh.
Camera
Speaker   In the sub menu click
Force Field   **Monkey**
Collection Instance

14

All New Objects added into a Scene are entered at the position of the **3D Viewport Editor Cursor. Yes! There is another Cursor.** By default the 3D Viewport Editor Cursor is located at the center of the 3D Space. The default Cube Object is also located at the same position and when Suzanne (Monkey) is entered she is also located at this position.

When a new Object is added to the Scene, the new Object becomes the selected Object, hence you see the orange outline and in this particular case you see part of Suzanne's Ear protruding from the surface of the Cube. To see Suzanne clearly hide the Cube using the **Outline Editor.**

1.10 Using the Outliner Editor   Figure 1.23

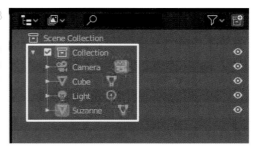

The **Outliner Editor** lists all the Objects in the Scene and provides a means of organising Objects into groups. This is a great help when compiling complicated Scenes.

In Figure 1.23 you see the Objects in the Scene listed in a group named **Collection**.

Figure 1.24

How to organise Collections will be explained in Chapter 20 but for the moment, click on **Cube** (highlights blue), then click on the little **Eye Icon** adjacent to Cube (Figure 1.24) to hide the Cube in the Scene. This does not delete the Cube, it merely cancels the display. You click the eye icon a second time to reinstate the Cube in the 3D Viewport Editor. If you click the eye icon adjacent to Collection the display of every Object in the Collection is cancelled.

1.11 Working in the 3D Viewport (Object Mode)

Rotating an Object (see 1.8 Rotating in 3D Space)

Figure 1.25

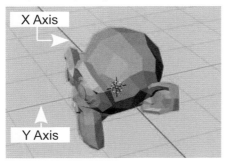

Suzanne with the Cube hidden

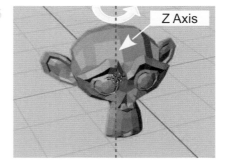

With Suzanne selected, press the **R Key + the Z Key** and drag the Mouse to see her pretty face.

Rotation: Pressing **R Key + Z Key** means, **Rotate** about the **Vertical Z Axis.**

Pressing **R Key + X Key** Rotates about the X Axis. Pressing **R Key + Y Key** Rotates about the Y Axis. Pressing **R Key** on its own Rotates about an Axis vertical to the plane of the Screen.

There are many functions which can be employed in the 3D Viewport Editor. Rotating an Object that has been selected is one. You also **Scale** the selected Object (Press the S Key and drag the Mouse) (S Key + X confines the Scale operation to the X Axis). You **Translate** (move and reposition) the Object in the 3D Viewport Editor (Press the G Key (G for Grab) and drag the Mouse) (G Key + Y confines the movement to the Y Axis).

The function of the Keystrokes are replicated by **Widgets** which are activated from the **Tool Panel in the 3D Viewport Editor**.

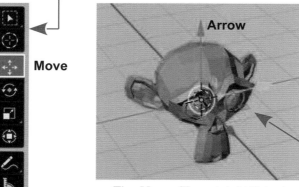

Figure 1.26

Arrow

Move

Rectangle

The **Move** (Translate) Widget

The colored **arrows** and **rectangles** are **Widget Control Handles** which you click (LMB), hold and drag to Translate (move) the selected Object in the Scene. Clicking an arrow confines the movement to an Axis in the Scene. Clicking a rectangles confines the movement to either the X,Y or Z Plane.

Widgets are explained in detail in Chapter 2 – 2.7, 2.14.

With the Cube hidden (see 1.10), using the Transform Widget, move Suzanne to one side of the center of the Scene, then in the Outliner Editor, click the eye icon adjacent to Cube to reinstate the display of the Cube in the 3D Viewport Editor.

1.12 Working in the 3D Viewport (Edit Mode)

Note: You will find there are many times when you want to switch between Object Mode and Edit Mode. Instead of using the Mode Selection Menu in the Header, simply press the **Tab Key** on the Keyboard to **Toggle** between the two Modes (have the Object selected).

In **Edit Mode** the default Cube displays with its **Faces** a different shade of gray, with orange dots at each corner called **Vertices**, connected by thin orange lines which are the **Edges**.

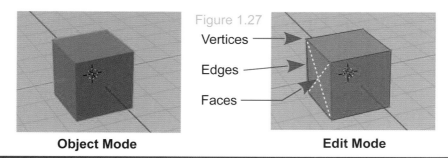

Figure 1.27

Vertices

Edges

Faces

Object Mode   **Edit Mode**

16

When changing from Object Mode to Edit Mode all **Vertices**, **Edges** and **Faces** are selected. Click **LMB** in the 3D Viewport Editor to deselect all the Vertices, Edges and Faces.

Note: In **Edit Mode**, the Mouse Cursor displays as a **white cross** . ——▶  Figure 1.28

Position the Mouse Cursor (white cross) over one of the Vertices and click LMB to select a single Vertex on the Cube (vertex turns white).

Note: Selection in 3D Viewport Editor, in Edit Mode, is by default, set to **Vertex Select.**

You change the **Selection Mode** in the 3D Viewport Editor Header.

3D Viewport Editor Header
Vertex, Edge and Face Selection Buttons (Vertex Select active, highlighted blue)

Figure 1.29

Face
Edge
Vertex (active highlighted blue)

Note: When changing to Edit Mode the array of buttons in the 3D Viewport Editor Header is different to Object Mode and the options in the Tool Panel change. You are able to select a Vertex since the Vertex Select button in the Header is active (highlighted blue). You have the options to select Edges or Faces.

With the Vertex selected, press the **G Key** and drag the Mouse to reposition the Vertex. Click LMB to set in place.

Figure 1.30

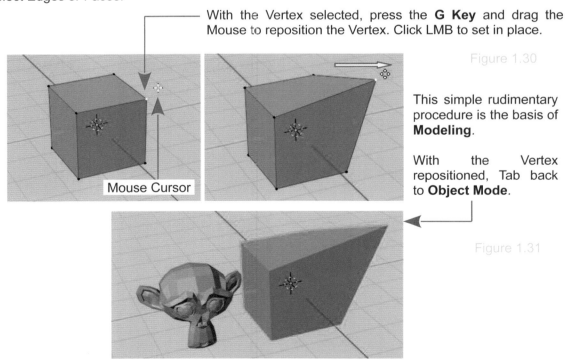

This simple rudimentary procedure is the basis of **Modeling**.

With the Vertex repositioned, Tab back to **Object Mode**.

Mouse Cursor

Figure 1.31

1.13 Adding Vertices by Subdivision

In the previous examples the Cube Object has eight (8) Vertices (one at each corner). Translating a single Vertex leaves the modified shape (Cube) with the same eight Vertices.

To produce even a simple Model you will require additional Vertices. This is particularly so when using Blender's Sculpting Tools. To add Vertices to an Object you Subdivide. Subdividing does not split the Object into parts, it merely adds Vertices.

For example; with the default Cube selected in Object Mode, Tab to Edit Mode. All Vertices will be selected (display orange). Click anywhere in the 3D Viewport Editor to deselect (display black). Press the A Key to re-select all Vertices (display orange). This procedure ensures that all Vertices are selected.

With the Mouse Cursor in the 3D Viewport Editor, RMB Click and LMB Click on Subdivide in the Vertex Context Menu that displays.

The surface of the Cube is Subdivided into 24 Faces with a Vertex at each Face corner. Repeat the procedure for additional subdivisions.

Figure 1.32

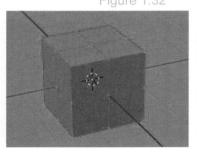

Note: In Blender there is usually more than one method of producing the same result.

1.14 The Last Operator Panel

When translating a Vertex, as previously described, you will observe a small panel display in the lower left of the Screen labelled **Move** (Figure 1.33).

This panel is called **The Last Operator Panel** and when expanded displays information about the last operation performed. In this particular case the operation is to **Move** or Translate the Vertex. By adjusting values in the panel you may affect the last operation.

Figure 1.33

Click LMB to expand

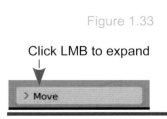

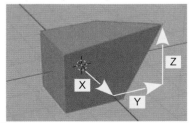

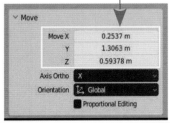

Applying the **Last Operator Panel** to **Subdivision** the following is observed.

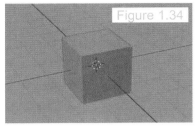

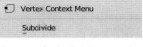

Vertex Context Menu

Subdivide

To Subdivide the surface of the Cube have all Vertices selected in Edit Mode (Figure 1.34).

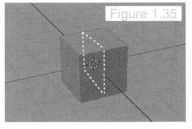

Press the **A Key** to select all Vertices – RMB click to display the **Vertex Context Menu** - RMB Click **Subdivide**. The surface of the Cube is Subdivided (Figure 1.35). In the **Last Operator Panel**, Subdivide, Number of Cuts: 1 displays (Figure 1.36). The **Cut** is referring to an Edge Loop Cut (Figure 1.35) where each Edge of the Cube is cut, dividing the Edge in two. Where the Loop Cut intersect an Edge, Vertices are created forming new Faces (Number of Cuts: 1 creates 24 Faces (Figure 1.36).

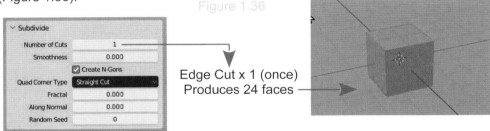

Figure 1.36

Edge Cut x 1 (once)
Produces 24 faces

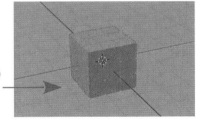

By altering the Number of Cuts value in the Last Operator, Subdivide panel you increase / decrease the number of Vertices.

Edge Cut x 2 (twice)
Produces 54 Faces

1.15 Using the Properties Editor

Bare in mind, the objective in this chapter is to familiarise you with the Graphical User Interface, not to explain all the functions available in Blender. You have been introduced to Editors and Headers and given a small insight into operating in 3D Space and working with Objects.

The **Properties Editor** contains controls which affect what happens in the 3D Viewport Editor. Some controls apply to the Scene as a whole and some specifically affect the properties of the Selected Object. There are usually multiple Objects in a Scene. The controls in the Properties Editor change depending on which Object is selected and affect only the Selected Object.

To demonstrate the basic operation, open a New Scene (New File) and replace the default Cube Object with Suzanne (Monkey Object). The Scene will be developed to create a rudimentary animated story by introducing color (Material) and using one of Blender's Quick Effects.

Remember: Objects added to the Scene have Default Properties which you modify to suit your requirements. Adding Susanne to the Scene displays her with a Default Gray **Material** (Color).

Figure 1.37

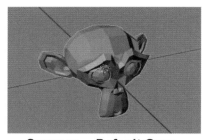

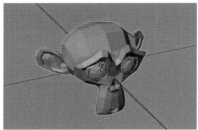

Suzanne – Default Gray

Suzanne – Modified Material

The Properties Editor will be used to modify the color of Suzanne. In Blender a color is called a **Material**. When considering coloring Objects in the 3D Viewport Editor, you should be aware that the Editor has several different display options.

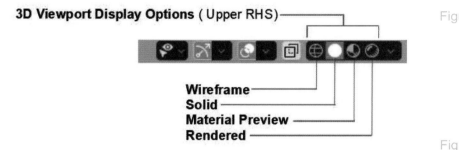

3D Viewport Display Options (Upper RHS)

Figure 1.38

Wireframe
Solid
Material Preview
Rendered

Figure 1.39

The default Display Mode is **Solid**. At this point only be concerned with **Solid Display**.

With Suzanne selected, click on the **Material Properties** button at the left hand side of the **Properties Editor** (Figure 1.38).

Remember: Monkey is called **Suzanne**. With Suzanne selected the Material button controls only affect Suzanne.

The Material button controls for Suzanne, at this stage, consist of the single **New Button**. This tells you that Suzanne has the default Material applied. At this point consider **Material** to mean **Color**.

The vertical array of buttons at the left hand side of the Properties Editor will be explained in due course but for the moment only be concerned with coloring Suzanne.

Material Properties Button ⟶

Why Color?

Color adds a new dimension to a Scene. Objects become more interesting and color in a Scene creates atmosphere which enhances the story or message being conveyed.   Figure 1.40

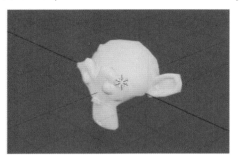

Adding Color: To add **Material** (color) to Suzanne (**the selected Object**) click the **New Button** in the **Properties Editor, Material buttons** (Figure 1.41). The display expands (Figure 1.42).

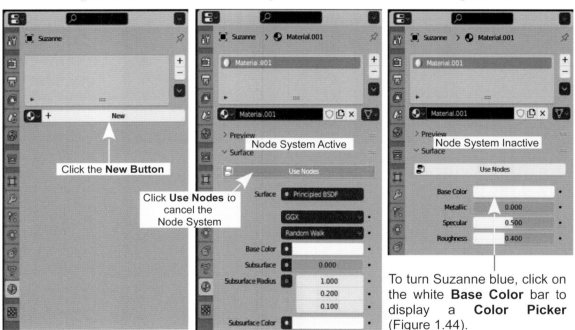

To turn Suzanne blue, click on the white **Base Color** bar to display a **Color Picker** (Figure 1.44).

By default, Material Color is being controlled by a hidden **Node System**. The blue bar with the notation **Use Nodes** indicates that the Node System is active.

Nodes are explained in Chapter 22, but for the moment click on the blue **Use Nodes** button (Figure 1.43) to **cancel the Node System**.

With the Node System inactive (cancelled) the Properties Editor, Material buttons display with a reduced number of functions (Figure 1.39) **Note:** diagrams are curtailed to save page space).

Remember the **Material Properties** button controls only apply to the selected Object in the 3D Viewport Editor, in this case Suzanne.

To turn Suzanne blue, click on the white **Base Color** bar (Figure 1.43) to display the **Color Picker** (Figure 1.44).

Figure 1.44

Color Schemes

Values for the **HSV** Color Scheme

Brightness Slider
Click LMB on the dot, hold and drag up/down.

The Color Picker gives the options to select one of three **Color Schemes**; **RGB**, **HSV** or **Hex**. By default the **HSV** color scheme is selected. Click on the **RGB** button to change the color scheme to **RGB** (**R**ed, **G**reen, **B**lue).

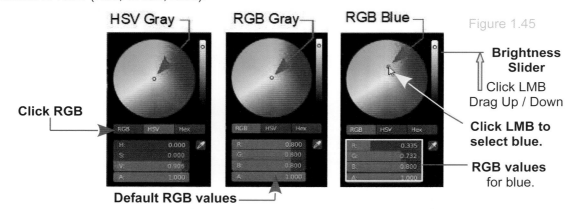

Figure 1.45

HSV Gray

RGB Gray

RGB Blue

Brightness Slider
Click LMB
Drag Up / Down

Click RGB

Click LMB to select blue.

RGB values for blue.

Default RGB values

When you add a Color to an Object the **Default RGB values are, R: 0.800, G: 0.800, B: 0.800 and A: 1.000.** The three RGB values generate the Blender default gray color, while the A (Alpha) value sets the transparency of the color (A: 1.000 = Opaque, A: 0.000 = Fully Transparent).

To make Suzanne blue in the face, click LMB in the RGB Color Picker Circle where it displays blue. To select the exact blue shown in the diagrams you may double click on a numeric value (displays a typing cursor) hit delete or backspace and retype a new value (Figure 1.46).

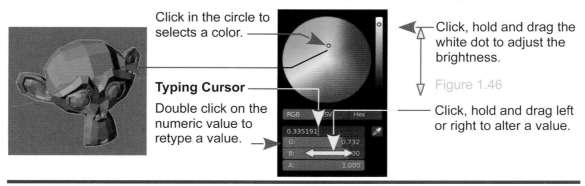

Click in the circle to selects a color.

Click, hold and drag the white dot to adjust the brightness.

Typing Cursor

Double click on the numeric value to retype a value.

Figure 1.46

Click, hold and drag left or right to alter a value.

When you select a color in the circle or alter the numeric values, the color of the selected Object changes. **Note:** This is a basic procedure demonstrating the application of Material color prior to understanding **Viewport Shading Modes** and **Material Nodes** (see Chapters 10 and 22).

1.16 Making a Plan - Storyboard

To efficiently utilise Blender's tools and techniques you should consider making a plan of what you intend to achieve. Even the simplest model can involve numerous aspects and a basic Animation can require multiple procedures. Performing procedures in the correct sequence can save you a lot of time and confusion. Making a plan is called creating a **Storyboard**.

To demonstrate, a simple Animation will be created. The plan will be to have Suzanne positioned to the side with a campfire at the center of the Scene. Susanne will move towards the fire changing color as she warms. As far as a Storyboard is concerned, the plan, in this case, can be depicted with three images (Figure 1.47).

Figure 1.47

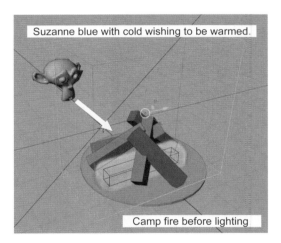

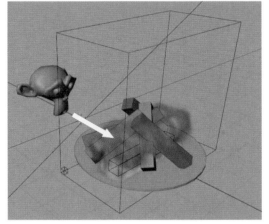

To tell this very simple story entails a surprising amount of detail.

To begin, Suzanne is animated to move closer to the fire and as she moves, her face is animated to change color.

At the same time Suzanne is moving, the camp fire is set alight.

With the Scene Animated the Blender data creating the display on the Screen is Rendered (converted) to a Movie File format.

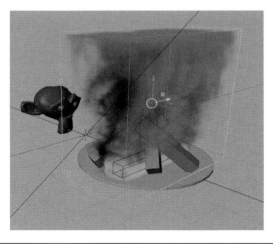

1.17 Camera View

You should be aware that only part of the Scene captured by the Camera (Camera View) is Rendered. It is, therefore, important to arrange components such that they fall within Camera View.

The Scene   Figure 1.48   **Camera View**

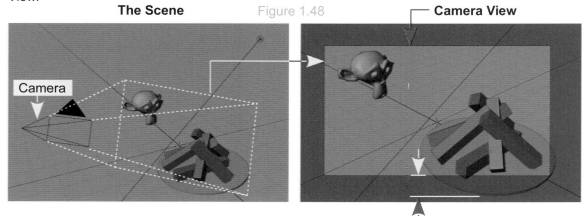

Note: Out of Camera View

Having Suzanne move in the Scene and having the Cube burn will be creating an **Animation**. This is a very simple unsophisticated example of **Animation** which will include a preview of a **Physical Simulation** (Fire and Smoke) using a **Quick Effect**.

1.18 Quick Effects

Blender allows you to create fantastic effects from first principles (from scratch) but also provides several **Quick Methods of** creating physical real world simulations. One of the **Quick Effects** is to cause an Object to catch on fire. Make note this is a **Quick Method** which has a limited application. You will be instructed in how to generate this effect from first principles later on and when you understand the procedures the results are limitless.

1.19 Something to Burn

The Scene depicted in Figure 1.47 includes a rudimentary campfire consisting a series of sticks or logs in a random pile. The logs are simply generated from a Cube Object scaled down, scaled on its Y Axis then Rotated and Grabbed and positioned.

Figure 1.49

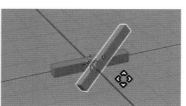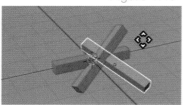

1.20 Saving Work to Start Over

Before proceeding you should consider saving your work. As a Scene is developed it can involve a considerable amount of effort, therefore, you won't wish to go back to the very beginning when procedures do not go to plan.

As Previously described, when you quit Blender or start over with a new Blender file you are prompted to save your work. You should, in fact, safe your work at regular intervals as you develop a Scene. It is inevitable, especially in the early stages of learning Blender that mistakes are made and you will not want to start over at the beginning of an exorcise.

How to save a Blender file and navigate the File System is described in Chapter 3.

The Undo Command

As you carry out separate procedures in Blender you can backtrack to alter or correct what you have done. For example, with Suzanne moved to the back of the Scene, the operation can be undone by simply pressing the **Ctrl + Z Key**. Alternatively you click **Edit** - **Undo** in the Screen Header. By default the number of **Undo Operations** is limited to 32 steps. If you have changed your mind or lost direction you can reload your work, providing you have saved the Blender file in which you are working.

1.21 Lighting the Fire

Creating an Animation is an illusion. The animation tricks the viewer unto believing they see something moving or an action taking place. Like a magician the animator uses trickery to deceive.

The Smoke and Fire shown in Figure 1.50 is created by one of Blender's **Quick Effects**. Look carefully and you will see that the Effect has been applied to only the bottom most log in the campfire. When the Effect is activated it creates the illusion that the whole campfire is burning.

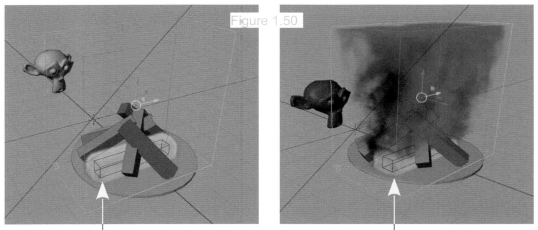

Figure 1.50

Quick Effect Smoke + Fire applied to the bottom log.

1.22 Smoke and Fire - Quick Effect

To apply the **Smoke and Fire Quick Effect** select the bottom log in the campfire in the 3D Viewport Editor.

Click on the **Object button** in the 3D Viewport Editor Header.

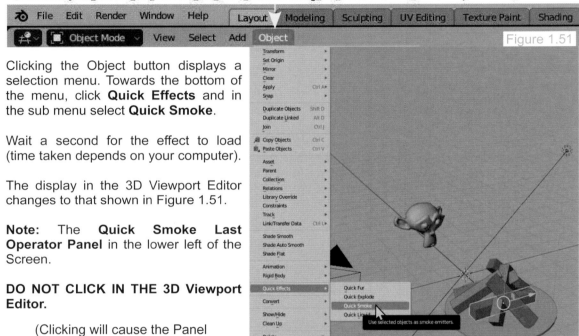

Clicking the Object button displays a selection menu. Towards the bottom of the menu, click **Quick Effects** and in the sub menu select **Quick Smoke**.

Wait a second for the effect to load (time taken depends on your computer).

The display in the 3D Viewport Editor changes to that shown in Figure 1.51.

Note: The **Quick Smoke Last Operator Panel** in the lower left of the Screen.

DO NOT CLICK IN THE 3D Viewport Editor.

(Clicking will cause the Panel to disappear.)

Quick Smoke Last Operator Panel Figure 1.52

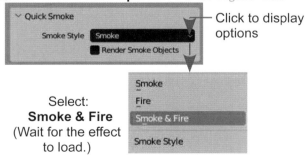

Click to display options

Select:
Smoke & Fire
(Wait for the effect to load.)

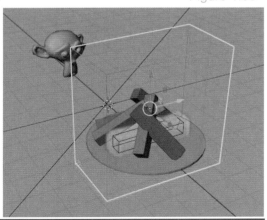

Figure 1.53

The display in the 3D Viewport Editor changes to that shown in Figure 1.53.

Loading the **Smoke & Fire** Quick Effect has automatically applied data to the log (modified Cube) which generates an Animated Physics Simulation. You see this as the orange glow surrounding the log and the orange cubic outline enclosing the campfire.

The orange glow is fire issuing from the log at the first Frame of the Animation. The orange cubic outline is called the Domain and is defining a cubic volume of space in which the simulation will take place.

Loading the Simulation has generated a 250 Frame Animation Sequence which you play in the **Timeline Editor** by clicking the **Play button**.

Figure 1.54   **End Frame**

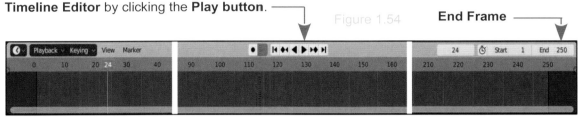

Timeline Editor

Pause the Animation at Frame 42 to see the simulation shown in Figure 1.55.

Figure 1.55   Figure 1.56

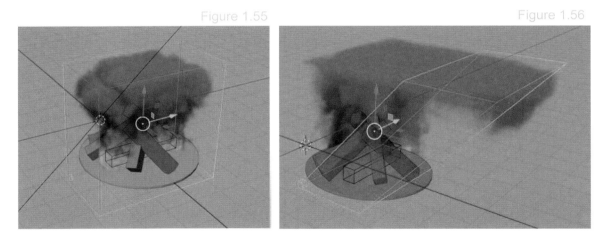

Note: In the Timeline Editor the default End Frame is 250, therefore, the simulation will continue to play until Frame 250 then automatically replay from Frame 1. During the simulation, flames (fire) will continually issue from the surface of the log and smoke will billow inside the Domain. The smoke, will not however, completely fill the Domain.

You may Scale, adjust and reposition the Domain to modify the effect (Figure 1.56) BUT in doing so the Object to which the Quick Effect is being applied (the lower log Cube) must remain entirely inside the Domain.

OK. You have a nice warm fire burning but Suzanne is patiently shivering with cold in the background. It's time to invite her to move closer to the fire.

1.23 Animating Suzanne

Animating Suzanne to move close to the fire will be done in two stages. First she will simply move closer and second her face will turn from blue to rosy red as she warms up.

With Suzanne selected in the 3D Viewport Editor and the Mouse Cursor in the Editor panel, press the **I Key** and click **Location** in the **Insert Keyframe Menu** that displays.

Figure 1.57

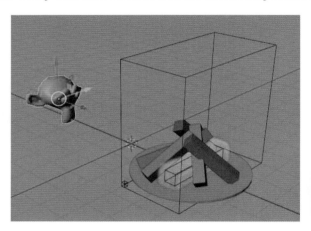

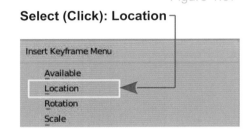

Select (Click): Location

Insert Keyframe Menu
- Available
- Location
- Rotation
- Scale

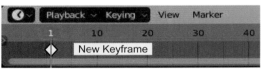

By default, the Timeline Editor Cursor will be located at Frame 1 in the Timeline. Inserting a Keyframe with the Cursor at Frame 1 inserts data which tells Blender the location of the selected Object in the 3D Viewport Editor. The new Keyframe is indicated by a small yellow triangle.

In the 3D Viewport Editor, move Suzanne closer to the camp fire (Figure 1.58).

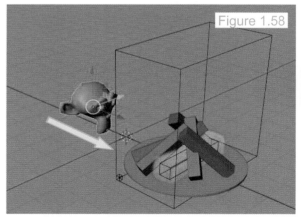

Figure 1.58

Position the Timeline Cursor at Frame 20 and with Suzanne selected, add a second Keyframe.

Figure 1.59

Adding a second Keyframe at Frame 20 with Suzanne repositioned tells Blender the position of Suzanne at Frame 20. When the Animation is played Blender will calculate where Suzanne is positioned at all Frames between Frame 1 and frame 20.

Suzanne is close to the campfire but she remains blue with cold. She needs to warm up.

To depict Suzanne warming, her face will change from Blue to rosy Red as the fire burns when the Animation plays.

Select Suzanne and examine her Material Properties (see 1.15 – Using the Properties Editor). You have already applied a blue Material (Figure 1.37) all you have to do is **Animate the color to change.**

In the Properties Editor, Material Properties Base Color, Color Picker you see that color is represented by numeric values.

Suzanne's blue, in the RGB Color Scheme is:

  R = 0.176
  G = 0.800
  B = 0.711

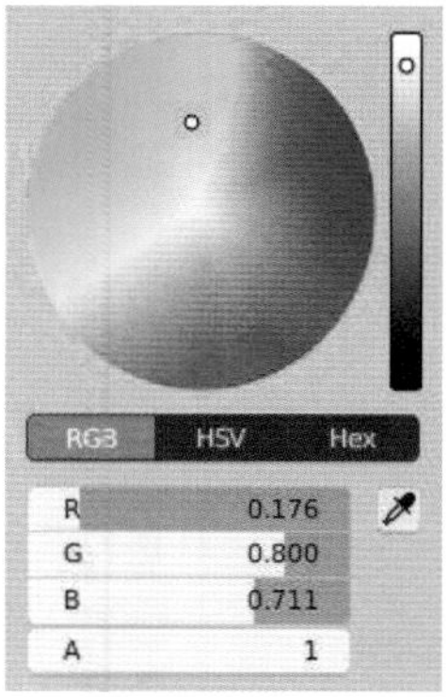

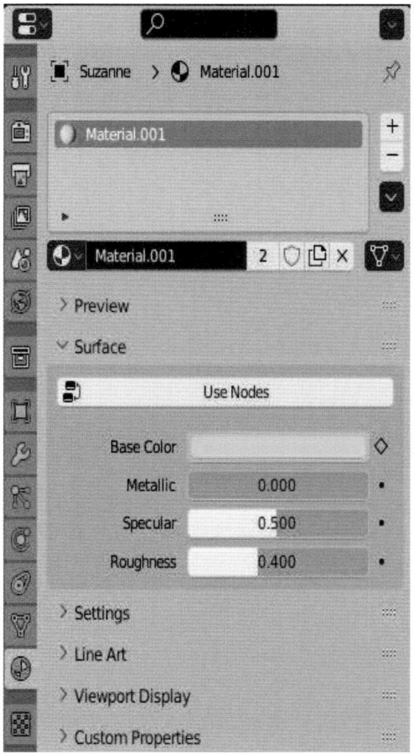

These values are in the range:

  RGB all 1.000 = white
  RGB all 0.000 = black

It follows that you can tell Blender what the Material color is, at any Frame in an Animation.

Figure 1.60

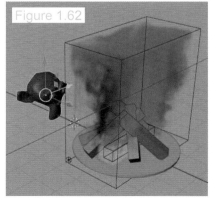

Position the Timeline Editor Cursor at Frame 20. Suzanne is located close to the fire with a blue face. Move the Timeline Cursor to Frame 30. Suzanne remains stationary but the fire has generated fire and smoke.

Right Mouse Click on the Base Color bar in the Properties Editor, Material buttons and select Diffuse Color: Insert Keyframe.

Figure 1.61

Diffuse Color

Insert Keyframe

Inserting a Keyframe at Frame 20 tells Blender to display Suzanne blue. A yellow diamond appears in the Timeline. Move the Timeline Cursor to Frame 60, change the Base Color to red, RMB Click and insert another Keyframe.

Figure 1.62

Timeline Editor

Position Keyframes   Material Keyframes
                                          (color)

Figure 1.63

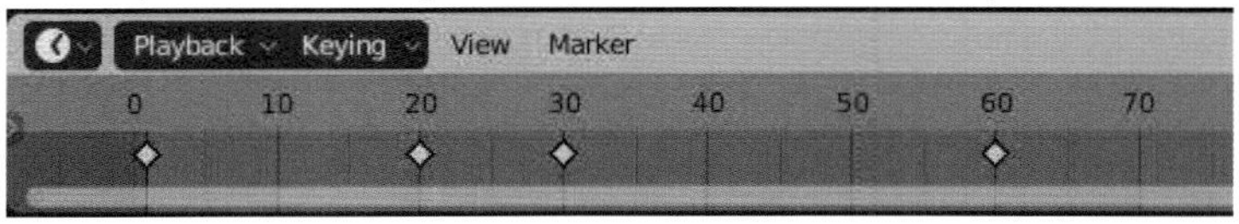

With Keyframes set to move Suzanne in the Scene and change her appearance as she moves closer to the fire you play the Animation by clicking the **Play button** in the **Timeline Editor** Header.

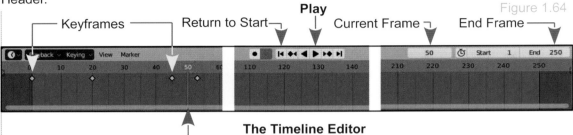

The Timeline Editor

If the **Timeline Editor Cursor is positioned at frame 50** as shown in Figure 1.64 the Animation will play from the current Frame (Frame 50) on to the End Frame (Frame 250) before restarting at Frame 1. To play the Animation from the beginning press the **Return to Start** button.

For full instruction on Animation see Chapter 19.

1.24 Render

Rendering means converting what you have created in the 3D Viewport Editor into a Image File or a Video File. An Image File will be what you see in Camera View at a single Frame in the Animation (see 1.17 Figure 1.48). A Video File consist of the entire Animation.

For full Render details see Chapter 14.

1.25 Summary

Chapter 1 has introduced Blender's Graphical User Interface and demonstrated a sample of the controls for operating Blender. At the same time you will have been subjected to the method of reading and applying instructions as you operate the program. The subjects selected for study have, hopefully, whetted your appetite and enticed you to continue with further study.

The samples, so far presented, are exactly that, a sample. There is so much more to learn and discover what can be achieved with this fantastic application. Before proceeding you should be fully conversant with the Blender interface and how it is configured for the different operational aspects of the program. There are built in arrangements of Editor Panels for different procedures and you may configure an arrangement for your own personal preference.

A particular arrangement of Editors is called a **Workspace**. How each Editor displays in regard to its aesthetic appearance is called a **Theme**. There are built in Themes from which to choose and you may construct a personal Theme.

Personal Workspaces and Themes are configured in a Blender file and saved on the computer for future use, therefore, knowing how to Navigate and Save files is essential.

2

Editors – Workspaces - Themes

Editors – Workspaces - Themes

Editors are the individual windows or panels which make up the Blender Interface. They contain the controls for editing data. Everything initially displayed in the 3D Viewport Editor (Window) is generated by a set of default data which you modify using the controls in the various Editors.

Workspaces are the arrangement of Editors in the Graphical User Interface (GUI). The Blender **GUI** opens with four separate Editors displayed. This arrangement constitutes a **Workspace** (working space) where you arrange models and characters and create Scenes. The default Workspace is called the **General** Workspace. There are alternative pre-constructed Workspaces available and you may configure your own.

Themes are how the Graphical User Interface displays as a whole and are purely cosmetic. Blender has several Themes for selection. You can create your own or download custom builds from the internet.

You may resize the Editor Panels, divide the Panels, creating additional Panels and change each Panel to a different type. In doing this you create a specialised Workspace which can be saved in a Blender file and reused. You can generate your personal Theme in a Blender file.

This chapter will introduce the controls for each of the above which will allow you to configure Blender for your personal requirements.

2.1 Editor Types

The **Default** Screen arrangement comprises four individual panels or windows, as shown in Figure 1.1 in Chapter 1. The panels are called **Editors**.

The default Editors displayed are: The **3D Viewport Editor**, the **Outliner Editor,** the **Properties Editor** and the **Timeline Editor**. Each has an icon representing the **Editor Type** in the upper left hand corner of the panel. Clicking LMB on this icon displays a menu for changing the Editor to a different Editor Type.

3D View Editor Icon – click LMB to display the **Editor Type Selection Menu**

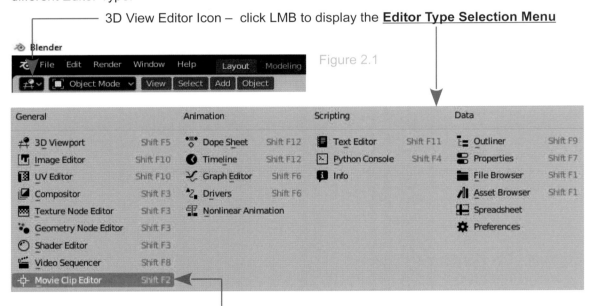

Figure 2.1

In the Editor Type menu, select (click) one of the Editors and the current Editor changes to that selected.

Here's an example; In the upper LH (Left hand) corner of the **3D Viewport Editor**, position the mouse cursor over the **Editor Icon** and click the left mouse button to display the Editor Type selection menu. Select (click on), **Graph Editor**, in the menu and the 3D Viewport Editor changes to the **Graph Editor**. In the upper left corner of this Editor click on the **Graph Editor** icon and select **3D Viewport** in the menu. The Graph Editor reverts to the 3D Viewport Editor. Any Editor may be changed to a different Editor type in this way.

Note: Make a note of the **Preferences Editor** in the selection menu.

2.2 Resizing Editors

Figure 2.2

Most Editors and panels may be resized. Place the mouse cursor on an Editor or panel border and it changes to a double headed arrow (Figure 2.2). Click and hold the LH Mouse button and drag the arrow to resize the Editor panel. This works on both horizontal and vertical borders.

2.3 Splitting Editors

Editors may be divided, to initially form a duplicate, then changed to a different Editor Type. When the mouse cursor is placed in the corner of an Editor panel it changes to a **white cross** Figure 2.3 Right). Click **RMB** and select a **Split Area** option in the menu that displays. Drag the Mouse **horizontally or vertically** into the Editor to be divided. The Mouse Cursor changes with a **dividing line attached (Figure 2.3 Left). Position the dividing line and click LMB.**

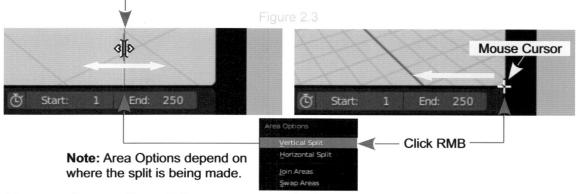

Figure 2.3

Mouse Cursor

Click RMB

Note: Area Options depend on where the split is being made.

Alternatively, to split an Editor, mouse over in the corner of an Editor panel (mouse icon becomes a cross), LMB click, hold and drag the Cursor into the Editor to be divided.

If you make a mistake with the Split direction (Vertical – Horizontal) press **Esc** before releasing the Mouse button.

Alternatively, where **View** displays in a **Header**, click **View** then select **Area** (at the bottom of the menu that displays) then choose Horizontal or Vertical Split. Position the line that displays where you want the split to be then click LMB.

With an Editor split in two, one copy may be changed to another Editor Type (Figure 2.4).

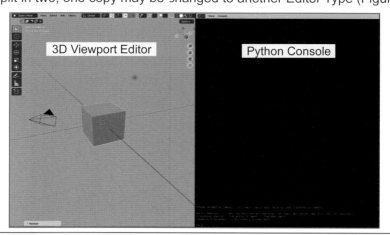

Figure 2.4

3D Viewport Editor

Python Console

Note: Henceforth the **3D Viewport Editor** may be abbreviated to the **3D Viewport**

2.4 Cancel an Editor

To cancel or join an Editor panel, position the Mouse cursor in the Editor corner (cursor becomes a cross). Click RMB and select **Join Area** in the menu that displays (Figure 2.5). The Mouse Cursor becomes a chevron. Drag the chevron into unwanted Editor. The Editor darkens (Figure 2.6). Click LMB to cancel the unwanted Editor.

Figure 2.5

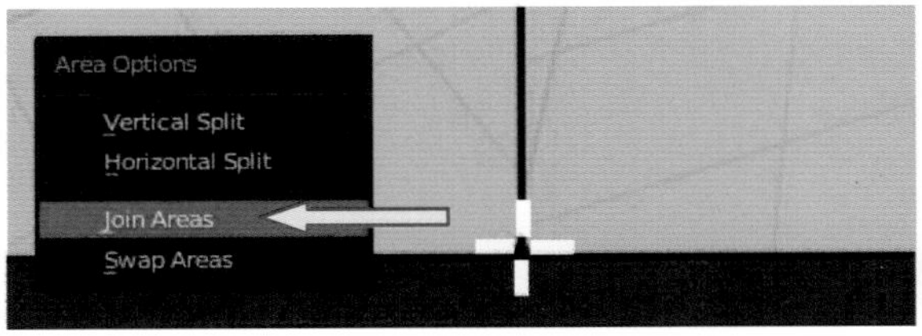
Area Options
Vertical Split
Horizontal Split
Join Areas
Swap Areas

Figure 2.6

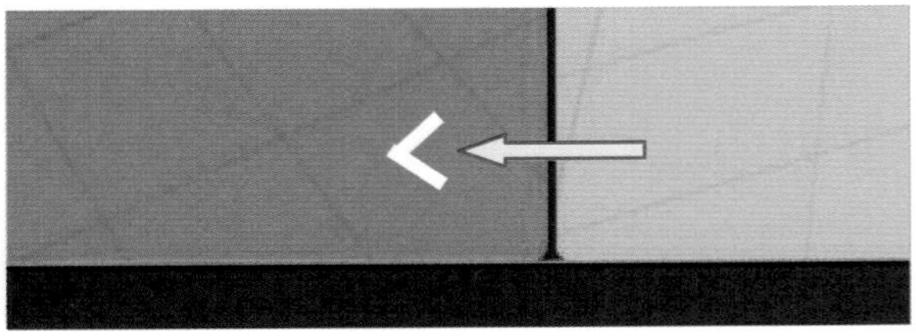

Note: While holding LMB with the chevron displayed you may reverse the direction from one Editor to the other. If you drag to the wrong Editor the Cursor displays as a No Go Signal:

170

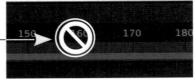

2.5 3D Viewport Features

Figure 2.7 shows the main features included in the **3D Viewport Editor** display.

Figure 2.7

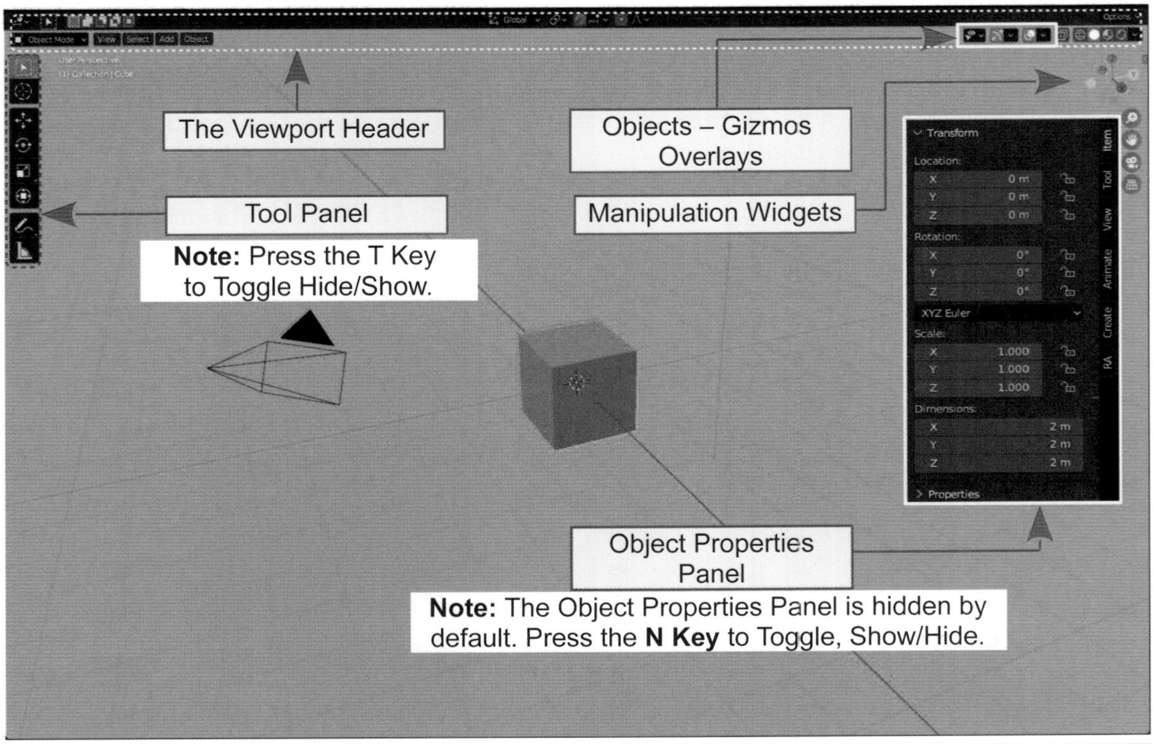
The Viewport Header
Objects – Gizmos Overlays
Tool Panel
Manipulation Widgets
Note: Press the T Key to Toggle Hide/Show.
Transform
Location:
Rotation:
XYZ Euler
Scale:
Dimensions:
Properties
Item
Tool
View
Animate
Create
Object Properties Panel
Note: The Object Properties Panel is hidden by default. Press the N Key to Toggle, Show/Hide.

Uncluttering the Scene

When a Scene becomes complicated it can be advantageous to turn off displays such as the User Perspective and Object notification in the upper left hand corner of the 3D Viewport or the Scene manipulation Widget at the right hand side or perhaps the background grid in the 3D Viewport panel.

As described in Chapter 1 – 1.8 some of the display in the 3D Viewport may be controlled in the **Outliner Editor** by clicking the eye icons adjacent to the entries.

Hiding and showing displays here applies to Objects in the 3D Viewport.

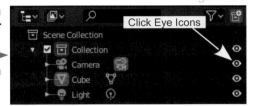

Figure 2.8

Click Eye Icons

Other displays are controlled by **Object Type**, **Gizmos** and **Overlays** from the 3D Viewport Header (Figure 2.9).

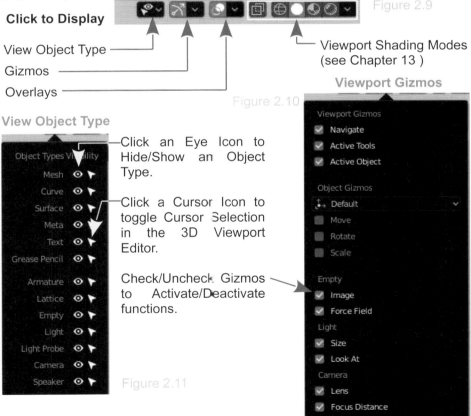

Figure 2.9

Click to Display

View Object Type

Gizmos

Overlays

Viewport Shading Modes
(see Chapter 13)

Viewport Gizmos

Figure 2.10

View Object Type

Click an Eye Icon to Hide/Show an Object Type.

Click a Cursor Icon to toggle Cursor Selection in the 3D Viewport Editor.

Check/Uncheck Gizmos to Activate/Deactivate functions.

Figure 2.11

Overlays: control what displays in the 3D Viewport.

Note: The Overlay selection is different in Object Mode and Edit Mode (Figure 2.12 over).

35

Object Mode Overlays   Figure 2.12   Edit Mode Overlays

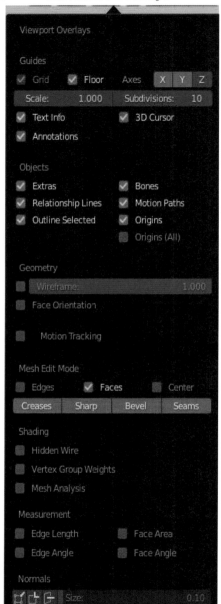

Note: The 3D Viewport has several different Modes. Overlays are only relevant to Object Mode and Edit Mode. You switch between the Modes by clicking on the Object Mode button in the 3D Viewport Header and selecting Edit Mode or vice versa. You may also toggle between Object and Edit Modes by pressing the **Tab Key**.

You set **Overlay** preferences in the relevant Overlay panels. The preferences are then toggled on / off by clicking the **Toggle Button** in the Header.   Figure 2.13

e.g. With **Floor** checked in Object Mode, clicking the Toggle button Hides and Shows the Grid Floor.

2.6 Scene Manipulation

Before adding new Objects and creating a Scene you should be conversant with how the 3D Viewport may be viewed and how to move in the three dimensional world.

Moving in 3D Space

In a 3D (Three Dimensional) program, not only do you have to consider where you are in two dimensions (height and width), but you also need to consider depth (how close or far away).

Moving around in the 3D Viewport is controlled by the Mouse and the Keyboard Number Pad.

User Perspective and Orthographic View

The Blender default Scene in the 3D Viewport, opens in the **User Perspective** view as indicated in the upper LH corner of the Editor. The Scene contains a Cube Object located at the center. There is also a Camera and a Light in the Scene. All three Objects are positioned relative to the center of the Scene which is the center of the 3D World, or if you like, a central point in 3D Space.

The Blender Scene may be viewed in either **Perspective** or **Orthographic** view. Toggle between the two views by pressing **Num Pad 5 on the Keyboard**.

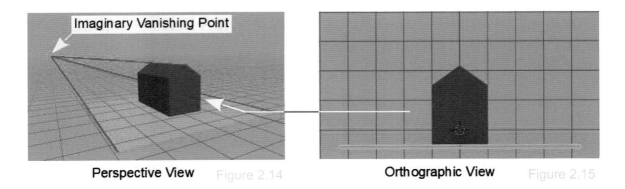

Perspective View   Figure 2.14   Orthographic View   Figure 2.15

A **Perspective View** projects parallel lines to a single vanishing point somewhere in the distance. In landscape drawing this will be on the horizon.

An **Orthographic View** is seen looking square on (90°) to a Face.

The position of Objects relative to each other is important when considering 3D Space especially with Lights (lighting) and the Camera (seeing). When taking a photograph with a camera the position of the camera relative to what you want to photograph and where the lighting is located determine what you get in your snapshot. This is the same in a Blender Scene.

By default the Camera in the default Scene is positioned such that it points towards the Cube and with the default settings, for the Camera, captures an image of the Cube in its viewport. This is the image that will render (convert what the Camera sees to an image). To understand this, perform the following demonstration.

With the default Scene, have the Mouse Cursor in the 3D Viewport and press the Keyboard **Num Pad 0.** This places the 3D Viewport in **Camera View** (what the Camera sees). Press **F12** on the Keyboard to **Render (Esc to Quit).**

Figure 2.16

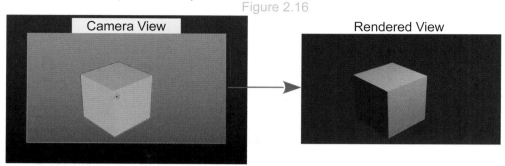

Camera View

Rendered View

Pressing **F12** Renders (converts) the Camera view to a format that may be saved as an image file. Note that the rendered view has been opened in a new Editor – the **Image Editor**.

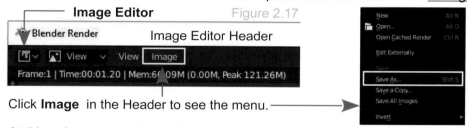

Image Editor   Figure 2.17

Image Editor Header

Click **Image** in the Header to see the menu.

At this point you could save the display as an image. To save an image you have to understand how to save a file into a folder (see Chapter 3).

Press the **Esc Key** to cancel the Image Editor window and return to Camera View in the 3D Viewport . Press the **Num Pad 5 Key** to enter **User Orthographic** view, then press the **Num Pad 5 Key** a second time for **User Perspective** view.

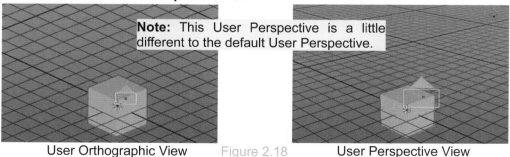

Note: This User Perspective is a little different to the default User Perspective.

User Orthographic View   Figure 2.18   User Perspective View

Pressing Num Pad 5 a second time displays a User Perspective view but it isn't the same as the original view in the 3D Viewport. To return to the original view press **Num Pad 6** or place the Mouse Cursor in the 3D Viewport, click the Middle Mouse Button (MMB), hold the button depressed and drag the Mouse to rotate the view.

Clicking, holding and dragging MMB is one of several methods for manipulating the Scene in then 3D Viewport. Clicking **View – Navigation** in the Header gives a menu with all the **options**.

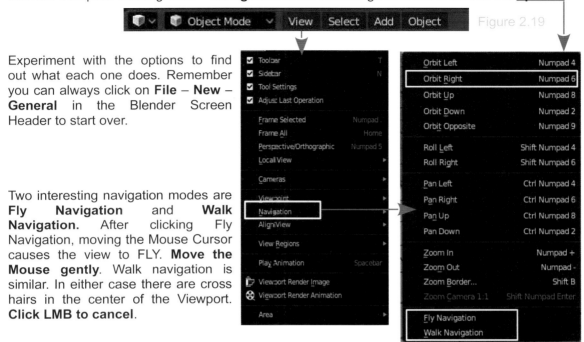

Experiment with the options to find out what each one does. Remember you can always click on **File – New – General** in the Blender Screen Header to start over.

Two interesting navigation modes are **Fly Navigation** and **Walk Navigation.** After clicking Fly Navigation, moving the Mouse Cursor causes the view to FLY. **Move the Mouse gently**. Walk navigation is similar. In either case there are cross hairs in the center of the Viewport. **Click LMB to cancel**.

2.7 Scene Manipulation Widget (another way to Navigate)

Place the Mouse Cursor in proximity to the Widget to display the circle. Click, hold and move the Mouse to rotate the view.

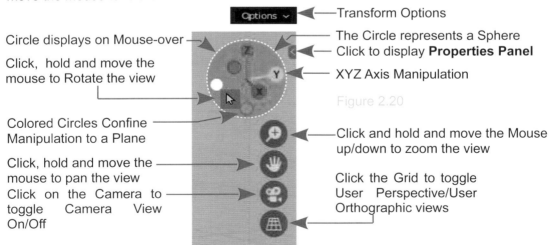

Note: The Red, Green and Blue circles on the rotation sphere align with the Red, Green and Blue Axis of the 3D Scene. Mouse over on a circle highlights the notation.

2.8 Multiple Scenes

At this point it is worth reinforcing the distinction between a **Scene** and a **Workspace**. The definitions have been presented at the beginning of the chapter but in introducing the concept of multiple Scenes clarification may be required.

The **Scene** is what you see in the 3D Viewport and consists of your models, characters, lighting effects and background. The **Workspace** is the arrangement of Editor Panels in the Graphical User Interface (what you see on the computer screen).

Workspaces are Screen Arrangements of Editors for working at specific tasks. The default Screen arrangement is the **Layout Workspace** as seen in the **Screen Header**.

Cursor Tool Selected in the Tool Panel   **Workspaces**   Figure 2.21

The main portion of the Layout Workspace is the 3D Viewport which shows a 3D View of the default Blender Scene. The Scene has a Cube Object at the center of the 3D World.

Figure 2.22

The Outliner Editor (Figure 2.22) displays **Scene Collection** which lists the Objects in the Scene in the 3D Viewport. At this point there is one single Scene in this Blender file.

At some stage you may wish to have more Scenes which is like having different sets on a stage or different sets for filming different parts of a movie.

In the Screen Header (upper RH side) you will see **Scene** displayed. Clicking on the Scene button shows a single entry **Scene** (highlighted blue).

To add additional Scenes click the **Add Scene button**.

Click **New** in the options menu. The 3D View Editor shows a new empty Scene. **Scene.001** is entered in the Header.

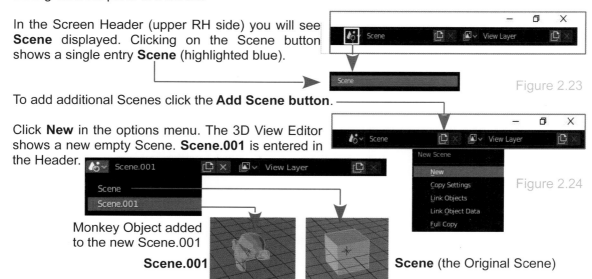

Monkey Object added to the new Scene.001

Scene.001

Scene (the Original Scene)

Figure 2.23

Figure 2.24

If you add a Monkey to the Scene you have the option to select the default Scene with the Cube or the New Scene with the Monkey. The New Scene is only available in the Blender File being worked on. Save the file for future use.

Click to display Scene selection

The demonstration shows the default Blender Scene containing the default Cube Object and a new Scene containing a Monkey Object. The default Scene is named: **Scene**, the new Scene is named: **Scene.001**.

With the two Scenes created make note of the content of the Outliner Editor when each Scene is selected in turn (Figure 2.25).

Figure 2.25

With **Scene** (the default Scene) selected, pressing Num Pad 0 will display Camera View (what the Camera sees). Pressing Num Pad 0 with Scene.001 selected has no effect since there is no Camera in Scene.001. There is also no Light in Scene.001, therefore, there will be no lighting effects until a Light is added to Scene.001.

If you wish to add items included in the original Scene to Scene.001 you simply copy and paste.

Fore example: To add the Camera and Light in Scene to Scene.001, in the 3D Viewport Editor, with **Scene** selected, hold Shift and LMB click on the Objects to be copied (Camera and Lamp) then RMB click and select Copy Objects in the menu that displays. Select Scene.001 in the Screen Header and in 3D Viewport Editor for Scene.001, RMB click and select Paste Objects.

Note: In the Outliner Editor with **Scene** selected the display shows the Objects listed under **Collection** which is listed under **Scene Collection**. With **Scene.001** selected the display shows the Objects listed under **Scene Collection** (no sub entry Collection).

Scene   **Scene.001**

Figure 2.26

For details of how Objects are listed in Collections see Chapter 20 **Outliner &Collections** .

2.9 Headers Menus and Panels

The default Blender Screen is made up with four Editor Panels and three Headers as seen in Figure 2.27. Each Editor Panel has a Header across the top of the Panel.

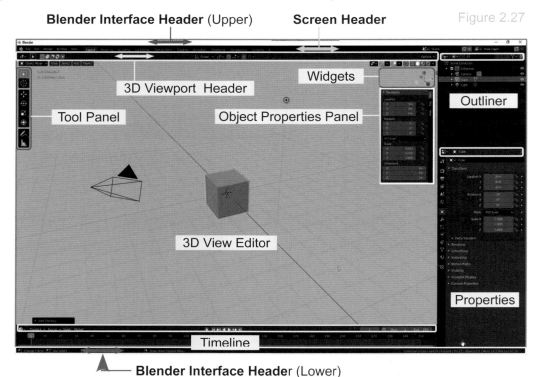

Blender Interface Header (Upper)   **Screen Header**   Figure 2.27

Widgets

3D Viewport Header

Outliner

Tool Panel   Object Properties Panel

3D View Editor

Properties

Timeline

Blender Interface Header (Lower)

The following diagrams will make you aware of the selection menus available in the Headers.

2.10 Headers and Panels

The Headers contain icons and text notations which are buttons that display Selection Menus containing options for activating functions affecting what takes place in the Editor. The options are numerous, therefore, it is not recommended that you attempt to memorise every option. Being aware of the different menus will help when reference is made in instructions. Specific references to selections will be made as required.

2.11 The Blender Interface Header

Quit the Program
Expand the Screen
Minimise (Hide) the Screen

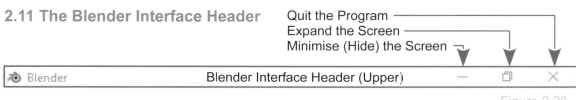

Blender   Blender Interface Header (Upper)   —   ⬜   ✕

Figure 2.28

2.12 The Blender Screen Header

Click a Button to Display a Menu

Figure 2.29

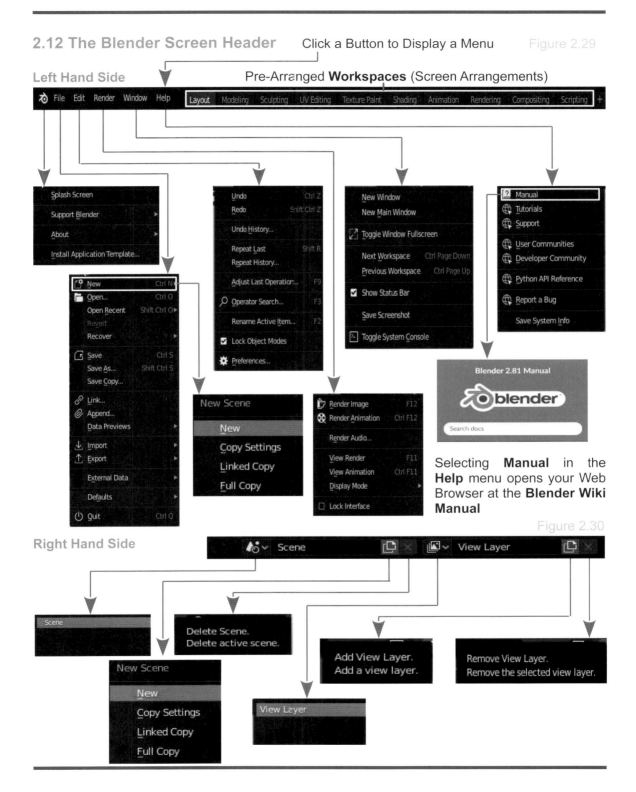

Left Hand Side

Pre-Arranged **Workspaces** (Screen Arrangements)

Selecting **Manual** in the **Help** menu opens your Web Browser at the **Blender Wiki Manual**

Figure 2.30

Right Hand Side

2.13 The 3D Viewport Header

The 3D Viewport Header is divided into three sections.

Note: The Header controls in Figure 2.31 are for the 3D Viewport when in **Object Mode**. The selection menus shown are a sample only.

The controls change when selecting an alternative Mode for the 3D Viewport Editor.

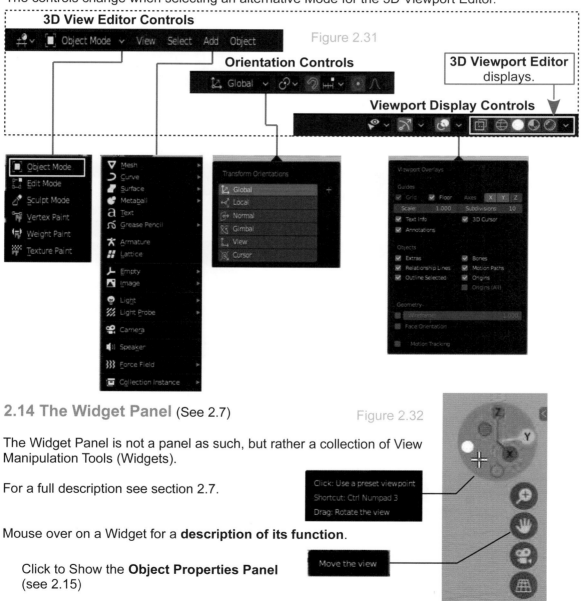

2.14 The Widget Panel (See 2.7)

Figure 2.32

The Widget Panel is not a panel as such, but rather a collection of View Manipulation Tools (Widgets).

For a full description see section 2.7.

Mouse over on a Widget for a **description of its function**.

Click to Show the **Object Properties Panel** (see 2.15)

2.15 The Tool Panel and Object Properties Panel

The Tool Panel at the left hand side of the 3D Viewport Editor houses Tools for performing operations on the Object which is selected. The Panel has three display arrangements.

Mouse over on the edge of the panel, click, hold and drag to increment the displays.

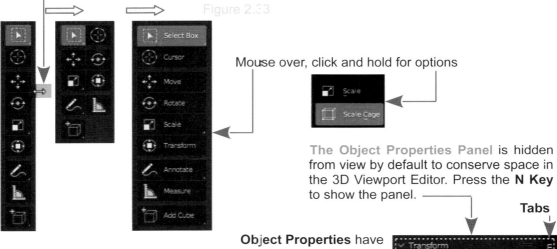

Figure 2.33

Mouse over, click and hold for options

The Object Properties Panel is hidden from view by default to conserve space in the 3D Viewport Editor. Press the **N Key** to show the panel.

Tabs

Object Properties have six display Modes.

Click a Tab to change Modes

Note: The **Object Properties Panel** allows you to adjust values affecting the Properties of the selected Object. For example increasing the X Location value in the positive direction moves the Object on the X Axis in the 3D Viewport Editor.

Note: To hide the Object Properties Panel press the **N Key.** You may show and hide the **Tool Panel** by pressing the **T Key.** Alternatively click on Chevrons in the upper corners of the 3D Viewport Editor when the panels are hidden

Chevron

Cheveron

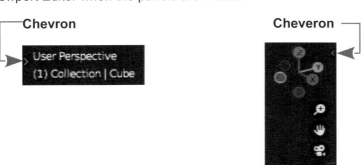

2.16 Properties Editor Tabs

The Properties Editor is the panel below the Outliner Editor which extends to the bottom of the Screen. This Editor is the engine room for Blender containing controls for actions in the 3D Viewport Editor. The controls will be explained as you progress through the book and encounter the different features of the program. What you see in the Properties Editor depends on which selection button is activated (Figure 2.34). There are fifteen **Properties** from which to choose, each will present a different display of controls. The Properties are arranged in two categories (Scene Controls and Object Controls).

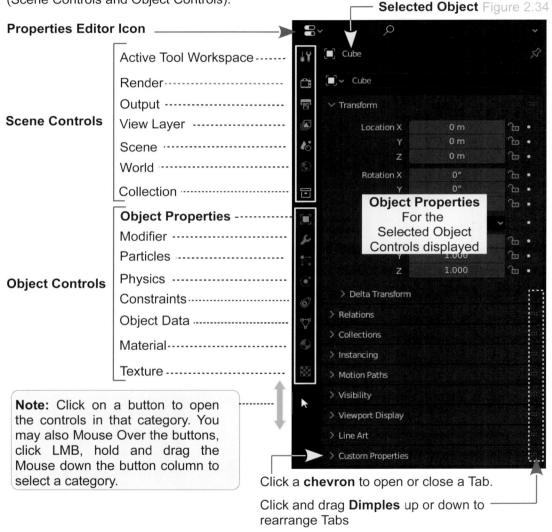

Selected Object Figure 2.34

Properties Editor Icon

Scene Controls
- Active Tool Workspace
- Render
- Output
- View Layer
- Scene
- World
- Collection

Object Controls
- **Object Properties**
- Modifier
- Particles
- Physics
- Constraints
- Object Data
- Material
- Texture

Object Properties
For the
Selected Object
Controls displayed

Note: Click on a button to open the controls in that category. You may also Mouse Over the buttons, click LMB, hold and drag the Mouse down the button column to select a category.

Click a **chevron** to open or close a Tab.

Click and drag **Dimples** up or down to rearrange Tabs

Figures 2.32 shows the Properties Editor with the **Object Properties** selected. The Object Properties control the properties of **the Object that is selected** in the 3D Viewport Editor Scene. The default Object is the Cube. The Object button displays controls and information about any Object which you have selected in the 3D Viewport Editor.

2.17 The Preferences Editor

The **Preferences Editor** is a behind scenes control panel for configuring and adding functionality to Blender. The controls are extensive, therefore, will be referenced as the various features are required while progressing through the book. At this point you should be aware of the Editors existence and have a general understanding of what it entails.

The **Preferences Editor** may be opened by clicking an Editor Icon and selecting **Preferences** in the Editor selection menu (Figure 2.1). This method will fill the entire Editor Panel. For example selecting the 3D Viewport Editor icon and selecting Preferences fills the 3D Viewport Editor Panel with the Preferences Editor.

For many operations opening the Preferences Editor in this way is fine but when configuring the 3D Viewport Editor from the Preferences Editor it is advantageous to see changes as they are made.

Access the Preferences Editor from the Blender Screen Header.

Click **Edit** and select **Preferences**

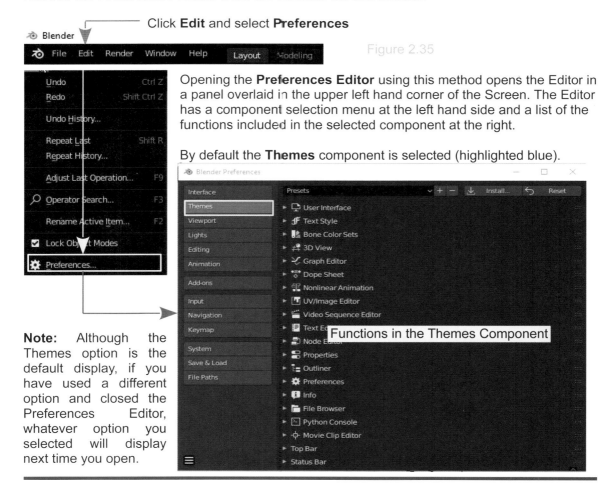

Figure 2.35

Opening the **Preferences Editor** using this method opens the Editor in a panel overlaid in the upper left hand corner of the Screen. The Editor has a component selection menu at the left hand side and a list of the functions included in the selected component at the right.

By default the **Themes** component is selected (highlighted blue).

Note: Although the Themes option is the default display, if you have used a different option and closed the Preferences Editor, whatever option you selected will display next time you open.

2.18 3D Viewport Editor - Background Color

In the **Preferences Editor, Themes**, click the triangle adjacent to **3D View**. With the **Mouse Cursor** in the right hand panel of the **Preferences Editor**, scroll down, **way way down**, until you see **Theme Space**. Expand this entry (click the triangle) and scroll way way down again to **Gradient Colors**. Expand this entry. You will find the **Gradient High/Off** color bar. This is where you change the color of the 3D Viewport Editor background.

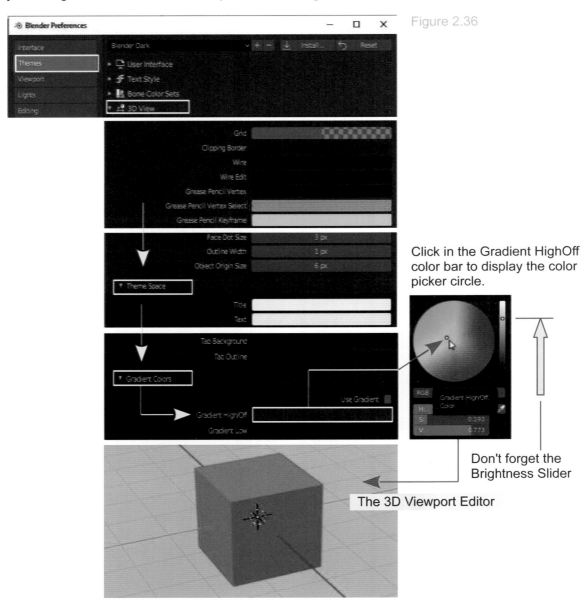

Figure 2.36

Click in the Gradient HighOff color bar to display the color picker circle.

Don't forget the Brightness Slider

The 3D Viewport Editor

2.19 Workspaces

Workspaces are the arrangement of Editor panels configured for specific working procedures.

The default arrangement of Editors is configured to provide a space for compiling a Scene, that is primarily to enter and position Objects. The Objects may be for creating models or they could be pre-constructed models of characters. The default arrangement is named the **Layout Workspace**.

In the default Screen arrangement Header you will see **Layout** highlighted white which indicates that this Workspace is the **Active Workspace**.

Also in the Screen Header is a selection of **alternative Workspaces** designed for a variety of operations (Figure 2.37).

The Active Workspace

Figure 2.37

Selecting the **Modeling** Workspace places the default 3D Viewport Editor in **Edit Mode**

Figure 2.38

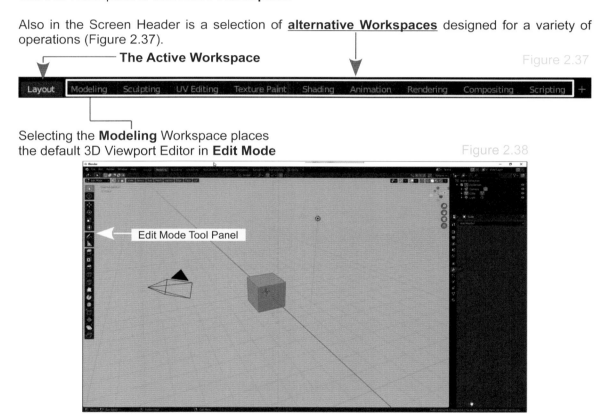

Edit Mode Tool Panel

2.20 Creating New Workspaces

As explained in Section 2.19, **Workspaces** are the arrangements of Editor Panels configured for specific working procedures. You may select one of the **Pre-Assembled Workspace** in the Blender Screen Header (Figure 2.39 over) or you can create a new unique Workspace.

Pre-Assembled Workspaces ⌐   Click ✚ to create a new Workspace ⌐

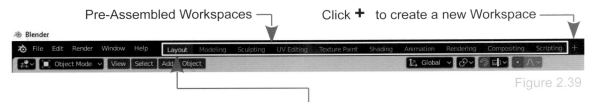

Figure 2.39

To create a new Workspace select the default **Layout** Workspace in the Header, that is, have the default Blender Screen arrangement opened.

Click the cross in the Blender Screen Header at the RHS of the Workspace options. Click **Duplicate Current** in the menu that displays. Duplicating Current generates a copy of the current Screen arrangement and automatically names it **Layout.001**. The new name is displayed in the Header.

Click on **Layout.001** in the Blender Screen Header to ensure you have Layout.001 displayed in the Screen. You may now reconfigure the Screen arrangement to suit your working requirements. Rearrange the Blender Screen by splitting Editors and moving borders and changing the Editor Types. This creates a new Workspace (Figure 2.40).

Figure 2.40

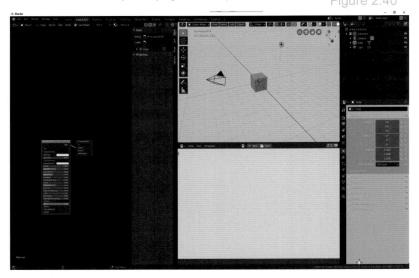

Note: The new Workspace is only available in the current Blender File. If the current file is the default Blender file, save the current file with a new name to make the new Workspace available for future work.

With **Layout.001** configured, selecting **Layout** in the Screen header changes the Screen back to the default Screen arrangement.

You may create as many Workspaces as you like by repeating the procedure outlined above. New Workspaces will be named: Layout.001, Layout.002, Layout.003, Layout.004 etc.

You rename a Workspace by double clicking on the name in the Screen Header, backspace and retype a new name.

Saving a Workspace

> **Note**: Creating a Workspace (Working Environment) in the default Blender Screen arrangement is, in fact, modifying the default Blender File. This procedure occurs whenever you change anything in the default Screen. This means, whenever you model something, change a color or create an animation, the changes are, therefore, only available in the Blender file that is open when the changes are made.
>
> To use changes in future work you have to save the Blender File, as a new file, then reopen it when you want to use something contained in the file. This applies to Workspaces.

How to save a Blender file is discussed in Chapter 3.

2.21 Themes

A **Theme** is the cosmetic appearance of the interface. This is purely a matter of taste and personal preference. Working in a pleasing environment has a beneficial effect on work output and changing the environment occasionally can give a new lease of life.

For your convenience Blender has a choice of nine Themes. You may download and install new Themes into Blender from the Internet.

Inbuilt Themes: are found in the **Preferences Editor**. You can change an Editor Panel to the Preferences Editor as demonstrated in Section 2.1 but for convenience, when changing the appearance of the Blender interface, it is better to open the Preferences Editor from the Blender Screen Header. This method opens the Editor as a small separate Panel over the top of the GUI allowing you to see changes as the occur .

In the Blender Screen Header click on **Edit**. Select **Preferences** at the bottom of the menu.

Figure 2.41

The Edit Menu

In the **Preferences Editor** click **Presets**

Figure 2.42

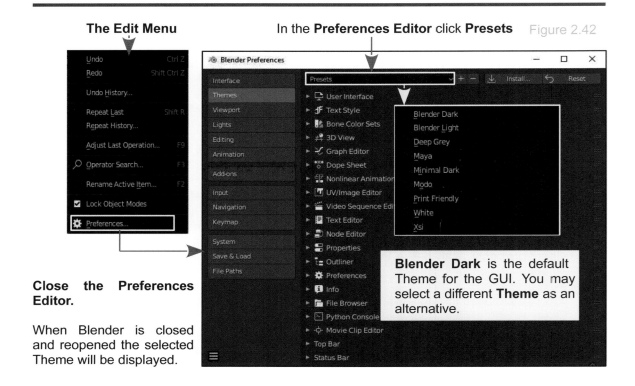

Blender Dark is the default Theme for the GUI. You may select a different **Theme** as an alternative.

Close the Preferences Editor.

When Blender is closed and reopened the selected Theme will be displayed.

Installing New Themes

You may download and install themes from the internet. Themes are downloaded as Blender 2.81 XML Files. One example is found at:

https://blenderartists.org/t/theme-awsome-theme-for-blender-2-8/1120656

Download [Theme] **Awesome** – Theme for Blender 2.8 XML File from:

Figure 2.43

With the XML file saved to your computer, open the **Preferences Editor** and click on **Install...** in the Header.

Figure 2.44

Navigate to the **XML file** in the **File Browser** (see Chapter 3), select the file and click **Install Theme** .

The **Awesome** Theme will be available in the **Theme Preset** menu.

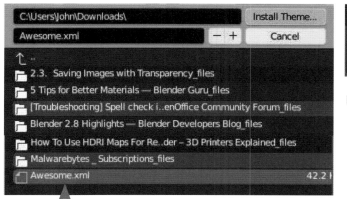

Figure 2.45

The **Theme: Awesome.xml** saved in the Downloads folder on the PC.

> **Note: Saving Files** and Navigating the **Blender File Browser** is explained in Chapter 3.

Creating New Themes

A new Theme may be created from within Blender. In Figure 1.1 in Chapter 1 the background colors of the Editor Panels were modified to make it easier to identify the individual Panels. These modification can be saved as a Theme for future use.

To change Editor background colors, open the **Preferences Editor** and have **Themes** selected in the left hand column. Click on a triangle adjacent to the Editor you wish to modify, for example the **Properties Editor**, then click the triangle adjacent to **Theme Space**. You will see Window Background and a gray color bar. Click the color bar and select a new color in the color picker.

Click Triangles to Expand   Figure 2.46   Drag the Brightness Slider Up

Selecting a color changes the color in the Color Bar and the background of the Editor Panel.

You may repeat this procedure for any Editor Type but be aware, the 3D Viewport Editor is different, as explained in section 2.18.

2.22 Saving a Theme

In the **Preferences Editor** Header click on **Add Theme Preset**. Figure 2.47

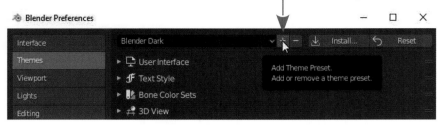

In the panel that displays click in the area next to **Name** to show a typing cursor and type a name for the Theme. Click **OK**.

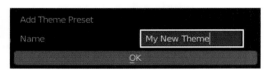

My New Theme is entered as one of the available Themes.

Note: A Theme, including a new Theme, may be applied to any Workspace. As with Themes, you can create your own unique Workspaces.

3

Navigate and Save

Saving Work

When you work in Blender you edit (modify) the default file which opens when you start Blender or a file that has been previously saved. Blender file names end with a **.blend** suffix and are peculiar to the Blender program. Saving work means you save the modifications or editing, that has been performed in a Blender file. You save the file, in a folder of your choice on your computer's hard drive. You should understand how and where to create a folder and how to retrieve a file when it has been saved. In other words you need to know how to navigate your file system. In Blender files are saved on your computer using the **File Browser Editor**.

Navigation

Navigation is the science of finding the way from one place to another. If you can see where you are going it's an easy process to head over to that place but sometimes where you want to go is hidden from view. In Blender you create files and store them away for future use. You can reuse the files and build on to them and then save the new material. Saved files are your library of information from which you extract elements and insert into future work. The saying is, **"There is no point reinventing the wheel"**. If you have created something that works use it again. But where did you put the wheel? That's where navigation comes in. You need to find the place where you safely stored that wheel or, in the case of Blender, where you saved a file containing the wheel. Navigation in Blender is performed in the **File Browser Editor**.

3.1 Files and Folders

Definition (from the internet)

A file is a common storage unit in a computer, and all programs and data are "written" into a file and "read" from a file. A folder holds one or more files, and a folder can be empty until it is filled. A folder can contain other folders (sub folders). Folders provide a method for organising files much like a manila file folder contains paper documents in a file cabinet. In fact, files that contain text are often called documents.

Folders are also called "directories," and they are created on the hard drive (HD) or solid state drive (SSD) when the operating system and applications are installed. Files are always stored in folders. In fact, even the computer desktop is a folder; a special kind of folder that displays its contents across the entire screen.

File Extensions

A file extension or suffix, is the bit at the end of a file name preceded by a dot or period. For example; My_Photo.JPEG, would be a JPEG image (photograph). The .JPEG extension tells the computer which application (App) or program to use when opening the file. With a .JPEG extension the computer would look for an image editor or viewer to open the file. With a .TXT extension, signifying a text file, the computer would use a text editor.

When writing file extensions to a file name they are usually written in lower case letters such as **.jpeg** or **.txt**.

Blender files have a **.blend** extension which tells the computer to open the file in the Blender program.

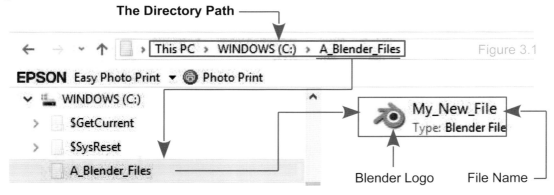

Windows 10 File Explorer

Figure 3.1 show a Blender file saved in the **C: Directory** (Hard Drive) in a Folder named **A_Blender_Files**. The Blender file is named **My_New_File**. Blender file names usually display with the Blender logo preceding the file name but the **.blend** file extension does not always display.

3.2 Saving a File

Outliner Editor ─── ─── Blender File Mode

On a computer, when you save a Blender file (.blend) you are saving the data which is producing the display on the computer screen. This set of data includes not only what you see but all the settings which control all the effects that will be displayed in the various Editors. The Blender file may be considered as a complete package. Saving a file for the default arrangement saves everything.

Figure 3.2

Figure 3.2 (Right) shows the data listed in the **Outliner Editor** which would be saved for the default Blender Scene. Even before any editing has taken place the list is extensive. All this data is saved to a single file.

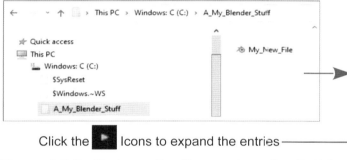

Click the ▶ Icons to expand the entries ─────

Figure 3.2 (Left) shows the file saved on the **C:** Drive (Hard Drive) of the computer in the Directory Folder named **A_My_Blender_Stuff**. The file has been named **My_New_File**. Although not shown, in this Windows file system the file does have a **.blend** suffix.

> **Note:** Figure 3.2 shows the **Outliner Editor in Blender File Mode.**
>
> **Note:** Placing an **A** in front of the Directory Folder name ensures that it is located at the top of the alphabetical directory list.

In Blender the **File Browser Editor** (Figure 3.3) is used to navigate through the file system on your computer. On a Windows operating system, **Windows Explorer** or **Windows File Explorer** are used. Blender's File Browser is a little different to the Windows system in appearance but uses the same work flow.

Blender File Browser   Figure 3.3

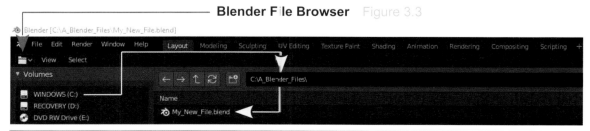

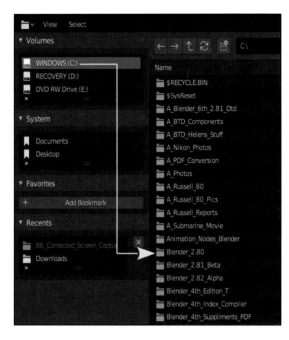

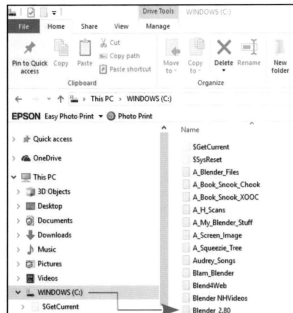

Blender – File Browser   Figure 3.4   **Windows – File Explorer**

3.3 Windows File Explorer

Take a short refresher to analyse what you do when you save something when using a Windows operating system.

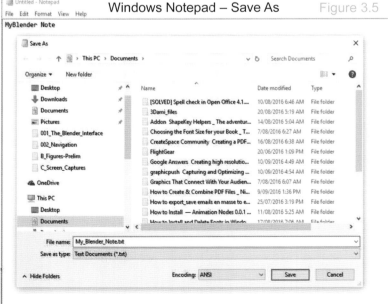

Windows Notepad – Save As   Figure 3.5

As an example, it is assumed you have written a note using **Windows Notepad** and you are about to save the file. You simply go to the top of the Notepad window, click on File, click on Save and the Save As window displays. In the panel at the top of this window you will probably see a panel showing This PC > Documents which is telling you that your file will be saved to the Documents folder on your computer (Figure 3.5). You enter a name for your file (My_Blender_Note.txt) and click Save. Simple!

The problem with this is; the file gets saved amongst your letters to your mother, the tax man, pictures of your pet dog and holiday snaps a l saved in the Documents folder. You should make a special folder for your **Blender Stuff**. You can create new folders in File Explorer by Right clicking on a folder or sub folder, selecting **New** then clicking **New Folder** and entering a name. You probably know how to do this but it is more important for you to understand how to do this is in Blender.

3.4 Windows File Explorer Diagram

Figure 3.6

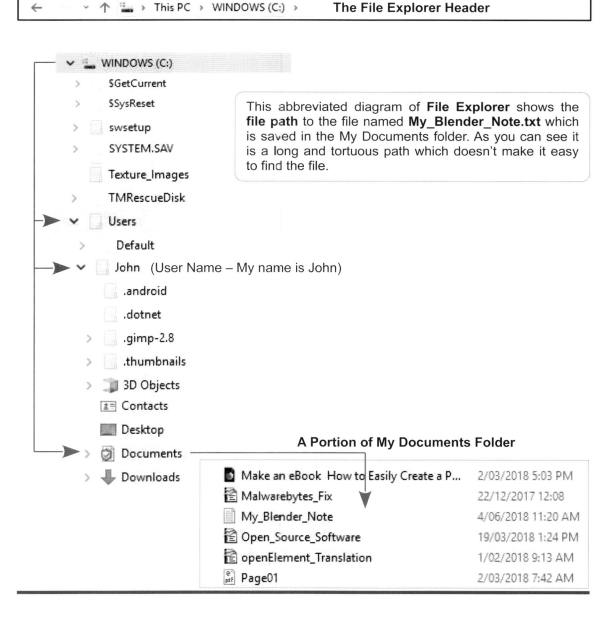

←   ∨ ↑ 🖳 › This PC › WINDOWS (C:) ›   **The File Explorer Header**

∨ 🖳 WINDOWS (C:)
> $GetCurrent
> $SysReset
> swsetup
> SYSTEM.SAV
Texture_Images
> TMRescueDisk

This abbreviated diagram of **File Explorer** shows the **file path** to the file named **My_Blender_Note.txt** which is saved in the My Documents folder. As you can see it is a long and tortuous path which doesn't make it easy to find the file.

➤ ∨ Users
> Default
➤ ∨ John (User Name – My name is John)
.android
.dotnet
> .gimp-2.8
> .thumbnails
> 3D Objects
Contacts
Desktop
➤ > Documents
> Downloads

A Portion of My Documents Folder

Make an eBook How to Easily Create a P...	2/03/2018 5:03 PM
Malwarebytes_Fix	22/12/2017 12:08
My_Blender_Note	4/06/2018 11:20 AM
Open_Source_Software	19/03/2018 1:24 PM
openElement_Translation	1/02/2018 9:13 AM
Page01	2/03/2018 7:42 AM

3.5 Blender File Browser

Blender's File Browser is the **File Browser Editor**. Click on the 3D Viewport Editor icon (upper left) and select **Editor Type: File Browser** in the menu. The 3D Viewport Editor is replaced by the **File Browser Editor** (Figure 3.8). This is where you navigate to find things and save things. You save your Blender files and rendered images and animation files and you search for pre-saved files from which you obtain data to use in new work. You can also create a new folder for your **Blender Stuff**.

To navigate the File Browser is very simple. As an example, go find the file named **My_Blender_Note.txt**. The **.txt** bit (suffix) on the end of the name tells you that the file is a Text file.

Figure 3.7

In the File Browser Editor click on **(C:)** or **Windows (C:)** in the **System Tab** panel in the upper LH part of the Editor panel. This is the C: drive on your PC. The PC used in this demonstration is a HP computer running Windows 10. The name on your computer is probably different but you will have something that tells you it is your C: Drive.

When you click on the C: Drive the main RH panel (in the File Browser Editor) displays the list of folders that you have in the C: Drive. The list is displayed in columns and by default is in alphabetical order. To follow the file path that was shown in Windows File Explorer:

C:\ Users\ John\ Documents\ My_Blender_Note.txt

File Browser Editor

My name is John. This will be your **User Name**.

In each panel, click the heading (highlights blue or gray) then double click to open the next panel.

Figure 3.8

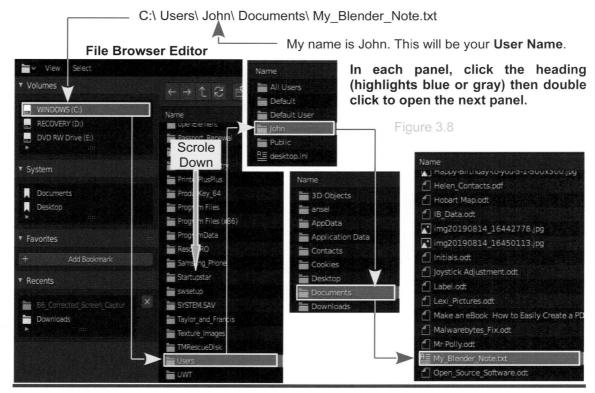

3.6 Opening Files

When the File Browser Editor has been opened, replacing the 3D Viewport Editor, it is merely allows you to search your file system to locate folders and files or create a new folder. **You can not open files.**

Blender opens different types of files in different Editors (see Chapter 04 Objects in the 3D Viewport Editor). **My_Blender_Note.txt** is a text file therefore you would open it in the **Text Editor**. Blender files with the **.blend** extension open in **Blender** in the 3D Viewport Editor. Image files would open in the UV Image Editor.

To demonstrate, consider the file named **My_Blender_Note.txt**. The **.txt** suffix indicates that it is a text file, therefore, it is opened in the Text Editor. Replace the 3D Viewport Editor with the Text Editor. To open My_Blender_Note.txt click **Text** in the Header and select **Open** or click **Open** (Figure 3.9).

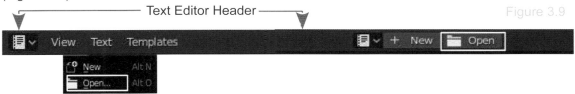

Clicking on either **Open** options displays the **Blender File View** panel which is essentially the Blender File Browser for the Text Editor. If you were in the Image Editor or the 3D Viewport Editor the Blender File View panel would be applicable to the Editor that was opened allowing you to select and open files applicable to the particular Editor.

Having navigated to the Documents Folder in the File View panel and scrolling you may be disappointed to find **My_Blender_Note.text** is nowhere to be found. Text files can be hidden? Click on the **Display button** in the upper RH corner of the panel and check **Text Files** in the display menu. Text Files will be shown, Select (click to highlight) and click Open Text.

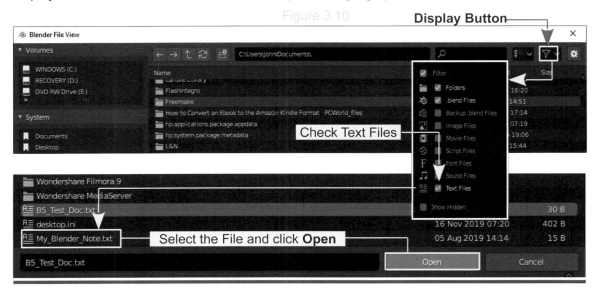

3.7 File Browser Header Features

Figure 3.11

Previous Folder
Next Folder
Parent File (Go Back)
Refresh the File display
Create a New Directory

File Display Options
Click to activate.
Editor Display Options

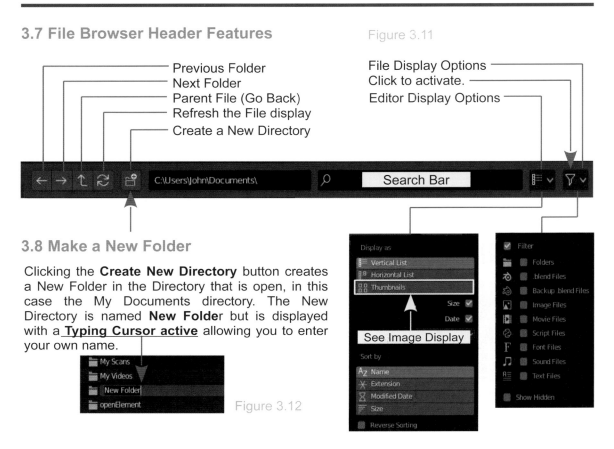

C:\Users\John\Documents\

Search Bar

Display as
Vertical List
Horizontal List
Thumbnails
Size ✓
Date ✓
See Image Display
Sort by
A-Z Name
Extension
Modified Date
Size
Reverse Sorting

Filter
Folders
.blend Files
Backup .blend Files
Image Files
Movie Files
Script Files
F Font Files
Sound Files
Text Files

Show Hidden

3.8 Make a New Folder

Clicking the **Create New Directory** button creates a New Folder in the Directory that is open, in this case the My Documents directory. The New Directory is named **New Folde**r but is displayed with a **Typing Cursor active** allowing you to enter your own name.

My Scans
My Videos
New Folder
openElement

Figure 3.12

3.9 Display Options

The way in which Folders and Files are displayed can be changed in the **Editor Display Options.**

Which Type of Files display is controlled in the **File Display Options.**

Image Display: By default Image File names are displayed as text. By activating **Thumbnails** in the **File Display Options** you can see Image Files as an Image.

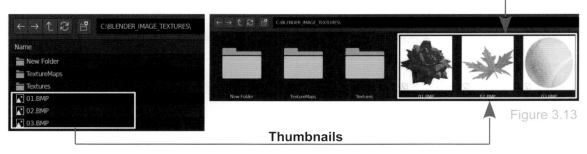

C:\BLENDER_IMAGE_TEXTURES\

Name
New Folder
TextureMaps
Textures
01.BMP
02.BMP
03.BMP

C:\BLENDER_IMAGE_TEXTURES\

New Folder   TextureMaps   Textures   01.BMP   02.BMP   03.BMP

Thumbnails

Figure 3.13

3.10 Saving Your Work

Besides being able to navigate the File Browser to find things that have been saved you will inevitably want to save your work. It's a good idea to be organised and create folders for different things.

Make a new folder in the C:\ Directory and name it **A_My_Blender_Stuff**.

Open the File Browser Editor.

Click on **Windows (C:)** under **Volumes** (upper LH). In the File browser Header click the Create New directory Button. New Folder is created. With the Typing Cursor active, backspace and retype **A_My_Blender_Stuff**. Press Enter.

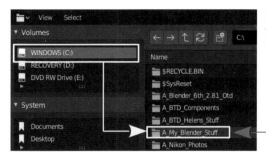

Note: Putting **A** at the beginning of the name places the New Folder at the top of the list in the C:\ Drive (makes it easy to find).

Figure 3.14

For the exercise a modified copy of the default Blender Scene will be saved to the new folder named **My_Blender_Stuff**.

With the new folder created, open the 3D Viewport Editor to display the default Blender Scene with the Cube Object. Replace the Cube with a Monkey Object. Adding the Monkey will distinguish the file to be saved from the original default Scene.

In the 3D Viewport Editor Header, click on **File** then click on **Save As** in the menu. The Blender File Viewer opens. Navigate to the Folder named **My_Blender_Stuff**. At the bottom of the File Viewer, where you see **untitled.blend**, click to display the Typing Cursor, backspace and retype a name for your new file, **My_New_File.blend** (If you forget the .blend suffix, Blender will obligingly add it for you). Click on **Save As** (highlighted blue).

Figure 3.15

Retype: **My_New_File.blend** ———

My_New_File.blend is saved in the My_Blender_Stuff folder.

3.11 The Concept of Files

To save a file? What does this mean? It's easy to say, **save a file,** but what are you actually doing when you save? The chapter started by discussing saving a file created in Windows Notepad. This was a simple text file. A text file contains data which displays letters and words on your screen i.e. Text. An image file contains data which displays a picture. A music file plays music. Each file type uses a different application (App) or program to generate the display or, in the case of a music file, play the music. Sure! You know all this but the point is; a Blender file contains a combination of data organised into separate parts or elements.

When you save a Blender file you save all the elements.

To show you what this means in practical terms, open Blender with the default Scene. Click on **File** in the **Blender Screen Header** then click on **Append**. The **File Viewer** opens. Navigate to the file you previously saved named **My_New_File.blend** (Figure 3.16).

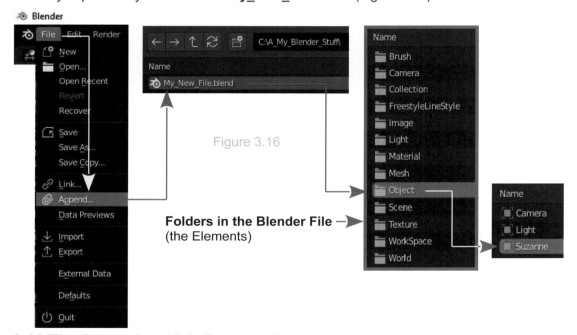

Figure 3.16

Folders in the Blender File →
(the Elements)

3.12 The Append or Link Command

You can insert elements from one Blender (.blend) file into another Blender file. To do this you select the **Append** or **Link** commands from the File pull-down menu in the Blender Screen Header (Figure 3.16). An element could be a model you have created.

Append takes data from an existing file and adds it to the current file. **Link** allows you to use data from an existing file in the current file but the data remains in the existing file. In the latter case the data cannot be edited in the current file if the data is changed in the existing file, the changes show in the current file the next time it is opened.

At this stage the foregoing is probably somewhat difficult to understand, therefore working through an example will help to clarify the meaning. You will have to jump the gun a little and follow some procedures without explanation. The detail of the procedures will be covered later but at the moment only be concerned with the file system navigation involved.

Selecting **Append** or **Link** opens the File Viewer allowing you to navigate to the Blender file you wish to select elements from. You can **Append** anything, including cameras, lights, meshes, materials, textures, scenes, and objects. Ey appending Objects, any materials, textures and animations that are linked to that object will automatically be imported with the Object. Clicking the LMB on an Object will select it. Pressing tne A key will deselect.

To clarify this procedure start a new Blender file (open Blender) with the default Scene containing the Cube Object. Select the **Append** command as previously described and navigate to the file **My_New_File.blend**. Open the **Object directory** (the Objects folder, Figure 3.15). Click on the Object named **Suzanne** to highlight it, then click on the **Append** button in the lower RH corner of the Viewer (Figure 3.17).

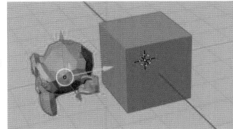

Figure 3.17

Suzanne Appended in the 3D Viewport Editor.

You can Append any Object from any Blender file.

Note: When Appended an Object is located in the Scene at its location in the the file from which it originated.

3.13 Importing Objects

One of Blender's strong points is its ability to accept several generic types of 3D files from other programs. Two examples are: The **.dae Collada** file format used by the **Make Human** program, which creates models of the human figure.

The **Make Human** prcgram is freely available. Other programs save files in one format but also give the option to export in another format. You will have to find the **Export** command in the program and match up the file type with one of the file types in Blender's import menu .

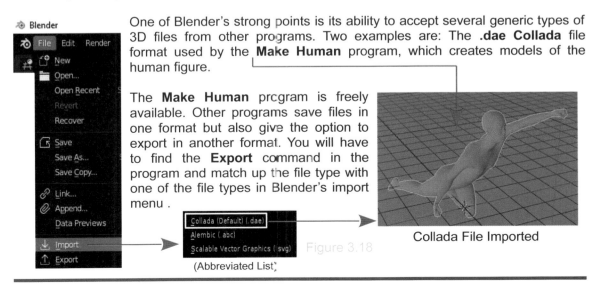

Collada (Default) (.dae)
Alembic (.abc)
Scalable Vector Graphics ('svg)
(Abbreviated List)

Figure 3.18

Collada File Imported

> **Note:** The file type options shown in Figure 3.18 have been abbreviated as has the actual selection menu. **Collada (.dae)** is shown while **Pointcache (.pc2)** is not. To conserve space in the GUI, Blender has limited the file type display. Other file types are available as **Add-ons** in the **Preferences Editor** in the **Import-Export** category.

3.14 Activating Import File Types

To import a **DXF file** (Autocad DFX Format-.dfx) into a Blender scene, open the **Preferences Editor** and click on **Add-ons** at the LHS of the Editor. In the list to the right select an **Import-Export Add-on**. Find the **File Type** you require and check (tick) the box adjacent to the name. The checked file type will display in white text and be available in the **Import** selection menu.

> **Note:** When importing Blender files into other Blender files, remember to use the **Append** command instead of Import. In the **Append** command, select the file, then select what you would like to bring into the current file. You will usually use the Objects option.

The Preferences Editor – Add-ons – Import-Export

Note: You may type **Import** in the Search Bar to find Import Add-ons.

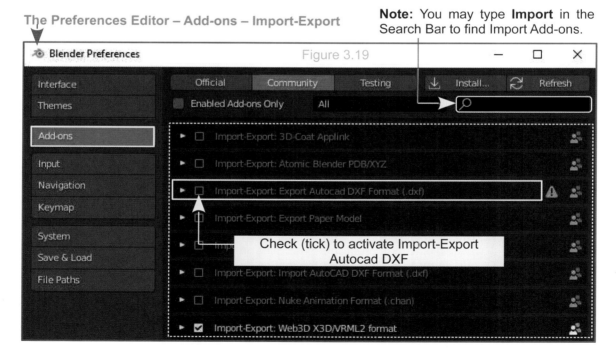

Figure 3.19

Check (tick) to activate Import-Export Autocad DXF

> **Note:** Although Autocad DXF is titled Import-Export, activating the Add-on only provides an Import Function. You can not export from Blender to Autocad.

Clicking the file type opens the File Browser Editor where you navigate to the file containing the Object you wish to import. As an example, a model of a human figure has been created using the **Make Human Program**. The model has been exported as a **Wavefront.obj** file. You will see that this type of file is included in the default Import file list, **Wavefront OBJ.** Click on this file type to display the **File Browser Editor**.

> **Important:** When you export a model from another program, know where it is saved on your computer and what the file name is.

The model exported from the **Make Human** program is named **Running_Man.obj.** The model was exported to:

C:\A_My_Blender_Stuff\

Figure 3.20

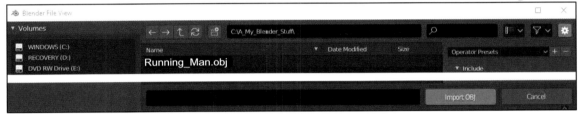

Figure 3.21

In the File Browser Editor navigate and find your file. Click on the file name to select it (highlight) then click on **Import OBJ** in the lower RH corner

The Object Running_Man (Figure 3.21) is entered into the Blender 3D View Editor. **Note:** You will probably have to scale the model to suit.

3.15 Packing Data

If you plan to open a Blender file on other computers, you will need to select the **Pack All into .blend** option in the **File** menu under **External Data**. Textures and sounds are not automatically included in your Blender file in order to keep the file size down. Every time your file opens, the textures and sounds are placed into your file. If the files can't be found, you won't have any textures and sounds. If you **Pack the Data**, those files are included with the .blend file so they can be opened anywhere. Remember, your file size may become very large. You can also unpack data to bring the file size back down.

You may alternatively check **Automatically Pack Into .blend**.

Objects in the 3D View Editor

The overview of Blender in Chapter 1 has introduced the Editors in the default Screen arrangement and demonstrates how they interrelate. The fundamental concept in using Blender is to create a model, place the model in a Scene and perhaps animate the model to move creating an animation sequence. In the creation process the models and components of the Scene may be colored and textured and the Scene illuminated for effect. The Scene or part of a Scene is then **Rendered** converting to an Image file or a video file.

To model an object or character, or a component of a Scene such as a landscape, a simple shape is placed in the 3D Viewport Editor and modified (modeled). The simple shape is called a **Primitive**. Blender has ten primitives from which to choose, which one you select will depend on what you want to create.

Instruction will be given with the default Screen Arrangement (GUI) with the **Eevee Render Engine** active (see Chapter 14 Rendering). **Eevee** is one of three Render options.

Bear in mind that you have the options to use the **Cycles** or **Workbench** Render Engines. Workbench provides a simplified working environments for modeling when Scenes become complicated. Cycles allows you to work in a viewport that continually renders a **photo-realistic** view.

4.1 Workflow Philosophy

Blender has been introduced in the Preamble and Chapter 1 by describing the **Graphical User Interface** and demonstrating a sample of the tools that may be used to create and Animate a Scene. Studying the **Graphical User Interface (GUI)** with its arrangement of **Editors** and panels and having a knowledge of Keyboard and Mouse input commands shows the practical aspect of operating the program.

Before you begin to create a Scene you should understand the philosophy of the Blender process.

When you open Blender you are presented with a default Scene in the 3D Viewport Editor containing a Cube Object.

Remember: In the context of Blender, **Default** means that which is displayed before any action has been taken.

The **Default Scene** displays in the 3D Viewport Editor with a Cube Object at the center. The Scene also has a Light and a Camera in place. To create something new, you start by saving this arrangement with a **new file name**. The new file is a starting point for developing a new Scene with new Models. You modify the default Scene in the new file to whatever you require. Modifying a Scene will involve such things as moving and repositioning objects, reshaping objects, adding new objects, applying color (Material), arranging lighting effects, positioning the camera, Animating etc.

4.2 Starting a New File

When beginning a new project it is advisable to **start a new file** with a new name. Start Blender and before changing anything in the default Scene click **File – Save As** in the **Blender Screen Header** and save the file in your **Blender_Stuff** folder with a meaningful name. You can save your work wherever you like as long as you remember what you named the file and where you saved it. Write down the name. Be familiar with saving and creating files and folders. Review Chapter 3 if necessary.

> **Note:** Depending on the version of Blender you have, the program may not prompt you to save your file when closing . Remember to always save your work often and don't forget to insert a **.blend** suffix at the end of the name.

After saving the default Scene as a new file, the new file will be open in the Screen ready to be modified. The new Blender file will display the default arrangement of Editors and the 3D Viewport Editor will display the default Scene. If you have closed Blender after saving you will have to reopen the new file.

When you restart Blender the default Screen arrangement is displayed. To reopen the file that you saved, click on **File** in the **Blender Screen Header** and click on **Open** in the **File** menu. The **File Viewer** opens (Figure 2.1) where you navigate to where you saved your file. Click on your file name then click **Open** in the lower RH corner of the Editor (Figure 4.1 over).

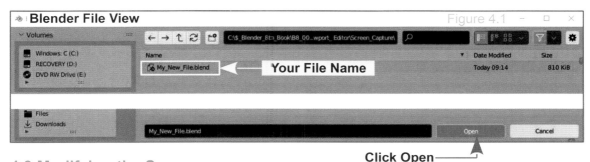

Your File Name

Click Open

4.3 Modifying the Scene

Any changes you make to the Scene will be construed as modifying the Scene. For example, changing the shape of an Object is a modification. Changing the shape of an Object is called modeling. Another basic modification would be to move an Object in the Scene. Another Scene modification is to add an Object. There are many modifications that can be made.

4.4 Object Mode and Edit Mode

As demonstrated in Chapter 1 – 1.9 and 1.11 the **3D Viewport Editor** has two basic working modes, **Object Mode** and **Edit Mode**. With an Object selected in the 3D Viewport, in Object Mode, you Translate (move), Rotate and Scale the Object. In Edit Mode you change the shape of the Object. Note: This is a simplistic description of the operations, there is more to it than that. Look at the Cube Object in the default Scene.

Switching Modes: Click in the 3D Viewport Editor Header and select **Edit Mode**.

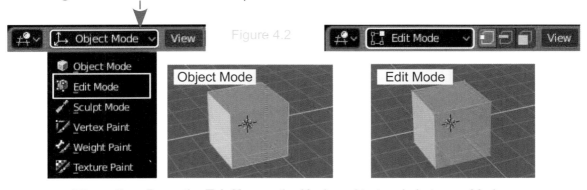

Figure 4.2

Alternative: Press the **Tab Key** on the Keyboard to toggle between Modes.

In **Object Mode** the Cube displays as a solid gray Object with an orange outline. The orange outline indicates that the Cube is **selected**. Being selected means that the Cube may be manipulated in the Scene (Translated (Moved), Rotated or Scaled).

In **Edit Mode**, when the Cube is selected, it is shown with an orange tint with orange edges and with little orange dots at each corner. The orange dots are called **Vertices**, the orange edges are **Edges** while the orange tinted surfaces are **Faces**. In Edit Mode you select either of these elements individually and manipulate them to change (model) the shape (see Chapter 4).

Also in Edit Mode, there are buttons which allow the display and select the different elements separately.

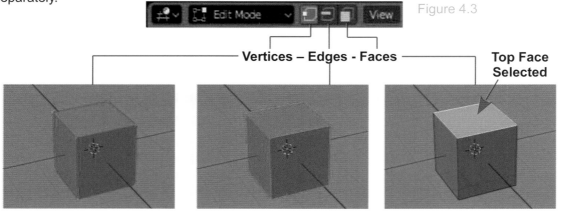

Figure 4.3

Vertices – Edges - Faces ———— **Top Face Selected**

Top Face selected (LMB Click) – Translated (G Key- Grab- Move Mouse – LMB Click to place) – Rotated about the X Axis of the Scene (R Key + X Key - drag Mouse – LMB Click to set).

Figure 4.4

Example: Edit Mode Manipulation ————→ **3D Viewport Editor Cursor**

4.5 3D Viewport Cursor

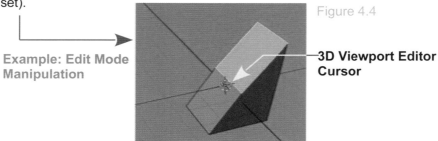

3D Viewport Editor Cursor ————→ ◆ ◄———— **Mouse Cursor** Figure 4.5

When working in the 3D Viewport Editor there are two **Cursors**; the **Mouse Cursor** and the **Editor Cursor**. By default the **Editor Cursor** is located at the center of the Scene. The center of the default Cube Object is also at the center of the Scene. Objects may be positioned by using the Editor Cursor. To understand positioning using the Editor Cursor you must first understand selecting, deselecting and adding Objects.

4.6 Selecting and Deselecting Objects

In the default Scene the **Cube Object is selected as shown by the orange outline.** To deselect the Cube **LMB click** (left mouse button) an empty space in the Editor (the orange outline cancels). To **select** the Cube again, position the Mouse Cursor on the Cube (mouse over) and click **LMB** .

> **Note:** If you deselect then press the **A Key,** all Objects in the Scene will be selected. If you inadvertently select all Objects click an empty space to deselect all Objects. Click LMB on a single Object to select.

An alternative selection method is to press the **B Key** on the Keyboard with the Mouse Cursor in the 3D Viewport Editor panel. In this case, pressing the B Key displays cross hair lines in the Editor panel which you drag, forming a rectangle, around an Object **or multiple Objects**. Release the mouse button to select (orange outline appears).

Press the B Key to display the cross hairs - Position the Mouse Cursor
Click LMB, hold and drag a rectangle – release the Mouse button   Figure 4.6

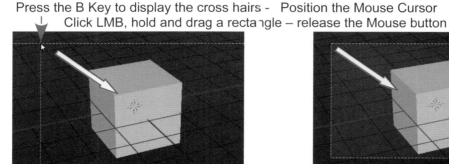
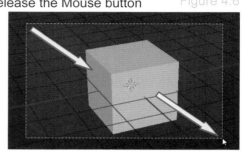

When Blender is first opened the **Select Box Tool** is active in the **Tool Panel** at the LHS of the 3D Viewport Editor (Figure 4.7). With the Border Select Tool active you can Click LMB and drag a rectangle, similar to B Key Select, to select multiple Objects.

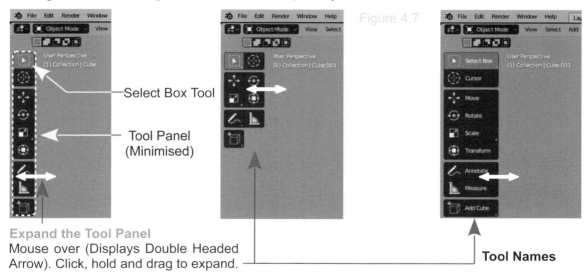

Figure 4.7

Select Box Tool

Tool Panel
(Minimised)

Tool Names

Mouse over (Displays Double Headed Arrow). Click, hold and drag to expand.

Yet another method of selection is to position the Mouse Cursor in the 3D Viewport Editor and press the **C Key**. In this case the Mouse Cursor becomes a **Selection Circle** which you position over the Object or Objects to be selected. When first displayed the circle is relatively small.

Unless the circle encapsulates a whole Object the Object will not be selected. To increase or decrease the size of the circle **Scroll MMB**. With the circle surrounding the Object click LMB to select. Press **Esc** to cancel the selection circle.

Selection Circle   Figure 4.8

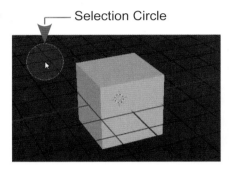

Scroll MMB to increase the size of the Circle.

Position over the Cube and click LMB to select. Press **Esc** to cancel the Circle.

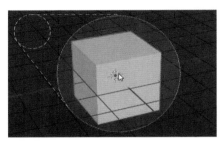

4.7 Adding Objects

As described in Chapter 1 – 1.7 the default Blender Scene contains three Objects; a Cube, a Camera and a Light. The Camera and Light are special Objects which perform functions but do not **Render** as part of an image or animation (see Chapter 14). The Cube, on the other hand, does render. The Cube is one of ten Objects called **Primitives**, which are the starting point for modeling. You modify the shape of a Primitive into a model of a character or as part of the Scene background. Multiple Primitives can be combined to form a single Object.

4.8 Object Primitives

3D Manipulation Widget shown on the Circle Primative

Figure 4.9

Mesh Object Primitives selection menu (Press Shift + A key)

Plane
Cube
Circle
UV Sphere
Ico Sphere
Cylinder
Cone
Torus

For the Menu see Figure 4.10 (over)

Grid
Monkey

Figure 4.9 above shows the ten default **Primitives** available for selection. They have been colored to distinguish them. When added to a Scene they are entered with the default gray color. The one exception being the Circle which displays with only an orange outline.

A **Primitive** shape entered into the scene is referred to as an **Object**. Blender automatically names Objects according to the shape i.e. **Cube**, **Sphere**, **Cone** etc. When you reshape (modify) the primitive Object to make a model you will rename it. Primitives are entered in the 3D Viewport Editor with the Editor in **Object Mode.**

To add a new Object into a Scene you click on **Add** in the **3D Viewport Editor Header** (Figure 4.10) then click **Mesh** to add a new Object. This displays the **Add - Mesh Menu**.

An alternative way to display the **Add - Mesh Menu** is to press **Shift + A Key** with the Mouse Cursor in the 3D Viewport Editor.

In either case, with the **Add Menu** displayed you click **Mesh** to display the selection menu where you click to select one of the Primitives. Selecting a **Primitive** enters it in the Scene at the location of the **3D Viewport Editor Cursor**.

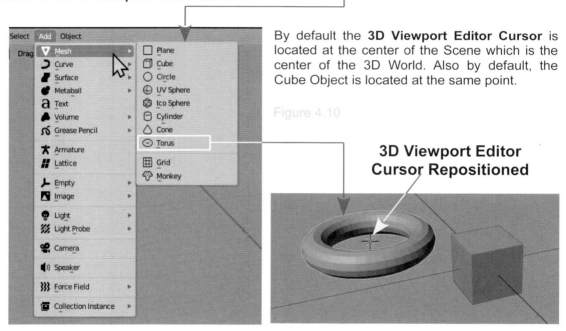

By default the **3D Viewport Editor Cursor** is located at the center of the Scene which is the center of the 3D World. Also by default, the Cube Object is located at the same point.

Figure 4.10

3D Viewport Editor Cursor Repositioned

4.9 Locating the 3D Viewport Editor Cursor

Remember; Objects added (entered) in the Scene are located at the position of the **3D Viewport Editor Cursor**, therefore, you may wish to relocate the Cursor to position Objects.

Hold Shift and **click RMB** to position the Cursor. Alternatively activate the **Cursor Tool** in the Tool Panel. With the Tool activated you can click **LMB** anywhere in the 3D Viewport Editor to position the Cursor. With the Tool activated you can click LMB to relocate the Cursor and click hold and drag the Cursor to a new location.

Don't forget to deactivate the Cursor Tool to allow selection and deselect of Objects. To deactivate the Cursor Tool click on the **Select Box** Tool (uppermost in the Tool Panel).

Yet another control for locating the Cursor and positing Objects is the **Snap Tool Pie Menu**. With an Object selected, press **Shift + S Key** to display the **Pie Menu.**

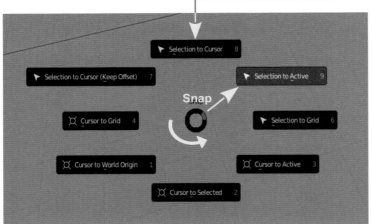

Clicking **Selection to Cursor** relocates the selected Object to the position of the 3D Viewport Editor Cursor.

Figure 4.11

You may also drag the Mouse to rotate the **Snap Ring** at the center of the Pie Menu to make a selection. With the blue segment located as shown, **Selection to Active** is selected.

4.10 Deleting Objects

To Delete (remove) an Object from the Scene, select the Object then press the **X Key**. The **OK Delete** panel displays. Click **Delete** to delete or **drag the Cursor away from the Object** to cancel.

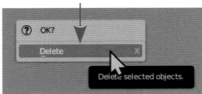

Figure 4.12

Note: You may select multiple Objects for deletion.

4.11 Duplicating Objects

When you want to duplicate an Object (make an identical copy), select the Object and press **Shift + D Key.** A new Object is created occupying the same space as the original. The new Object is in **Move Mode** (able to be moved by dragging the Mouse) as indicated by a white outline. To reposition in the Scene, drag the Mouse and click LMB when in place.

Figure 4.13

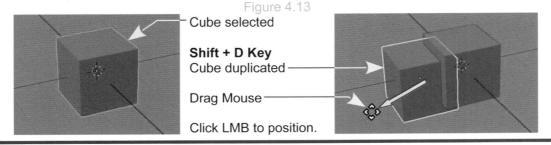

Cube selected

Shift + D Key
Cube duplicated

Drag Mouse

Click LMB to position.

4.12 Object Mode Manipulation

The three basic manipulation controls are: **Translate, Rotate and Scale**.

Translate: To move an Object freely in the plane of the view, press the **G Key** (Grab Mode) with the object selected and drag the Mouse. In Grab mode the outline turns white. To lock the movement to a particular axis, press the **G Key + X**, Y, or Z. G key + Y restricts the movement to the Y (green) Axis (Figure 2.14).

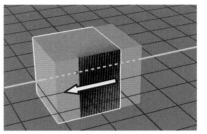

Figure 4.14

Scaling: To scale an Object (make larger or smaller), press the **S Key** and drag the mouse. To lock the scale to a particular axis, press S Key + X, Y, or Z. To scale by a specific value press S Key + Number Key (S + 2 + Y = Scale twice on the Y Axis (Figure 4.15)

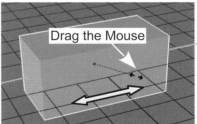

Figure 4.15

Rotating: To rotate an Object, press the **R Key** and move the mouse about the **Object's center**. To lock the rotation to an axis, press the R Key + X, Y, or Z. To rotate a set number of degrees, press R + the number of degrees of rotation and press Enter. R+30 rotates the Object 30 degrees. R + Y + 30 rotates the Object 30 degrees about the Y- Axis (Figure 4.16).

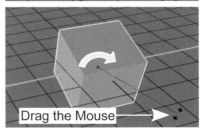

4.13 The Last Operator Panel

Figure 4.16

The Last Operator Panel has been introduced in Chapter 1 – 1.4 in relation to performing operations in Edit Mode. The panel also displays and is applicable to operations in Object Mode.

For example; when an Object is Translated (Moved) a panel displays at the lower left hand side of the 3D Viewport Editor. When expanded this panel shows information relating to the last operation performed in the Editor. The panel also allows values to be adjusted, providing a means of fine tuning or correcting the operation.

Figure 4.17

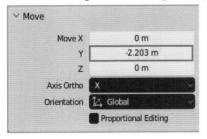

Last Operator – Move Panel

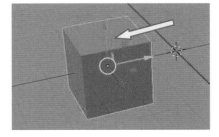

Cube Translated (Moved) – 3D Viewport

The controls in the Last Operator Panel are replicated in the **Object Properties Panel** in the 3D Viewport Editor (Upper RHS – Press N Key to display) and in the **Properties Editor, Object Properties Buttons.**

Object Properties Panel   **Properties Editor**

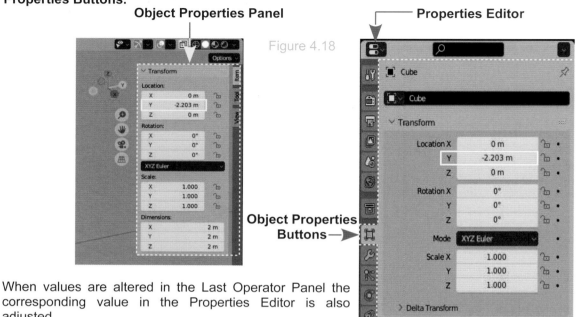

Figure 4.18

Object Properties Buttons ➤

When values are altered in the Last Operator Panel the corresponding value in the Properties Editor is also adjusted.

Note: The **Move Y** value in the Last Operator Panel shows the distance moved from the original location. The Location Y value in the Properties Editor shows the actual location on the Y Axis of the Scene. Moving the Cube a further 1m on the Y Axis will show 1m in the Last Operator panel (distance moved) and 3.5m in the Properties Editor (the Location).

4.14 Tool Panel – Widgets   Expand the Tool Panel to display the Tool Names (Figure 2.7).

In the **3D Viewport Editor, Tool Panel** (Object Mode- upper left hand side) you will see **Move, Rotate, Scale** and **Transform** buttons. Clicking on a button (highlights blue) displays a **Manipulation Widget** at the center of the selected Object. To use a Widget click LMB on a red, green or blue handle, hold the mouse button and drag the mouse.

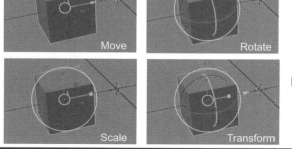

Figure 4.19

Transform combines
Move, Rotate and Scale

4.15 Manipulation Units

By default Translation and Scaling units are expressed in **Metric** values and Rotation is in **Degrees**. You can change the values in the <u>**Properties Editor, Scene Properties**, **Units tab.**</u>

Figure 4.20

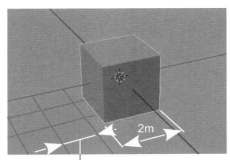

1 m Grid – 2m Scale

When using Metric values the Background Grid in the 3D View Editor is considered to represent One Meter by One Meter divisions.

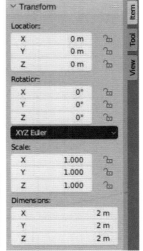

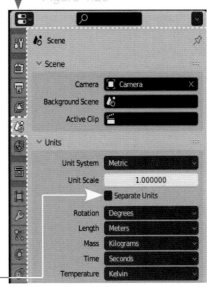

Check **Separate Units** to display values in M, cm, mm etc.

With the Cube Scaled up the default Dimensions display as 2.17m. With Separate Units checked 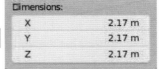 the display will be 2m 17cm.

Dimensions:	
X	2.17 m
Y	2.17 m
Z	2.17 m

Dimensions:	
X	2 m 17 cm
Y	2 m 17 cm
Z	2 m 17 cm

Scale Units: By default the size of an object is expressed in **Metric Units**. You may elect to change this. In the **Properties Editor, Scene Properties, Units tab** you will see **Unit System Metric**. Clicking the unit bar will display options to select **None** or **Imperial**.

Unit System – Metric is the default setting in which case the mid plane grid in the 3D Viewport Editor is considered as representing a 1M x 1M Grid.

Values in the 3D View Editor display during Manipulation
(upper LH corner of the Screen).

Figure 4.21

Cube Translated (Moved)

79

None: Changing the **Unit System – Unit Preset** to **None** means you chose to work in Blender units as represented by the division of the mid plane grid (each grid segment = 1 Unit by 1 Unit)

Rotation or Angle: Changing the Unit Preset **Degrees** to **Radians** means you are choosing the measurement where there are **2π Radians** in a circle (Figure 4.22). Angular values are, therefore given in Radians instead of Degrees.

Succinctly, pi (**π**) is the Greek letter for p.

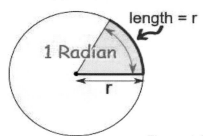

2π = 2 x 3.142 = 6.284

Note: Pi (**π**) is not an absolute value. Pi = 3.141592653589793238462643383279502884197169399375105820974944592307816406286 .

4.16 Measuring Ruler / Protractor

At the bottom of the Tool Panel you will see the **Measure button** (Figure 4.23). This button allows you to take liner and angular measurements in the 3D View Editor.

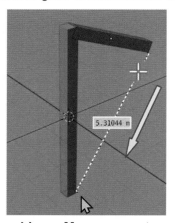

Cube, Scaled down, then Scaled up on the Z Axis and duplicated with the duplicate Rotated and repositioned in the Scene.

Figure 4.23

Tool Panel

Linear Measurement
Position the Mouse Cursor, click, hold and drag from Start point to Finish.

Angular Measurement
Position the Mouse Cursor, (Cross) mid way between points. Click, hold and drag to apex of angle.

Note: When using the Measure Tool measurements are made on the plane of the monitor Screen. True measurements can only be made in Top, Front and Side Orthographic Views.

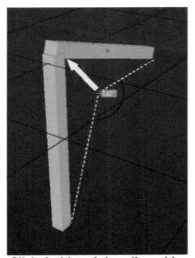
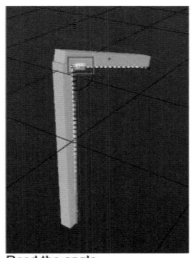
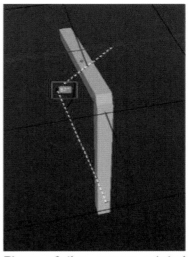

Click, hold and drag the mid point to the Apex.	Read the angle.

Figure 2.44

Plane of the screen rotated showing where measurement were taken (See Note).

4.17 Precision Manipulation

Precise Manipulation, precise Translation (location), Rotation and Scaling can be performed in the **3D Viewport Editor, Object Properties Panel, Item Tab** (press the N Key to display). Remember, the values shown in this panel are for the Object that is selected in the 3D Viewport Editor.

In Figure 4.25 the values are for the default Cube Object in its default position at the center of the Scene. The location is, therefore, X, Y and Z = 0m.

Figure 4.25

To move the Cube a precise distance away from the center, position the Mouse Cursor over a value. The cursor changes to a double headed arrow. ──────────────▶

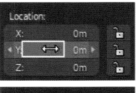

Click LMB and drag left or right to change the value. The value bar displays the value as you drag the cursor. Release the Mouse button to set the value. The Cube is moved in the 3D View Editor as the value alters. Clicking the **little arrows** incrementally alters the value. ──

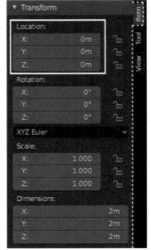

You may also click LMB on the value bar to display a typing cursor

Backspace to delete the existing value and retype a new value.

31

4.18 Camera View

Figure 4.26

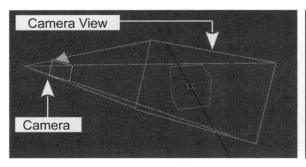 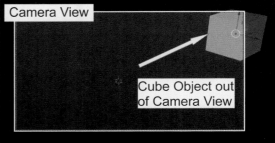

Note: When manipulating an Object in the 3D Viewport Editor you may be moving the Object out of **Camera View.** When you **Render** an image your model may not be included. Press **Num Pad 0** to see what is included in the shot (Camera View Figure 4.26).

Render: See the **Command Instruction Example** in the **Preamble**.

To return to the original User Perspective View press Num Pad 5 twice, click and hold RMB to rotate the Viewport or press Num Pad 6.

4.19 Other Types of Objects

Figure 4.27

3D Viewport Editor Header

Object Primitives accessed in the 3D Viewport Header, Add Mesh Menu are the starting point for modeling a character or shape. The Add Mesh Menu lists Mesh Objects which produce Objects that have volume and surface properties (Faces) which Render in a Scene. You will see, however, that the Add Menu includes other Object categories that do not have these properties and do not Render. They do, however, provide functionality in Scene construction. For example **Curves, Armature** and **Empty**.

How the different Object types are used will be explained as you progress through the book.

From the menu you will see that you may add additional Cameras and Lights into a Scene. These influence how you see Objects.

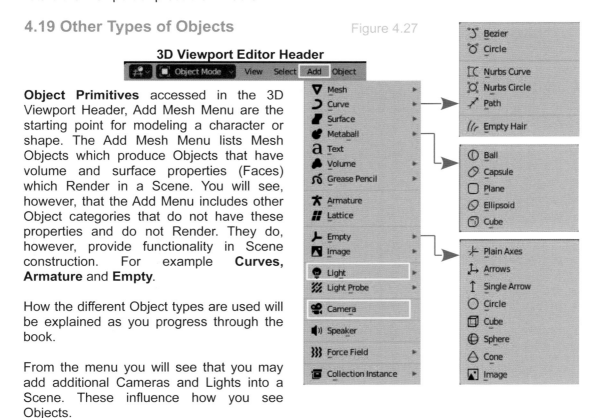

82

4.20 Naming Objects

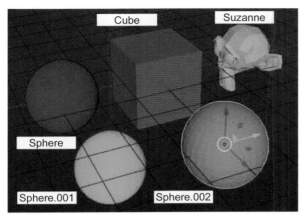

As you enter Objects in a Scene Blender automatically assigns a name. In Figure 4.28 the Cube Object has been named **Cube**, the Monkey Object has been named **Suzanne** and the UV Spheres have been named **Sphere, Sphere.001** and **Sphere.002**.

Figure 4.28

The names are displayed in the **Outliner Editor** under **Scene Collection** (Figure 4.29).

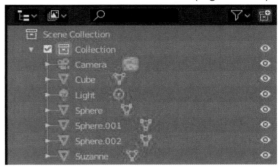

Figure 4.29

You will also see an Object's name in the **Properties Editor** with the **Object Properties** selected (Figure 4.30).

Figure 4.30

The automatic names are all very well, but as you build a Scene and add many Objects, it is obvious that automatic names could become meaningless and confusing. For example; **UV Spheres** are named **Sphere, Sphere.001** and **Sphere.002**.

Suzanne

Blender has a monkey head that's affectionately referred to as **Suzanne**, a reference to the ape in two of Kevin Smith's films: *Jay and Silent Bob Strike Back* and *Mallrats* (close to the end). Many 3D modeling and animation suites have a generic semi-complex primitive that is used for test renders, benchmarks, and examples that necessitate something a little more complex than a cube or sphere.

The name **Suzanne** will definitely distinguish Monkey unless you add more Monkeys, in which case they will be named Suzanne, Susanne.001, Suzanne.002 etc. Even though the UV Spheres have been colored the question arises, *which one is which?*

Obviously it is preferable to name Objects with meaningful names especially when they have been reshaped into Characters or components of a complex Scene.

You rename Objects in the **Properties Editor, Object Properties** or in the **Outliner Editor** by double clicking on the Object name, backspacing or deleting the name and retyping a new name.

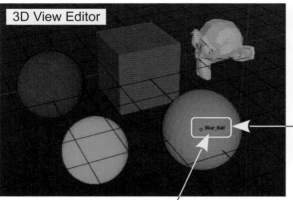

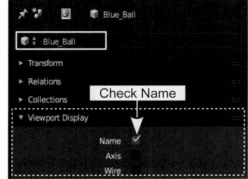

Object Name Displayed   Figure 4.31

A handy way of identifying Objects in the 3D Viewport Editor is to check (tick) **Name** in the **Properties Editor, Object Properties, Viewport Display Tab**. The name of the Object is displayed in the Editor (Figure 4.31).

Note: When Objects are renamed they are alphabetically listed in the Outliner Editor (Figure 4.29).

> **Note:** Objects in the 3D Viewport Editor are listed in the Outliner Editor in groups called **Collections**.The arrangement and management of Collections are detailed in Chapter 21.

4.21 The Header Button Menus

The 3D Viewport Editor **Header,** buttons provide menus for selecting a variety of functions. The individual functions will be called upon as required in specific instructions. Some functions have already been covered such as switching between Object Mode and Edit Mode, Object Selection (Select button) and adding Objects (Add button). The menus allow you to activate a function by clicking the function name and in many cases provide a Keyboard shortcut. For example; in the Select button menu you will see Box Select (Tweak Left – LMB Clk Drag) and Select Circle (C Key). You either click the select type name in the menu or press the Keyboard shortcut with the Mouse cursor in the 3D Viewport Editor panel. The Add button displays the Object Add Menu which is the same as pressing Shift + A Key. The Object button displays a comprehensive menu with sub menus. As you progress in Blender you will become familiar with the functions in the menus but for now, the following are worth mentioning:

Join (Ctrl + J Key)　　　Selecting two or more Objects at the same time (Hold Shift + LMB Click) then clicking Join in the menu or pressing Ctrl + J Key joins the selected Objects into a single Object.

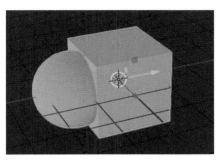

Figure 4.32

Copy and Paste - Objects may be copied from one Blender file and pasted into another file.

Smooth and Flat Shading

In the previous diagrams describing naming and coloring Objects you will observe that the surface of the UV Sphere is made up from a series of rectangular flat surfaces (Flat Shading). In the **3D Viewport Editor Header** selecting **Object – Shade Smooth** in the menu produces a smooth spherical surface which is much nicer for coloring the sphere. Alternatively RMB click in the 3D Viewport Editor to display the **Object Context Menu** with the shading options.

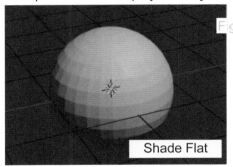

Figure 4.33

Shade Flat

Shade Smooth

4.22 Meta Shapes

Meta Shapes: Are described as *mercurial, or clay-like forms that have a rounded shape.*

When two **Meta Objects** (Shapes) get close, they begin to interact with one another. They merge, as water droplets do. When they are moved apart, they restore their original shape.

There are several **Meta Shapes** you can use in Blender (Figure 4.27 Metaball). Meta Shapes are added to a Scene in Object mode like any other shape: press **Shift + the A key – Add – Metaball** and select either Ball, Capsule, Plane, Ellipsoid, or Cube. Be sure to deselect one shape before adding another, or they will be automatically joined. When **Meta Shapes** get close to one another, they begin to pull and flow together like droplets of liquid (Figure 4.34).

The shapes can be animated and textured, and reflection and transparency can be applied to create some stunning effects.

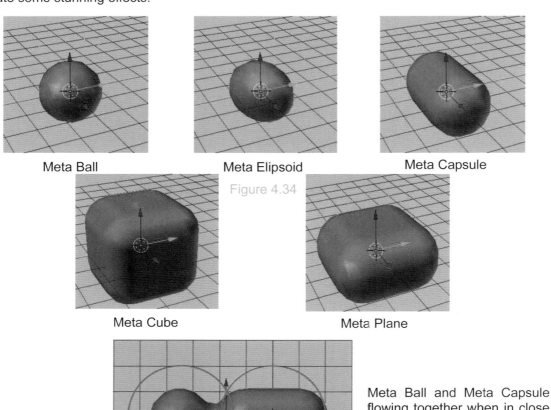

Meta Ball

Meta Elipsoid

Meta Capsule

Figure 4.34

Meta Cube

Meta Plane

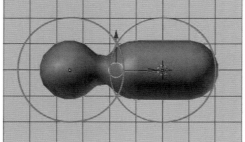

Meta Ball and Meta Capsule flowing together when in close proximity.

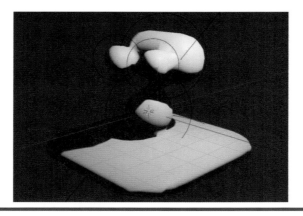

4.23 Coloring Objects

In the course of this chapter you will have observed that some Objects shown in diagrams have been colored to distinguish one from another, For example, in Figure 4.28 the different Spheres.

Coloring in Blender is termed **Applying a Material**. At this point consider **Material** to mean **Color**.

Applying a Material opens up a whole can of worms which will be explained as you progress through the book but for the time being you may color Objects by using the following procedure.

Select the Object in the 3D Viewport Editor.

Figure 4.35

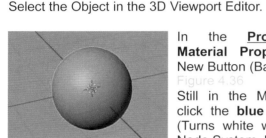

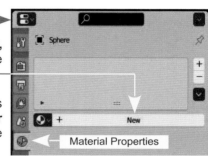

In the **Properties Editor, Material Properties** click the New Button (Bar)

Figure 4.36

Still in the Material Properties click the **blue Use Nodes Bar** (Turns white which cancels the Node System. Nodes are explained in Chapter 11).

With Nodes cancelled click the **Base Color Bar** to display the **Color Picker Circle**.

Figure 4.37

Click in the Color Circle to select a Color.

The Color (Material) displays on the Object in the 3D Viewport Editor.

Note: 3D Viewport Editor Display Modes. The default mode is **Solid Viewport Display**.

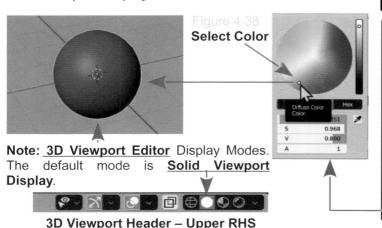

Figure 4.38

Select Color

Note: 3D Viewport Editor Display Modes. The default mode is **Solid Viewport Display**.

3D Viewport Header – Upper RHS

5

Editing Objects

Editing Objects

Editing or modifying one of the basic shapes (Primitives) in Blender is the process of Modeling.

Creating a model begins by introducing a Primitive to the Scene. Blender's Primitives are Mesh Objects, that is to say, they are constructed with surfaces formed by a mesh. The mesh can be imagined as a fishing net or a piece of chicken coop wire with strands of twine or wire crisscrossing and joined where they intersect. The spaces between the strands are filled in forming a surface.

The shape of a primitive is altered by manipulating the mesh. This is achieved by selecting (grabbing) the intersection points (**Vertices**) or the strands (**Edges**) or the filled in pieces (**Faces**) and moving them in 3D Space.

Vertices, Edges and Faces can be extruded to build onto a Primitive. Edges and Faces may be scaled and rotated to twist the shape of the Primitive.

Several Primitives can be joined together to shape a single Object.

Figure 5.1

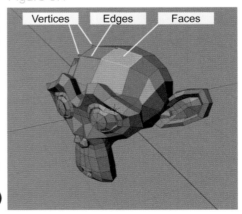

Vertices   Edges   Faces

Suzanne is a Mesh Object (Model)

5.1 The Mesh Object

The default Blender Scene contains a **Cube Mesh Object** which, by default, is selected in **Object Mode**. With the Cube selected (orange outline) press the **Tab ke**y to enter **Edit Mode** to see the basic components of the Cube Mesh (Figure 5.2).

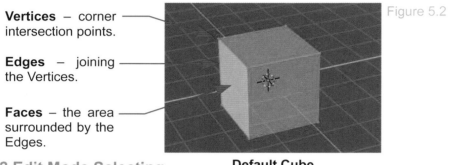

Vertices – corner intersection points.

Edges – joining the Vertices.

Faces – the area surrounded by the Edges.

Figure 5.2

Default Cube

5.2 Edit Mode Selecting

With the 3D Viewport Editor In **Edit Mode**, you work with the individual **Vertices** (mesh intersections) to Model the shape. You know you're in Edit Mode when you see orange lines and dots on the selected Object (Figure 5.2). When you tab into Edit Mode, the whole of your selected Object is in Edit Mode with all the Vertices selected. By default, Edit mode is in **Vertex Select Mode**.

Selection Options

In **Edit Mode**, the default selection Mode is **Vertex** which means you may select Vertices. You can elect to enter **Edge** or **Face** select Mode (Figure 5.3). These options are available in the 3D Viewport Editor Header.

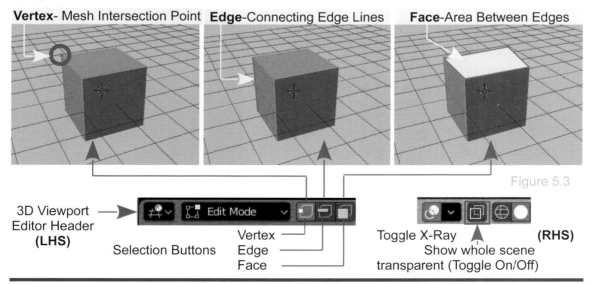

Vertex- Mesh Intersection Point   **Edge**-Connecting Edge Lines   **Face**-Area Between Edges

Figure 5.3

3D Viewport Editor Header **(LHS)**

Selection Buttons

Vertex
Edge
Face

Toggle X-Ray   **(RHS)**
Show whole scene transparent (Toggle On/Off)

Also, by default, only visible Vertices, Edges or Faces are available for selection. This means that you can only select the Vertices, Edges or Faces on the front that you actually see in the Editor. Blender has a **Toggle X -Ray** function, which allows you to see and select hidden Vertices, Edges or Faces (Figure 5.4). This function is toggled on and off in the 3D Viewport Editor Header by clicking the **X-Ray** button.

Figure 5.4

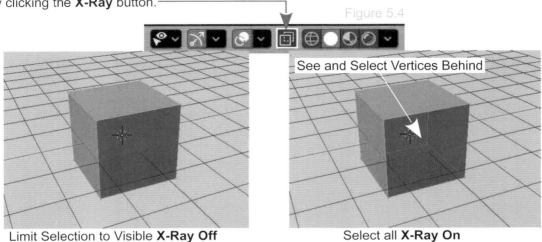

See and Select Vertices Behind

Limit Selection to Visible **X-Ray Off**   Select all **X-Ray On**

Toggling **X-Ray On** allows you to see Vertices in Edit Mode which are hidden behind front Faces. You should be aware that this feature exists for Object Mode. You can not select Vertices in Object Mode but there are occasions when you may wish to see hidden geometry.

The 3D Viewport Editor displays Objects in several different Display methods referred to as **Viewport Shading Modes** (see Chapter 13 – Viewport Shading). The default display is Solid Viewport Shading. The options are accessed in the 3D Viewport Editor Header.

Show Whole Scene Transparent   **Wireframe**
(**Toggles X-Ray On - Off**)   **Solid Viewport Shading**

3D Viewport Editor Header (RHS)

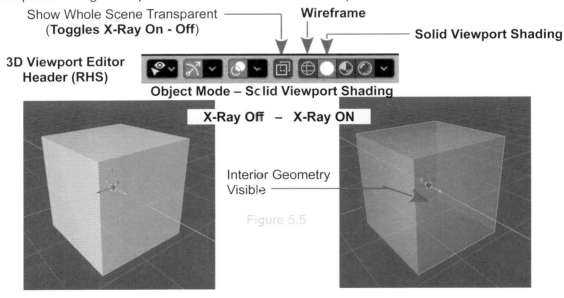

Object Mode – Solid Viewport Shading

X-Ray Off – X-Ray ON

Interior Geometry Visible

Figure 5.5

Object Mode – Wireframe Display

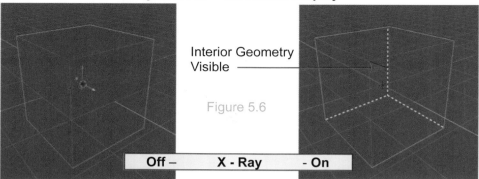

Interior Geometry
Visible

Figure 5.6

| Off – | X - Ray | - On |

5.3 Selecting Vertices, Edges and Faces

While in **Edit Mode**, to select a single Vertex, first press **Click LMB,** in an empty part of the Editor, to deselect all the Vertices. In **Edit Mode** this does not deselect the Object, only the Vertices. Click with the left mouse button (LMB) on a single Vertex to select it (Vertex displays white). To select multiple Vertices, hold down **Shift** while using the LMB to click. You can also drag a rectangle around the Vertices. Press the **B Key**, hold and drag a rectangle to select a group of Vertices. Pressing the **C Key** will bring up a circle selection tool. Holding the LMB and dragging the circle, selects Vertices on the move. The circle can be sized by scrolling the center Mouse Wheel (MMB). Pressing **Esc** will get you out of the circular selection tool. In order to deselect all Vertices or deselect those currently selected, press the **Alt + A Key** or **LMB** click on an empty space in the **3D Viewport Editor**. The selection and deselection procedures are the same for Vertices, Edges and Faces.

5.4 Manipulating Selected Vertices, Edges and Faces

After selecting Vertices, Edges or Faces, you can use the basic controls used for manipulating Objects (**G Key** to grab or move (Translate), **S Key** to scale, and **R Key** to rotate) (Figure 5.7). Obviously you cannot scale a single vertex but you can scale two or more selected Vertices which constitute a **Vertex Group**. **Note:** The **Edit Mode Tool Panel** at the LHS of the 3D Viewport Editor provides **Manipulation Widgets** for Translating, Scaling and Rotating (see Chapter 6 - Editing Tools).

Examples of Translation (Move), Scale and Rotation   Figure 5.7

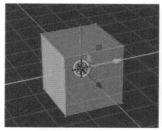

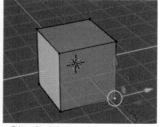

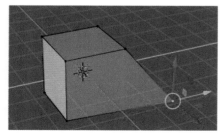

Default Cube – All Vertices
Selected

Single Vertex Selected
EDIT MODE

Single Vertex Moved (Translated)

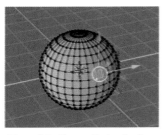

Four Vertices Selected
Hold Shift – Click **LMB**

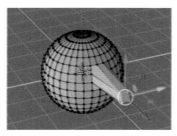

Vertex Group **Translated**
Using the Widget

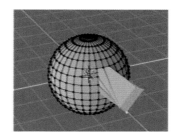

Vertex Group Scaled and Rotated
S Key Scale – R Key Rotate

Figure 5.8

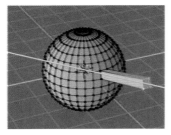

Vertex Group **Extruded** Along
the Axis Normal to the Face

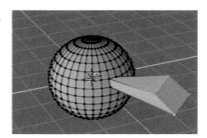

Vertex Group Scaled and Rotated

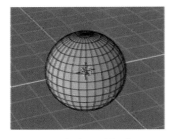

Face Select Mode

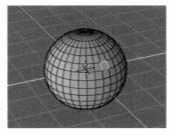

Single Face Selected

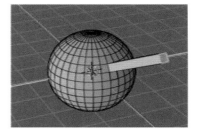

Face Extruded Along Axis

Note the difference between **Translating (Moving)** a **Vertex Group** and **Extruding** a **Vertex Group**. Extrusion creates new Vertices (see Chapter 6- 6.5 Editing Tool – Extrude Region).

5.5 Creating Vertices by Subdivision

There are occasions when you need to add more Vertices to part or **all of the mesh** in order to create detail. To do this, you must be in **Edit Mode** with Vertices selected. To add Vertices to a specific area select Vertices surrounding the area where you wish to add detail. Click **RMB** in the Screen to display the **Vertex Context Menu** and select **Subdivide.**
Figure 5.9

Selecting **Subdivide** inserts a new Vertex at the mid point of each Edge defined by the selected Vertices. Opening the Last Operator **Subdivide Panel** (Lower LHS) shows **Number of Cuts = 1**. Each Edge has been divided once. You may increase the Number of Cuts, further dividing.

RMB click to display the **Vertex Context Menu**

Vertices Selected

Figure 5.10

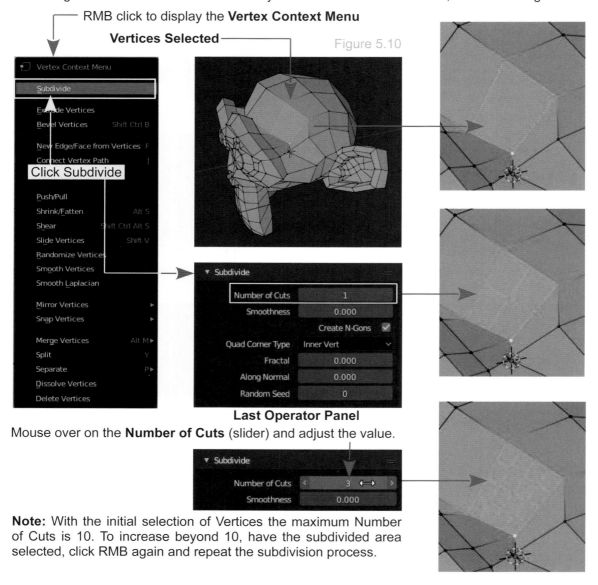

Last Operator Panel

Mouse over on the **Number of Cuts** (slider) and adjust the value.

Note: With the initial selection of Vertices the maximum Number of Cuts is 10. To increase beyond 10, have the subdivided area selected, click RMB again and repeat the subdivision process.

Alternative Subdivision Method

Note: With the initial Vertices selected you may also click **Edge** in the 3D Viewport Editor Header and click Subdivide for the same result.

5.6 Adding and Deleting Vertices, Edges, or Faces

Deleting: If you want to make a hole in a mesh, enter **Edit Mode** and select the Vertices, Edges or Faces you wish to remove, then hit the **X Key or Delete Key**. Select (click) the item from the menu that displays (Figure 5.11).

Figure 5.11

Adding Vertices and Faces: Place the Object in **Edit Mode**. Deselect all Vertices. **Press Ctrl** and click **RMB** where you wish to place a new Vertex. Shift select three or more Vertices. Press the **F key** to **Face** (fill in between the selected Vertices Figure 5.12).

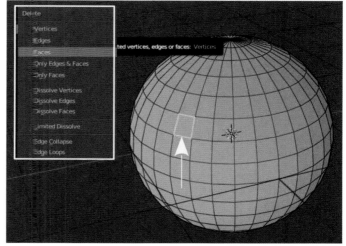

UV Sphere in Edit Face Select Mode

New Vertex Ctrl + RMB click

Figure 5.12

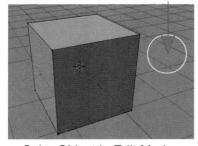

Cube Object in Edit Mode

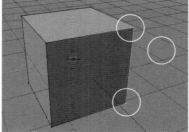

Selec Three Vertices

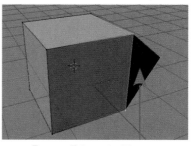

Press **F key** to Face

Note: If you get the sequence of operations wrong you will get unexpected results.

Two Vertices Selected   Mouse positioned to add a Vertex

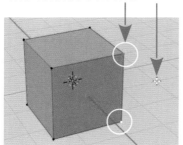

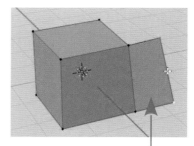

Ctrl + RMB Clicked

When you add a new Vertex in **User Perspective View** the Vertex is placed on the mid plane of the view. This means it is placed on an imaginary plane located at the center of the 3D World. The plane is normal (at right angles) to your computer screen.

Top Orthographic View

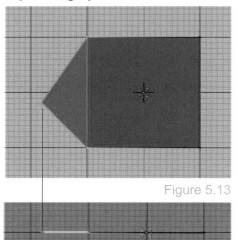

New Vertex added. Three Vertices are selected then Faced (Figure 5.13).

All Vertices are located on the same plane in elevation.

Front Orthographic View (Figure 5.14)

Side Orthographic View (Figure 5.15)

Figure 5.13

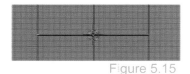

Figure 5.14   Figure 5.15

User Perspective View

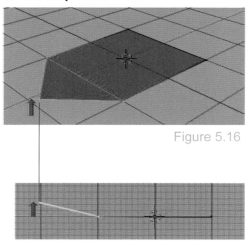

New Vertex added. Three Vertices are selected then faced (Figure 5.16).

The new Vertex is displaced in elevation.

Front Orthographic View (Figure 5.17).

Side Orthographic View (Figure 5.18).

Figure 5.16

Figure 5.17   Figure 5.18

5.7 Center Points

Every Object you create in Blender has a small dot somewhere in the center (by default, usually at the center of geometry of the Object).This is the Object's **Origin**, or pivot point (Figure 5.19). With the Object selected in **Object Mode**, moving the Object moves the origin at the same time. In **Edit Mode** the origin does not move when Vertices are moved.

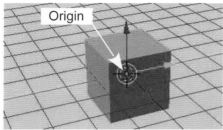

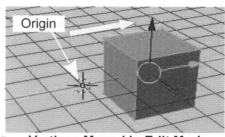

Origint at Center of Geometry   Figure 5.19   **Vertices Moved in Edit Mode**

Having the Origin located somewhere else is advantageous when you want to set a Rotation point.

Top Orthographic View (Press Num Pad 7)

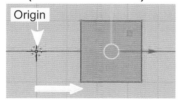

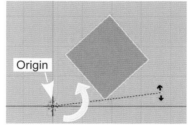

In Top Orthographic View – Object Mode – Vertices moved, Rotation is about the original Origin position.

R Key (Rotate)- Drag the Mouse

Rotation occurs about the Origin. To rotate about a different position, relocate the Origin to the location of the **3D Viewport Editor Cursor,** when it has been relocates. Press **Shift and RMB click** in the Editor to locate the Cursor. With the Mouse Cursor in the 3D Viewport, **RMB click** to display the **Object Context Menu**. Mouse over on **Set Origin** then click, **Origin to 3D Cursor**. Rotating the Cube will be about the Origin located at the position of the 3D Viewport Cursor.

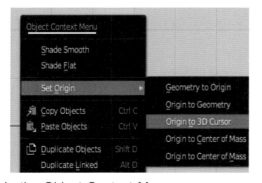

Figure 5.20

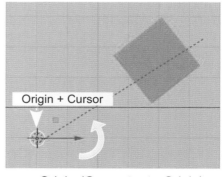

In the Object Context Menu you can move the Cube to the new Origin (Geometry to Origin) or move the Origin back to the Cube (Origin to Geometry).

5.8 Joining and Separating

Individual Objects can be joined together to make a single Object. The Objects may be separated under certain conditions or parts of a mesh can be separated from the main Object.

Joining in Object Mode

In Figure 5.21, a UV Sphere Object has been added to the default Scene and positioned such that it intersects with the default Cube. After positioning, the Sphere is deselected and the Cube selected. **Note:** The Move Tool has been selected in the Tool Panel displaying the Translate Manipulation Widget. <u>The Manipulation Widget</u> is located at the center of the Cube.

Figure 5.21

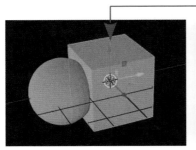
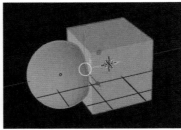
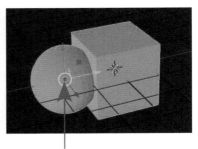

Cube Selected After Positioning   Widget Locates Mid Way   New Center of Rotation

To join the two Objects, have the Cube selected and **Shift select the UV Sphere**. Note: The Sphere was the last Object to be selected and now the Manipulation Widget is located mid way between the center of the Sphere and the Cube. Press **Ctrl + J Key** to join the two Objects. Note: There is an orange outline encapsulating both the Sphere and the Cube which indicates they are a single Object. Note Also: The Widget has located at the center of the Sphere, the last Object selected. The center of geometry for the combined Object is at the center of the Sphere. Rotation of the combined Object will be about this center.

Joining in Edit Mode

Consider the following with the default Blender Scene; The Cube Object is selected in Object Mode. Press **Tab** to enter Edit Mode. Press the **Alt +A Key** deselecting the Vertices. The Cube remains selected since it is the active Object selected in Object Mode. While remaining in Edit mode, add a UV Sphere Object to the Scene. The Sphere will display with its verticies selected but since it coincides with the Cube only the polar and cardinal vertices at the equator are visible.

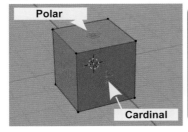
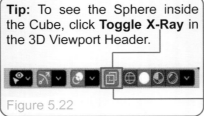
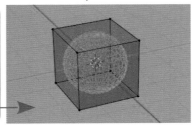

Polar

Tip: To see the Sphere inside the Cube, click **Toggle X-Ray** in the 3D Viewport Header.

Cardinal   Figure 5.22

> Objects added to a Scene in **Edit Mode** are automatically joined to the last object selected while in **Object Mode**.

When the UV Sphere is added all its Vertices are selected and may be manipulated (**T**ranslated **R**otated and **S**caled) manually using the T, R and S Keys or by using the manipulation widgets from the Tool Panel. When manipulated press **Alt + A** Key or click LMB in an empty part of the Editor to deselect the Sphere's Vertices. Pressing the **A Key** following this will select the joined UV Sphere plus the Cube. They have been joined and form a single Object (Figure 5.23).

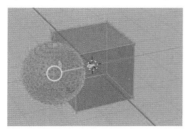
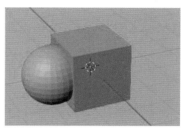

Figure 5.23

In the **Outliner Editor** you will see a single Object named **Cube** listed (the combined Object).

Figure 5.24

Separating in Edit Mode

To demonstrate separation in Edit Mode, use the same Cube – Sphere arrangement as shown in Figure 5.23. Have the Cube and the Sphere joined into a single Object.

Figure 5.25

Place the **3D View Editor** in **Right Orthographic view** and with the combined Object selected, **Tab** to Edit Mode. Press **Alt + A key** to deselect all Vertices. Press the **B key** (Box Select) and drag a rectangle around the LH side of the spherical part. **Don't forget to Toggle X Ray On** to enable selection of Vertices behind the visible Vertices.

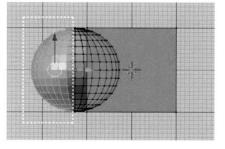

The selected Vertices will be displayed orange.
(Figure 5.25)

With the selection made, press the **P Key** to display the **Separate Menu** and in this case, click on the **Selection** option. The **Selection** option separates the selected Vertices creating a new Object as shown by the orange outline. (Figure 5.26).

Figure 5.26

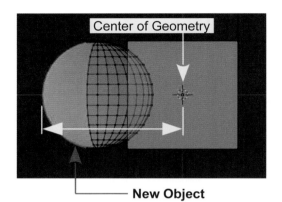
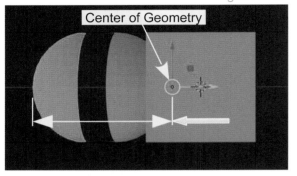

New Object   **New Object Moved**

Tab back to Object mode. With the Manipulation Widget turned on, move the new Object along the Y Axis. You can move the object anywhere you like, rotate it, scale it etc.

Note: In joining the Sphere to the Cube in Object Mode by pressing **Ctrl + J**, in this case the Cube was the last Object selected, therefore, the center of geometry of the combined Objects was at the center of the Cube. After separating part of the Sphere mesh, its' center of geometry is also located, coinciding with the center of the Cube. When moving the separated part of the Sphere you see the center of geometry, i.e. center of rotation, displaced from the mesh.

The Separate Menu Options

In the previous example you used the **Selection option** in the **Separate** menu. There are two alternatives (Figure 5.27):

Separate by Material: When joined objects have different Materials (Color) applied they will be separated into single Objects according to their color.

Figure 5.27

> Material (Color) is discussed in Chapter 16

Separate by Loose Parts: Consider the Objects automatically joined in Edit Mode (Figure 5.23).

With the UV Sphere and Cube joined in Edit Mode, and displayed in Edit Mode, press the **P Key** to display the **Separate** menu and select **By Loose Parts**. Immediately one of the Objects will display a red outline. **Tab to Object Mode**. You may now select either part as a separate Object. Note the center of Geometry (Origin).

5.9 Creating Vertex Groups

On occasion you will want to manipulate a **group of vertices**. You can select multiple vertices on an Object and manipulate them, but once deselected you could have trouble selecting the exact same group the next time. To assist with this you can assign multiple Vertices to a designated group for re-selection. Working through the following example will show you how.

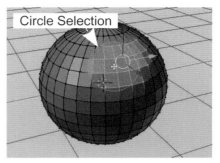

Figure 5.28

Start the default Scene and replace the Cube with a **UV Sphere**. Zoom in on the Scene to give a better view (press the Number Pad **+** sign). Tab to **Edit mode** and then press **Alt + A key** to **deselect** all the Vertices. Press the **C key** for circle select (scroll the mouse wheel to adjust the circle size) and click, hold and drag the circle over the Sphere to select a group of Vertices (Figure 5.28). Press **Esc** to cancel the circle selection. The Vertices remain selected.

In the **Properties Editor, Object Data Properties, Vertex Groups tab**, click on the **+** sign to create a **Vertex Group Data Slot**. By default, this will be named simply **Group** (Figure 5.29). If you wish you can change the name to something meaningful by clicking on **Group** in the **Name** slot, deleting it, and retyping a new name.

Properties Editor

Figure 5.29

With the group of vertices still selected on the Sphere, click on the **Assign button** in the **Vertex Groups Tab -** this assigns the selected vertices to **Group**.

By clicking on the **Select** and **Deselect** buttons, you will see the vertices on the Sphere being selected or deselected, respectively.

Deselect the Vertices and repeat the circle select with a different group. Click on the **+** sign again in the **Vertex Groups Tab** and you should see a new data block created named **Group.001**. Click the **Assign button** to assign the new group of vertices to **Group.001**. Deselect the Vertices on the Sphere in the 3D Viewport Editor, and you can now select **Group** or **Group.001** (Figure 5.30).

Weigh Paint Method

Figure 5.30

An alternative method for selecting Vertices for assignment to a Vertex Group is to use Blender's **Weigh Paint Tool.**

With a **UV Sphere** selected in the **3D Viewport,** go to the **Properties Editor, Object Data Properties**. In the **Vertex Group Tab** click the **Plus** sign to create a new **Vertex Group**. The Vertex Group will be named simply **Group** (Figure 5.32).

Place the 3D Viewport Editor in **Weigh Paint Mode** (Figure 5.31).

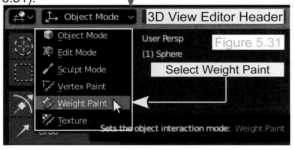

3D View Editor Header

Figure 5.31

Select Weight Paint

Figure 5.32

In the **Weigh Paint Mode, Tool Panel** click on **Draw.**
The 3D Editor cursor becomes a red circle which is the paint **Brush** (Figure 5.32).

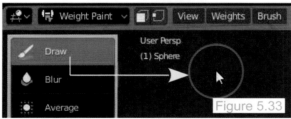

Figure 5.33

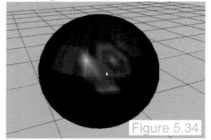

Figure 5.34

The UV Sphere displays blue. Click, hold and drag the brush over the surface of the UV Sphere painting an area until it is red (Figures 5.34, 5.35). Painting selects Vertices.

Press the **Tab Key** to place the 3D Viewport in **Edit Mode** and **deselect all Vertices** (press Alt + A Key).

In the **Properties Editor, Object Data Properties, Vertex Groups Tab,** with the new Vertex Group named Group highlighted, click the **Assign button** (Figure 5.36).

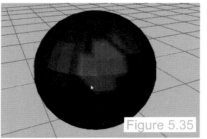

Figure 5.35

Click the **Select button** to see the painted vertices assigned to the **Vertex Group** (Figure 5.37).

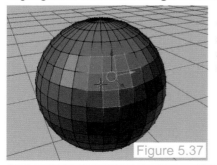

Figure 5.37

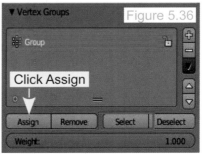

Figure 5.36

Click Assign

5.10 Proportional Vertex Editing

Proportional Vertex Editing is used to create a flow in the shape when editing Vertices. To turn **Proportional Vertex Editing on**, in **Edit Mode**, click the **Proportional Editing** button in the **3D View Editor Header** (Figure 5.38) .

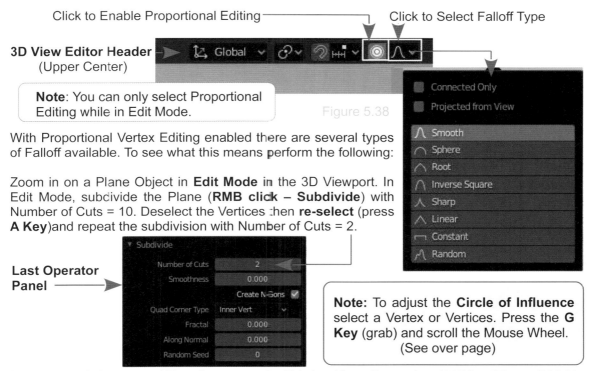

Click to Enable Proportional Editing

Click to Select Falloff Type

3D View Editor Header (Upper Center)

Note: You can only select Proportional Editing while in Edit Mode.

Figure 5.38

With Proportional Vertex Editing enabled there are several types of Falloff available. To see what this means perform the following:

Zoom in on a Plane Object in **Edit Mode** in the 3D Viewport. In Edit Mode, subdivide the Plane (**RMB click – Subdivide**) with Number of Cuts = 10. Deselect the Vertices then **re-select** (press **A Key**)and repeat the subdivision with Number of Cuts = 2.

Last Operator Panel

Note: To adjust the **Circle of Influence** select a Vertex or Vertices. Press the **G Key** (grab) and scroll the Mouse Wheel. (See over page)

Select a single Vertex and Translate up on the Z Axis without Proportional Editing (Figure 5.39 L).

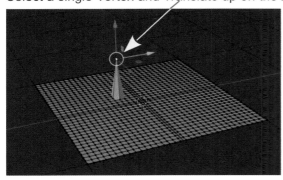

Plane Subdivided – Single Vertex Translated
Note: Proportional Vertex Editing has **NOT** been activated.

Figure 5.39

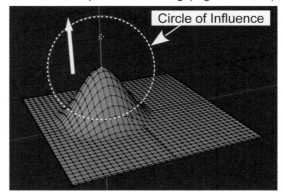

Circle of Influence

Single Vertex Translated on the Z Axis
Proportional Vertex Editing Activated

When a single Vertex is selected and Translated **with Proportional Vertex Editing activated** a **Circle of Influence** determines how many surrounding Vertices are influenced in the Translation.

The diameter of the circle is adjustable. Select the Vertex to be Translated. Press the G Key (places the Vertex in Grab Mode) to display the circle. Without moving the Mouse, scroll the mouse wheel. Click LMB. The circle display is cancelled but the influence is retained. Pressing the G Key and moving the Mouse displays the circle again and moves the selected Vertex. Clicking the Move button in the Tool Panel displays the Manipulation Widget and allows Translation of the Vertex. The Circle of Influence previously set is in effect. Experiment with the different types of Falloff.

Figure 5.40

Having moved the Vertex, the Last Operator – **Move Panel** displays which includes a Proportional Size slider for adjusting the Circle of Influence.

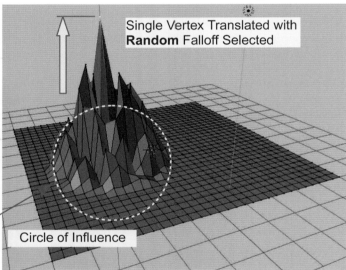

Single Vertex Translated with **Random** Falloff Selected

Circle of Influence

It doesn't take much imagination to see that Proportional Vertex Editing as seen in Figure 5.40 can be employed to create a landscape (see Chapter 8 – 8.1 Editing Techniques and Examples).

5.11 Inset Faces

The **Inset Faces** command causes new Faces to be created inside or outside a selected geometry.

To demonstrate, delete the default Cube in the 3D Viewport and add a **Plane** Object. Zoom in (Scroll MMB), Tab into **Edit** mode and Subdivide the Plane (Number of Cuts = 3). Deselect the Vertices (LMB Click in Editor). Change from **Vertex Select** mode to **Face Select** mode.

Select a single Face and with the Mouse Cursor in the 3D Viewport Editor, **moved to one side**, press the **I Key** and move the Mouse Cursor towards the center of the Face.(Figure 5.41). Alternatively, with a **Face** selected, click **Face** in the 3D Viewport Editor Header and select **Inset Faces** Move the Mouse towards the center of the Face. Another method is, click **Inset Faces** in the **Tool Panel**. Click on the yellow paddle that displays and move it towards the center. With either method, and you see new Faces created. Click LMB to set the new Faces in position.

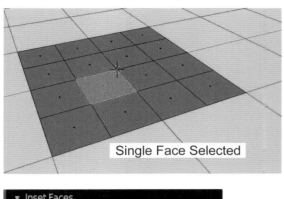

Single Face Selected

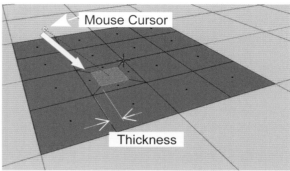

Mouse Cursor

Thickness

Figure 5.41

Last Operator Panel

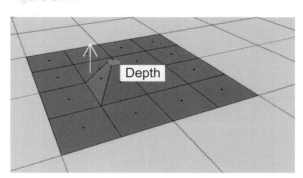

Depth

Figure 5.42

Note: **Inset Faces** displays in the **Last Operator Panel** (Figure 5.42). While this panel is displayed you can make adjustments. The **Thickness Slider** controls the size of the new Face. The **Depth Slider** displaces the face normal to the Plane. Positive values above the Plane, negative values below the Plane.

Note: The procedure can be processed in both **Vertex Select Mode** and **Edge Select Mode** by selecting the perimeter of an area on the surface of the plane. The principle can be applied to the surface of any mesh Object.

5.12 Parenting

In **5.8 Joining and Separating**, it was demonstrated how two Mesh Objects may be joined together to form a single combined Object. There are, however, occasions when you will want two or more Objects to act as a single unit but not actually have the mesh joined. For example, you may want one Object to follow another when the first Object is moved. This can be achieved by **Parenting** or creating a **Child Parent Relationship** between Objects.

To demonstrate, add a UV Sphere Object to the default Scene (Figure 5.43).

Note: In the diagram the Move Tool in the Tool Panel has been activated and the Manipulation Widget employed to position the UV Sphere.

With the UV Sphere selected press Shift and select the Cube. For the demonstration make the selection in this order (Sphere selected – Shift select the Cube).

Press **Ctrl + P Key** and click on **Set Parent To Object.**   Figure 5.43

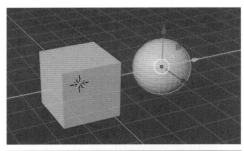

With the Move Tool activated displaying the Manipulation Widget, you will observe that the **Widget relocates mid way** between the two Objects. This indicates that Parenting is in place. Using the Widget to move along the Y Axis will demonstrate that the Objects are Parented. They both move together.

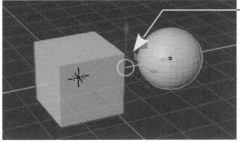

Note: The selection order in the Parenting operation is important.

Having the UV Sphere selected then selecting the Cube has made the UV Sphere the child of the Cube. Selecting the Cube individually and moving, will see the UV Sphere follow. If the UV Sphere is selected individually it can be moved independently.

6

Editing Tools

Editing Tools

In the previous chapter some of Blender's basic mesh editing techniques were introduced which allowed you to manipulate and reshape Primitives. These techniques are the beginning of the process and are essential for mastering more sophisticated practices. Blender incorporates many techniques for performing a variety of functions some of which are automated. The automated techniques may be considered as **Tools**.

Like any trades person, mechanic or engineer, knowing what tools are available, how each functions and most importantly what tool to use for a particular application is the key to success. And, yes! where to find the tool.

As you have seen many editing techniques are simple Key and Mouse commands applied to an Object or to an Object's mesh surface. Other tools automate some fantastic and complex operations. In this chapter some of the Tools will be introduced with examples showing how they are employed.

Other Tools will be introduced in context with specific operations as you progress through the book.

6.1 The Edit Mode Tool Panel

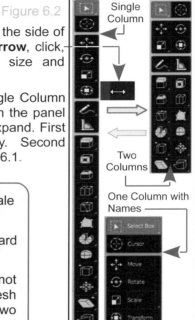

The **Tool Panel** at the left hand side of the **3D Viewport Editor** in **Edit Mode** contains a variety of tools for automating editing processes (Figure 6.1).

The top eight Tools are identical to those found in the Object Mode Tool panel and function in the same way when applied to a selection of Vertices, Edges or Faces. The Tools are activated by clicking (LMB) on a Tool (highlights blue – see **Select Box Tool** at the top of the Tool Stack).

Figure 6.1   Figure 6.2

To gain Screen space you may mouse over at the side of the Tool Panel to reveal a **double headed arrow**, click, hold and drag, to expand or reduce the size and arrangement of the panel (Figure 6.2).

By default the Tool Panel displays with a single Column as shown in Figure 6.2 (LHS). Mouse over on the panel edge and drag the double headed arrow to expand. First expansion created a two column display. Second expansion displays names as shown in Figure 6.1.

> **Note:** You cannot apply the Rotate, Scale or Ruler Tools to a single Vertex.
>
> Pressing the **T Key** on the Keyboard toggles hide and show the Tool Panel.
>
> **Note:** When in Object Mode you can not enter Edit Mode unless you have a Mesh Object in the 3D Viewport Editor. With two or more Objects in the 3D Viewport Editor, the selected Object or the last Object that was selected will be the active Object when entering Edit Mode.

6.2 The Add Menu

Figure 6.3

Objects may be added to the Scene with the **3D Viewport Editor in Edit Mode** by clicking **Add** in the 3D Viewport Editor Header (Edit Mode).

Remember: Objects added to a Scene in **Edit Mode** are automatically joined to the last object selected while in **Object Mode** (see Chapter 5 – 5.8).

6.3 Last Operator Panels

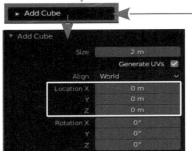

◄─────── Click to Expand the Panel

When an action has been performed in the 3D Viewport Editor, the **Last Operator Panel** is displayed in the bottom LH corner of the Editor. **Click to Expand**, allowing values in the panel to be adjusted affecting the action.

The Last Operator Panel (Figure 6.4) shows that a Cube Object was added at the center of the Scene (Location X, Y, Z = 0 m)

Figure 6.4

6.4 Extrusion

Before examining the **Extrude Region Tool** consider Extrusion in general.

Extrusion means, stretching such that the shape is altered. Shapes can be altered by selecting a single Vertex or a group of Vertices, then Translating, Rotating or Scaling. You may also select Edges or Faces and apply the same processes (Figure 6.5).

Vertices are selected with the Object in Edit Mode. When the selected **Vertices** are **Extruded duplicate Vertices are created**, which may be Moved, Scaled or Rotated. The new Vertices remain attached to the original Object's surface mesh thus altering the shape of the Object.

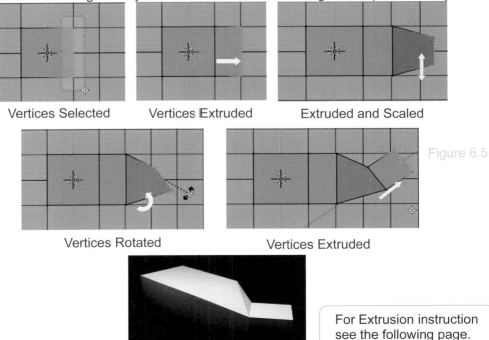

Vertices Selected   Vertices Extruded   Extruded and Scaled

Figure 6.5

Vertices Rotated   Vertices Extruded

For Extrusion instruction see the following page.

Rendered Image of Camera View

In Figure 6.5 the RH Vertices of a Cube (Top Orthographic View) are selected in **Edit Mode** by pressing the **B Key** (Box Select) and dragging a rectangle (don't forget to have **Toggle X-Ray on** - Chapter 5 – 5.2 – Figure 5.3). With the Vertices selected press the **E key** (Extrude) + **X Key** (confines Extrusion to the X Axis) and drag the Mouse. The Vertices are duplicated and repositioned. With the Vertices remaining selected the Extrusion process is repeated, and the selection Scaled down by pressing the **S Key** and moving the Mouse in. The selection is Rotated by pressing the **R Key** and moving the mouse. Finally, the selection is Extruded again.

6.5 The Extrude Region Tool

 Activating the **Extrude Region Tool** displays a manipulation Widget located at the center of the selection. In Figure 6.6 the selection is the top Face of the default Cube. Click, hold and drag the Widget to Extrude the selection.

The Tool has four options. Mouse over on the Tool and click and hold to expand the panel.

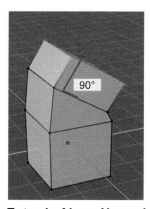

Figure 6.6

Extrude Region ──────▶

Extrude Along Normal means Extrude at right angles to the selected Face.

Extrude Individual allows Extrusion of an individual Face.

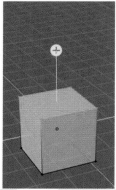

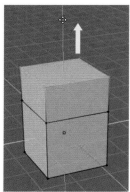

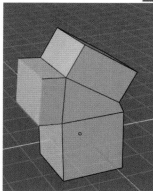

Mouse Cursor

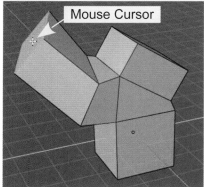

Extrude Along Normal   **Extrude Individual**   **Extrude to Cursor**

With **Extrude to Cursor** selected the selected Face will be Extruded to wherever you click the Mouse Cursor (click the Select Box Tool at the top of the Tool Panel to cancel).

Note: The Extrusion methods can be applied to Faces, Edges and Vertices.

6.6 Inset Faces

Figure 6.7

Inset Faces creates new Faces inside a selected geometry (see Chapter 5 – 5.11).

To demonstrate, select the top **Face** of the default Cube while in Edit Mode. Press the **I Key** (Insert - Figure 6.7) and move the **Mouse Cursor** towards the center of the selected Face. You see new Faces created. Click LMB to set the new Faces in position.

Note: The **Inset Faces Last Operator Panel** displays (Figure 6.8). While this panel is displayed you can make adjustments. The **Thickness slider** controls the size of the new Face. The **Depth slider** displaces the Face normal to the surface (positive values above the surface, negative values below). Note: The procedure can be processed in both **Vertex Select Mode** and **Edge Select Mode** by selecting the perimeter of an area on the surface. The procedure can be applied to the surface of any mesh Object.

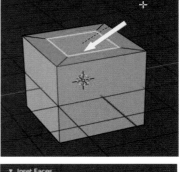

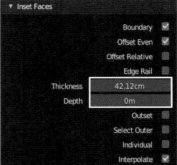

Figure 6.8

6.7 The Inset Faces Tool

Activating the **Inset Faces Tool** replicates the above procedure. Click the Tool to activate. Click hold and drag the yellow paddle that displays (Figure 6.9). While the Tool is activated you can select any Face in the 3D Viewport and apply the procedure.

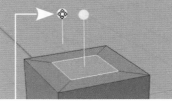

6.8 The Bevel Tool

Figure 6.9

The **Bevel Tool** bevels the Edges of a selected Face (Figure 6.10).

Mouse Cursor Over the Paddle

Figure 6.10

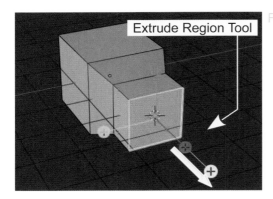

Extrude Region Tool

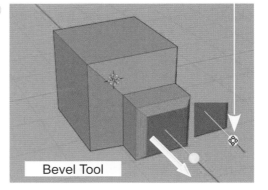

Bevel Tool

The default Cube with the front face Extruded and Scaled down then Extruded a second time.

With the face selected activate the Bevel Tool. Place the Mouse Cursor, click hold and drag to bevel the edges of the Face.

6.9 Edge and Loop Selection

When working with Vertices, it is sometimes useful to select Vertices which form an Edge or a Loop.

Cylinder Object in Edit Mode

Figure 6.11

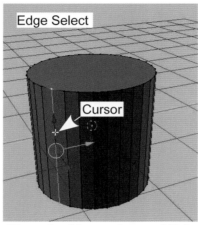

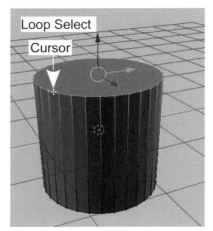

Place the Mouse Cursor (White Cross) over an Edge – Press **Alt – Click LMB**

Place the Mouse Cursor (White Cross) over a Loop – Press **Alt – Click LMB**

6.10 Loop Cut Tool

The **Loop Cut Tool** allows you to create new Edges and Loops without selecting Vertices.

Note: This Tool has two options;

Mouse over on the Loop Cut Tool in the Tool Panel, Click LMB and hold to see the options. Drag the Mouse Cursor over the option required and release to select the option.

Have the Object selected in Object Mode, Tab to Edit Mode and deselect all Vertices. To demonstrate, a Cylinder will be used, in Vertex Select Mode.

With the Loop Cut option selected, you may create a new **Edge** or a new **Edge Loop**.

To Create a New Edge (Vertices connected by a vertical Edge), hover the Mouse Cursor (white cross) over either the upper or lower ring of Vertices to display the new intended Edge as a vertical yellow line between any two Vertices on either ring. You position the yellow line between sets of Vertices line by dragging the Mouse (Figure 6.12a). Click LMB to set the new Edge. By default the Edge is positioned mid way between Vertices. If you wish to locate the new Edge other than mid way, Click LMB, hold and drag the mouse (Figure 6.12b, c), release to set. You can only drag the new Edge in between two vertices.

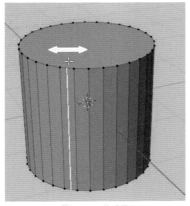

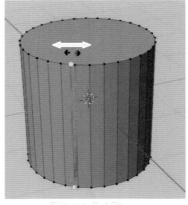

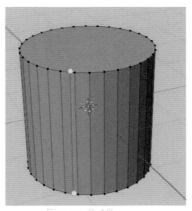

Figure 6.12a Figure 6.12b Figure 6.12c

To Create a New Edge Loop mouse over (white cross) on the side of the Cylinder to display the new Edge Loop as a yellow circle (Figure 6.13a). By default the yellow circle will display mid way between the upper and lower Edge Loops or mid way between any loops previously created. Click LMB, hold and drag the Mouse to position the new Edge Loop and release to set in position (Figure 6.13b, c).

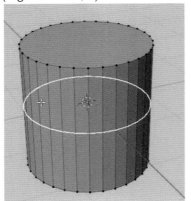

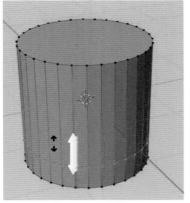

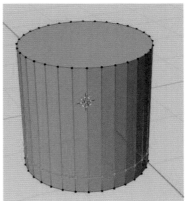

Figure 6.13a Figure 6.13b Figure 6.13c

After setting the new Loop Cut in position you can create additional Loop Cuts by adjusting the Number of Cuts in the Last Operator Panel (Figure 6.14).

Alternativy you can preset the number of Loop Cuts to be created in the 3D Viewport Header (Figure 15).

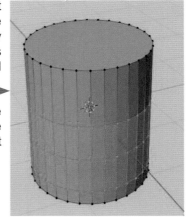

Figure 6.15

113

Offset Edge Loop Cut

Having created a new Edge Loop you may duplicate Edge Loops either side of the cut using the Offset Edge Loop Cut Tool. Activate the Tool, position the Mouse Cursor adjacent to the cut, clickand hold LMB and drag the Mouse (Figure 6.16).

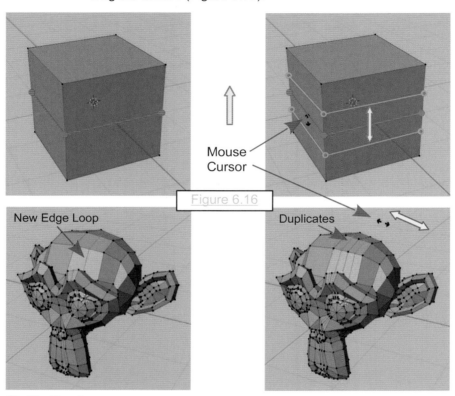

Mouse Cursor

Figure 6.16

New Edge Loop

Duplicates

6.11 The Knife Tool

Figure 6.17

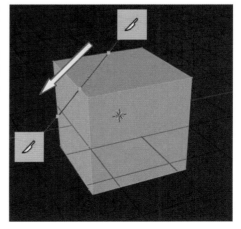

With the **Knife Tool** activated clicking LMB in the Editor displays the Mouse Cursor as a knife. Hold and drag across Edges creating Vertices and Edges. Release the Mouse button and press Enter.

6.12 The Poly Build Tool

 **Poly Build** allows you to create Polygon Surfaces generating shapes by simply clicking LMB in the 3D View Editor.

With the **Poly Build Tool** activated, in **Vertex Select Mode**, Mouse Over on an **Edge** (highlights). Click **LMB, hold and drag** to generate a new Face. Click LMB to place.

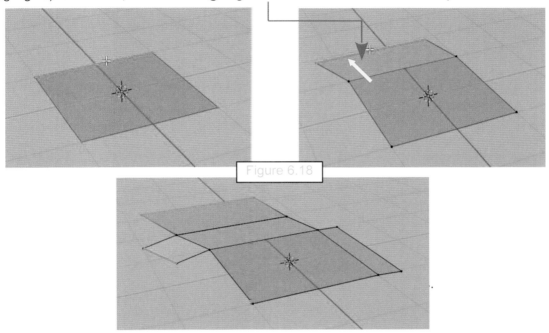

Figure 6.18

6.13 The Spin Tool

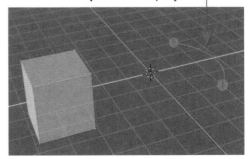 To see what the Spin Tool accomplishes, have the default Cube Object in Edit Mode displaced from the center of the Scene (Figure 16.19).The Viewport Editor Cursor is located at the center of the Scene. The Cursor is the center of rotation for the Spin Action. Click on the Spin Tool in the Tool Panel. The **Spin Arc** displays.

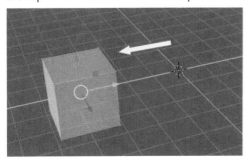

Figure 6.19

Figure 6.20

With all Vertices selected, Click LMB on a cross, hold and drag the Mouse to create a partial Spin (Figure 6.21. Release LMB. To Spin the Cube 360° about the center of rotation (the **3D View Editor Cursor**) (Figure 16.22) enter Angle 360° in the Last Operator Panel (Figure 16.23).

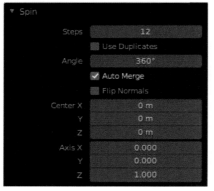

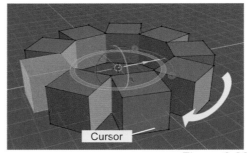

Figure 6.21

Figure 6.22

Release the Mouse button then click on the manipulation Widget that displays and skew the Spin profile (Figure 16.24).

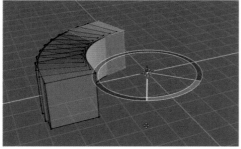

Figure 6.23

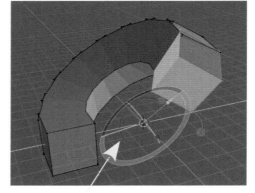

Manipulation Widget   Figure 6.24

6.14 Creating a Spin Profile

A Spin Profile is a line drawing of a shape representing the cross section through an object you wish to generate. As an example a wine glass or goblet will be created.

Figure 6.25

To create a Spin Profile you start with two vertices in Edit Mode in the 3D Viewport Editor. One way to do this is to have a **Plane Object** in a new Scene and delete two Vertices in Edit mode

A Plane Object is always added to a Scene laying flat in Top Orthographic View, therefore, flick it on edge by pressing **R Key** (Rotate) + **X Key** + **90** (rotate about the X Axis 90 degrees) press **Enter.**

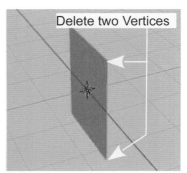

116

Have the Plane in **Front Orthographic View**, in **Edit Mode** and delete two Vertices. This leaves the remaining two Vertices from which you build your profile.

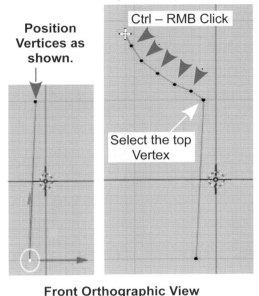

Position Vertices as shown.

Ctrl – RMB Click

Select the top Vertex

Front Orthographic View

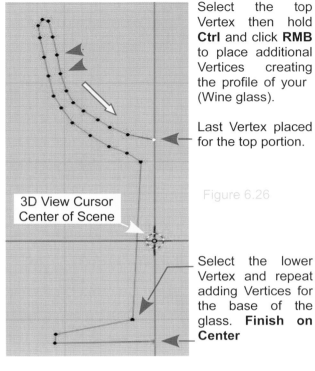

Select the top Vertex then hold **Ctrl** and click **RMB** to place additional Vertices creating the profile of your (Wine glass).

Last Vertex placed for the top portion.

Figure 6.26

3D View Cursor Center of Scene

Select the lower Vertex and repeat adding Vertices for the base of the glass. **Finish on Center**

Spinning: To generate the glass the completed profile will be spun around the position of the **3D View Editor Cursor** with the **3D View Editor** in **Top Orthographic View** in **Edit Mode**. In creating the profile the 3D View Editor has been in **Front Orthographic View** and **Note: The 3D View Editor Cursor is at the center of the Scene.**

Important: If the 3D View Editor Cursor is located other than at the center of the Scene, spin rotation will take place about that point with unexpected results.

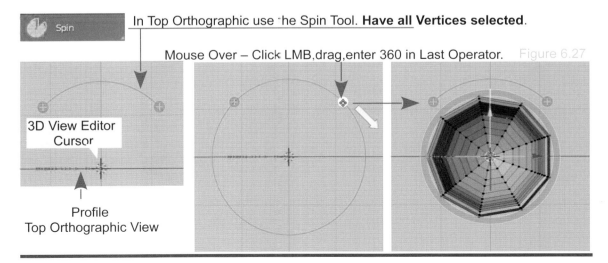

Spin

In Top Orthographic use the Spin Tool. **Have all Vertices selected.**

Mouse Over – Click LMB,drag,enter 360 in Last Operator.   Figure 6.27

3D View Editor Cursor

Profile
Top Orthographic View

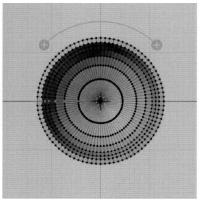

In the **Last Operator Spin Panel** increase the number of **Steps** to add Vertices create a rounding effect.

In Object Mode, LMB click and select **Shade Smooth** in the **Object Context Menu.**

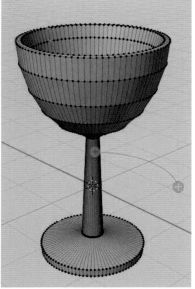

User Perspective View

Figure 6.28

Add a Glass Material (more on this later – Chapter 9).

6.15 Spin Duplication

The Spin Tool may be used to duplicate an Object around a circular path. The Spin is always about the Z Axis on the XY Plane, therefore, place the 3D Viewport Editor in **Top Orthographic View**. The Spin uses the location of the **3D Viewport Editor Cursor** as the center of rotation.

In a new Scene in **Top Orthographic View** with the default **Cube Object** selected and located at the centre of the Scene, Tab to **Edit Mode**. Place the 3D Viewport Editor Cursor off to one side (Shift + RMB click to place). Alternatively, with all Vertices selected move the Cube away from the Cursor which is at the center of the Scene. Activate the **Spin Tools** and click **LMB, hold and drag** on either of the crosses in the blue circles that are displayed. (Figure 6.28).

By default the Spin creates twelve duplications of the Cube spaced in a circle around the 3D Viewport Editor Cursor. The number of duplications depends on the value set in the Last Operator Panel for the Spin (Figure 6.29).

The Vertices of the original Cube are selected (in Edit Mode). You may press the G Key and move the Vertices but if you Tab to Object Mode you will discover that although you appear have separate Cubes, they are in fact joined as one Object. Tab back to Edit Mode. Press the **P Key** and select **Separate by Loose Parts**. In Object Mode you may select individual Cubes and move them but note where the center of each Cube is located. With one Cube selected Tab to Edit Mode and reposition the individual Vertices of the Cube over the center point.

Top Orthographic View
Click LMB on a Blue Cross   Figure 6.29

Eight Duplication
Nine Steps in the Last Operator Panel

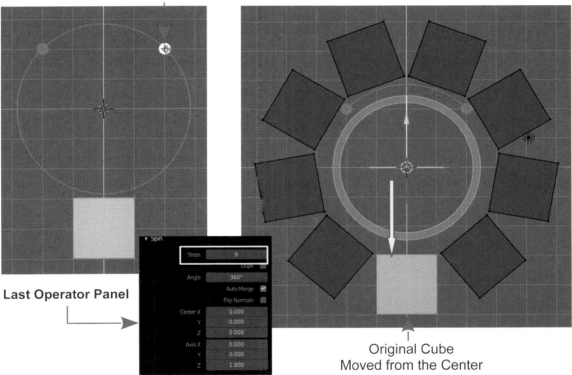

Last Operator Panel

Original Cube
Moved from the Center

6.16 The Screw Tool   Figure 6.30

Previous versions of Blender included a Screw Tool which spun vertices and at the same time generated duplications at right angles to the spin producing a Screw effect. This procedure is now accomplished by the **Screw Modifier** (see Modifiers Chapter 7). You may, however, use the Manipulation Widget of the Spin Tool to skew the Spin Duplication.

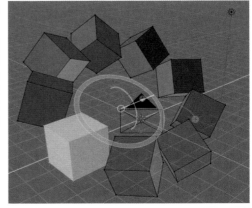

6.17 The Smooth and Randomize Tools

The effect of the **Smooth Tool** is to smooth or round transitions at the corners of a mesh. Randomize displaces Vertices in a Random order. The Tools are best demonstrated with an Object that has been Extruded and Subdivided (see Section 6.4).

In the **3D Viewport Editor Header** select **Edge** and click **Subdivide with all Vertices selected**.

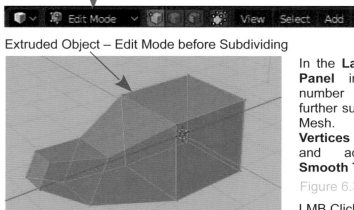

Extruded Object – Edit Mode before Subdividing

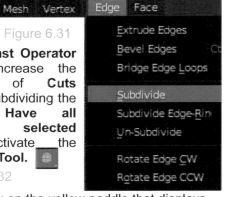

Figure 6.31

In the **Last Operator Panel** increase the number of **Cuts** further subdividing the Mesh. **Have all Vertices selected** and activate the **Smooth Tool.**

Figure 6.32

LMB Click on the yellow paddle that displays, hold and drag.

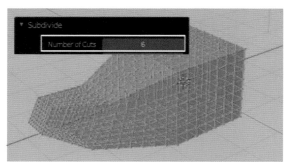

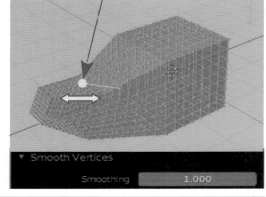

In the Smooth Vertices Panel increase Smoothing to 1.000.

After Subdividing and Smoothing

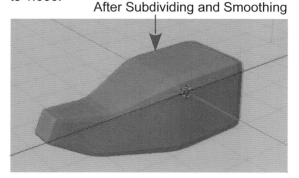

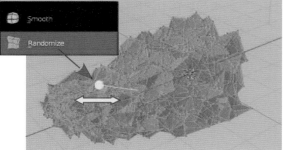

6.18 The Edge Slide And Vertex Slide Tool

Select an **Edge** (in Edit Mode) on an Object. Activate the **Edge Slide Tool**. Click on the yellow paddle and drag the Mouse. The Edge will be translated within the space occupied by the Object.

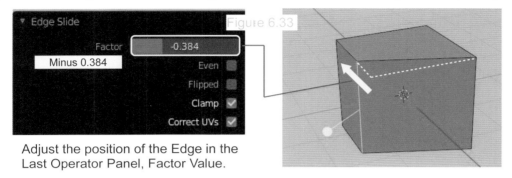

Figure 6.33

Adjust the position of the Edge in the Last Operator Panel, Factor Value.

6.19 The Shrink Fatten Tool

The **Shrink Fatten** Tool allows you to expand (fatten) or shrink a selection.

Figure 6.34

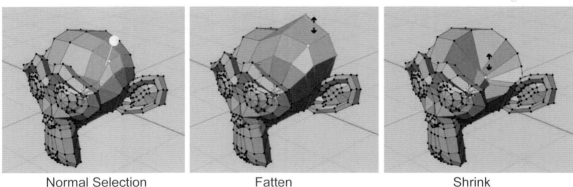

| Normal Selection | Fatten | Shrink |

6.20 The Shear Tool

Figure 6.35

Click LMB on a handle to Shear the Object. Selected handle turns white.

 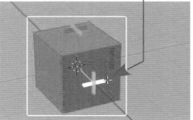 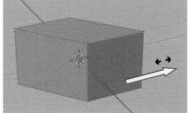

Shear Handles   Click LMB, hold and drag the double headed arrow to Shear

6.21 The Rip Region Tool

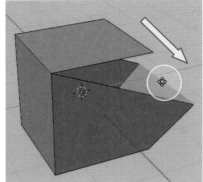

Figure 6.36

Select an Edge (Edit Mode – Edge Selection Mode). Activate the **Rip Region Tool**. With the Mouse Cursor in the Editor, click, hold and drag to translate the selected Edge.

7

Editing with Modifiers

Modifiers, in Blender, are pre-assembled code that apply a process or algorithm to an Object, changing the Object's properties and affecting the way the Object behaves or how it is displayed. Modifiers may, therefore, be considered as Editing Tools.

The Modifiers are designed to automate some of the otherwise tedious processes involved in shaping Objects and controlling their behaviour. Some Modifiers can only be used in conjunction with other processes.

The following chapters are offered as a guide. You will be shown how a Modifier is added to an Object and provided with examples showing the Modifier's basic features.

Modifiers are found in the **Properties Editor, Modifier Properties**.

The Object Modifier Properties are only displayed when an object to which a Modifier can be applied is selected in the 3D Viewport Editor. Some objects can not have Modifiers applied.

> **Note:** If there are Objects in the 3D Viewport Editor to which Modifiers may be applied (not necessarily selected), clicking the **Add Modifier** button and selecting a Modifier will apply the Modifier to the last Object that was selected. This occurs even though that Object is not selected at the time.

7.1 Modifiers in General

Modifiers are found in the **Properties Editor, Modifiers Properties.**

> **Note:** The **Modifiers Properties** button is only displayed when an Object to which a Modifier can be applied is selected in the 3D Viewport Editor. Some Objects cannot have Modifiers applied.

With an Object selected in the 3D Viewport Editor (in Object Mode), clicking the Modifier Properties button in the Properties Editor displays the empty panel shown in Figure 7.1.

In this chapter **Modifiers in general** will be briefly described. Some Modifiers are complex and beyond a basic introduction and will be better understood having undergone further studies. New Modifiers are continually being added to the program and the selection menu changes accordingly. Click on the **Add Modifier** button to view the menu (Figure 7.2).

The menu is divided into **four categories** to aid selection.

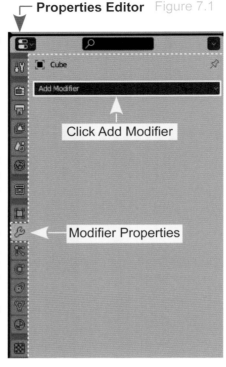

Properties Editor Figure 7.1

Click Add Modifier

Modifier Properties

Figure 7.2

Modify	Generate	Deform	Physics
Data Transfer	Array	Armature	Cloth
Mesh Cache	Bevel	Cast	Collision
Mesh Sequence Cache	Boolean	Curve	Dynamic Paint
Normal Edit	Build	Displace	Explode
Weighted Normal	Decimate	Hook	Fluid
UV Project	Edge Split	Laplacian Deform	Ocean
UV Warp	Geometry Nodes	Lattice	Particle Instance
Vertex Weight Edit	Mask	Mesh Deform	Particle System
Vertex Weight Mix	Mirror	Shrinkwrap	Soft Body
Vertex Weight Proximity	Multiresolution	Simple Deform	
	Remesh	Smooth	
	Screw	Smooth Corrective	
	Skin	Smooth Laplacian	
	Solidify	Surface Deform	
	Subdivision Surface	Warp	
	Triangulate	Wave	
	Volume to Mesh		
	Weld		
	Wireframe		

To demonstrate the basic procedure for adding a **Modifier** the **Generate – Bevel Modifier** will be used. Begin by having the default Cube Object selected in the **3D Viewport Editor**. In the **Properties Editor, Modifier Properties**, click the **Add Modifier** button to display the selection menu (Figure 7.2).

This instruction has been purposely repeated

Under the **Generate** heading select (click LMB) **Bevel**.

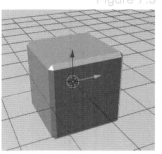

The **Bevel Modifier panel** opens in the **Properties Editor** and the Cube object in the 3D Viewport Editor displays with its edges bevelled (Figure 7.3). Values in the Modifier panel may be adjusted to affect the bevel.

Figure 7.3

By default, when panels are opened in Blender, they tend to open with a minimal display to save space in the interface. The Modifier panel is no exception.

Blue border indicates Modifier selected.

Before attempting an exercise in using a Modifier you should understand a few basic features of the typical Modifier panel. Keep in mind that each type of Modifier will display a different panel configuration. The bevel Modifier panel will be used as an example.

Figure 7.4 shows the upper part of the Modifier panel which is typical of all Modifiers.

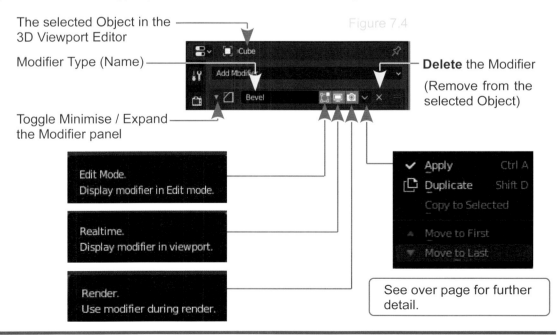

The selected Object in the 3D Viewport Editor

Figure 7.4

Modifier Type (Name)

Delete the Modifier
(Remove from the selected Object)

Toggle Minimise / Expand the Modifier panel

Edit Mode.
Display modifier in Edit mode.

Realtime.
Display modifier in viewport.

Render.
Use modifier during render.

✓ Apply   Ctrl A
⊡ Duplicate   Shift D
Copy to Selected
▲ Move to First
▼ Move to Last

See over page for further detail.

Edit Mode (Display modifier in Edit Mode):

Figure 7.5

Object Mode

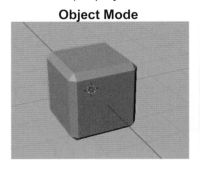

Edit Mode

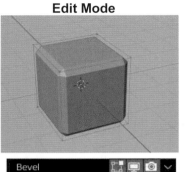

Active ——

Edit Mode

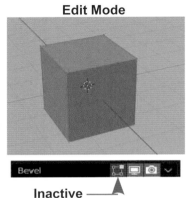

Inactive ——

Realtime (Display Modifier in Viewport)

Figure 7.6

Object Mode

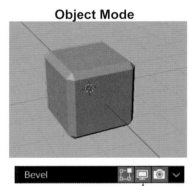

Active ——

Object Mode

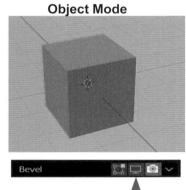

Inactive ——

Render (Use Modifier during Render)

Figure 7.7

Object Mode

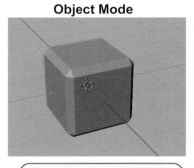

Pressing the **F12** Key Renders a view of Camera View

Rendered Views (Press F12)

Active ——

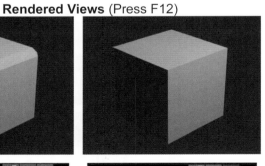

Inactive ——

126

When adjusting values **in the Modifier Panel** you should be aware of the **Apply button.**

Adding and Applying Modifiers

At this point how to Add a Modifier to an Object has been described. You should understand that using a Modifier entails two stages. The first stage is to **Add the Modifier to the Object** and adjust values in the Modifier panel. The second stage is to **Apply the Modifier**. Applying assigns data to the Object permanently affecting the Object.

In the case of the Cube Object, Adding the Bevel Modifier sees the edges of the Cube bevelled in the 3D Viewport Editor when in Object Mode. In Edit Mode, with Display Modifier in Edit Mode Active, you will see the bevelled Edges with the Viewport in Edit Mode but observe the original eight Vertices forming the Cube still exist. The Modifier has been Added but has NOT been Applied. To Apply the Modifier you click the hidden **Apply** button in the Modifier panel.

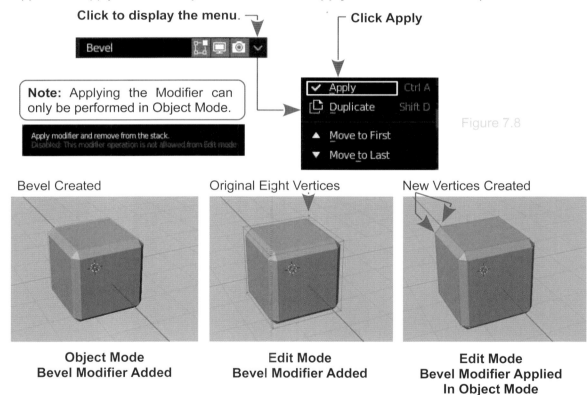

Click to display the menu.

Click Apply

Bevel

Note: Applying the Modifier can only be performed in Object Mode.

Apply modifier and remove from the stack.
Disabled: This modifier operation is not allowed from Edit mode

✓ Apply   Ctrl A
🗐 Duplicate   Shift D

▲ Move to First
▼ Move to Last

Figure 7.8

Bevel Created   Original Eight Vertices   New Vertices Created

Object Mode
Bevel Modifier Added

Edit Mode
Bevel Modifier Added

Edit Mode
Bevel Modifier Applied
In Object Mode

Note: You may delete a Modifier **before Applying,** cancelling all the modifications made (see the **Delete** button in Figure 7.4. Once a Modifier has been Applied all modifications are permanently set and the Delete option is no longer available in the Modifier panel. However, if the Modifier has been Applied within the range of the **Undo function** you can press **Ctrl + Z** with the Mouse Cursor in the 3D Viewport Editor and back step through operations until you reach the point before the Modifier was Added to the Object.

7.2 The Modifier Stack

Figure 7.9

In some cases it is appropriate to apply more than one Modifier to an Object. The modifiers are placed in a stack in order of priority. A Modifier at the top of the stack takes precedence over Modifiers lower down. The priority can be changed by moving a Modifier up or down in the stack. Although Modifiers are generally applied in Object mode, some may be used in Edit mode. Figure 7.9 shows an **Array Modifier**, a **Bevel Modifier** and a **Weld Modifier** in a stack.

The **Bevel Modifier** has been added first followed by the **Array Modifier** then the **Weld Modifier**.

With the Modifiers arranged in this order (Bevel at the Top) the Bevel Modifier takes precedence over the other two.

The priority can be changed by selecting a **Move Option** to move the Modifier up or down in the stack.

The Bevel Modifier bevels the edges of the Cube and the Array modifier duplicates the Cube in the 3D Viewport Editor.

Figure 7.10

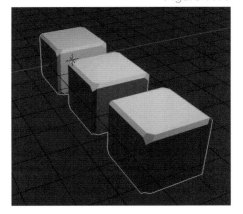

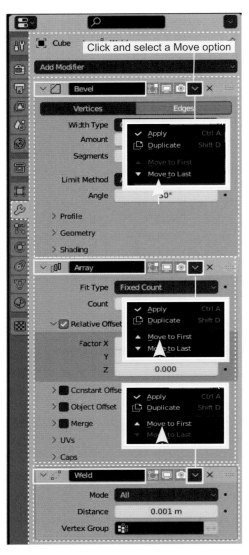

In this particular instance the **Weld Modifier** is not used and is only shown to demonstrate the Modifier Stack.

7.3 The Modify Group

The Modifiers under the heading **Modify** (Figure 7.2) do not directly affect the shape of an object but rather other data such as Vertex Groups and appearance. The demonstration of this group will be left in abeyance at this point since you will have to study some of Blender's more advanced features before being able to understand what they do.

7.4 The Generate Group

The Bevel Modifier previously demonstrated falls into this group of Modifiers and as you have seen alters (Modifies) the shape of the selected Object in the 3D Viewport Editor. A detailed description of each Modifier would require a dedicated publication, therefore, at this point only the following samples are offered.

Mirror Modifier

Figure 7.11

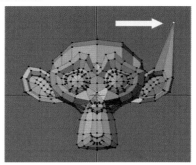

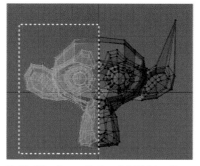

Edit Mode – Single Vertex Translated

Edit Mode – Select LH Vertices

Apply a Mirror Modifier

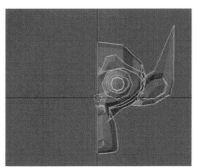

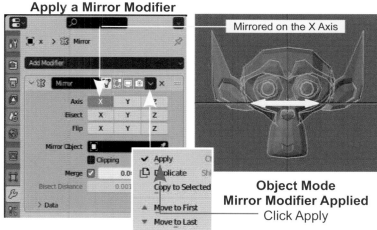

Mirrored on the X Axis

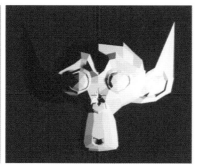

**Object Mode
LH Vertices Deleted**

**Object Mode
Mirror Modifier Applied**
Click Apply

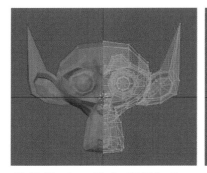

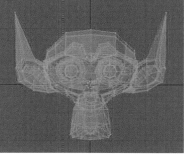

Edit Mode – Only RH Vertices

Mirror Modifier **Applied**

A Spooky Look

Subdivision Surface Modifier   Figure 7.12

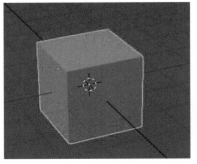

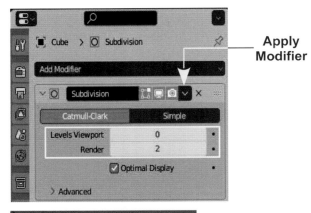

Apply
Modifier

**Default Cube – Subdivision Surface
Modifier Added – Viewport Levels 0**

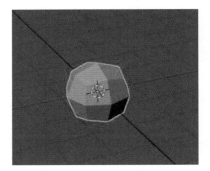

Apply the Modifier
after setting the
Viewport and
Render Levels.

Viewport Levels 1   **Viewport Levels 2**

7.5 The Deform Group

Cast Modifier - Example   Figure 7.13

The **Cast Modifier** is used to deform a primitive Object
such as the Cube Object in the default Scene.

Select the Cube Object. In **Edit Mode,** Subdivide
(number of Cuts 4) then **Tab** back to **Object Mode**.

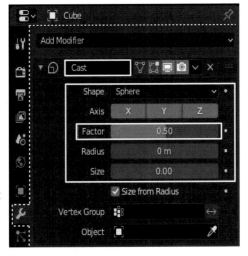

In the **Properties Editor, Modifier Properties** add a
Cast Modifier (Figure 7.13). By changing the **Cast
Type**, altering the **Factor**, **Radius** and **Size** values and
or limiting the effects to the X,Y and Z axis the
deformation of the cube is controlled.

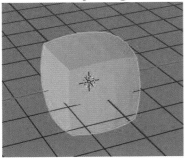

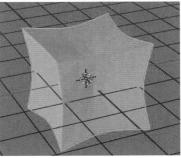

Default Cube
Subdivided Four Times
Cast Modifier Added
Type Sphere Factor: 0.50

Cast Type: Sphere
Factor: 2.000

Cast Type: Sphere
Factor: -2.000

Displace Modifier - Example

The Displace Modifier is used to displace an Object in the 3D Viewport Editor from its original position or to displace Vertices designated as a Vertex Group on the surface of an Object.

3D Viewport

Figure 7.15

Displace Modifier

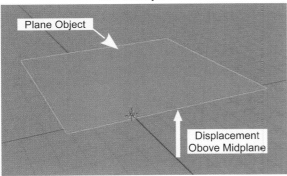

Plane Object

Displacement
Obove Midplane

**Modifier
Properties**

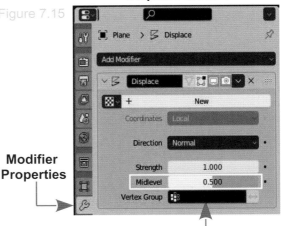

The Displacement of the Plane is controlled by the **Midlevel Slider** in the Displace Modifier panel.

Enter the name of the Vertex Group

Vertex Group in Edit Mode   Figure 7.16

Displacement in Object Mode

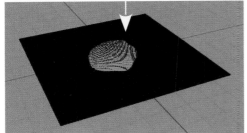

7.6 The Physics Group

The **Physics** group of modifiers, activate simulations (animated physical sequences such as fluid or gas flow). In most cases, these modifiers are automatically added to the Modifier stack whenever a **Particle System** or **Physics Simulation** is enabled.

Figure 7.17

Their role is to define the place in the modifier stack used as base data by the tool they represent. Generally, the attributes of these modifiers are accessible in separate panels. The demonstration of this group will be left in abeyance at this point since you will have to study some of Blender's more advanced features before being able to understanc what they do.

Wave Surface Displacement – Using the Dynamic Paint Modifier

Figure 7.18

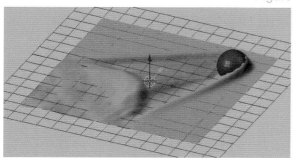
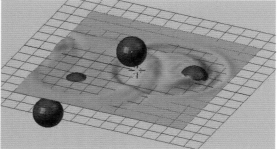

Sphere Dragged through the Surface

Sphere Dragged from below surface then back into the Surface

8

Editing Techniques - Examples

Introduction

Becoming proficient at Modeling requires a knowledge of the tools that are available and how to combine the use of tools to create what you want. There are no hard and fast rules concerning which tool is used for any particular application. You use whatever suits what you are doing.

This chapter shows a very brief sample of how different tools are used in creating some basic models and effects.

What you can model using Blender is only limited by your imagination and your knowledge of what tools are available and where to find them.

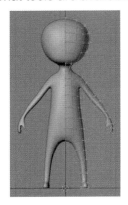
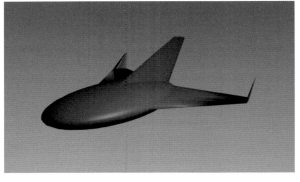
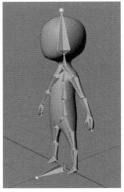

8.1 Proportional Editing

Proportional Editing means changing the properties of one Object based on the change in properties of a second Object. The properties include, Translation, Rotation and Scale and apply to Objects as a whole in Object Mode and Vertices and Vertex Groups in Edit Mode.

For example, scaling the Monkey Object in Figure 8.1 causes the Cube Object to be Proportionally scaled at the same time (Figure 8.2).

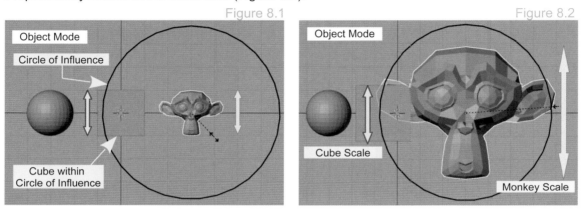

Figure 8.1   Figure 8.2

Figures 8.1 and 8.2 show that the Cube Object is scaled up when the Monkey Object is scaled. The Cubes Scale is Proportional to the Scale of the Monkey as determined by the **Falloff Type**.

The Cube scales when the Monkey is scaled since the Cube lies within the Circle of Influence of the Monkey. The Circle of Influence only displays when Proportional Editing is activated in the **3D Viewport Editor Header.**

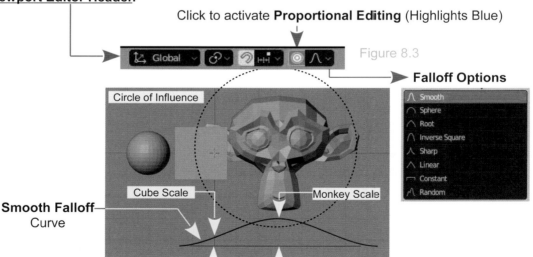

Click to activate **Proportional Editing** (Highlights Blue)

Figure 8.3

Falloff Options

Circle of Influence

Cube Scale   Monkey Scale

Smooth Falloff Curve

To Scale the Monkey and Cube, select Monkey with Proportional Editing active. Press the S Key (Scale). Before dragging the Mouse to Scale, Scroll MMB to adjust the Circle of Influence to include the Cube. Drag the Mouse to Scale Monkey and the Cube.

Translation and Rotation of Objects in Object Mode may also be accomplished using Proportional Editing.

In Edit Mode the shape of an Object can be influenced by manipulating Vertices on the Object's Mesh Surface. Proportional Vertex Editing allows the manipulation a Vertex or a group of Vertices to influence adjacent Vertices which fall within a Circle of Influence.

Proportional Vertex Editing can, therefore, be employed to create a landscape or ground as a background for a Scene. Simply select Vertices on a subdivided Plane and move them up or down the Z Axis. Vertices moved down forming depressions can be turned into lakes or rivers by positioning a second Plane below the original and giving it a different color (Chapter 9). When the landscape is formed in Edit Mode, Tab to Object Mode, select the ground and select **Shading Smooth** in the **Object Context Menu** (RMB click in the Editor).

Figure 8.4

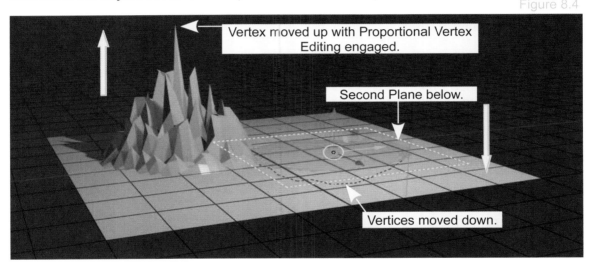

Vertex moved up with Proportional Vertex Editing engaged.

Second Plane below.

Vertices moved down.

Cook Book Instructions

Note: The Add Mesh: A.N.T. Landscape Add-on for Blender automates landscape generation. There are also external programs.

Delete the Cube from the default 3D Viewport Editor.
Add a Plane Object and scale up four times.
Tab to Edit Mode.
Subdivide the Plane.
In the Last Operator Panel increase the Number of Cuts to 10.
Subdivide again. Increase the Number of Cuts to 3 (10 + 3 = 13).
Deselect the Vertices and select a single Vertex.
Enable Proportional Editing and select Random Falloff.
Press G Key plus Z Key and drag the Mouse Cursor up.
Deselect the Vertex and select a second Vertex. Repeat the process for another mountain or with Spherical Fall off drag down creating a depression for a lake.
Add a second Plane to the Scene just below the first scaled to sit in the depression.
Give the new Plane a green-blue color.

Note: When following these instructions, at this point, you will not see the view of the Scene in the 3D Viewport Editor exactly as shown in the diagram. What is seen in the Editor is dependent on how Material (Color) is applied (Chapter 9), what lighting (Lamps) have been introduced (Chapter 12) and the Viewport Shading that is implemented (Chapter 13).

8.2 Dupliverts

Dupliverts means **Duplicating at Vertices**, which means creating an Array of Objects by duplication. Each duplicated Object is positioned at the location of a Vertices of a secondary Object. To demonstrate, a **UV Sphere** Object will be duplicated at the position of each Vertex of a **Plane** that has been Subdivided. Delete the default **Cube** Object in the default Blender Scene. In the **3D Viewport Editor** add a **Plane** Object. Scale the Plane up four times (S Key + 4, LMB click) then **Tab** to **Edit Mode** and **Subdivide.**

To replicate the Subdivision in the diagrams, in 3D View Editor Header, RMB click in the Editor and select Subdivide in the Object Context menu. In the Subdivide Last Operator Panel increase the Number of Cuts to 10. Press the A Key to select all Vertices. RMB click again, Subdivide a second time. In the Last Operator Panel the Number of Cuts resets to 1. Increase to 2. If you like to examine the subdivision in detail you will find you have 1156 Vertices. How many times you Subdivide is arbitrary but having a decent number of Vertices produces a good effect.

Figure 8.5

Tab to **Object Mode** deselect the Plane. Add a **UV Sphere** Object to the Scene, Scale it down (Figure 11.2). In the Sidebar Object Properties Panel (N Key) make the Scale values = 0.158.

With the **Sphere selected** (in Object Mode), **Shift** select the **Plane**. Press **CTRL + P key** and select **Object** to parent the Sphere to the Plane (Figure 8.6).

UV Sphere Scaled Down

Deselect the Sphere and the Plane. Select the Plane only.

Figure 8.6

With the Plane selected go to the **Properties Editor, Object Properties (NOT Object Data), Instancing Tab** and select **Vertices** (Figure 8.7). The **Sphere** is duplicated at the location of each Vertex on the Plane (Figure 8.8).

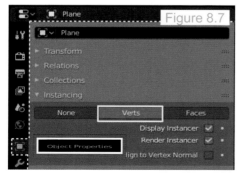

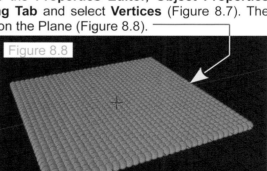

Deselect the Plane.

Scale the **Sphere** to adjust its size and create separation between the duplicates. Since the original Sphere is at the center of the Plane it is more than likely hidden among the duplicates and difficult (impossible) to select.

To select the Sphere, go to the **Outliner Editor** and locate the Sphere in the File tree (Figure 8.9). Select the Sphere in the **Outliner Editor** (Click LMB) then in the **3D Viewport Editor** Scale the Sphere down to make gaps between the duplicates (Figure 8.10).

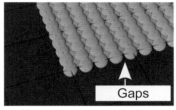

Figure 8.10

Gaps

With Sphere selected (**Object Mode)** move up on the Z Axis (Figure 8.11). Deselect the Sphere.

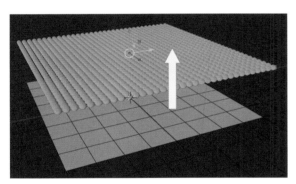

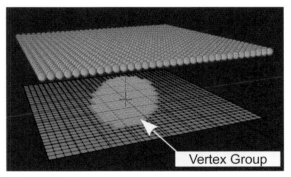

Vertex Group

Figure 8.11   Figure 8.12

Select the **Plane,** then in **Edit Mode** a group of Vertices may be selected (Figure 8.12) and with **Proportional Editing** turned on, translated deforming the Array of Spheres (Figure 8.13).

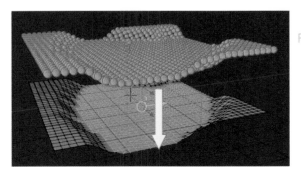

Figure 8.13

By animating the Vertices on the Plane to move and combining sound effects the Spheres can be made to dance in time to music.

8.3 Modeling Exercise – Aircraft

Figure 8.14

Vertical Z Axis

Figure 8.15

To model the aircraft shown in Figure 8.14 open a new Blender Scene. Delete the default Cube and add a **UV Sphere**. Zoom in (scroll MMB or press Num Pad +). Scale down on the Z Axis (S Key + 0.5 + Z Key). Scale the Sphere times 2 on the Y Axis (press S key + Y Key + 2 and LMB click) (Figure 8.15).

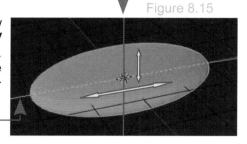

Y Axis (Green Line) ──────

You will be modeling the reshaped Sphere and want it to be identical either side of the Y Axis (the green line). That is to say you want it to be mirrored **on the X Axis** (along the red line).

In Top Orthographic view, place the UV Sphere in **Edit Mode** and delete all the vertices on the LHS of the Y Axis (press the B key for Box select, place the Cursor as shown by the white cross, click and hold drag a rectangle around the LHS Vertices). **Don't forget; Activate Show X-Ray**. With the Vertices selected press the **X Key** and select **Delete Vertices** .

Figure 8.16

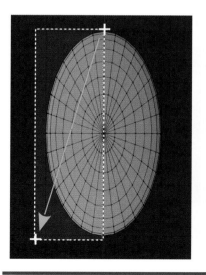 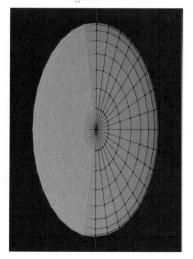 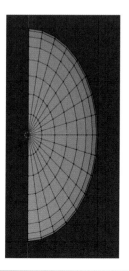

Place the UV Sphere in **Object Mode** (press Tab). Add a **Mirror Modifier** (Ref: Chapter 7) which by default is set to mirror on the X Axis. Change to **Right Orthographic** view (press the Num Pad 3 Key)

Figure 8.17

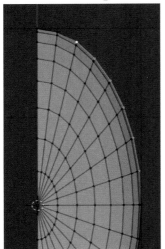

Tab to Edit Mode and select the Vertices as shown in Figure 8.17 (hold Shift and RMB click on each Vertex).

Change back to **Top Orthographic** view. Press the **G Key** (Move) and use the **Widget** to move the Vertices to the right (Figure 8.18).

With the **Vertex Group** still selected press the **S Key** (Scale) and Scale the group in.

Figure 8.18

Use the **Widget** to move the group towards the back of the aircraft forming a wing (Figure 8.19).

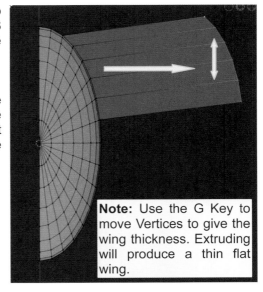

Note: Use the G Key to move Vertices to give the wing thickness. Extruding will produce a thin flat wing.

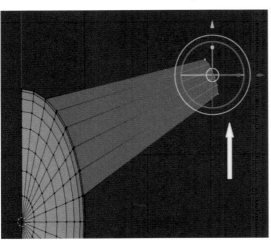

Figure 8.19

Rotate to align with the fuselage (Figure 8.19).

Extrude up, Scale the group in and move back forming the wing stabiliser (Figure 8.20)

Figure 8.20

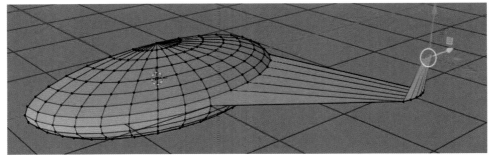

Select vertices at the rear of the fuselage on the centerline, Move up and repeat the procedure for the wing stabiliser forming a tail (Figure 8.21)

Figure 8.21

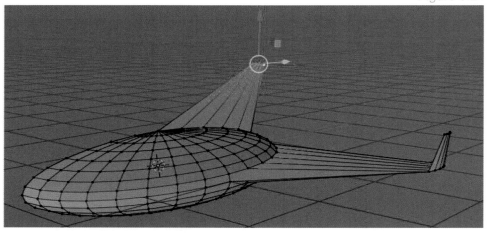

Go into **Object Mode**, **Apply the Mirror Modifier**, add a **Material**. In the **3D View Editor Header** click on **Object** and select **Shade Smooth**. Rotate the 3D View Editor to see your super duper aircraft.

Figure 8.22

Note: Change the 3D Viewport Editor background color to get the blue sky effect.

8.4 Sculpting

Sculpting, in Blender, allows you to add detail to the surface of a model by manipulating the Mesh Vertices. The process produces results similar to kneading a piece of clay. Vertices are pulled or pushed or added, by using of Tools which deform the mesh surface.

Sculpting is performed after you have created a model. To demonstrate the basics of the process a UV Sphere will be employed. The UV Sphere has a reasonable number of Vertices forming its surface but for Sculpting to be effective a high vertex count is required. Replace the default Cube Object with a UV Sphere in the 3D Viewport Editor. In the demonstration the whole surface of the Sphere will be used but in reality you would Subdivide the surface of a model in the area where detail is to be added.

With the UV Sphere selected in Object Mode, Tab to Edit Mode and with all Vertices selected, Subdivide with Number of Cuts 10 (Figure 8.23) (reference Chapter 5 – 5.5)

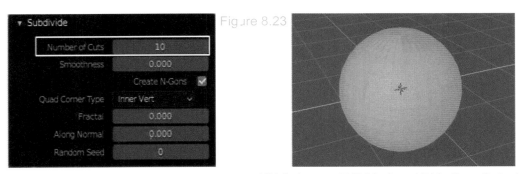

Last Operator Panel   UV Sphere – Edit Mode – All Vertices Selected

With the UV Sphere Subdivided, either **change to Sculpt Mode** or **select the Sculpting Workspace.**

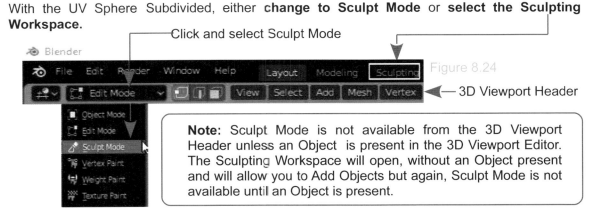

Note: Sculpt Mode is not available from the 3D Viewport Header unless an Object is present in the 3D Viewport Editor. The Sculpting Workspace will open, without an Object present and will allow you to Add Objects but again, Sculpt Mode is not available until an Object is present.

The first thing you will notice when changing to Sculpt Mode is the change in the 3D Viewport Editor Header and the arrangement of Tools down the LHS of the Screen. The second observation is, the subdivided UV Sphere is displayed as it would be in Object Mode with Flat Shading. Changing back to Object Mode and selecting Shading - Smooth has no effect.

A third significant change is; the 3D Viewport Editor Cursor has a blue circle attached **when you mouse over the Sphere**. The circle is called the **Brush** (Figure 8.25).

Note: The color of the Brush Circle changes depending on the Tool selected.

Figure 8.25

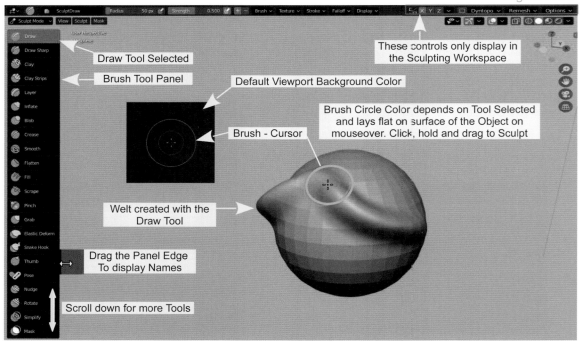

Draw Tool Selected

Brush Tool Panel

Default Viewport Background Color

These controls only display in the Sculpting Workspace

Brush Circle Color depends on Tool Selected and lays flat on surface of the Object on mouseover. Click, hold and drag to Sculpt

Brush - Cursor

Welt created with the Draw Tool

Drag the Panel Edge To display Names

Scroll down for more Tools

Note: This display shows the 3D Viewport Editor in Sculpt Mode when the **Sculpting Workspace** is selected in the Screen Header.

Figure 8.26

To Sculpt you select a Tool, click, hold and drag over the surface of the selected Object. In Figure 8.25 the Draw Tool has been selected (blue icon in the Tool Panel = blue Brush Circle). The Sculpt effect is dependent on the Strength setting in the Header and the Brush Radius.

For example, with the Draw Tool selected (highlighted blue) click, hold and drag the mouse cursor (blue circle) over the surface of the UV Sphere. With the default settings Vertices forming the surface will be raised forming a welt. Note the deformation may be mirrored about a centerline with Mesh Symmetry set in the Header.

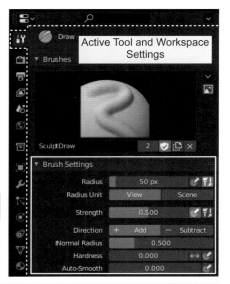

For detailed Sculpting you would select the Sculpting Workspace. Detailed controls for each Brush Type are found in the Properties Editor, **Active Tool and Workspace settings** (Figure 8.26).

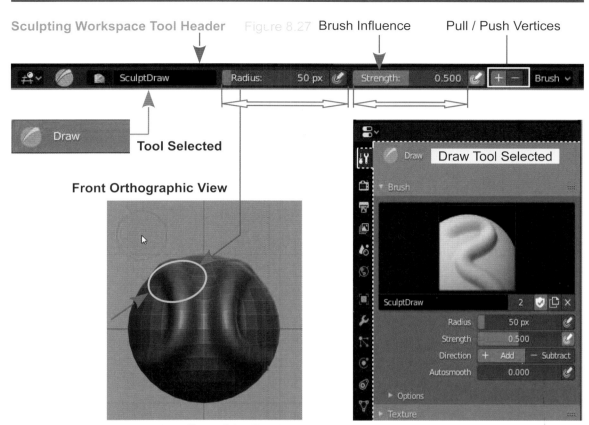

Sculpting Workspace Tool Header Figure 8.27 **Brush Influence** **Pull / Push Vertices**

Tool Selected

Front Orthographic View

Draw Tool Selected

Controls duplicated in the Properties Editor

Note: In this instance the affect of the Brush is cumulative. The Brush has been dragged over the same Vertices three times **with the Strength value = 0.500**

8.5 Sculpting Demonstration (Basic)

The Sculpt demonstration will be limited to the Draw Tool. Each Tool affects the Mesh Surface in a different way and the results vary depending on what settings are applied to the individual tools. As with any graphics drawing application proficiency is obtained by experimentation and practice.

It is worth noting that instead of the Mouse a Graphics Drawing Tablet with a Stylus may be substituted.

To see how the Draw Tools operates, select a Draw tool in the Tool Panel. The buttons in the Tool Header will control the properties of the Draw Tool. Set the Radius slider to approximately 30 px (pixels) and have the plus **+** setting for Pull engaged. Change the Strength value to 1.000 (drag the slider). The effect of the Tool will have a more pronounced effect with a higher value.

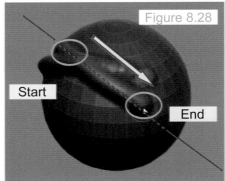

Figure 8.28

Start
Start

End

Position the Brush in the 3D Viewport Editor as shown in Figure 8.28, click and hold LMB and drag the Brush over the surface of the UV Sphere (generally along the red X Axis). At the end of the stroke release the mouse button.

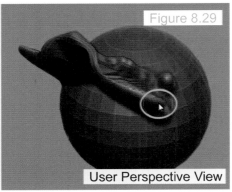

Figure 8.29

User Perspective View

As the Brush moves over the surface a welt appears as the Vertices are pulled away from the surface. Repeatedly dragging the Brush over the top of the welt further increases the deformation (Figure 8.29).

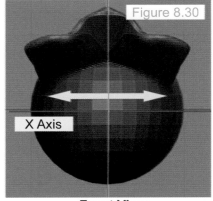

Figure 8.30

X Axis

Front View

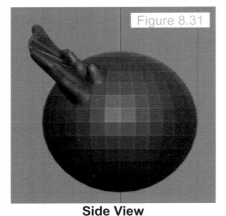

Figure 8.31

Side View

Click to activate X Axis Mirror Sculpting (highlights blue)

Controlling the Mirror Sculpt ➔

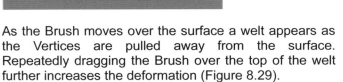

3D Viewport Editor Header Sculpting Workspace RHS

Options

Figure 8.32

In the Front View you see that the deformation of the surface has been mirrored along the X Axis, that is mirrored either side of the Z Axis. To turn the mirror effect off, in the 3D Viewport Editor Header (in Sculpt Mode) click on **X** to toggle **X Axis Mirror.** You may also elect to mirror the Sculpting about the Y or Z Axis.

With Mirror toggled off you can stroke over the surface in any direction modeling freehand.

At this stage clarification in respect to the relationship between the options available in the Headers is required. Figure 8.33 shows the options available in the Headers.

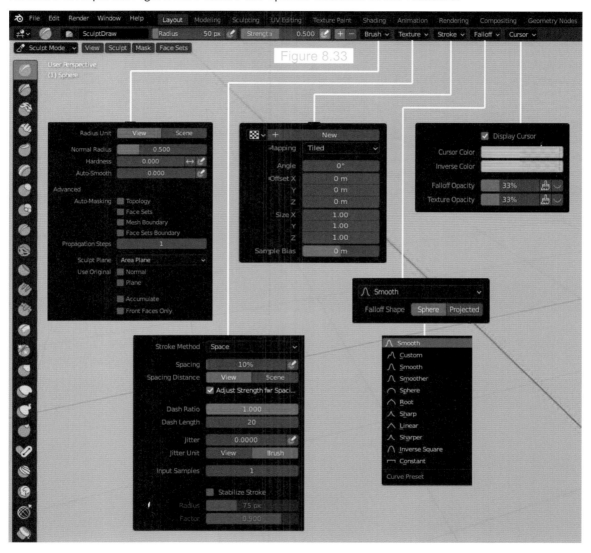

Figure 8.33

Controls in the Header alter depending on the particular Brush selected from the Brush Panel. In the diagram the Draw Brush is selected (highlighted blue). You see the icon representing Draw at the LHS of the Header.

The Headers provide a variety of options for selecting how the Brush affects the mesh surface. Many of the selection options are duplicated. Knowing what Tools are available and where to access them will allow you to experiment and practice sculpting.

8.6 Creating a Humanoid Figure

At some stage you will want to make a character figure for animation. As with the Aircraft Modeling Exercise this starts with one of Blender's primitives (a Cube) and by a process of selecting Vertices, Extrusion, Scaling, Manipulation and the application of Modifiers a simple figure may be generated. The following is intended to demonstrate the technique and not to produce a refined result. Modeling requires time and patience and plenty of practice. Add a **Bevel Modifier** to the default Cube with Width = 0.401. Apply the Modifier and place the Cube in **Edit Mode – Front Orthographic View. Remember: Modifiers can only be Applied in Object Mode.**

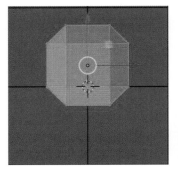
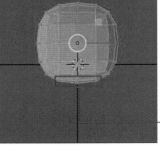
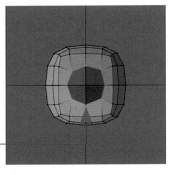

Cube with Bevel Modifier applied. Width = 0.401

Apply a Subdivision Surface Modifier to add Vertices.

Figure8.34

Remove the center Vertex and reshape perimeter of the hole on the base.

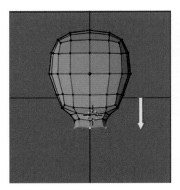
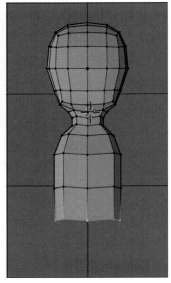
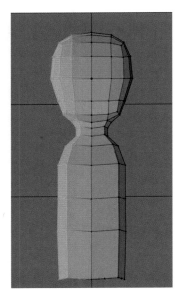

Select perimeter Vertices and Extrude down to form the neck.

Continue extrusions and Scale out forming the body.

With the body formed select one half of the Vertices and delete (Front View).

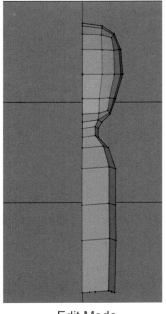

Edit Mode

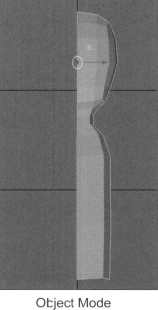

Object Mode

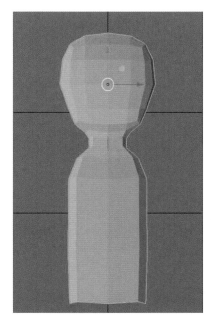

Add a Mirror Modifier in Object Mode (Do **NOT** Apply).

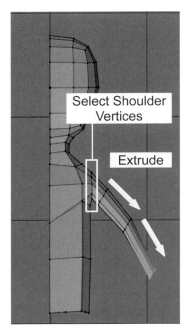

Select Shoulder Vertices

Extrude

In Edit Mode, select Vertices in the shoulder. Delete one Vertex to create a hole. Extrude and Scale the arm.

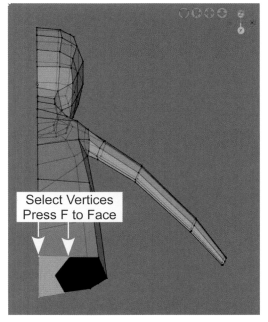

Select Vertices Press F to Face

At the base, Subdivide to create Vertices and Face the center portion leaving a hole for the leg.

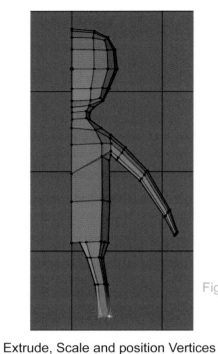

Extrude, Scale and position Vertices
forming a leg and foot (not shown).

Figure 8.36

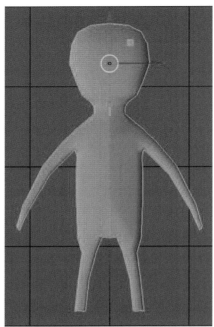

In Object Mode set Shading to Smooth
and **Apply the Mirror Modifier**.

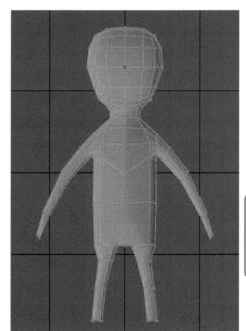

Edit Mode showing Vertices when the Mirror Modifier is Applied

Note: This is a very rough crude model shown for modeling technique only.

See Chapter 16

9

Materials - Textures - Nodes

9.1 Material Definition

Considered **Material** as the color of an Object which is how the visible spectrum of light reflects from the Object's surface. A Material also defines whether the surface appears dull (matt) or shiny (metallic).

How the surface of an Object displays is determined by three factors; **Material, Texture and Lighting**.

Material: The Base Color of the surface.
Texture: The physical characteristics of the surface.
Lighting: The background illumination or light emitting from Lights (Lamps).

Figure 9.1

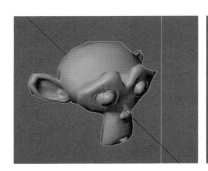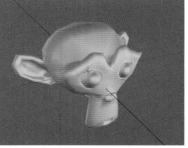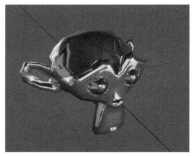

9.2 Materials in Practice

In Blender, **Materials** are said to be, **Applied to an Object**. Simplistically this means coloring an Object. In Chapter 1-1.15 the Monkey Object (Suzanne) was colored by disabling the default **Node System** and adjusting controls in the Properties Editor. The Node System was disabled to allow the color to display on the Object's surface in the 3D Viewport Editor, when the Editor is in **Solid Viewport Shading Mode**.

The **Viewport Shading Modes** are discussed in detail in Chapter 13 but for the moment be aware of the different modes and the fact that, in **Solid Viewport Shading Mode**, you can not display color when the **Node System** is controlling Material.

Viewport Shading   Figure 9.2   **Viewport Shading Modes**

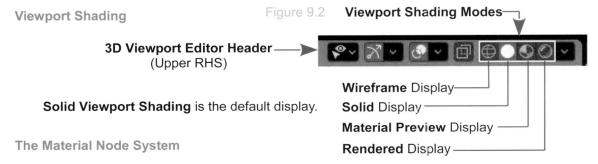

3D Viewport Editor Header ——▶
(Upper RHS)

Wireframe Display
Solid Viewport Shading is the default display.   **Solid** Display

The Material Node System   **Material Preview** Display
                                                         Rendered Display

The **Blender Material Node System** is a graphical representation of computer data or instruction which is arranged in a **pipeline** producing the display of color. Think about mixing colors. The primary colors are Red, Green and Blue, which when mixed in equal proportions produce White In a **Node System** this would look like:

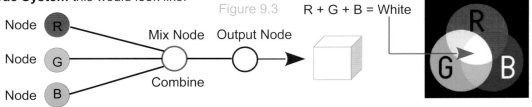

Figure 9.3   R + G + B = White

Node R

Node G   Mix Node Output Node

Node B   Combine

The Blender Node system looks like this: Figure 9.4

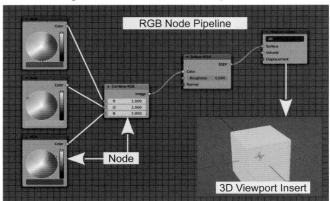

RGB Node Pipeline

Node

3D Viewport Insert

Note: Nodes are used to control many features but in this instance the Nodes control **Material Color**.

Nodes may be connected and disconnected and rearranged in the pipeline to create effects.

The Node System shown in Figure 9.3, 9.4 is a very simplified diagram.

To understand the application of Materials (Color) examine the default Blender interface with the Cube Object at the center of the Scene. Have the Cube selected (orange outline) and select the **Material Properties** button in the **Properties Editor** (Figure 9.5).

At this point the **Cube Object** is selected, the **3D Viewport Editor** is displaying in **Solid Viewport Shading Mode** and the **Properties Editor, Material Properties** contain controls for the **Material** color of the Cube.

Note: In the **Properties Editor, Material Properties** buttons, **Use Nodes** is highlighted blue indicating that the **Blender Node System is active**. The 3D Viewport Editor is in **Solid Viewport Shading Mode.**

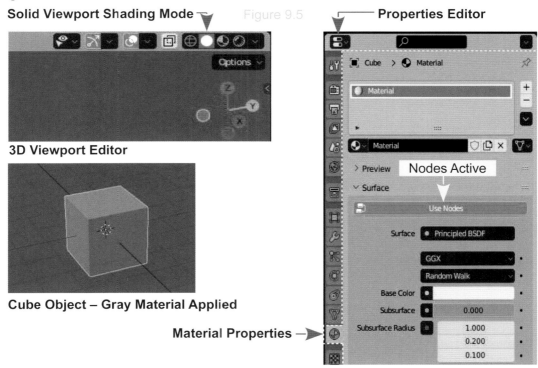

Solid Viewport Shading Mode — Figure 9.5 — Properties Editor

3D Viewport Editor

Cube Object – Gray Material Applied

Material Properties ➔

Nodes Active

Important: In the Default Blender Interface the Default Cube Object has a Material Color pre-applied hence the controls displaying in the Properties Editor, Material Properties. This is the only time this occurs. New Objects entered in a Scene do not have a Material applied despite the fact that they display in the 3D Viewport Editor with the default gray color.

When a new Object is added to a Scene, Blender uses the default gray color so you see the Object but initially a Material **has not been applied**. The Material Properties panel is empty.

To understand this concept step through the following exercise in adding an Object and applying a Material.

Applying a Material

In the 3D Viewport Editor, delete the default Cube. Deleting the Cube removes all the Material Properties from the Properties Editor.

Properties Editor

Add a new Cube Object to the Scene.   Figure 9.6

The Material Properties are reinstated in the Properties Editor but they would appear to only contain the **New button**.

The **New Cube** displays with the default gray color in the **3D Viewport Editor.**

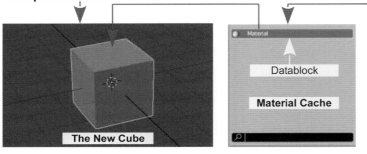

New

Browse Material to be linked

Material

Datablock

Material Cache

The New Cube

To color the new Cube gray, Blender is using data stored in a **Cache** (The Material Cache). You access the Cache by pressing the **Browse Material to be linked button**.

The data or **Datablock** in the Cache is named **Material** (the default gray).

When the new Cube Object is entered into the Scene or any new Object is entered, Blender automatically uses the datablock named **Material** to display the Object in the 3D Viewport Editor.

Figure 9.7

Clicking the **New** button reinstated the Material Property controls indicating that a Material, the default gray, has been added to the new Cube Object in the 3D Viewport Editor.

Note: Use Nodes is active (highlighted blue Figure 9.7).

Reinstating the Material Properties controls has automatically created a new material Datablock named **Material.001**. This is the data applied to the new Cube. By default the new data is identical to the original producing the default gray.

The color for the new Material can be changed (modified) by clicking the **Base Color bar** in the Material Properties and selecting a color in the color picker circle that displays but **REMBER** (see over).   **Material Properties→**

Cube   >   Material.001

Material.001

Material.001

Nodes Active

Preview

Surface

Use Nodes

Surface   Principled BSDF

GGX

Random Walk

Base Color

Subsurface   0.000

Subsurface Radius   1.000

0.200

152

REMBER: By default the 3D Viewport Editor is in **Solid Viewport Shading Mode** and Material colors **will not** display when the Material Node System is active.

Change the 3D Viewport Editor to **Rendered Viewport Shading Mode.**

3D Viewport Editor Header
(Upper RHS)

Figure 9.8

Changing the Base Color changes the data for Material.001. In **Rendered Viewport Shading Mode** you see the color change in the 3D Viewport Editor and you will find that there are two material Datablocks in the Material Cache named **Material** and **Material.001**.

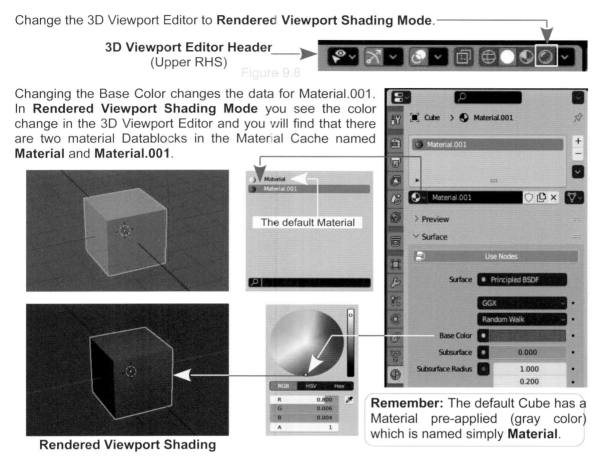

The default Material

Rendered Viewport Shading

Remember: The default Cube has a Material pre-applied (gray color) which is named simply **Material**.

To continue, of necessity, some of the forgoing instruction will be repeated to reinforce the concepts presented.

One point to emphasise is the necessity to have the 3D Viewport Editor displaying in **Rendered Viewport Shading Mode** to enable you to see Material colors. Viewport Shading is discussed in detail in Chapter 18, for the moment, accept being in **Rendered Mode**.

This Chapter is outlining the application of Materials in terms of what you find in the Blender interface and again, of necessity, is limited to describing Material colors. You will observe that the controls in the Properties Editor, Material Properties are extensive, therefore, a detailed description of each function is impractical. That being the case instruction will be provided on a need to know basis as a function is required.

At this point, be aware of the relationship between the Material Properties in the Properties Editor and the default Node Tree that displays in the Shader Editor (14.3 - Figure 14.9 following).

9.3 Materials and the Shader Editor

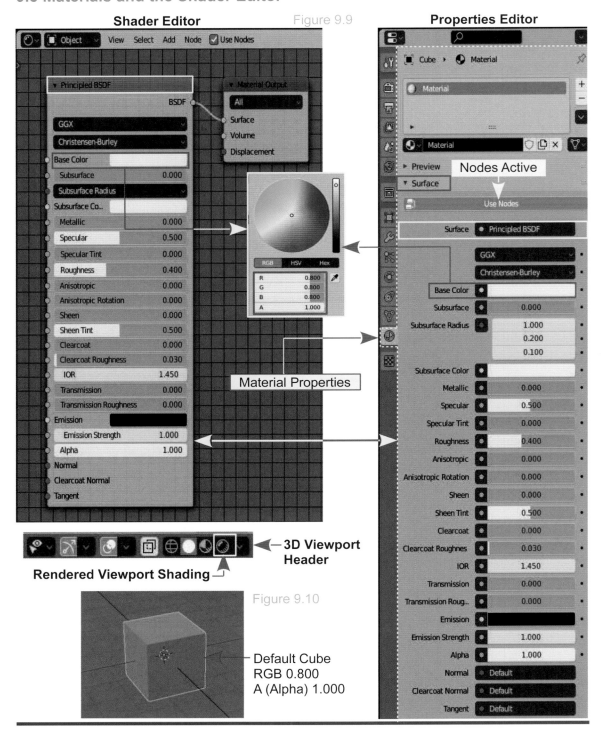

Shader Editor

Figure 9.9

Properties Editor

Object · View · Select · Add · Node · ☑ Use Nodes

▼ Principled BSDF

BSDF

GGX

Christensen-Burley

Base Color

Subsurface	0.000
Subsurface Radius	
Subsurface Co...	
Metallic	0.000
Specular	0.500
Specular Tint	0.000
Roughness	0.400
Anisotropic	0.000
Anisotropic Rotation	0.000
Sheen	0.000
Sheen Tint	0.500
Clearcoat	0.000
Clearcoat Roughness	0.030
IOR	1.450
Transmission	0.000
Transmission Roughness	0.000
Emission	
Emission Strength	1.000
Alpha	1.000
Normal	
Clearcoat Normal	
Tangent	

▼ Material Output

All

Surface
Volume
Displacement

RGB	HSV	Hex
R	0.800
G	0.800
B	0.800
A	1.000

Material Properties

🔲 Cube › ● Material

Material

Material

► Preview
▼ Surface

Nodes Active

Use Nodes

Surface ● Principled BSDF

GGX

Christensen-Burley

Base Color	
Subsurface	0.000
Subsurface Radius	1.000
	0.200
	0.100
Subsurface Color	
Metallic	0.000
Specular	0.500
Specular Tint	0.000
Roughness	0.400
Anisotropic	0.000
Anisotropic Rotation	0.000
Sheen	0.000
Sheen Tint	0.500
Clearcoat	0.000
Clearcoat Roughnes	0.030
IOR	1.450
Transmission	0.000
Transmission Roug...	0.000
Emission	
Emission Strength	1.000
Alpha	1.000
Normal	Default
Clearcoat Normal	Default
Tangent	Default

◄— **3D Viewport Header**

Rendered Viewport Shading ⌐

Figure 9.10

Default Cube
RGB 0.800
A (Alpha) 1.000

9.4 Adding Material Properties

Summarise what is known so far;

The default Cube has a default Material pre-applied which displays as the gray color on its surface.

The data for the default Material is stored in a Cache and named simply **Material**.

Deleting the default Cube from the 3D Viewport Editor removes the Material Properties from the Properties Editor but the data for the default gray Material remains in the Cache.

Adding a new Cube to the Scene in the 3D Viewport Editor and pressing the New Button in the Properties Editor, Material Properties reinstates Material Properties with a new set of data named Material.001. By default Material.001 data is identical to the original default data named Material, therefore both produce the gray color.

Selecting a different Base Color for Material.001 modifies the data for Material.001 thus creating two different datablocks in the Material Cache. This process is, therefore, **Adding Material Properties** to the Cache.

It is important to understand that adding Material Properties is adding properties to the Material Cache in the Blender File being worked. If the file is not saved before closing all new data is destroyed.

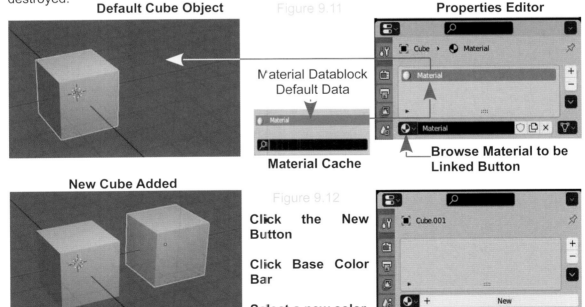

Default Cube Object   Figure 9.11   **Properties Editor**

Material Datablock
Default Data

Material Cache

Browse Material to be Linked Button

New Cube Added   Figure 9.12

Click the New Button

Click Base Color Bar

Select a new color.

Rendered Viewport Shading Mode

Clicking the New Button creates a New Material Datablock (Material.001).

Datablock named **Material.001** is identical to the original datablock named **Material**.

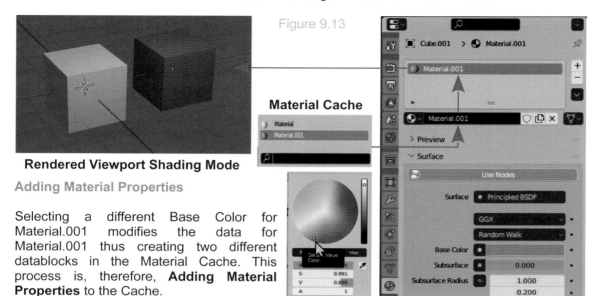

Figure 9.13

Material Cache

Rendered Viewport Shading Mode

Adding Material Properties

Selecting a different Base Color for Material.001 modifies the data for Material.001 thus creating two different datablocks in the Material Cache. This process is, therefore, **Adding Material Properties** to the Cache.

9.5 Alternative Material Assignment

Figure 9.14

With a new Cube entered in the 3D Viewport Editor and selected, click the **Browse Material to be Linked** Button instead of the New Button then click on the Datablock named **Material**.

The Datablock named **Material** will be assigned to both the default Cube and the new Cube and Material Properties will display in the Properties Editor. Both Cubes will display gray in the 3D Viewport Editor.

Figure 9.15

Changing the **Base Color** with either Cube selected changes the color of both Cubes. Changing any value in the Properties Editor changes the value for both Cubes.

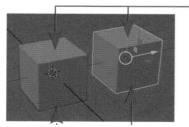

Default Cube   New Cube

Note: If **Use Nodes** is activated the same will apply.

Note: there is only one Material Datablock in the Cache.

9.6 Multiple Material Datablocks

Assigning Material Properties by clicking the New Button when new Objects are added to the Scene generates new Material Datablocks in the Cache.

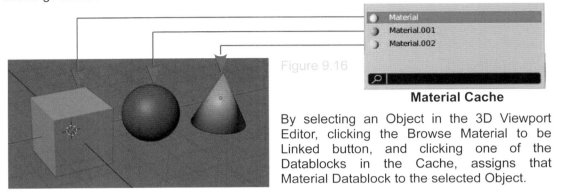

Figure 9.16

Material Cache

By selecting an Object in the 3D Viewport Editor, clicking the Browse Material to be Linked button, and clicking one of the Datablocks in the Cache, assigns that Material Datablock to the selected Object.

9.7 The Material Slot

Figure 9.15 shows a **Material Datablock** selected from the **Cash** and entered in the **Material Slot** the Datablock assigns the Material to the selected Object in the 3D Viewport Editor.

Figure 9.16 demonstrates that with multiple Objects each with a different Material color there are multiple Datablocks available for selection.

Selecting a Datablock from the Cash automatically enters the Datablock in the Material Slot hence applying it to the selected Object.

Adding Material Slots

With an Object selected you may add Material Slots and apply multiple colors to an Object. One method of doing this is to create **Vertex Groups** (Reference Chapter 5 -5.9) and apply a Material to a group.

To demonstrate, open a new Blender File, delete the default Cube and enter a **UV Sphere** into the Scene and give it a new Material .

Figure 9.17

Note: When giving the UV Sphere a New Material it is automatically named **Material.001**. In the Cache you will see **Material** and **Material.001**.

Material is the default Material used on the deleted Cube Object

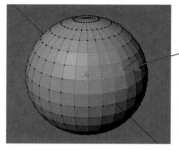

Create a **Vertex Group** on the surface of the UV Sphere.

Figure 9.18

Remember: If you are are working in a Blender File where you have entered several Objects, given them different Materials (Reference: Figure 14.16) and deleted the Objects, the Materials that were applied to the Objects will remain in the Material Cache.

With the UV Sphere in question, it will be assumed you have started a new Blender File, deleted the default Cube and entered a new UV Sphere. In this case the Cache will show the default Material named **Material** and the Material named **Material.001** (Figure 9.19).

With the UV Sphere selected, click on the **plus button** adjacent to the Material slot to add a second Slot.

Figure 9.19

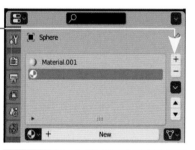

You may open the Cache and select a Material to enter in the new Slot or alternatively, click the New button, cancel the Node System and select a new Base Color to create a new Material.

The new Material is entered in the new Material Slot and is automatically named **Material.002** (Figure 9.20).

Properties Editor, Material Properties, Object Mode —▶

Figure 9.20

The UV Sphere does not change color since Material.001 is being applied from the original Slot.

Have the UV Sphere with the Vertex Group created in **Edit Mode** in the 3D Viewport Editor.

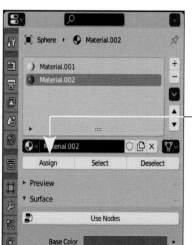

Figure 9.21

In the Properties Editor, Material Properties with the new slot selected (highlighted) containing Material.002, click the **Assign** Button

Figure 9.22

Material.002 is displayed on the Vertex Group in the 3D Viewport Editor. **Edit Mode** —▶

Note: The Assign button only displays with the 3D Viewport Editor in Edit Mode.

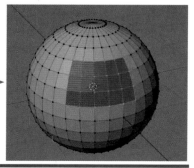

9.8 The Color Picker

The Color Picker is activated from a variety of locations in the interface such as clicking the Base Color bar in the Properties Editor, Material Properties.

In practice, a Material (color) is selected in the Color Picker Circle.

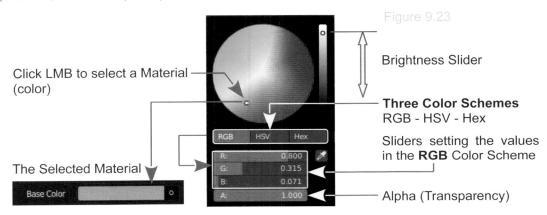

Figure 9.23

Brightness Slider

Click LMB to select a Material (color)

Three Color Schemes
RGB - HSV - Hex

Sliders setting the values in the **RGB** Color Scheme

The Selected Material

Alpha (Transparency)

Materials (color) can be displayed in three color schemes i.e. **RGB**, **HSV** or **Hex**. How the color appears in each scheme is also dependent on an Alpha value which is the amount of transparency the material (color) is given and the brightness of the color. (Chapter 1, 1.15 – Coloring).

9.9 Material Display

In the foregoing Material (color) has been applied to the selected Object in the 3D Viewport Editor with the Node System deactivated. When the Node System is inactive you see the Material in all Viewport Shading Modes. Up to this point, apart from the Base Color that has been selected, how you see the Materials has been determined by the **default settings** in the Properties Editor, Material Properties.

How you see, the Material may be controlled by adjusting the values in the Properties Editor. To demonstrate, have a Monkey Object, shaded smooth with the following settings. Figure 9.24

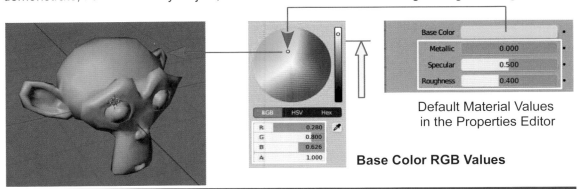

Default Material Values in the Properties Editor

Base Color RGB Values

Adjust values in the Properties Editor, Material Properties to see the difference.

Figure 9.25   Figure 9.26   Figure 9.27

Base Color			Base Color			Base Color	
Metallic	0.000		Metallic	0.500		Metallic	1.000
Specular	0.500		Specular	0.500		Specular	0.500
Roughness	0.000		Roughness	0.500		Roughness	0.333

Adjust Values

In the above, the **Specular** value has been maintained at 0.500 since the effect is very subtle. The Specular value is responsible for the highlights such as those seen on the tips of eyebrows and the pupils in the eyes.

9.10 Lighting Affects on Materials

How the Scene is illuminated (Chapter 12) and the **Viewport Shading Mode** employed has an effect on how you see Materials in the 3D Viewport Editor. Consider the Monkey Object.

3D Viewport Editor - Viewport Shading Modes   Figure 9.28

Solid   **Material Preview**   **Rendered**

Properties Editor Light Settings

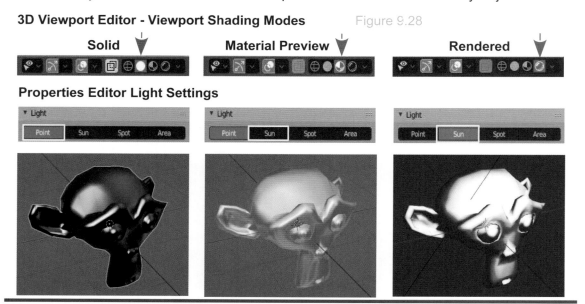

In the preceding examples Materials have been demonstrated with the Material Node System **disabled**.

9.11 Materials using Nodes

When Blender first opens with the default Cube Object in the 3D Viewport Editor the Properties Editor, Material Properties show the controls for the Material of the Cube with the default Blender **Material Node System** active. This is indicated by the **Use Nodes** button being highlighted blue.

Figure 9.30 (below) shows the default Node arrangement controlling the Material for the default Cube Object (the selected Object). This arrangement is displayed in the **Shader Editor**. Material Nodes are sometimes called Shaders. Figure 9.34 shows the Material Properties in the Properties Editor which for the default Material replicate the controls in the Principled BSDF Node. **Principled BSDF** is the name of the Node.

Blender has four different **Node Systems** which you see in the see in the Editor Type menu in the **3D Viewport Header**.

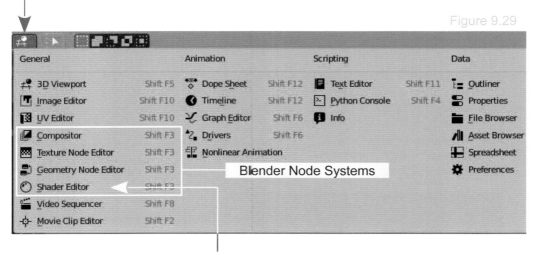

Figure 9.29

Material Nodes are seen in the **Shader Editor**.

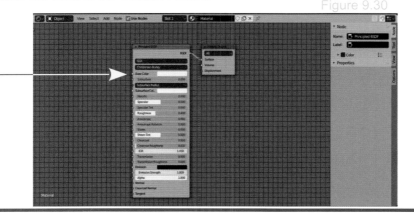

Figure 9.30

9.12 A Simple Node Arrangement

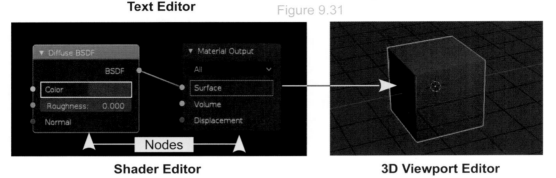

```
Computer Code

shader simple_material(
    color Diffuse_Color = color(0.6, 0.8, 0.6),
    float Noise_Factor = 0.5,
    output closure color BSDF = diffuse(N))
{
    color material_color = Diffuse_Color * mix(1.0, noise(P * 10.0), Noise_Factor);
    BSDF = material_color * diffuse(N);
}
```

Text Editor

Computer Code written in **Python**, is represented by the **Diffuse BSDF Node**, which outputs data to the **Material Output Node.** This in turn applies Material (color) to the surface of the **Cube** Object in the 3D Viewport Editor.

Figure 9.31

Shader Editor

3D Viewport Editor

9.13 Accessing and Viewing Node Effects

To view Material Node effects it is advantageous to have an Object with a nice smooth surface.

Start over with a new Blender file. Delete the default Cube and replace it with a UV Sphere. Scale the UV Sphere down in the Z Axis forming a flat disk and set Shading Smooth (3D Viewport Editor Header in Object Mode – Click Object – Click Shade Smooth in the menu).

Note: How Figures and Diagrams display depends on how your version of Blender is configured (Reference Chapter 2 – 2.17).

Figure 9.32

It is also advantageous to have the Scene adequately illuminated. Set the Scene lighting similar to that described in Chapter 12- 12.7 You may also position a ground Plane below the modified Sphere.

Nodes are accessed in the **Shader Editor**. You could change the 3D Viewport Editor to the Shader Editor but it is useful to have both Editors displayed at the same time allowing you to see the effect in the 3D Viewport Editor as you compile a Node Arrangement.

To work with Nodes, divide the 3D Viewport Editor in two, horizontally and make the lower half the **Shader Editor** (Figure 9.33). Having both Editors displayed allows you to see changes to Objects in the Scene as adjustments are made via the Nodes.

Figure 9.33

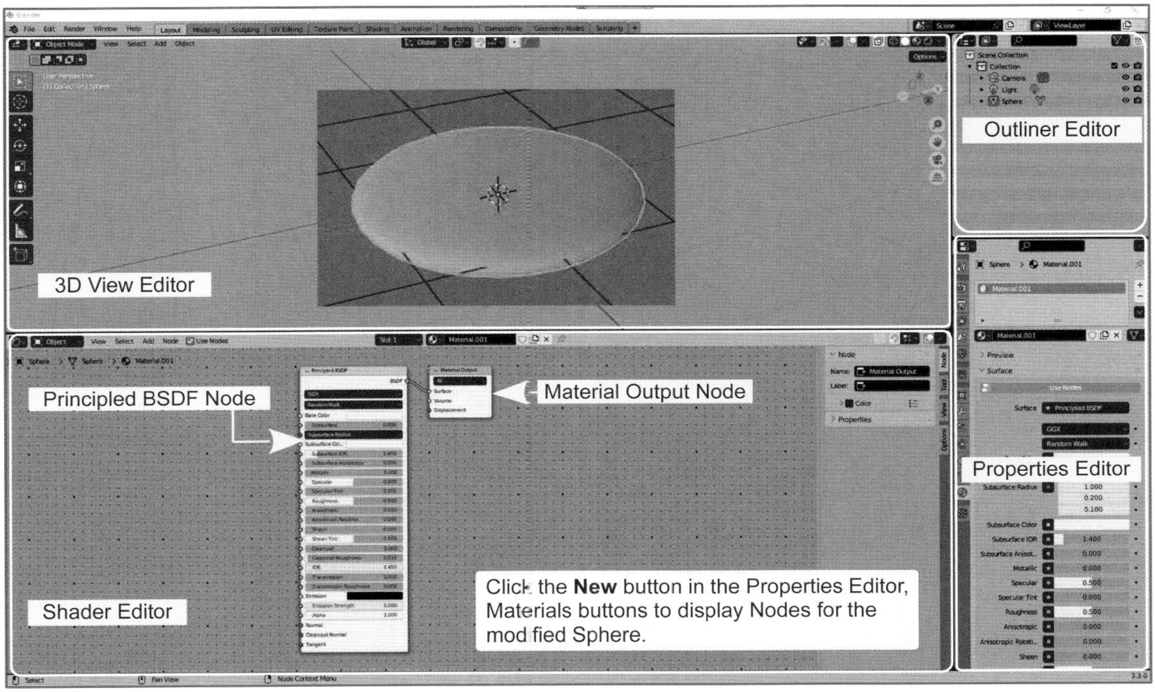

In the new Scene with the flat disk selected (New Object) go to the Material Properties in the Properties Editor and click **New**. Before clicking **New** the Shader Editor will be empty.

> **Note:** If you open the Shader Editor with the default Cube Object selected in the 3D Viewport Editor, Nodes are displayed which control the Material color for the Cube. This occurs since the default Cube has a Material pre-applied (default Gray).

The Material Properties display with **Use Nodes** highlighted blue indicating that the Node System is active. In the **Shader Editor** two rectangles are displayed, one labelled **Principled BSDF** and the other **Material Output**. The rectangles are the Nodes. (zoom in – scroll MMB or press plus + or minus – on the Keyboard). You may also click **MMB**, hold and drag the Mouse to pan the view.

Note: The **Principled BSDF Node** is not typical of all Nodes. This Node is what you might call a Super Node when you compare it with the **Diffuse BSDF Node** shown in Figure 9.31. It is shown here since it is displayed by default when Nodes are activated by clicking **Use Nodes** in the **Properties Editor**.

Note: The **Principled BSDF Node** displays values and controls identical to the controls in the Properties Editor, Material Properties when the Node System is active (Figure 9.34).

Compare the Principled BSDF Node to the content of the Properties Editor, Material Properties. You will see that the controls are identical.

Nodes in the Shader Editor
Figure 9.34

Properties Editor Material Properties

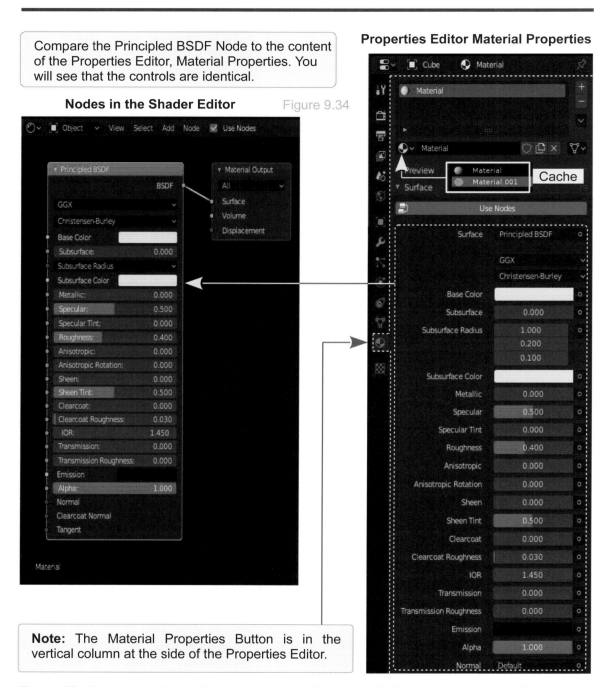

Note: The Material Properties Button is in the vertical column at the side of the Properties Editor.

To simplify the introduction to Nodes replace the Principled BSDF Node with the **Diffuse BSDF Node**. With the Mouse Cursor in the **Shader Editor**, press Alt + A Key on the Keyboard to deselect both Nodes. LMB click on a blank part of the Principled BSDF Node. The outline of the Node will display red. Press the **X Key** on the Keyboard to delete. Only the Material Output Node remains.

In the **Shader Editor Header** click **Add**, then navigate the menu that displays and click on **Diffuse BSDF**.

Note: You may alternatively press **Shift + A Key**

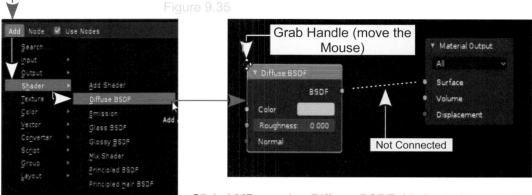

Figure 9.35

Click LMB on the Diffuse BSDF Node, hold and drag to displays a **Grab Handle** attached which follows Mouse movement allowing you to position the Node in the Editor. Release LMB to set in position. The handle is cancelled.

To adjust the position LMB click and hold on the Node (Grab Handle reappears) hold and drag the Mouse. Release.

The purpose of the **Diffuse BSDF Node** is to add a **Diffuse Material** (color) to the surface of the Object selected in the 3D Viewport Editor. To achieve this it has to be connected to the **Material Output Node**. At this point the Diffuse BSDF Node is not connected (Figure 9.36). To connect, click LMB on the green dot at the RHS of the Node, hold the Mouse button down and drag over to the green dot next to **Surface** at the LHS of the Material Output Node. Release the Mouse button to connect the Nodes (Figure 9.36 - 37). The connecting line is called a **Noodle**. The green dots are called **Sockets**.

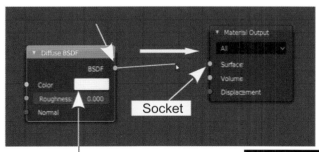

Figure 9.36

Diffuse: The color displays on the surface is the same, no matter where the light source or the camera is positioned in the Scene.

Note: Clicking the Color bar in the Diffuse BSDF Node displays the color picker allowing you to change the surface color of the selected Object in Rendered Viewport Shading Mode.

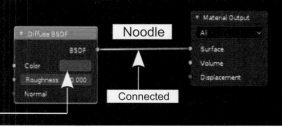

Figure 9.37

9.14 Noodle Curving

Note: The **Shader Editor** is sometimes called the **Node Editor**.

The default Noodle is drawn as a Curved line connecting Sockets. You may adjust the curve between 0 (straight line) or 10 in the **Preferences Editor** (Chapter 2 – 2.17). Go to **Themes** – click the triangle to expand the **Node Editor** entry and scroll down to **Noodle curving** and adjust the value.

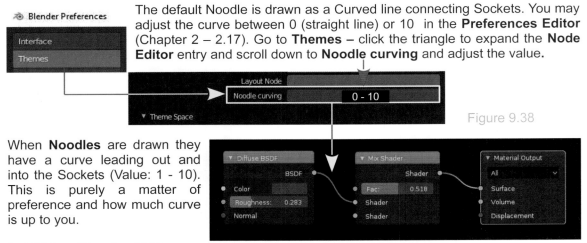

Figure 9.38

When **Noodles** are drawn they have a curve leading out and into the Sockets (Value: 1 - 10). This is purely a matter of preference and how much curve is up to you.

9.15 The Shader Editor

Examine the content of the **Shader Editor Header**. The buttons generally display selection menus which, by and large, are self explanatory. One button of note is the **View button** with the **Toggle Sidebar (N)** and **Toggle Tool Shelf (T)** entries in the menu (Toggle display On / Off).

Figure 9.39

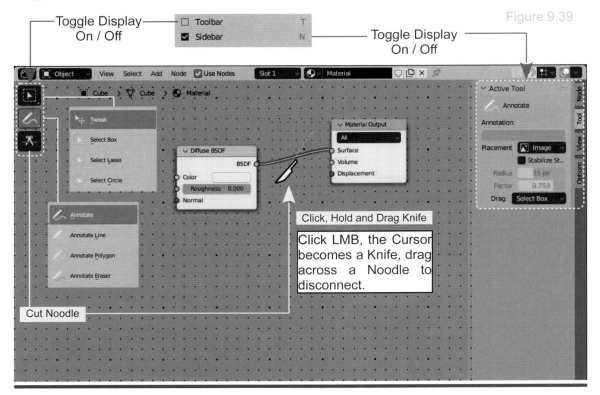

9.16 The Shader Node Menu

Click the **Add Button** in the **Shader Editor Header**.

Clicking the **Add Button** displays the **Main Category Menu**. Mouse over on a category to display a **Node Selection Menu** for the Category. Click on a Node name to open the Node in the **Node Editor**, i.e click on **Diffuse BSDF** to enter the Diffuse BSDF Node in the Node Editor.

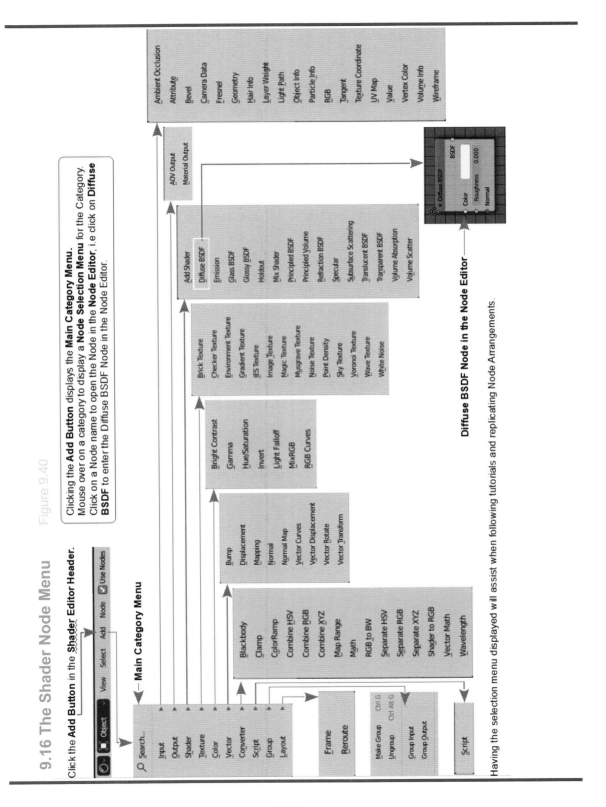

Figure 9.40

Having the selection menu displayed will assist when following tutorials and replicating Node Arrangements.

9.17 Adding Nodes

Figure 9.35 introduced the procedure for adding Nodes into the Editor by entering a Diffuse BSDF Node. Clicking the **Add button** in the Shader Editor Header opens a category list where you select a category to display the relevant Nodes. The categories assist when you are conversant with the function of each Node and how to arrange them to produce an effect. Knowing which Node to select and how to connect comes from experience, which in the beginning, is gained by following tutorials and copying and experimenting. In practical terms the Add button in the Shader Editor Header is the gateway to the maze of Nodes. When following tutorials you find a particular Node by either entering the name of the Node in the search panel at the top of the Category list or by navigating through the different categories.

Figure 9.40 on the preceding page displays the different categories which will assist in your search.

Becoming proficient in the use of Nodes comes with a certain amount of experimentation and organisation. When you have created a Node arrangement which produces a result, save it in a Blender file for future use. You may wish to use it again in another project or use it as a starting point for further development.

9.18 The Shading Workspace

You may arrange the Blender Screen as previously described in 9.13 and shown in Figure 9.33 or alternatively activate the **Shading Workspace** in the Screen Header.

Figure 9.41

Figure 9.42

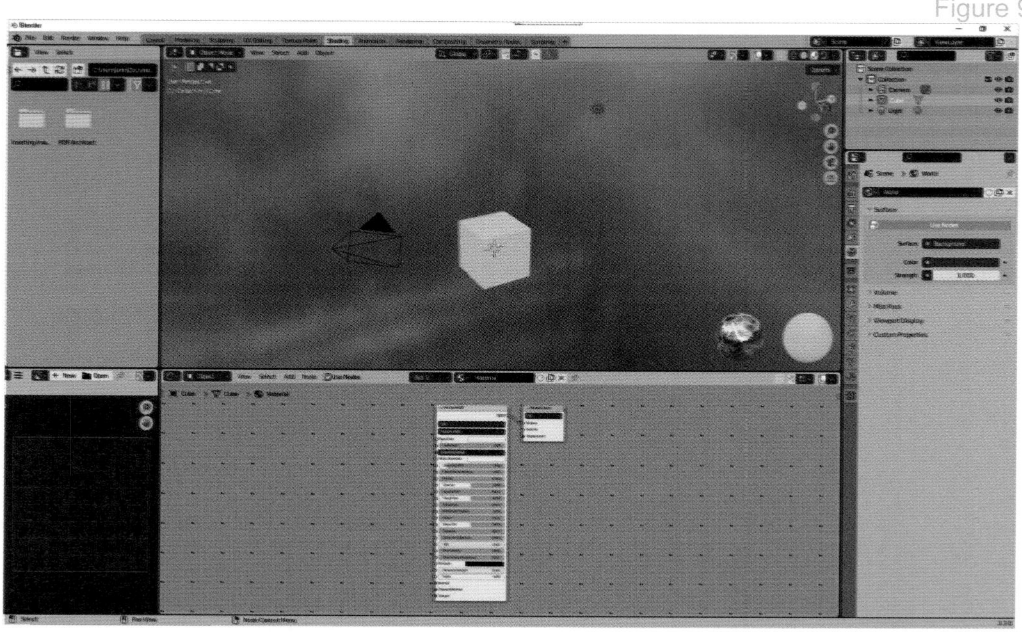

The **Shading Workspace** displays with six Editors forming a working environment for working with Nodes. At this stage it is suggested you work with the Screen Arrangement as shown in Figure 9.33.

9.19 Scene Arrangements

Before trying examples of Node Arrangements set up a Scene as previously described, with a smooth UV Sphere scaled down on the Z Axis forming a flat disc. Have the disc sitting above a Plane and place Lamps similar to those in Chapter 12 – 12.7 (Basic Lighting Arrangement). Have the 3D View Editor in Camera View with Material Preview Viewport Shading and Scene Lights checked in the Sub Options. Alternatively be in Rendered Viewport Shading Mode.

To understand how Nodes operate replicate the Node arrangements in the following examples.

9.20 Mixing Material Example

With the Node arrangement in Figure 9.43 two Material colors (red and blue) may be mixed together. The colors for mixing are selected in the **Diffuse BSDF** Nodes and mixed by adjusting the Factor slider in the **Mix Shader** Node.

In this instance the Nodes are found in the **Add menu** in the **Shader** category.

Figure 9.43

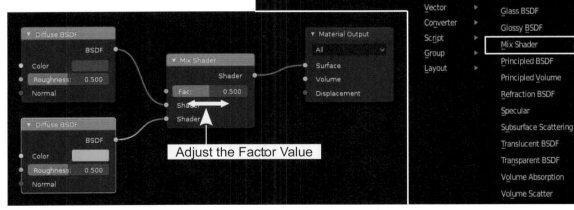

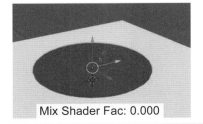
Mix Shader Fac: 0.000

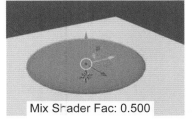
Mix Shader Fac: 0.500

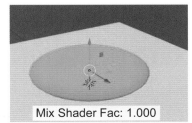
Mix Shader Fac: 1.000

9.21 The Principled BSDF Node

The default Node arrangement in the Shader Editor for Materials shows the **Principled BSDF Node** connected to the **Material Output Node** when the New button is pressed in the Properties Editor, Material Properties. This applies a Material to the selected Object entered into the Scene.

Figures 9.44, 9.45 show that the Principled BSDF Node replicates the controls displayed in the Properties Editor. Adjusting controls in the Properties Editor or in the Principled BSDF Node affects the selected Object in the 3D Viewport Editor i.e. selecting a Base Color and adjusting the Metallic, Specular and Roughness values.

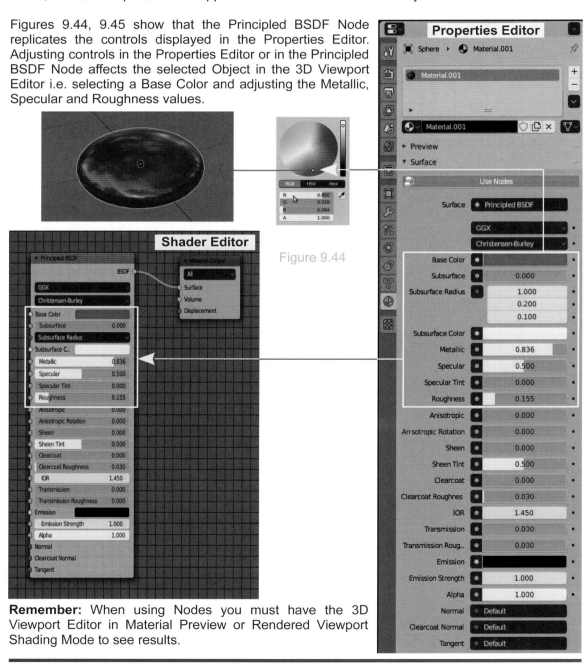

Figure 9.44

Remember: When using Nodes you must have the 3D Viewport Editor in Material Preview or Rendered Viewport Shading Mode to see results.

This default Node arrangement may be considered as a starting point for generating a Material. Additional Nodes are entered into the Shader Editor and connected to the input sockets at the left hand side of the Principled BSDF Node (Figure 9.45).

There are two methods of adding Nodes; click the Add button in the Shader Editor Header and select from the menus, then manually connect sockets or click the buttons at the left hand side of the values in the Properties Editor. In the later case the Node being added is automatically connected to the Principled BSDF Node.

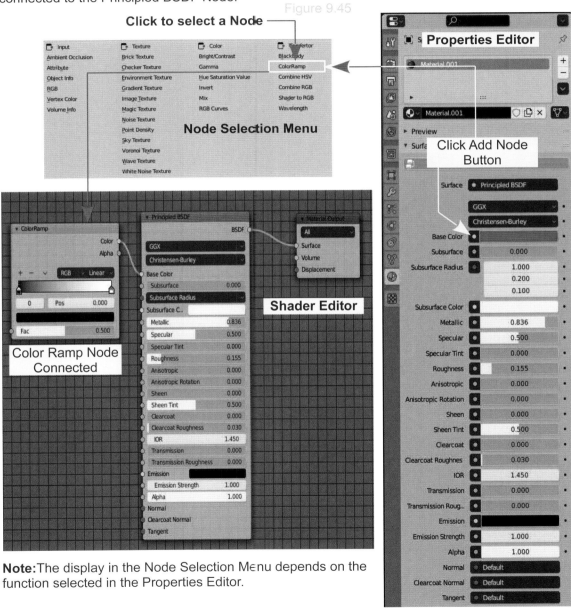

Figure 9.45

Note: The display in the Node Selection Menu depends on the function selected in the Properties Editor.

171

Figure 9.46 shows the **Principled BSDF Node** in the **Shader Editor** listing some of the functions contained in the Node.

Figure 9.46

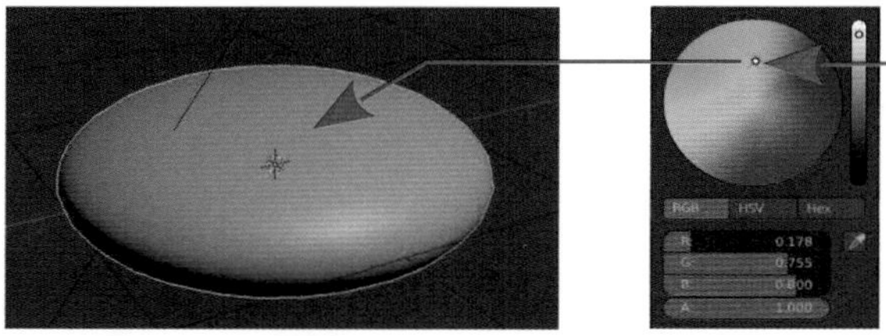

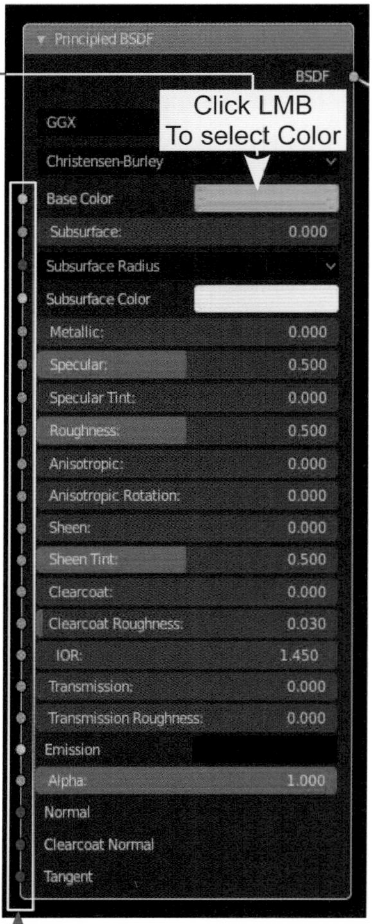

Base Color: The Material color of the selected Object in the 3D Viewport Editor.

Subsurface: Controls how much light shines through translucent substances e.g. wax.

Metallic: Defines weather the Object appears Metallic (1.000) or Non Metallic (0.000).

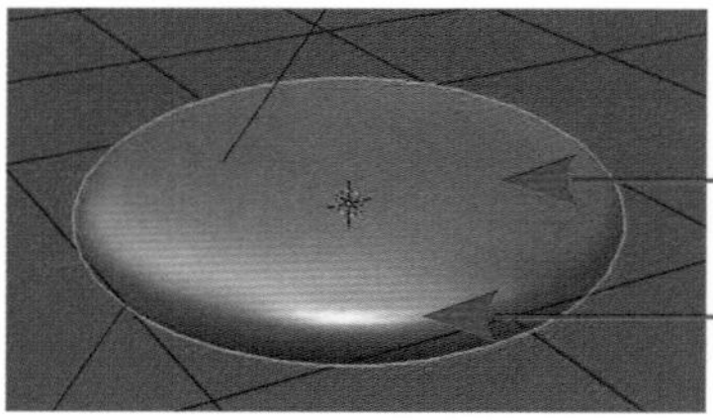

Figure 9.47

Specular: Controls the amount of Specular Reflection (shiny highlights on smooth rounded corners).

Specular Tint: Uses some of the Base Color in highlights.

Roughness: Controls how blurry or sharp reflections are.

Clearcoat: Produces extra layers of gloss, like car paint.

IOR: Transmission factor for Glass materials

Node Connection Sockets

With the **Principled BSDF** Node connected to the **Material Output** Node in the Shader Editor, adjusting controls (sliders) in the Node, affects the surface appearance of the selected Object in the 3D Viewport Editor.

Adding and connecting Nodes to the Principled BSDF Node was demonstrated in Figure 9.46 by the introduction of the **Color Ramp Node**.

The Color Ramp is of particular interest since it provides the means for creating a color gradient over the surface of an Object.

9.22 The Color Ramp Node

The Color Ramp is Material Node which implements a color gradient over the surface of a Mesh Object. The Node may be connected to the Principled BSDF Node as shown in Figure 9.45 but may also be configured in a simple arrangement comprising a **Converter - Color Ramp Node**, a **Shader - Diffuse BSDF Node** and a **Material Output Node**.

Remember: Material Nodes produce color on the surface of an Object which is selected in the 3D Viewport Editor. To see Material Color the 3D Viewport Editor must be in Material Preview or Rendered Viewport Shading Mode.

To add Nodes in the Shader Editor you must have a Material applied in the Properties Editor, Material Properties with Use Nodes active.

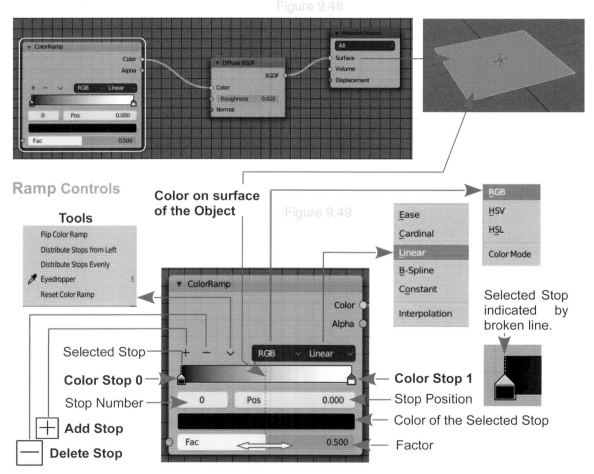

As you see the Color Ramp Node packs a considerable number of controls. Although not evident in the default configuration, the Node will generate a graduated Color Shading across the surface of the selected Object to which the Node is applied.

You see the shading, being applied to the Plane Object, in the **Color Ramp bar** in the center of the Node between **Color Stop 0** (Black) and **Color Stop 1** (White).

> **Note:** The Node itself does not create the color gradient shown in the Color Ramp bar. Additional Nodes have to be connected to Map the gradient to the surface.

As it stands, the color of the Object's surface is being set by the **Factor Slider**. With the Slider mid way between **Stop 0** and **Stop 1** (Fac: 0.500) the surface color is the gray color half way along the Color Ramp Bar. Adjusting the Factor Slider alters the color between Black and White.

Broken line indicates that the Stop is selected ——————▷

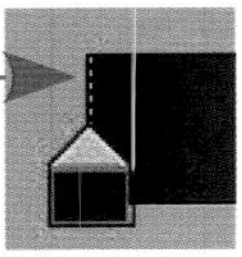

Figure 9.50

With a Color Stop selected, as indicated by the broken line above the Stop, you click in the color bar to set the Material Color **at the Stop position** in the Gradient bar.

Add a New Color Stop   Figure 9.51

A **New Stop** is created at the center of the Gradient ─

▲
┊
Click the plus sign to add a **New Stop**

Click the Color bar to select a Material (color) for the New Stop

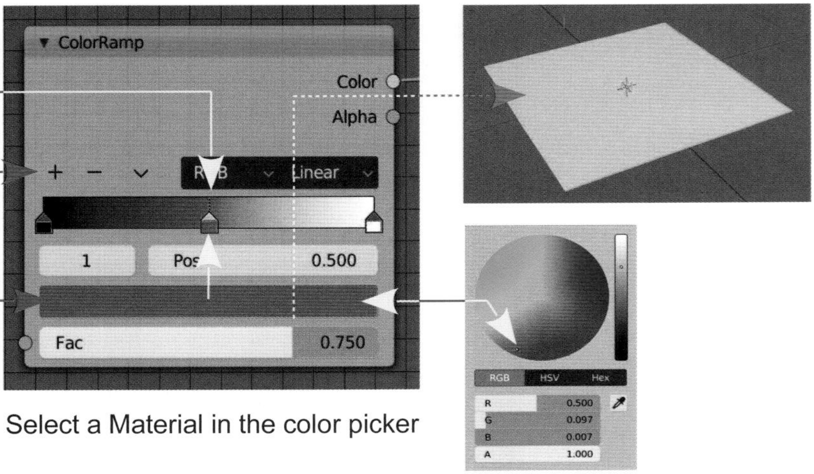

Select a Material in the color picker

Remember: The Color Ramp Node is connected to the Diffuse BSDF Node which in turn is connected to the Material Output Node (Figure 9.48).

Figure 9.52

With a New Stop added, the Stops are renumbered from left to right. The Material at Stop 0 is Black, the material at Stop 1 (the New Stop) is the color selected for the Stop and the material for Stop 2 is White. The Material gradient is, therefore, from Black to Stop 1 material, to White.

Note: With the Factor Slider positioned at 0.750 the Material at that location in the gradient is displayed on the selected Object in the 3D Viewport Editor.

You may click, hold and drag any Stop left or right in the gradient bar to reposition Materials. The Material displayed on the surface of the Object will be determined by the position of the factor Slider.

Apply the Color Gradient

To apply the Material (color) gradient to the surface of the selected Object you add a Texture Coordinate Node and a Mapping Node to the Node configuration as shown in Figure 9.53.

Material Preview or Rendered Viewport Shading Mode

Note: You may use the **Diffuse BSDF Node** in place of the **Principled BSDF Node**.

Tip: Changing the Point Light to an Area Light has a dramatic effect.

Figure 9.53

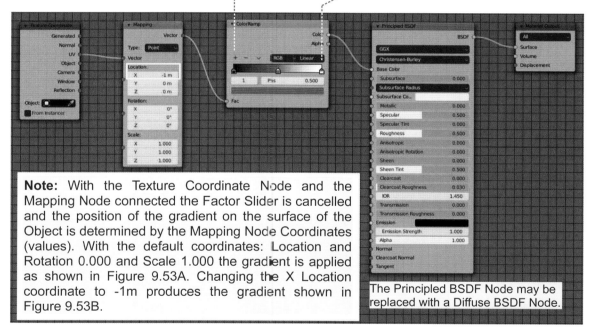

Note: With the Texture Coordinate Node and the Mapping Node connected the Factor Slider is cancelled and the position of the gradient on the surface of the Object is determined by the Mapping Node Coordinates (values). With the default coordinates: Location and Rotation 0.000 and Scale 1.000 the gradient is applied as shown in Figure 9.53A. Changing the X Location coordinate to -1m produces the gradient shown in Figure 9.53B.

The Principled BSDF Node may be replaced with a Diffuse BSDF Node.

Figure 9.53A

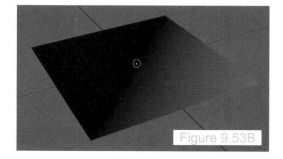

Figure 9.53B

Gradient Examples

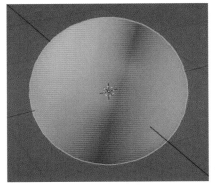
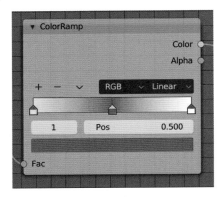

Figure 9.54

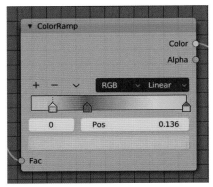

9.23 Saving Screen Space

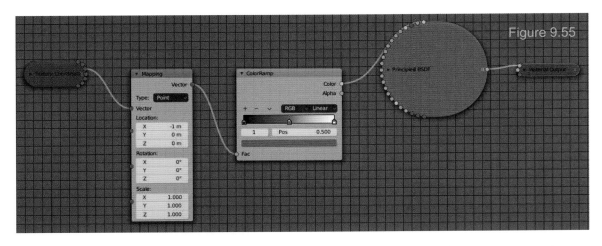

Figure 9.55

To save Screen Space with complicated Node Systems, click on a Node to select, right click on a the Node and select **Hide** from the menu that displays to minimise a Node.

9.24 Vertex Paint

With an Object (Model) selected in the 3D Viewport Editor in Object Mode, placing the Editor in **Vertex Paint Mode** allows you create a **Color Mask** for the Object.

Superficially, Vertex Painting, appears to let you paint color on to the surface of the Object but this is a deception. Placing the 3D Viewport Editor in Vertex Paint Mode creates an exact copy (duplicate) of the selected Object (Model). When you paint you are applying color to the duplicate. The colored duplicate is a **Mask** which is <u>placed over the Model</u>.

Colored Mask　　**Selected Object**　　Figure 9.56

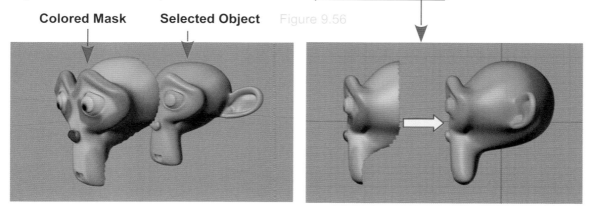

Note: The forgoing is an analogy which will assist in understanding the Vertex Paint process. With this concept in mind you will be better placed to follow instruction.

Consider the application of color to an Object using Vertex Painting as a three stage operation. The first stage is to prepare the surface of the Model, the second stage is to create a Color Layer or Mask which will be applied to the Model in the third stage. You may create multiple layers. The Color Layers supersede any Material that has been previously applied to the Model.

Remember: A new Object entered in the 3D Viewport Editor does **NOT** have a Material (color) applied although it displays with Blenders default gray color (see Chapter 1 – 1.15).

To demonstrate the process of **Vertex Painting** the following exercise will create a Color Mask for **Suzanne** (the Monkey Object). You may create a Mask for any Object but to paint detail, the Object's Mesh Surface should contain an adequate number of Vertices. In a new Blender File delete the default Cube Object and add **Suzanne**.

Figure 9.57

Edit Mode Default Vertices

Vertices Added

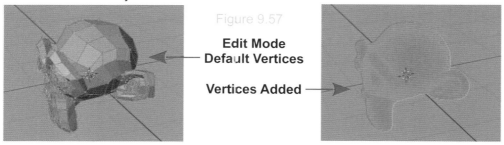

Properties Editor

You can paint the surface of Suzanne with the default number of Vertices forming the mesh but to perform detailed painting you will be required to add Vertices. The best way to do this is, apply a **Subdivision Surface Modifier** to Suzanne. Make **Levels Viewport** and **Render** in the Modifier = 4.

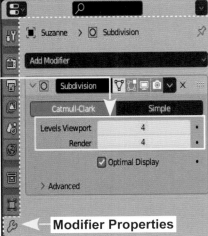

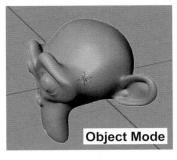

Object Mode

Edit Mode

Modifier Properties

Remember: The Modifier is Added to Suzanne with Suzanne selected in the 3D Viewport Editor in Object Mode. After Adding the Modifier you **Apply the Modifier** which fixes the Vertices that you see in Edit Mode.

Vertex Paint Mode

Figure 9.59

With Suzanne selected in the 3D Viewport Editor change from **Object Mode** to **Vertex Paint** Mode.

Click to see the **Viewport Mode** menu.
Select **Vertex Paint**.

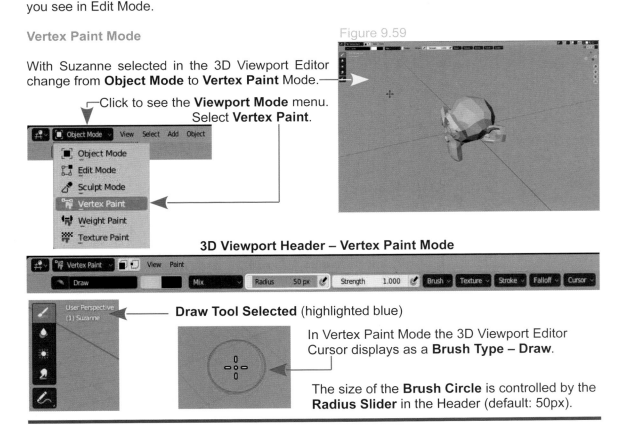

3D Viewport Header – Vertex Paint Mode

Draw Tool Selected (highlighted blue)

In Vertex Paint Mode the 3D Viewport Editor Cursor displays as a **Brush Type – Draw**.

The size of the **Brush Circle** is controlled by the **Radius Slider** in the Header (default: 50px).

When entering **Vertex Paint Mode** (with the Object – Suzanne selected in Object Mode), Blender automatically creates a Mask or Layer called a **Color Attribute**.

Figure 9.60

By default the Color Attribute is named **Col.** You see the Color Attribute in the **Properties Editor, Object Data Properties, Color Attributes Tab** (Figure 9 60).

Make note of the **Color Attributes Tab** with the Color Attribute named **Col** and also the **Attributes Tab** also with the Attribute named **Col**. The distinction between the two Tabs will be held in abeyance. Figure 9.61

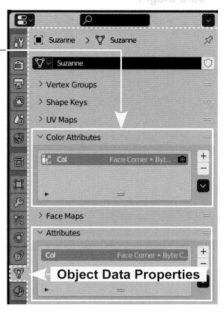

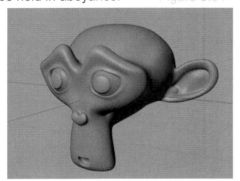

At this point Suzanne has been selected in Object Mode. Her surface has been Subdivided, creating additional Vertices and you have changed to Vertex Paint Mode. If you haven't messed with any colors Suzanne displays with the default gray.

Blender has created a **Color Mask** which is the **Color Attribute** named **Col**. What you see in the 3D Viewport Editor (Vertex Paint Mode) is the Mask not Suzanne (the Model). The Mask is an exact 3D replica of Suzanne and is ready to be Painted (Colored). Rotate the Viewport to present her face towards the front of the Screen (Figure 9.61).

Painting

Start by giving the Mask a new Color. Make note that in doing this you are not applying a Material (Color) to Suzanne (the Model) you are simply coloring the Mask.

You will, however, need to have Suzanne selected in the 3D Viewport Editor while in Object Mode. To reinforce the procedure for Vertex Painting the following is offered:

> Select the Object or Model in the 3D Viewport Editor while in Object Mode.
> (You may have several Objects in a Scene, in the 3D Viewport)
> With the Object selected, change the 3D Viewport to Vertex Paint Mode.
> All Objects in the Scene will be displayed in Vertex Paint Mode.
> You can only paint the Object that was selected in Object Mode.
> You will be painting a Mask, NOT the actual Object.

Applying a Base Color – Vertex Paint Mode

The Base Color is the overall surface color of the Object. When a new Object is added to a Scene it comes with **Blender's default gray** color as seen in **Solid Viewport Shading Mode.**

Figure 9.62

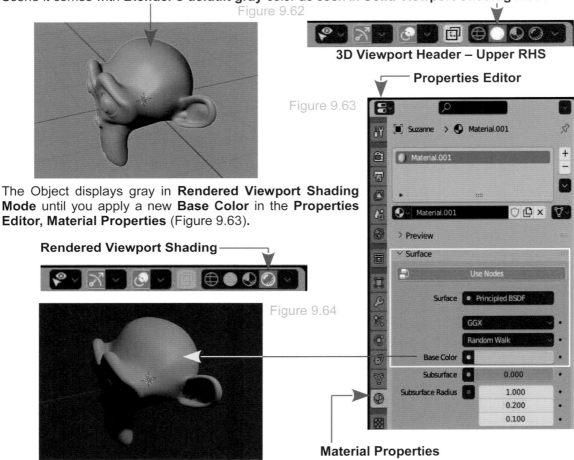

3D Viewport Header – Upper RHS

Properties Editor

Figure 9.63

The Object displays gray in **Rendered Viewport Shading Mode** until you apply a new **Base Color** in the **Properties Editor, Material Properties** (Figure 9.63).

Rendered Viewport Shading

Figure 9.64

Material Properties

Changing back to **Solid Viewport Shading Mode** will show the Object again with the gray color.

Remember; The Material Node System is active as indicated by the blue **Use Nodes button** in the Properties Editor, Material Properties, Surface Tab.

Changing the 3D Viewport Editor to **Vertex Paint Mode** will show the **Mask** of Suzanne gray.

Gray is the Base Color of the Mask.

To apply a different Base Color to the Mask **select a color** in the **Vertex Paint Header**.

Figure 9.65

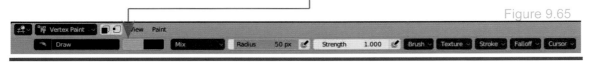

In the Vertex Paint Header, <u>select a color</u>. Click on **Paint – Set Vertex Colors**.

Figure 9.66

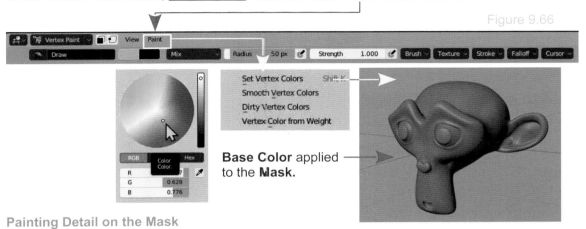

Base Color applied to the **Mask**.

Painting Detail on the Mask

With the Base Color applied, **select a different color in the Header** or Right Click in the Viewport and select a color.

Figure 9.67

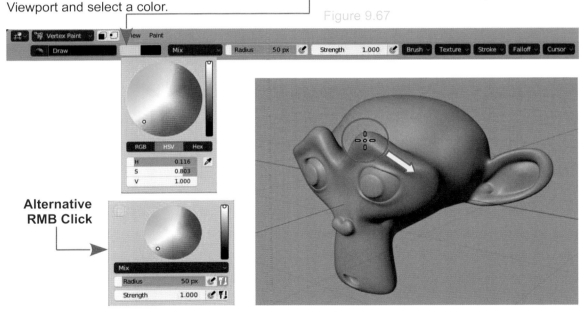

Alternative RMB Click

Click, hold and drag the Cursor Brush over the area you wish to paint. Rotate the Viewport to paint on hidden features. Adjust the Radius of the Brush to refine the detail of painting. Adjust the Strength value to soften the color.

While painting, bear in mind, you are painting the Mask not the Model.

Dragging the Brush over the features of the Mask is actually associating the data producing the chosen color with the Vertices encapsulated by the Brush Circle. To see what this means see Figures 9.59, 9.60 following.

In Figures 9.59 - 9.60 Suzanne has not been Subdivided prior to entering Vertex Paint Mode.

Select a Color ——— To see the association of the color to a Vertex, position the Cursor Brush over a Vertex and click LMB (Figure 14.69).

Figure 9.68

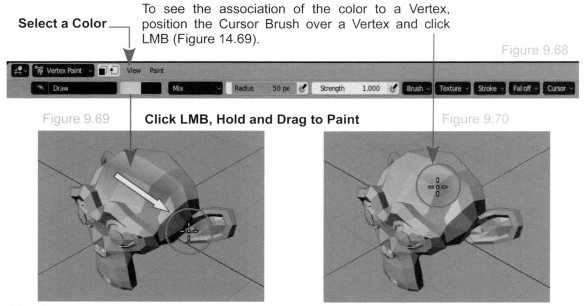

Figure 9.69 **Click LMB, Hold and Drag to Paint** Figure 9.70

Click, hold and drag the Brush over several Vertices to see color applied (Figure 9.69).

Painting More Detail

To paint detail on the Mask simply select colors, adjust the Brush controls in the Header and click, hold and drag the Brush over the surface. Rotate the Viewport and zoom the View to paint hidden features.

You will observe that the diameter of the Brush Cursor remains constant irrespective of the zoom applied to the Scene.

Figure 9.71

Brush Controls in the **Vertex Paint Mode Header** are used to adjust the Brush Paint Effect in conjunction with the Tool Panel at the left hand side of the Viewport. By default the **Draw Tool** in the Tool Panel is active (highlighted blue) and the name is displayed just below where you see **Vertex Paint**. Also by default Brush Type **F Draw** is active. There are several Types for selection.

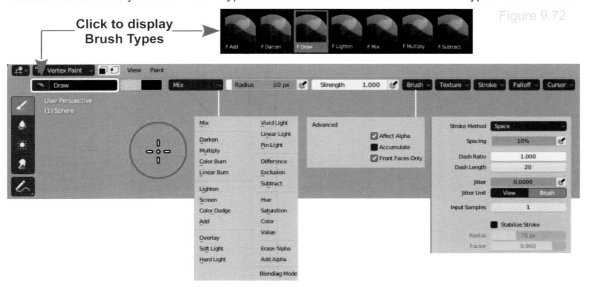

Figure 9.72

Be aware that the buttons in the Header open selection menus for selecting an array of functions. There are too many here for a comprehensive description of each but being aware of their existence will see you better placed to follow detailed tutorials.

You should also be aware that, having created a **Mask** (Color Attribute) you have to enter the Attribute in a Node in the Shader Editor for the selected Object. How you see your paintwork in the final Rendered View will depend on the lighting effects such as Lamp Types that you introduce to the Scene (see Chapter 12).

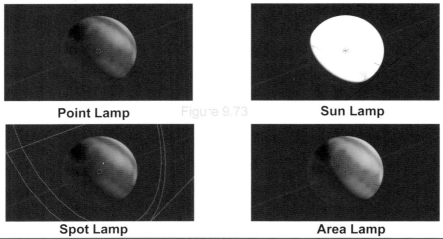

Point Lamp   Figure 9.73   **Sun Lamp**

Spot Lamp   **Area Lamp**

Viewing your Artwork

Figure 9.74

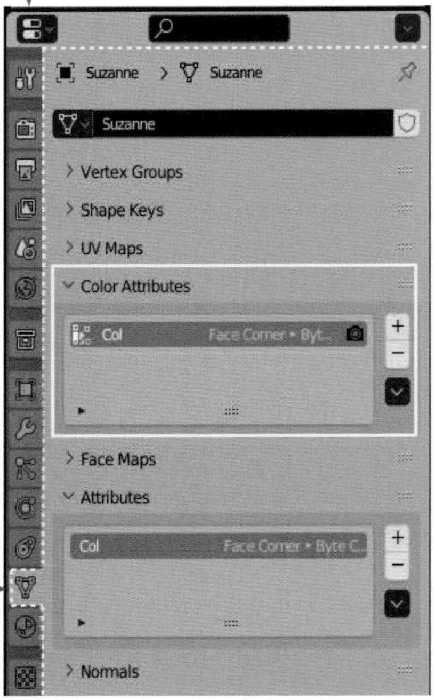

Properties Editor

At this point you will be disappointed to find that your paintwork does not display when you change the 3D Viewport to Object Mode. This applies to the Viewport in Solid, Material Preview and Rendered Viewport Display Modes (reference Chapter 18 Viewport Shading).

It was previously explained that Blender automatically creates a Mask or Layer called a **Color Attribute** when an Object is selected in Object Mode and you change to Vertex Paint Mode.

Attributes – The Painting Concept

The Concept: When you paint in Vertex Paint Mode you are not actually painting the surface of the Model. You are instead, using the Model as a template for creating a **Paint Layer** or **Mask**, which will be placed on the surface of the Model at a later stage. The Layer is called an **Attribute** or **Color Attribute (see Note following)**.

Object Data Properties

In Painting colors over Suzanne (Figure 9.71) you have generated a **multi colored Attribute**. You will see the Attribute in the **Properties Editor, Object Data Properties, Attributes** and **Color Attributes Tabs**. The Attribute has, by default, been named **Col** which is is applicable to Suzanne only.

Note: You will observe that there are two **Attribute Tabs** in the **Object Data Properties**, one named **Attribute** the other named **Color Attribute**. Both Tabs contain the single Attribute named Col. For the purpose of this discussion it will be assumed they are identical.

Additional Attributes

Figure 9.75

There will be times when you will want to have different Paint Masks for your Model, therefore, you create new Attributes.

In the Properties Editor, Object Data Properties, click on the plus button in either Attributes Tab to create a new Attribute.

In the **Add Color Attribute** panel that displays click **OK**.

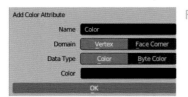

Figure 9.76

Click the Plus Sign

Object Data Properties →

When a New Attribute is entered in the Properties Editor, Object Data Properties a new Mask is created. Remember; Suzanne is selected in the 3D Viewport Editor in Object Mode.

A new Attribute named **Color** is created. Suzanne turns black in the 3D Viewport Editor.

You may paint over Suzanne's black face but be warned, in doing so you will be creating a mask with a black Base Color.

Figure 9.77

The mask (Attribute) named Col was created with Suzanne having her default gray color then subsequently Resetting the Vertex Colors by clicking the Paint button in the Header. The mask consists of the set color plus the colors that have been painted over. For a new Mask (New Color Attribute) you can set the base color to anything you like.

With the base color for the new mask reset go ahead and paint over.

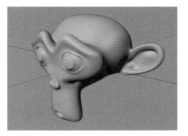

Figure 9.78

When painting you will have the Color Attribute named Color selected in the Object Data Properties.

Figure 9.79

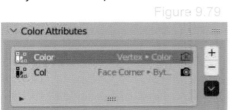

Figure 9.80

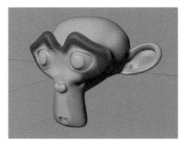

Using the Attributes

At this point you have two Color Attributes (Col and Color). You can rename if you wish. When creating the Attributes the 3D Viewport Editor has been in Vertex Paint Mode using Solid Viewport Display.

Figure 9.81   **Solid Viewport Display**

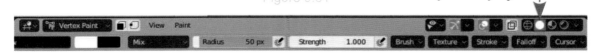

Changing the Viewport to **Object Mode** with **Rendered Viewport Display** shows Suzanne with her gray default color or the Base Color that you have previously set (see Figure 9.62).

The Color Attributes have to be applied to use the Masks.

Rotate Suzanne about the Z Axis to illuminate her face with the default Scene Light.

Figure 9.82

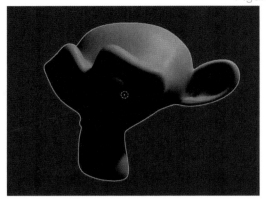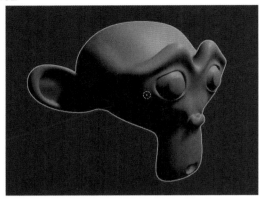

To use the Masks (Attributes) created by Vertex Painting you must have a Material, Base Color applied using the Blender Node System. You then configure a **Color Attribute Node**.

Drag the Timeline Editor panel edge up and change the window to the Shader Editor.

If you have previously applied a Base Color to Suzanne you will see a Principled BSDF Node connected to a Material Output Node otherwise, click the New button in the Shader Editor Header. Clicking the New button adds the default Principled BSDF Node connected to the Material Output Node.

In the Shader Editor Header click Add – Input and select Color Attribute to introduce a Color Attribute Node. Connect the Node to the Base Color socket on the Principled BSDF Node.

Figure 9.83

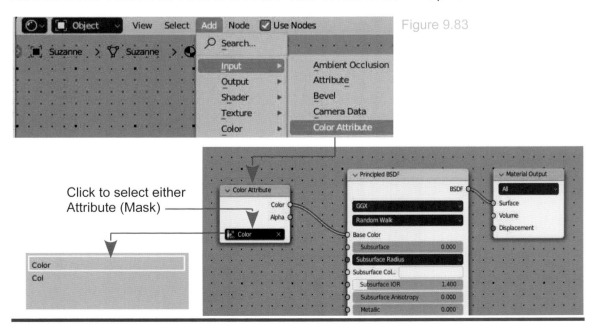

In the Color Attribute Node, enter either of the Color Attributes that have been created. The paint masks will display on Suzanne in the 3D Viewport (Rendered Viewport Display Mode) and will be Rendered to an Image (Press F12). Note the Image will be of Camera View not the 3D Viewport display.

Figure 9.84

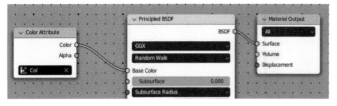

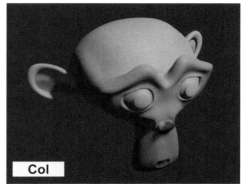

Rendered View – Camera View

Figure 9.85

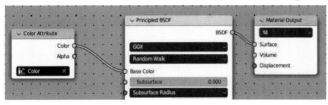

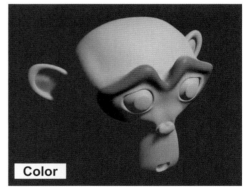

Rendered View – Camera View

10

Textures

Textures define the Object's composition such as whether it is glass, brick, sand, wood etc. Textures are also used to simply apply a pattern of color or shading. Textures, by and large, are images placed or mapped on to the surface and, therefore, superimpose over Material color. This type of Texture is referred to as; an **Image Texture**.

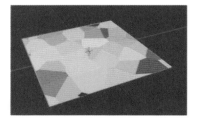

There are also **Procedural Textures** and **PBR Textures**.

Procedural Textures are patterns generated with mathematical formula and applied by computer code. **PBR Textures** are a Texture workflow to simulate the lumps and bums on a surface which react with light (Physically Based Rendering). These types of Texture are special JPEG or PNG images which deform a surface and react with light adding surface characteristics.

To introduce Textures they will be considered to be; **Material Textures** since they are applied to an Object's surface using the **Properties Editor, Material Properties** and configured using **Nodes** in the **Shader Editor**. (**Note:** The Material Properties **NOT Texture Properties**)

10.1 Procedural Texture

To apply a Texture to a surface of an Object, have the Object (default Cube) selected in the 3D Viewport Editor. To see a Texture in the 3D Viewport Editor, on the surface of the Object, the Editor must be in **Material Preview** or **Rendered Viewport Shading** Mode (see Chapter 13).

The starting point for applying a Texture to an Object is in the **Properties Editor, Material Properties, Surface Tab.**

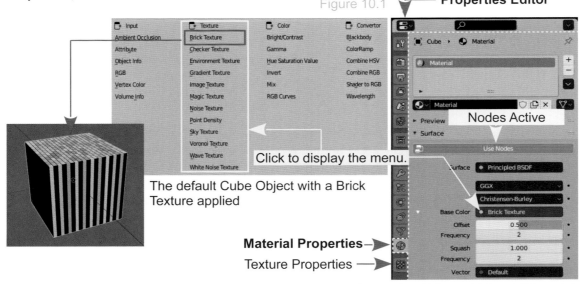

Figure 10.1 — **Properties Editor**

The default Cube Object with a Brick Texture applied

Click to display the menu.

Nodes Active

Material Properties →

Texture Properties →

You will note, there is a **Texture Properties** button in the Properties Editor which, at this point, contains no entries (Figure 10.4). This will be explained later (see 15.6 Texture Properties).

Remember; the default Cube Object has a Material pre-applied. New Objects entered into a Scene **Do NOT** have Materials until the **New Button** is pressed in the **Properties Editor, Material Properties**. Pressing the New Button applies a Material and displays Material Controls.

Applying a Material to an Object in the Properties Editor, **with Nodes activated** automatically places a **Principled BSDF Node** connected the **Material Output Node** in the **Shader Editor**.

To apply a Texture, click on the dot adjacent to the **Base Color** bar in the Properties Editor, Material Properties and in the selection menu that displays select one of the Textures in the **Texture Category** (Figure 10.1).

The Textures listed are called **Procedural Textures** which are built into Blender. This means the Texture is produced by code which generates a pattern in accordance with mathematical formula. There is one exception in the Texture Category which is the **Image Texture**.

The Image Texture enables the use of an Image saved on the computer being used. In this case the image would be **Mapped** to the surface of the Object (explanation to follow).

Since the application of the Texture is emanating from the Material Properties the Textures will be considered **Material Textures** (Procedural and Image).

In Figure 10.1 a Procedural Brick Texture is applied to the default Cube Object in the 3D Viewport Editor. When the **Shader Editor** is opened you see the **Node arrangement** creating the Texture.

Figure 10.2

The default Cube Object rotated and scaled to produce a brick wall.

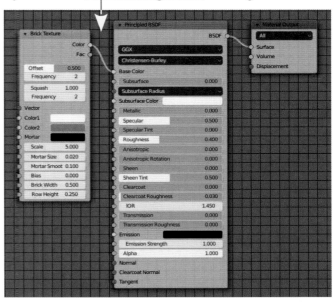

Values may be adjusted in the Brick Texture Node to alter the Texture Output (Figure 10.3).

Figure 10.3

Properties Editor →

The size of the Wall is unaltered. Only the Scale of the bricks and mortar change.

Figure 10.4

The **Brick Texture** is one of Blender's **Procedural Textures**. Experiment with different Textures on different Objects.

Texture Properties——→

Texture Cache: By clicking the **Browse Texture to be linked button** in the **Properties Editor, Texture Properties** you display the **Texture Cache** (Figure 10.4). At this point the Cache is empty despite having applied a Texture. The Cache may be used as a repository for Image Textures (see 10.7 **Texture Properties** following).

Procedural Texture Examples

Voronoi Texture   Figure 10.5

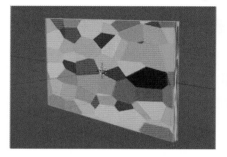

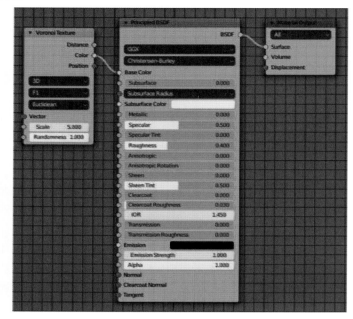

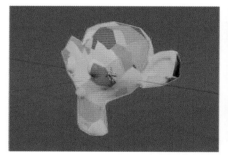

Magic Texture   Figure 10.6

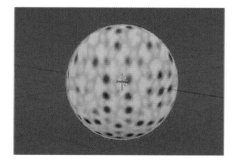

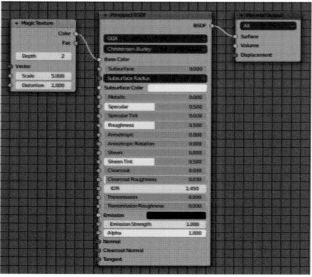

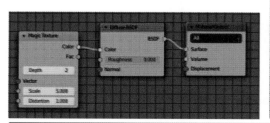

10.2 Adding Texture Nodes

As demonstrated in Figure 10.1, clicking the button in the Materials, Base Color bar and selecting a Texture from the menu applies a Texture by automatically connecting a Texture Node to the Base Color Socket of the Principled BSDF Node in the Shader Editor.

The Principled BSDF Node is the default Material Node for the application of a Material. When a Texture Node is connected the Texture supersedes the Material as the display on the selected Object in the 3D Viewport Editor.

The alternative method of introducing a **Texture Node** is to select a Node in the **Shader Editor Header** and manually connect to the Principled BSDF Node.

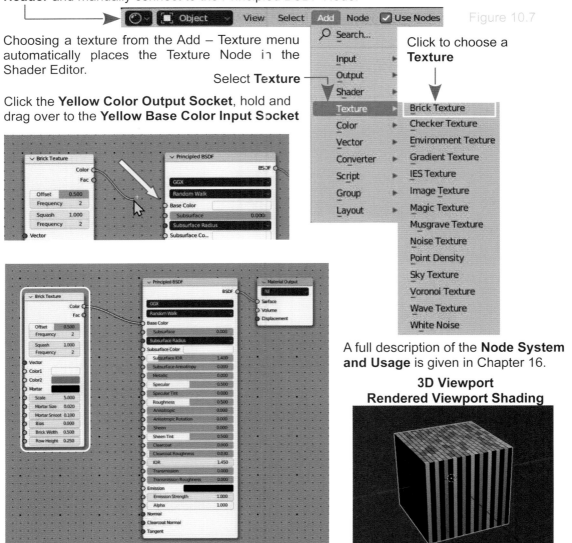

Choosing a texture from the Add – Texture menu automatically places the Texture Node in the Shader Editor.

Select **Texture**

Click the **Yellow Color Output Socket**, hold and drag over to the **Yellow Base Color Input Socket**

Click to choose a **Texture**

Figure 10.7

A full description of the **Node System and Usage** is given in Chapter 16.

3D Viewport
Rendered Viewport Shading

193

In the examples the **Texture Nodes** have been connected to the **Base Color input socket** of the **Principled BSDF Node**. Since this is the only function of the BSDF Node being used the Principled BSDF Node may be replaced by the **Diffuse BSDF Node** producing the same result (Figure 10.7).

The **Procedural Textures** included in the default Blender file are but the tip of the iceberg. As you have seen, selecting one of the Textures from the menu connects a Texture Node to the Base Color input socket of the BSDF Node which outputs the result to the surface of the selected Object in the 3D Viewport Editor. Introducing other Nodes into the pipeline in the Shader Editor modifies the Texture output creating new Textures. The combination of Nodes and the output results are infinite and, therefore, impossible to demonstrate in a single publication. To discover the possibilities you will have to experiment and research the internet for examples. Having found a result you then record the findings for future use.

One excellent source is to be found on the Blender Artists website:

https://blenderartists.org/t/my-100-free-cycles-procedural-textures-blend-files-and-or-settings-included/1113432

An example of a Texture Node System Figure 10.8

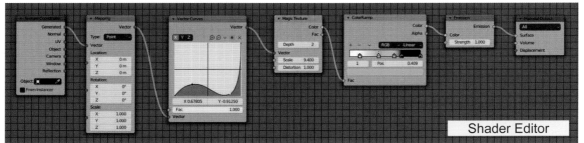

Shader Editor

The Node Arrangement in Figure 10.8 produces the pattern on the surface of a Plane Object (Figure 10.9).

Figure 10.9

Note: The original Texture example has been designed for use with **Cycles Render** activated but also works with **Eevee Render.**

Rendered Viewport Shading Mode ——▶

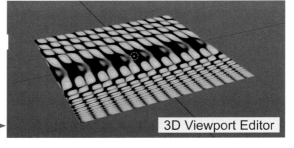

3D Viewport Editor

10.3 Image as a Texture

As previously mentioned an Image may be used as a Texture. The Image, such as JPEG, BMP or PNG, must be saved on your computer. One source of free Texture Images is: https://texture.ninja. These images are provided by Joost Vanhoutte; https://www.patreon.com/textureninja.

When downloading images to be used as Textures it is a good practice to save them to a dedicated folder which creates a Texture Library. Figure 10.10

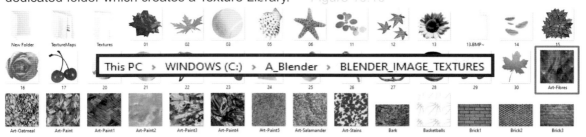

Applying an Image Texture

To use an Image as a Texture, apply a Material to an Object selected in the 3D Viewport Editor. Click the New Button, then in the **Properties Editor, Material Properties**, click the **Base Color button** and select, **Image Texture** from the menu. In the **Shader Editor** you will see an Image Texture Node connected to the Base Color input socket of the Principled BSDF Node (Figure 10.11).

In the **Material Properties** or in the **Image Texture Node** click on **Open**, navigate to the folder containing your Image and select it. **Shader Editor** ⌐ Figure 10.11 ⌐ **Properties Editor**

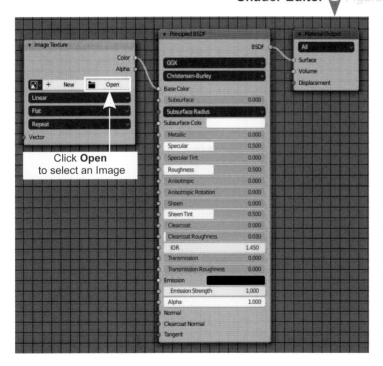

You will see the Image mapped to the surface of the selected Object in the **3D Viewport Editor** (in Material Preview or Rendered Viewport Shading Mode – Figure 10.12) .

Image Texture named **Art-Fibres** (Figure 10.12) selected, **Mapped** to a Plane Object in the 3D Viewport Editor.

Figure 10.12   **Rendered Viewport Shading Mode**

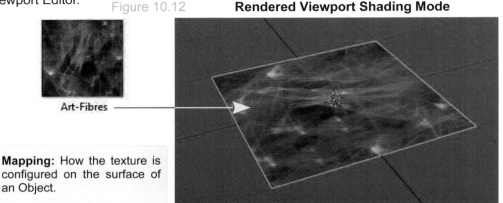

Art-Fibres

Mapping: How the texture is configured on the surface of an Object.

10.4 Texture Mapping

Mapping is best demonstrated with an Object a little more complicated than a flat Plain Object which for all tense and purposes has a single surface if you disregard its reverse side. The default Cube Object will do nicely. A Cube has six sides, therefore, six surfaces.

The default Cube has a Material pre-applied (gray).

Figure 10.13

For the demonstration a JPEG Image of a landscape will be used which provides a variation in detail instead of an indistinguishable pattern of color.

Mapping the Image to the surface of the Cube means that the Image or parts of the Image will be transferred to the six sides of the Cube. To do this the Cube will be laid out flat as if it were a cardboard box undone at the seams.

To see the unwrapping effect have the default Cube Object in the 3D Viewport Editor selected in **Edit Mode**. Divide the 3D Viewport Editor in two and change the left hand part to the **UV Editor**.

The default Cube is automatically laid flat (Unwrapped) in the **UV Editor** when the Object is in **Edit Mode**. The unwrapping fits inside the confines of what will be the outline of your Image when the Image is loaded in the UV Editor (Figure 15.14 over).

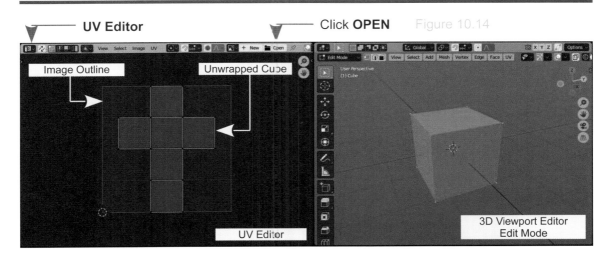

UV Editor   Click **OPEN**   Figure 10.14

Image Outline

Unwrapped Cube

UV Editor

3D Viewport Editor
Edit Mode

At this point the Image has not been loaded in the UV Editor nor has it been assigned as an Image Texture for the Cube Object. You will not see the Image applied to the surface of the Cube.

In the **UV Editor**, click on **Open** in the Header (Figure 10.14), navigate to your image and select it. This enters the Image in the UV Editor where the original Image confines change to fit the Image selected and the unwrapped Cube deforms to fit the new confine Figure 10.15).

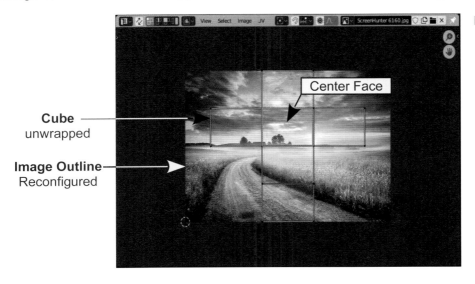

Figure 10.15

Center Face

Cube
unwrapped

Image Outline—
Reconfigured

Note: At this point the Image has not been assigned as an Image Texture to the Cube Object and, therefore, **does not** display on the surface of the Cube in the 3D Viewport Editor.

You assign the Image as a Texture, in the **Properties Editor, Material Properties,** click the **Base Color button**, select **Image Texture** and open the Image in the **Image Texture Node** (Figure 10.11).

With the Image assigned as a Texture it displays in the 3D Viewport Editor, Mapped to the surface of the Cube Object. Note the center face of the Cube in the UV Editor and the equivalent face of the Cube in the 3D Viewport Editor and the orientation of the Mapped Image.

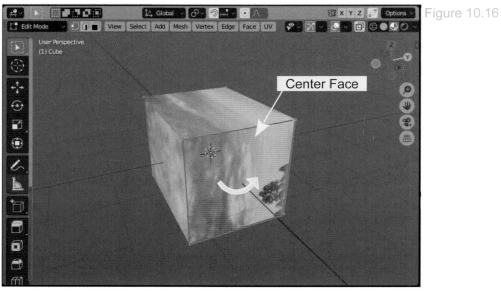

Figure 10.16

Note: To see the Texture in the 3D Viewport Editor be in Material Preview or Rendered Viewport Shading Mode.

By clicking a point or points (vertices) in the **UV Editor**, pressing the **G Key** and moving the points you may change which portion of the Image is mapped to a Face on the Cube. In Figure 10.17 the Cube has been rotated about the X Axis in Object Mode and returned to Edit Mode.

Figure 10.17

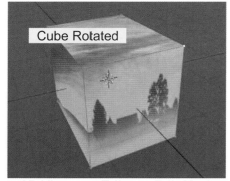

UV Editor　　　　**3D Viewport Editor – Edit Mode**

10.5 Unwrapping Options

The Unwrapping method has been demonstrated using the default automatic **Unwrap**. Different options are found in the **UV Editor Header, UV Button** (Figure 15.18).

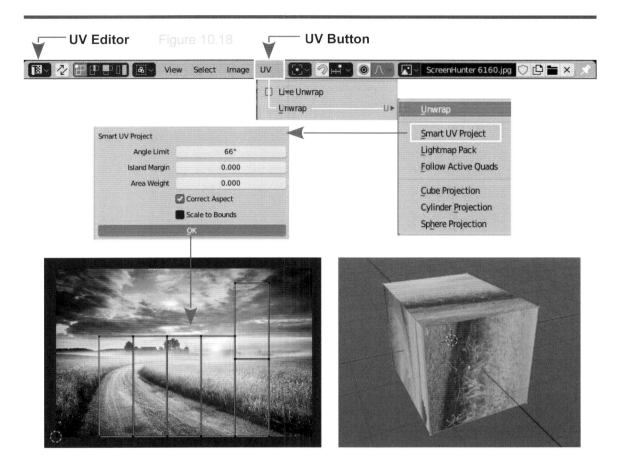

Figure 10.18

10.6 PBR Textures

PBR Textures (Physically Based Rendering) are a Texture workflow to simulate the lumps and bums on a surface which react with light, as do real life Materials. PBR Textures in practice are JPEG or PNG Images configured to represent dark and light areas on a surface which include highlights and shadows. A combination of PBR Texture Images are employed to create a Textured surface. The Images are entered into Texture Nodes and configured in the Shader Editor.

PBR Texture Images may be generated for specific applications but are generally downloaded from Texture Repositories on the internet similar to downloading blocks of computer code.

To demonstrate the basics of PBR Texturing a **Texture Pack** (series of Images) has been downloaded from: https://www.virtualtweaks.com/ **Free PBR Shader – terraCottaBB.zip**

When unzipped **terraCottaBB.zip** creates seven (7) Images and an Information file giving permission to use and explaining that the Images are low resolution and intended for practice.

In demonstrating the use of the PBR Textures not all images will be used. When downloading any Texture Pack the first hurdle in using the Textures is understanding which Images are applicable.

A detailed explanation will not be attempted at this stage, instead a practical example of implementing the Images will be presented.

Download terraCottaBB.zip and unzip the file to a folder. The folder will contain: Figure 10.19

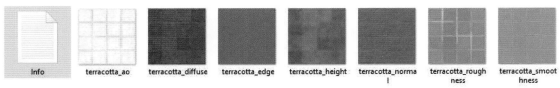

| Info | terracotta_ao | terracotta_diffuse | terracotta_edge | terracotta_height | terracotta_norma l | terracotta_rough ness | terracotta_smoot hness |

In Blender change the default Layout Workspace to the **Shading Workspace** (select in the Header).

Figure 10.20

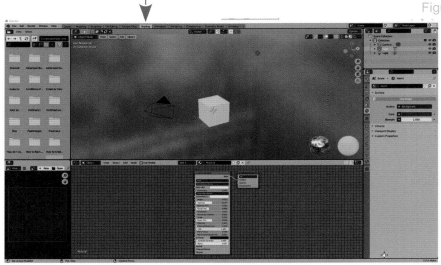

In the **File Browser Editor** (upper LHS) navigate to and open the folder containing the **PBR Texture Files**. By default the folder opens in **Thumbnail display mode** where the names of the files are obscured. By changing to one of the **List display modes** you see details of each file.

Thumbnail Display Figure 10.21 **List Display**

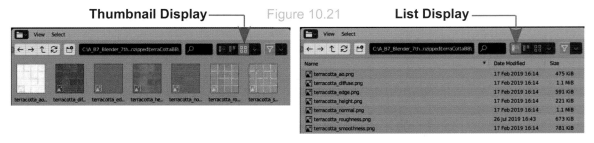

To demonstrate the application of PBR Textures, delete the default Cube from the 3D Viewport Editor and replace it with a Plane Object. **Add a Material**. Remember; the default Cube has a Material pre-applied. A new Object added to the Scene does not have a Material until you press the New Button in the Properties Editor, Material Properties.

With a Material applied and Use Nodes active you see the Principled BSDF Node connected to the Material Output Node in the Shader Editor.

The PBR Texture Thumbnails may be selected in the File Browser and dragged into the Shader Editor automatically entering an **Image Texture Node** with the PBR Texture Image entered in the Node.

Part A. Select and drag the **terracotta_diffuse.png** PBR Image into the Shader Editor and connect the Color output socket of the Image Texture Node to the Base Color input socket of the Principled BSDF Node. Figure 10.22

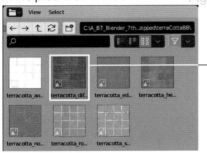

File Browser

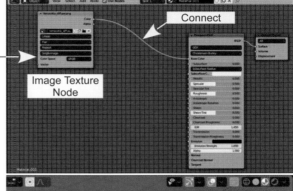

With the Nodes connected and with the 3D Viewport Editor in Material Preview or Rendered Viewport Shading Mode you see the Terracotta Image Mapped to the surface of the Plane. Note: The Plane is a flat surface without any detail of surface imperfections (Lumps or Bumps).

The PBR Texture Images are entered into the Shader Editor and connected to the Principled BSDF Node in the following sequence (**Note:** Not all the PBR Texture Images in the texture Pack are used).

A. terracotta_diffuse.png   provides the base color information for the Texture.
B. terracotta_normal.png   simulates bumpiness on the base color.
C. terracotta_height.png   allows adjustment of the bumpiness.
D. terracotta_roughness.png   provides fine imperfections to the surface for realism.

Apart from **A. terracotta_diffuse.png** which is connected directly to the Diffuse BSDF Node the other Images/Nodes are connected and employed via intermediary Nodes.

Part B. Select and drag the **terracotta_normal.png** PBR Image into the Shader Editor and connect as shown. In the terracotta_normal.png Node change **Color Space** to **Non-Color** and change the values in the **Normal map Node** as shown.

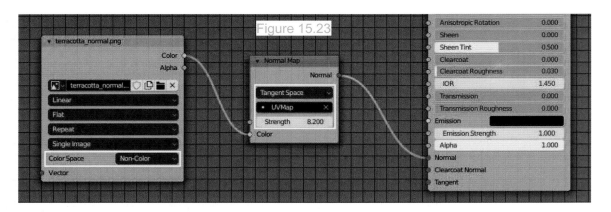

Figure 15.23

With the Nodes connected you will see how light reacts with the surface. Have the 3D Viewport Editor in rendered Viewport Shading Mode and locate the default Point Lamp down close to the Plane. In Figure10.24 the Point Lamp Power is set at 708.2 W.

Figure 10.24

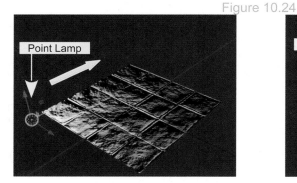

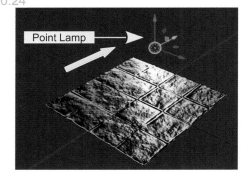

Part C. The surface of the Plane may be further enhanced by the introduction of an **Image Texture Node** with **terrracotta_height.png** inserted. The Node is connected via a **Converter -RGB to BW Node** and a **Vector- Bump Node** Figure 10.25

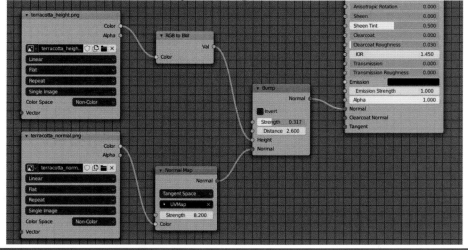

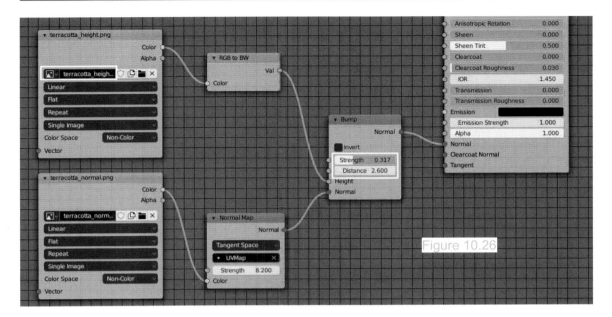

Figure 10.26

The affect is controlled by adjusting the Strength and Distance values in the Bump Map Node.

By placing the 3D Viewport Editor in Front Orthographic View you will see that the Plane remains a flat surface (Figure 10.28).

Figure 10.27

Figure 10.28

Part D. A final adjustment is obtained by introducing an Image Texture **terracotta_Roughness.png,** inserted and connected to the Roughness input socket of the Principled BSDF Node via a **Color Ramp Node**. By moving the Color Ramp Stops (Reference Chapter 9 – 9.22) fine tuning of the surface imperfections are made.

Figure 10.29

PBR Texturing Node Configuration

The completed PBR Texture Node configuration is shown in Figure 10.30.

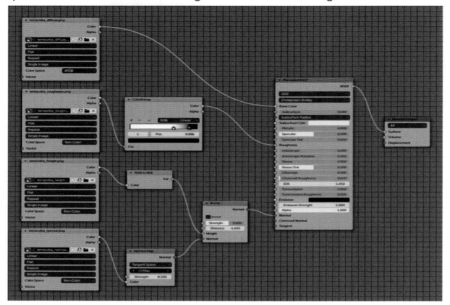

Figure 10.30

Node Wrangler

A quick way to set up a BBR Node Arrangement is to use Blender's **Node Wrangler**. This is an **Add-on** included with the program which you activate in the **Preferences Editor** (Reference Chapter 2 -2.17).

Figure 10.31

Have the PBR Texture Images saved on your computer.

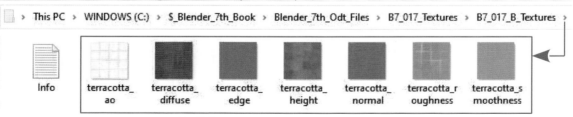

> This PC > WINDOWS (C:) > S_Blender_7th_Book > Blender_7th_Odt_Files > B7_017_Textures > B7_017_B_Textures >

| Info | terracotta_ ao | terracotta_ diffuse | terracotta_ edge | terracotta_ height | terracotta_ normal | terracotta_r oughness | terracotta_s moothness |

PBR Image Textures - .png Files

Figure 10.32

In the 3D Viewport Editor have the Object to which the Texture is to be applied selected. Remember; the Object must have a Material applied (default gray is fine).

In the Shader Editor you will see the Principled BSDF Node connected to the Material Output Node which produces the default gray Material on the selected Object.

In the Shader Editor, mouse over on the Principled BSDF Node then press **Ctrl + Shift + T Key**. The Blender File View displays. Navigate to the Folder containing the PBR Texture Images (.png).

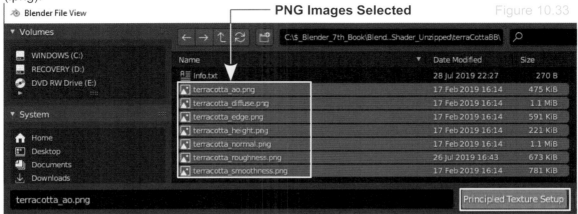

PNG Images Selected

Figure 10.33

Shift select the Texture Files you wish to use then click **Principled Texture Setup** at the bottom of the panel (Figure 10.33).

A **PBR Texture Node Arrangement** is automatically generated in the **Shader Editor** with the result exported to the Object in the 3D Viewport Editor (Figure 10.34)

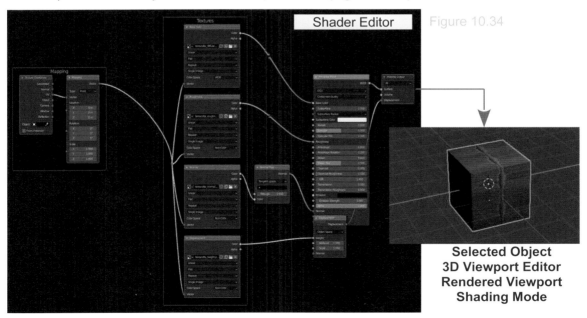

Shader Editor

Figure 10.34

**Selected Object
3D Viewport Editor
Rendered Viewport
Shading Mode**

10.7 Texture Properties – Properties Editor

As previously described **Textures** are applied to an Object's surface in the **Material Properties** and configured in the **Shader Editor**. The **Texture Properties** panel in the **Properties Editor** is used as **Texture Repository** allowing quick access to Image Textures for assignment to Objects in the 3D Viewport Editor.

To demonstrate, have several Images save on your computer to be used as Image Textures.

Figure 10.35

Mosaic-Glass.jpg   Art-Fibres.jpg   Art-Paint5.jpg   Fabric-Yellow.jpg   Pebbles.jpg   Wall paper2.jpg

In the default Blender Screen, delete the default Cube Object from the 3D Viewport Editor. Select **Texture Properties** in the Properties Editor.

Figure 10.36

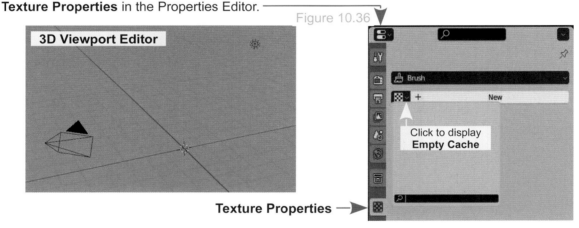

At this point there is **NO Object** in the 3D Viewport, **NO Material**, **NO Texture** and **NO Image**.

By clicking the **New button** in the **Texture Properties** you create an empty **Texture Channel**.

By default, the Channel is named **Texture** and is assigned **Type, Image or Movie** which indicates that you may assign an Image file as the Texture to the Texture Channel.

Figure 10.37

Alternatively you may elect to assign a **Procedural Texture** to the Channel (Reference 10.1).

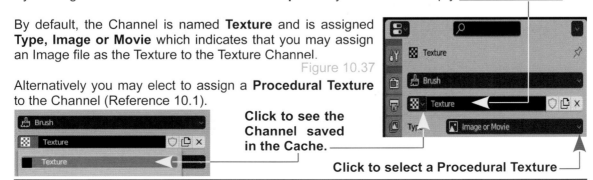

206

With the Texture Channel created, click Open in the Texture Properties, navigate to your saved Image and click Open Image to assign the Image as a Texture.

Figure 10.38

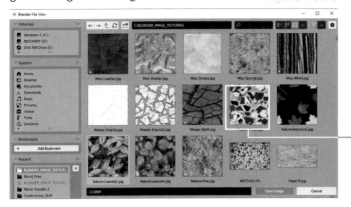

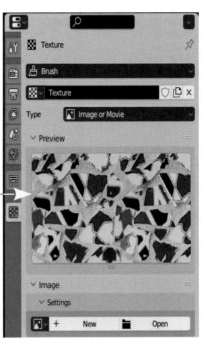

The Image is assigned to the Texture Channel and displays in the **Preview Panel**.

By clicking the **Browse Texture to be linked button** you see the Texture assigned to the Channel in the Texture Cache.

Figure 10.39

Browse Texture to be linked

Channel in the Texture Cache

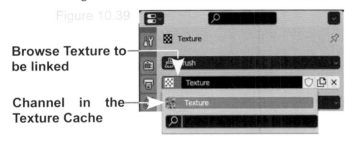

At this point you have created a Texture Channel and assigned an Image to the Channel as a Texture.

Remember: There is NO Object in the 3D Viewport, therefore, you have merely created a Texture for future use.

You may now proceed to create additional Channels and assign different Images as Textures.

To create a new Texture Channel click the New Texture button.

Figure 10.40

The new Channel is named **Texture.001** by default and has the previously assigned Image as the Texture.

Figure 10.41

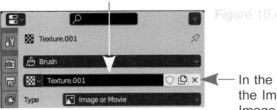

In the Image Settings Tab click the **X** to unlink the Image Datablock then reassign a different Image (click Open etc.).

By repeating the procedure you create a **Library of Texture Channels** (Figure 10.42).

The Texture Cache constitutes a **Texture Library**. Bear in mind, at this stage, the Library Cache is applicable only to the particular file in which you are working.

Click to open the Cache Figure 10.42

Texture Cache

To use the Library have a new Object entered in the 3D Viewport Editor. With the Object selected go to the **Properties Editor, Material Properties**. Click the **New button** to open the Material Properties controls for the selected Object.

In the **Surface Tab** click the yellow dot at the RH end of the **Base Color bar** and select **Image Texture** in the menu that displays.

Entering **Image Texture** <u>opens a bar</u> for entering a Texture.

Figure 10.43

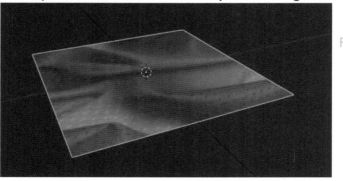

Clicking the **Browse Image to be linked button** will display the **Texture Cache – Library**. Clicking on one of the entries enters the assigned Image as the **Base Color – Image texture.**

Figure 10.44

With the 3D Viewport Editor in **Rendered Viewport Display Mode** you see the Texture mapped to the surface of the Object.

3D Viewport Editor – Rendered Viewport Shading Mode

Figure 10.45

Texture Image – Fabric-Yellow.jpg mapped to a Plane Object

10.8 Texture Painting

Texture Painting is the process of modifying a Texture that has been Mapped to the surface of an Object by **Painting over the Texture** with a Material Color or a different Texture saved in a Blender Texture File Cache.

To demonstrate the process a Texture will be applied to Suzanne (Monkey Object) and painted over to make her beautiful ("beauty is in the eye of the beholder").

In a new Blender file delete the default Cube Object and add a Monkey Object. Rotate Suzanne in the 3D Viewport Editor to display her face. By default Susanne displays with her surface features made up from a series of flat planes which you see when she is placed in Edit Mode. This display will suit the purpose for the Painting demonstration.

Properties Editor

Have Susanne in Object Mode in the 3D Viewport Editor. The process being demonstrated is painting over a texture (Texture Painting), therefore, the first step is to apply a Texture to Susanne.

Figure 10.46

A Texture is applied in the Properties Editor, Material Properties which enforces the golden rule that a Material must be added before a Texture. Remember; the default 3D Viewport displays in Solid Viewport Shading Mode and Textures will only display in Material Preview or Rendered Viewport Shading Modes.

Since the Texture is to be painted over it is best to use a simple plain bland Image Texture (reference 10.2). For this demonstration the JPEG Image shown in Figure 10.47 will be used which has been made by adding a bland Material (color) to a Plane Object and taking a Screen Capture.

Figure 10.47

Material Properties

Suzanne in the 3D Viewport Editor Figure 10.48

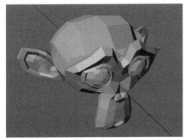

Solid

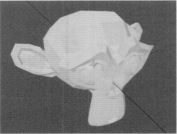

Material Preview

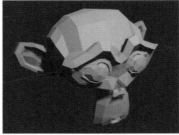

Rendered

Viewport Shading Modes

Change the default **Layout Workspace** to the **Texture Paint Workspace** and make sure the **3D Viewport Editor** is in **Texture Paint Mode**.

Figure 10.49

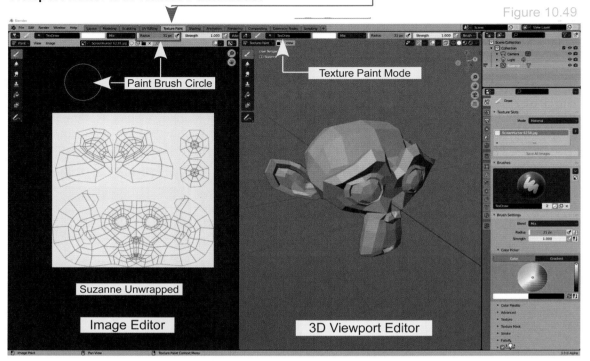

The **Texture Paint Workspace** displays with the **Image Editor** in **Paint Mode** and the **3D Viewport Editor** in **Texture Paint Mode**. In the Image Editor Suzanne has been automatically unwrapped laying out the surfaces on a flat plane.

Note: The 3D Viewport Editor is in Solid Viewport Shading Mode. To see Textures change this display to Material Preview or Rendered Viewport Shading.

The flat plane in the Image Editor and the surface of Suzanne in the 3D Viewport Editor display with the Texture (ScreenHunter 6229.jpg) that has been applied in the first step of the process.

At this point you can Paint, in the Image Editor over the Texture or in the 3D Viewport Editor. You Paint by clicking, holding and dragging the Brush Circle. The intention is; to Paint in specific Faces in the Image Editor which will Paint on to the corresponding Face on the surface of Suzanne, therefore, reduce the Brush Circle diameter to 5 px or 6 px in the Image Editor Header.

You Paint using a Material Color selected in either **Color Bar** in the Editor Headers (see over).

Figure 10.50

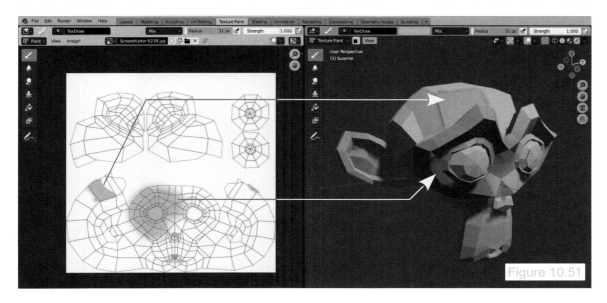

Figure 10.51

Tip: To adjust the Brush Circle diameter hold the F Key and drag the Mouse.

Painting with a Texture

Painting a Material color is painting the color over the Texture that has been applied to Susanne (the Monkey Object). Susanne is also the selected Object in the 3D Viewport Editor. With multiple Objects in a Scene the Texture Paint Mode is applicable to the Selected Object.

Besides painting a Material Color you may also paint with a Texture (Paint a Texture over the applied Texture).

Figure 10.52

Create a Texture in the Properties Editor, Texture Properties (reference Section 10.6).

In the example a Texture has been generated using a JPEG Image named Art-Fibres.

The Texture is placed in the **Texture Cache**.

Note: Source: **Single Image**.

With the Texture created and placed in the Cache you can paint the Texture in the Image Editor or in the 3D Viewport Editor.

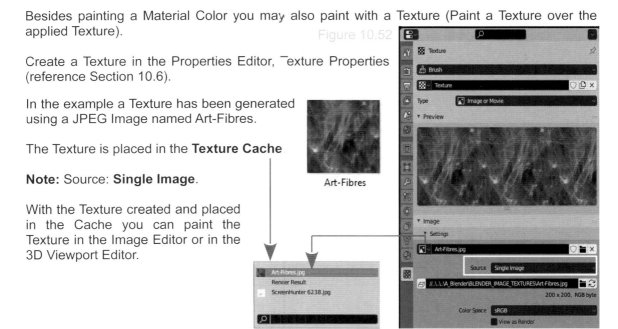

Art-Fibres

Blending Material Color with Texture   Figure 10.53

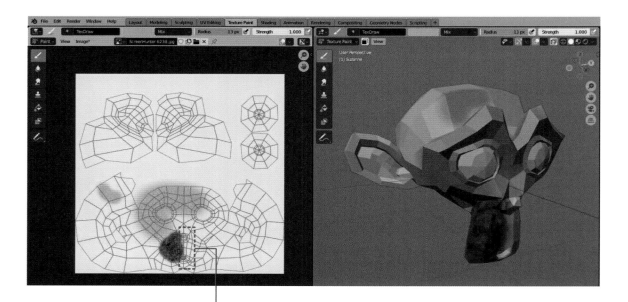

Note: MIX in the Viewport Headers. When painting with a Texture the Texture is blended with the Material color. Mix is one of several options for blending.

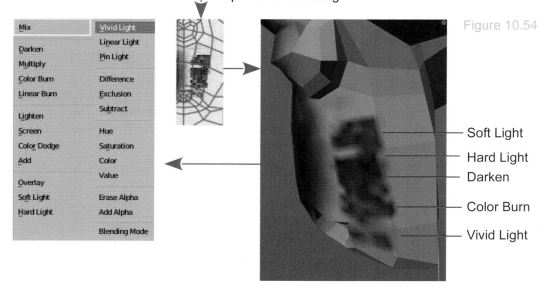

Figure 10.54

Soft Light

Hard Light

Darken

Color Burn

Vivid Light

10.9 Texture Displacement

Image Textures may be used to displace the Vertices forming the surface of an Object. The displacement is determined by the color shades in the Image. The Vertex displacement may be applied to the entire Mesh surface or a Vertex Group.

Figure 10.55

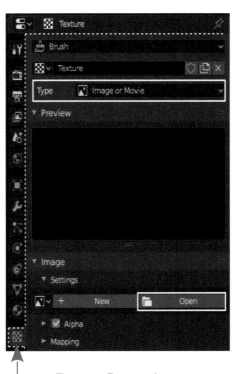

Prerequisites: 1. You must have an Image saved on your PC to be used as a Texture. To demonstrate Texture Displacement the image shown in Figure 10.55 will be used.

2. Have the surface Mesh (Plane Object) subdivided creating plenty of Vertices (Chapter 5 – 5.5).

Art-Paint.jpg

Note: Images may be used as a Texture to simply color a surface, in which case, the image is displayed on the surface of the mesh (Ref. Section 10.3).

Remember: To see color, be in **Material Preview** or **Rendered Viewport Shading Mode**.

Coloring using Texture

Figure 10.56

With the Object in the 3D Viewport Editor selected, **Open** the **Material Properties** in the Properties Editor with **Use Nodes** active. Click on the button at the end of the **Base Color** bar and select **Image Texture** from the menu. The Base Color will show **Image Texture** in what was the color bar. Click on **Open** and navigate in the File Browser to find your image file. Select a file and click **Open Image**. In **Material Preview** or **Rendered Viewport Shading Mode** the Texture Image is mapped to the surface of the Object.

Displacement using Texture

The displacement is performed by entering a Texture in a **Displace Modifier** (Ref: Chapter 7 – 7.5). To enter a Texture in the Modifier the Texture must first be entered in the **Texture Cache**.

In the **Properties Editor, Texture Properties** click **New**. The buttons display with **Type Image or Movie** (Figure 10.56). In the Image Tab, Settings, click **Open** (the File Browser opens). Navigate to your Texture Image and open it. This enters the Texture in the Texture Cache (Ref. 10.6 Texture Properties).

Texture Properties

Note: To use a texture for surface displacement it is not necessary to have it entered as a Material. The surface deformation will still occur in accordance with the color shading of the image but the colors do not show on the deformed surface. If you wish to display the colors enter the Texture Image in the Material Properties as previously described.

Texture Cache

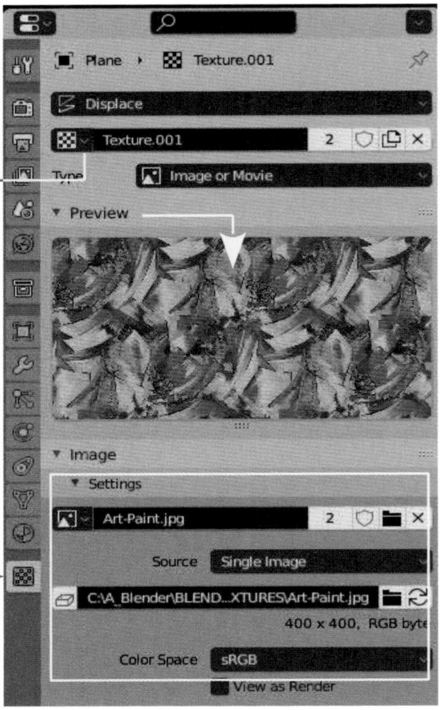

Figure 10.57

With the Texture Image entered in the texture Cache have the Object surface selected in the 3D Viewport Editor and add a **Displace Modifier** (Figure 10.57). In the Displace Modifier click on the **Browse Texture to be Linked button** to display the Texture Cache and select the Texture you previously entered (Figure 10.58).

Properties Editor Texture Properties

Figure 10.58

Texture Cache

Properties Editor, Modifier Properties

The Objects Mesh surface is deformed (Figure 10.59). The amount of deformation is controlled using the **Midlevel** and **Strength** sliders in the Modifier panel.

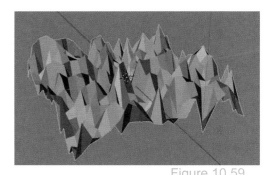

Figure 10.59

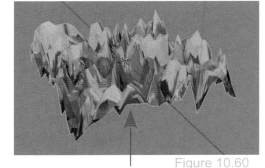

Figure 10.60

If you wish to see color on the deformed Mesh enter the Image as a **Color Image Texture** in the Material Properties (see Coloring using Textures above).

Node Systems and Usage

Nodes are an integral part of the application of Materials and Textures. There are, however, many other uses for Node Systems. The following examples will show a small sample with the **Eevee Render System** engaged. The **Cycles Render System** also uses Nodes although the Node selection differs.

Nodes are a graphical representation of code processing blocks which may be arranged and connected to produce effects. The Blender interface may be configured to display four (4) different **Node Systems** as seen in the **Viewport Editor Type**, selection menu.

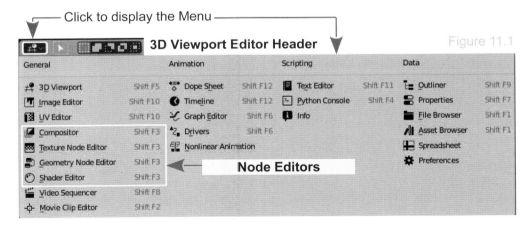

Figure 11.1

Nodes have been discussed in the **Shader Editor** when considering the application of Materials and Textures. The Textures were described as Material Textures since they were applied in the **Properties Editor, Material Properties** using the **Shader Editor**.

In Figure 16.1, in the Editor selection menu, you will find the **Compositor Editor**, the **Texture Node Editor,** the **Geometry Node Editor** and the **Shader Editor**, all of which employ Node Systems.

11.1 Compositing Nodes

Compositing Nodes (or composite, for short) allow you to create and enhance image files and video files. The contents of the Blender Scene can be Rendered to an Image and combined with other elements such as another Image saved on your computer. The combination or Composite Image is then available for use.

Compositing Workspace

In the default Blender GUI Screen Header you will find the **Compositing Workspace** with five Editors displayed.

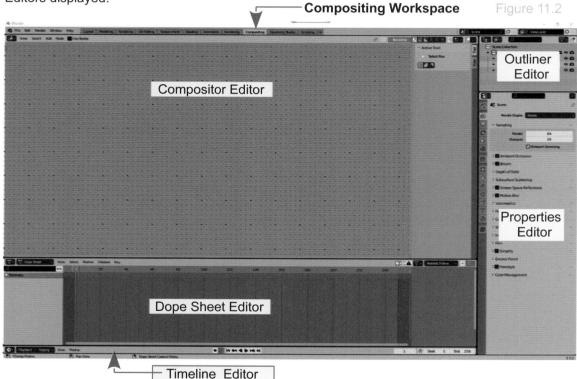

Compositing Workspace   Figure 11.2

The **Dope Sheet** and **Timeline Editors** are included since Compositing applies to Animation as well as still Scenes. To simplify the understanding of Compositing revise the Compositing Workspace to that shown in Figure 16.3 over. The Dope Sheet and Timeline are only used when Animation is employed.

For a basic demonstration a Render of the Scene in the 3D Viewport Editor will be combined with an Image saved on the computer. This will be accomplished using Blender's **Compositing Node System**. At this point you require the 3D Viewport Editor in which to construct the Scene, the Compositor Editor to arrange a Node Tree and the Image Editor to view the final result (Figure 11.3).

Revised Workspace

Figure 11.3

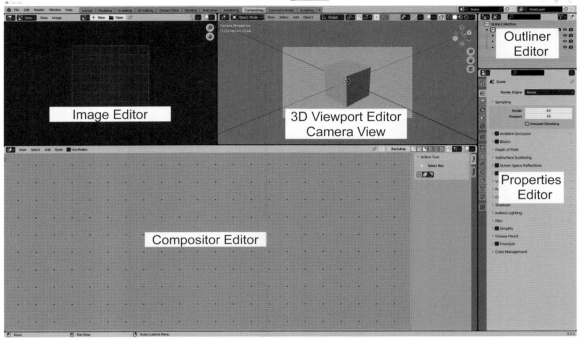

Outliner Editor

3D Viewport Editor
Camera View

Image Editor

Properties Editor

Compositor Editor

Properties Editor Figure 11.4

Since one element of the composition will be a Render of the Scene in the 3D Viewport Editor, change the Editor to **Rendered Viewport Shading Mode** and be in **Camera View**.

Remember: A Render of the Scene is what the Camera sees (see the Preamble).

Properties for the Egg (UV Sphere) →

You could use the default Cube Object as the subject in the Scene but to make something a little more appealing, replace the Cube with a UV Sphere, set smooth and elongated into an egg shape. Apply a nice shiny Material Color to the egg and change the default Point Light to an Area Light (Figures 11.4, 11.6).

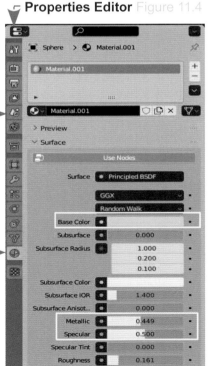

Figure 11.5

Material →
Properties

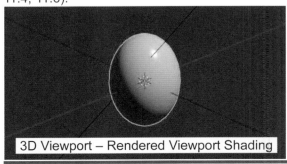

3D Viewport – Rendered Viewport Shading

217

Image saved on your computer

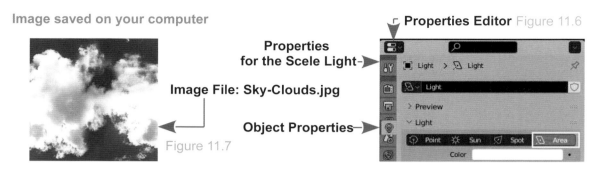

Properties
for the Scele Light→

Image File: Sky-Clouds.jpg

Object Properties→

Figure 11.7

Properties Editor Figure 11.6

The Scene – 3D Viewport Editor

Camera View - Rendered Viewport Shading

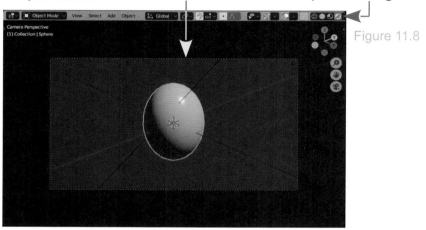

Figure 11.8

With the Scene in the 3D Viewport Editor as shown (Figure 11.3), place the Mouse Cursor in the Editor and press **F12** on the Keyboard to **Render an Image of Camera View**. The Rendered Image will display full Screen in a new version of the Image Editor. **Note:** In the Header, **Render Result** (center) and **Slot 1** (RHS). Press **Esc** to cancel the View.

The Rendered Image is automatically saved to a Cache. At this point the Image Editor View in the Compositing Workspace is empty. In the Header, Click and select **Render Result**.

Figure 11.9

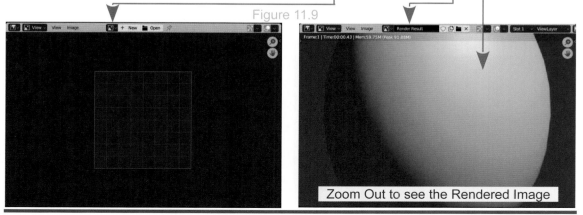

Zoom Out to see the Rendered Image

Note: If you save the Blender file and reopen at a later time the Render will not display in the Image Editor until you re-Render the 3D Viewport. The Image saved to the Cache is temporary.

Withe the Render in the Cache and the Image you have previously saved you combine (composite) the two using the **Node Editor** and the **Compsitor Node System**. By default the **Compositor Node Editor** is empty. In the Header check **Use Nodes** to start a **Node Tree** comprising a **Render Layers Node** connected to a **Composite Node**. Render the 3D Viewport Camera View (Press F12).

The Rendered Image displays in the Image Editor. You may have to zoom the Image Editor.

Compositing

To combine (Composite) the Rendered Image with the Image saved on your computer you add Nodes to the Node Tree. Click **Add** in the Compositor Editor Header to display the Node selection menu.

Figure 11.10

Figure 11.11

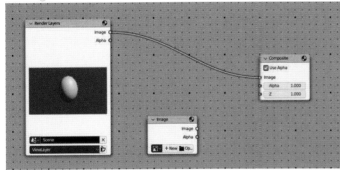

Since you are about to combine the saved Image with the Rendered View select **Input** then **Image**.

An **Image Node** is entered in the Compositor Viewport and the previously Rendered View Image displays in the Render Layers Node (Figure 11.11). To combine the Images two additional Nodes are required. Think of combining as mixing, therefore, add a **Color- Mix Node**.

When you use the saved Image you will probably want to Scale it to fit the rendered View, therefore, Add a **Distort – Scale Node** (Figure 11.12).

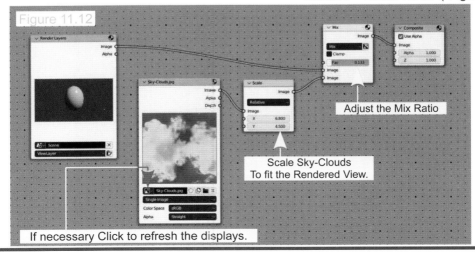

Adjust the Mix Ratio

Scale Sky-Clouds
To fit the Rendered View.

If necessary Click to refresh the displays.

219

With the Nodes and arranged and connected as sown in Figure 11.12 the composite Image displays in the Image Editor and may be saved as a new Image.

Figure 11.13

Figure 11.14

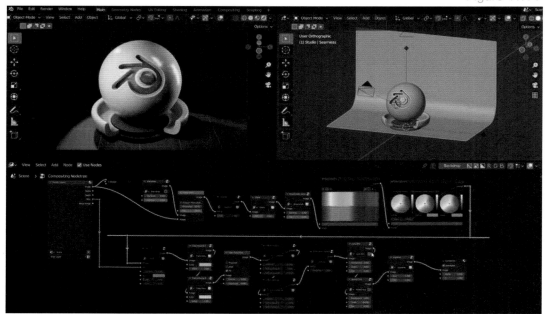

This example is a very basic Composite. As you will see by examining the **Node Add** menu on the Compositor Editor there are many Nodes to choose. To become conversant with which Node to select and how to arrange Nodes for different effects you will have to study examples and record which particular arrangement or part of an arrangement is applicable to your application.

11.2 Texture Nodes

The **Texture Node Editor** is accessed from the **Editor Type Selection Menu** (Figure 11.1). To introduce the Texture Node Editor the **Texture Paint** operation in the 3D Viewport Editor will be demonstrated.

In the default Screen arrangement, drag the upper edge of the Timeline Editor up and change the Timeline Editor to the **Texture Node Editor** Put the Editor in **Brush Mode** (Figure 11.15).

Have the 3D Viewport Editor in **Texture Paint Mode**.

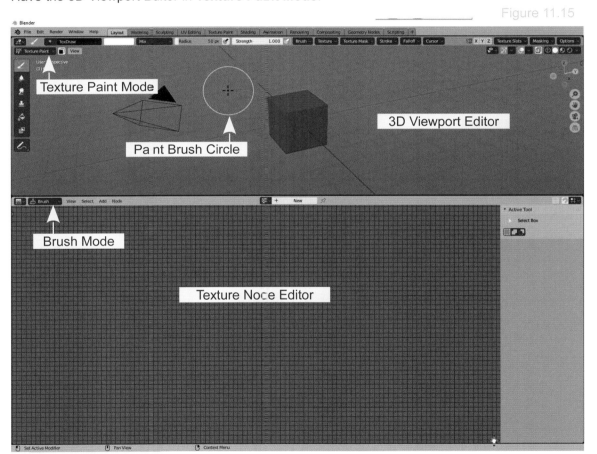

Figure 11.15

Note: In the default Screen Header you will see that there is a **Texture Paint** Workspace option. For the time being stay with the Workspace you have just created (Figure 11.15).

The default Cube Object in the 3D Viewport Editor is displaying purple. Remember; the default Cube has a Material pre-applied. If you enter a New Object it will not have a Material. The purple color indicates that the Cube does not have any Texture applied. As with Material Texture Painting (reference Chapter 10 – 10.7) a Texture has to be painted over an existing Texture.

Have the default Cube Object selected in Object Mode in the 3D Viewport Editor and apply a base Image Texture (Ref. Chapter 10 Texture Painting). **Note:** It is not necessary to have the 3D View Editor displaying Object Mode as long as the Cube is selected. With the base Texture applied the Cube in the 3D Viewport Editor in Texture Paint Mode displays with the Base Texture applied.

Base gray JPEG Image Texture **NOT** default gray Material.

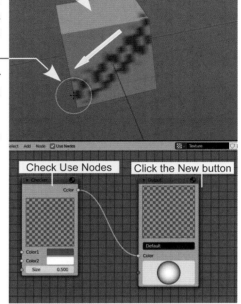

In the **Texture Node Editor** in **Brush Mode**, click the **New button** in the center of the Header (New becomes Texture) then check the **Use Nodes** button that displays in the Header. By default you immediately see a **Checker Texture Node** connected to an **Output Node**.

In the 3D Viewport Editor position the **Brush Circle** over the Cube, click, hold and drag the Mouse to paint a Checker Texture on the surface of the Cube.

Adjust values in the Checker Node to alter the Texture drawn in the 3D Viewport Editor.

Figure 11.16

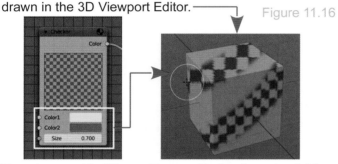

Check Use Nodes   Click the New button

Experiment with different Texture Nodes from the **Add menu** in the Texture Node Editor Header.

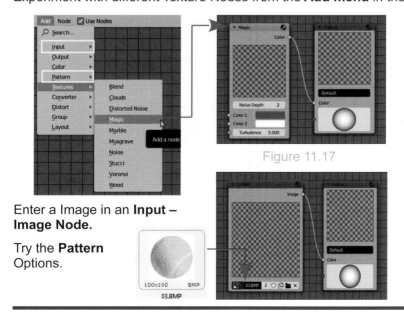

Magic Texture

Figure 11.17

Enter a Image in an **Input – Image Node.**

Try the **Pattern** Options.

Image Texture

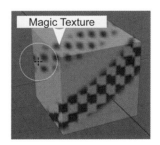

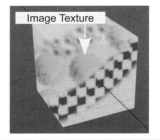

222

11.3 The Geometry Node Editor

The **Geometry Node Editor** is accessed from the Editor Type selection menu in an Editor Panel (Figure 11.1). At the time of writing Geometry Nodes are under development and will no doubt require a dedicated publication to describe the comprehensive scope of the subject. At this time the Geometry Node Editor will be introduced by demonstrating a simple example using **Blender Version 3.3.1** (**Note:** In earlier versions of Blender the Node selection and interface are different).

You may reconfigure the default Blender Screen arrangement creating a **Geometry Node Workspace** by dragging the upper edge of the Timeline Editor up and changing the Timeline Editor to the Geometry Node Editor. It is suggested, however, that you engage the **Geometry Node Workspace** from the Workspace selection button in the Screen Header. Activating the Workspace from the Header displays the **Spreadsheet Editor**, the **3D Viewport Editor**, the **Geometry Node Editor** with the **Outliner** and **Properties Editors**.

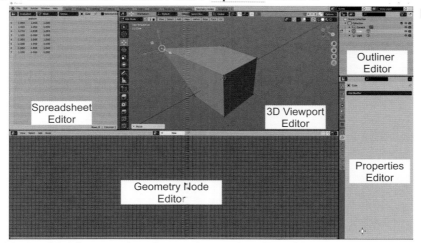

Figure 11.18

In Figure 11.19 the 3D Viewport has been changed to **Edit Mode** and a single Vertex on the Cube Object has been Translated. In Translating the Vertex you will observe that the relative location of the Vertex is recorded in the **Spreadsheet Editor**.

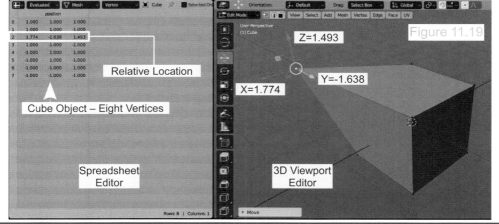

Figure 11.19

With an Object selected in the 3D Viewport Editor, clicking the **New Button** in the Geometry Node Editor Header places a **Group Input Node** connected to a **Group Output Node** in the Editor (Figure 11.20). You may consider these as the beginning and the end of the **Node Pipeline**. Other Nodes entered will be connected between the Input and Output.

The geometry **Node selection menu** is accessed by clicking the **Add Button** in the Header.

Figure 11.20

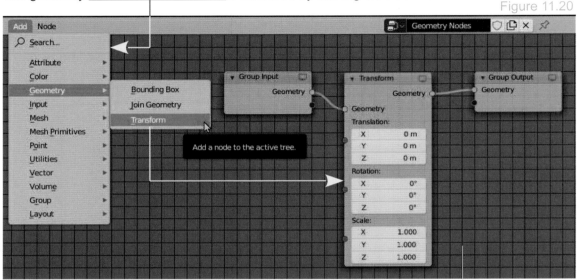

> **Note:** At the time of writing Geometry Nodes are a developing component of the Blender program. Additional Nodes are being created and new methods of deployment are being applied. You will, therefore, find that diagrams and instruction provided here for Blender 3.3.1 may not be applicable to other versions of Blender.

As an introduction a simple vertex displacement demonstration will be employed. In a new Blender Scene delete the default Cube Object in the 3D Viewport Editor and add a Plane. In Edit Mode subdivide the Plane. Number of Cuts: 20 (Figure 11.21).

Figure 11.21

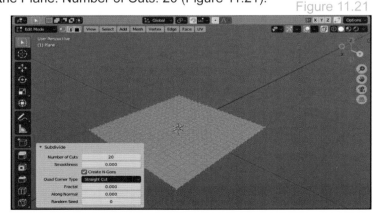

There are two methods for entering the **Input** and **Output** Nodes in the Geometry Node Editor (**GNE**). You either click The **New button** in the Header or in the Properties Editor, Modifier Properties you select **Geometry Node** in the Modifier Generate category. Clicking the New button in the Geometry Node Editor Header inserts a Geometry Modifier in the **Modifier Properties**.

Figure 11.22

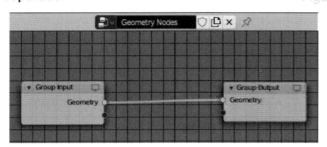

Note: The Nodes in the **GNE** are applicable to the Object selected in the 3D Viewport Editor.

In the **GNE** click the **Add button** in the Header or with the **Mouse Cursor** in the **GNE** press **Shift + A Key** for the **Add Node Menu**. Select a **Geometry – Transform Node**.

A **Transform Node** is entered in the GNE in **Grab Mode** as indicated by the change to the Mouse Cursor. Drag the Mouse and position the Transform Node between the Input and Output Nodes. The Transform Node will be automatically connected to the **Geometry Sockets.**

Figure 11.23

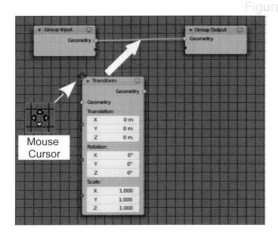
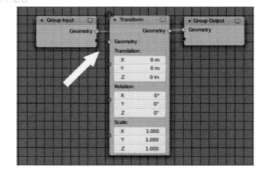

Note: The Nodes are applicable to the Plane Object which is selected in the 3D Viewport Editor. The Plane has been subdivided in Edit Mode, therefore, the **Spreadsheet Editor** displays the coordinates for each Vertex of the subdivided Plane.

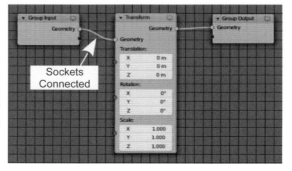

In the Transform Node increase the Translation Z Axis value to 0.9 m. By placing the 3D Viewport Editor in Edit Mode and having all Vertices selected (Press the A Key) you will see the Plane Translated 0.9 m above the Mid Plane Grid. The vertices remain in situ.

Figure 11.24

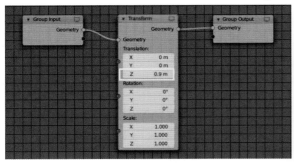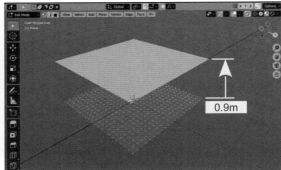

The foregoing has demonstrated how values set in a geometry Node in the GNE affect an Object in the 3D Viewport Editor. To develop the concept perform the following exercise.

In a new Blender Scene replace the default Cube with an **Icosphere**. The Icosphere is a little more interesting while having a relatively low number of Vertices. There are some fantastic demonstrations of Geometry Node applications on the internet but be aware that with high vertex count comes a demand on computer power.

Scale the **Icosphere** way down and park it to one side in the Viewport. Add a nice bright Material to the Icosphere.

Add a **Plane Object** to the Scene and in **Edit Mode**, Subdivide X 1 creating 9 Vertices and Scale up X 4.

Have the **Geometry Node Workspace** open and with the Plane selected click **New** in the GNE Header creating **Group Input** and **Output Nodes**.

In the GNE Header click the **Add button** and select a **Point Instance Node.**

An **Instance** of an Object is a Copy of the Object. In this particular case, **Point** refers to a Vertex. The Point Instance Node creates a copy of an Object and places a copy at the position of each Vertex of an Object entered in the Node.

Figure 11.25

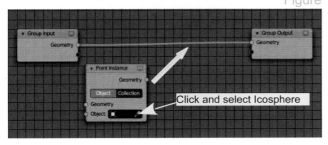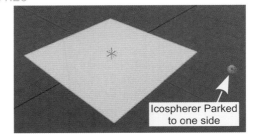

Position the Point – Instance Node between the Input and Output Nodes.

Figure 11.26

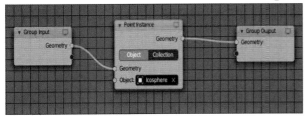

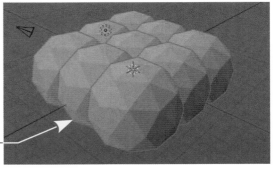

An Instance of the Icosphere is created at the position of each Vertex on the Plane.

Insert a **Point – Scale Node** entering X: 0.300, Y: 0.300, Z: 1.000   Figure 11.27

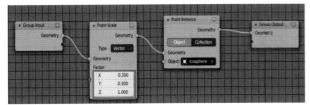

With the **Point – Scale Node** placed before the Instance Node in the Pipeline, the **Factor** values in the Node control the Scale of the Instance Objects.

Note: To see Material color of the Instance Objects have the 3D Viewport Editor in **Material Preview Mode**.   Figure 11.28

At this point the original Plane Object is not visible in the 3D Viewport Editor. To ensure that the Plane is selected make sure it is selected by clicking **Plane** in the **Outliner Editor**.

With the Plane selected, in the Properties Editor, Modifier Properties add a **Subdivision Surface Modifier**. The Modifier is placed in the Modifier Stack below the Geometry Node Modifier. With the default Modifier values the surface of the Instance Objects are refined but you will no longer see Material Color.   Figure 11.29

Move the Subdivision Surface Modifier to the top of the stack.

When the Subdivision Surface Modifier is at the top of the Stack the default Level and Render values increase the number of Instances in the 3D Viewport Editor. Make Level Viewport: 0.

Change the 3D Viewport Editor to Edit Mode, Wireframe Display Mode. Select a single Vertex. Press the G Key (grab), increase the Circle of Influence to encapsulate other Vertices then Translate the selected Vertex to deform the Instance display.

Figure 11.30

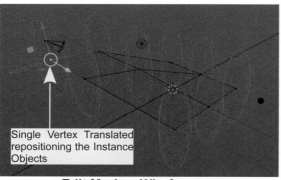

Single Vertex Translated repositioning the Instance Objects

Edit Mode – Wireframe

Object Mode

This simple procedure demonstrates that a display in the 3D Viewport Editor is controlled by Geometry Nodes in conjunction with Modifiers in the Properties Editor.

Add a Cube Object to the Scene. Apply the Cube as an Instance Object to the Icosphere. This is applying an Instance to an Instance.

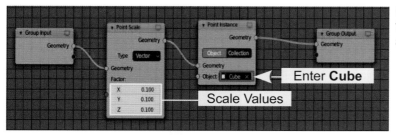

Enter **Cube**

Scale Values

Geometry Nodes applied to the **Icosphere** used previously as the Instance Object

Figure 11.31

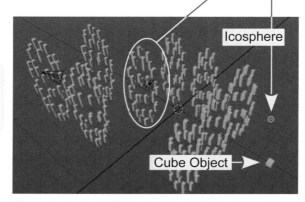

Icosphere

Remember: Geometry Nodes are under development. The intention in this section is merely to make you aware of their existence and introduce their capabilities.

Cube Object →

228

11.4 Transparency

To demonstrate Transparency a Plane Object will be turned into a pane of glass. Add a Plane to the default Blender Scene. Stand the Plane on edge and position in front of the default Cube. Give the Cube a Material with Nodes active (Figure 11.32).

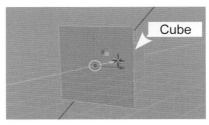
Figure 11.32

Change the default Point Lamp to an Area or Area Light.

Ensure that the **3D Viewport Editor** is in **Rendered Viewport Display Mode.**

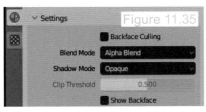
Figure 11.33

In the **Properties Editor, World Properties, Surface Tab** set the Background as shown in Figure 11.33 with the settings in Figure 11.35.

Select the Plane Object, add a Material, then in the Shader Editor create the Node arrangement in Figure 11.34. Pay attention to the settings.

Node categories in the Node Selection Menu Figure 11.34

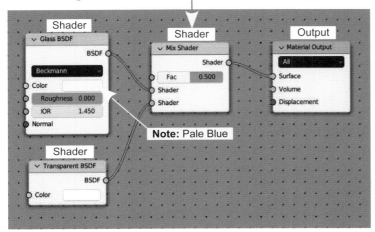

Figure 11.35

In the **Material Properties**, Settings Tab change the Blend Mode to **Alpha Blend** (Figure 11.35).

In the **Render Properties**, check **Screen Space Reflections** and **Refraction** (Figure 11.36).

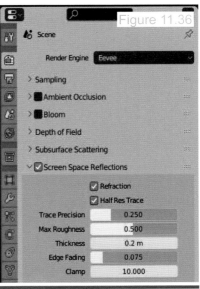
Figure 11.36

The 3D Viewport Editor will show the Plane as Transparent Glass with a slight blue tint (Figure 11.37 over).

Transparent Glass

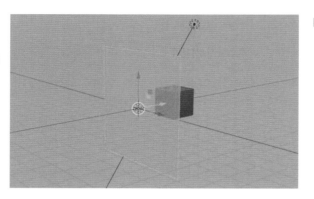

Figure 11.37

With the identical Node arrangement but with an HDRI image used in the World Background fantastic results can be generated (Ref Chapter 10).

Figure 11.38 shows the pane of glass standing on a desktop partially in front of the Cube on the windowsill. The desk and scenery are created by a HDRI Image as the background. With the view rotated the glass reflects light cast by the background HDRI image.

Figure 11.38

11.5 Volumetric Lighting

Volumetric Lighting is a technique used in 3D computer graphics to add lighting effects to a rendered scene. It allows the viewer to see beams of light shining through the environment. Seeing sunbeams streaming through an open window is an example of Volumetric Lighting, also known as God rays. Adding a mist effect is another example.

Volumetric Lighting requires that a cubic volume of space is defined in which the lighting effect will take place. Objects are encapsulated by the volume and, therefore, affected by the light. The camera in the Scene is positioned to capture the effect.

To demonstrate the effect, the Scene arrangement shown in Figure 11.39 will be used. The Camera and the Point Light are in the default positions.

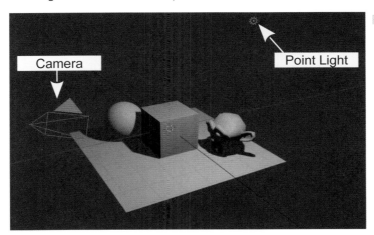

Figure 11.39

With the 3D Viewport Editor in Wireframe Viewport Shading Mode, add a new Cube Object and scale to encapsulate the original Objects (Figure 11.40). The scaled Cube defines the volume of space defining the lighting effect.

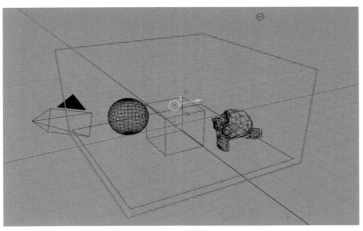

Figure 11.40

Select the **Point Light** then in the Properties Editor, Object Properties, change the Light to an **Area Light**.

Figure 11.41

Give the Area Light a bright pale Material Color.

Note: The Camera and the Area Light are located outside the defining volume.

Select the Defining Volume Cube.

Have the Shader Editor opened.

With the Cube selected, replace the Principled BSDF Node with a **Principled Volume Node** and connect the Volume to Volume sockets as shown in Figure 11.42.

Figure 11.42

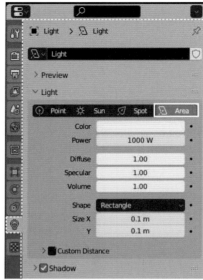

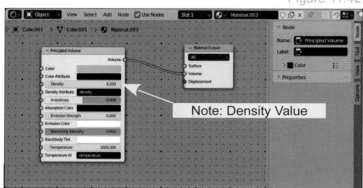

Note: Density Value

Note: In the **Properties Editor, Render Properties, Volumetrics Tab, Volumetric Lighting** is checked (active) by default (Figure 11.43).

Figure 11.43

Figure 11.44

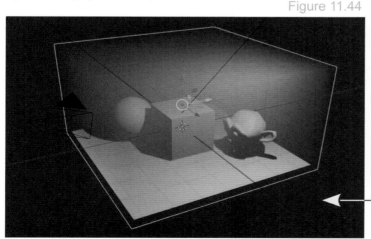

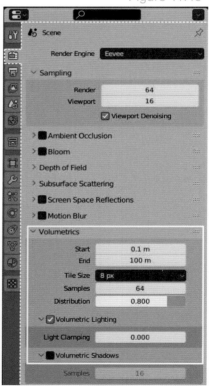

Volumetric Lighting in the 3D Viewport – **Rendered Viewport Display Mode**

In the **Principled Volume Node** set values as shown taking particular attention to the **density value**.

With the 3D Viewport Editor in **Rendered Viewport Shading Mode** you see the Light dispersed through the volume defined by the new Cube. Camera View shows the Objects in the Scene bathed in the pale misty light (Figures 11.45 and 11.46).

Figure 11.45

Figure 11.46

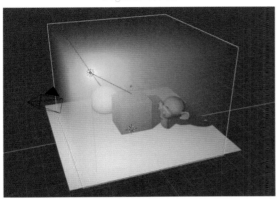
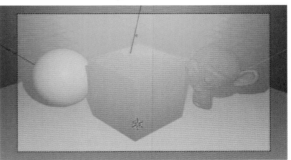

By having Objects inside a room with a window with the Light outside. The Camera inside the room and everything encapsulated by the Light Volume you see light streaming in.

Figure 11.47

Figure 11.48

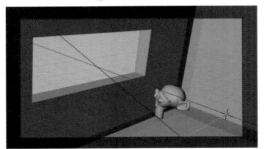

Camera View- Solid Viewport Shading

Camera View- Rendered Viewport Shading

12

Scene Lighting & Cameras

Introduction

The **Camera** or cameras in the 3D Viewport Editor capture the part of the Scene that is to be Rendered as a still Image File or Movie File. That part of the Scene is termed **Camera View**. **Scene Lighting** creates the mood of a Scene determining whether it depicts a bright happy sunny event or something that is dark and sinister. Lighting is, therefore, a significant factor in creating a still Image or creating atmosphere in a Video Clip or Movie.

It is important to understand that Scene Lighting only has effect when the 3D Viewport Editor is in **Rendered Viewport Shading Mode**.

The default Blender Scene is displayed in **Solid Viewport Shading Mode** with **Lighting: Studio** and **Color: Material** set in the Shading Options Panel. Solid Viewport Shading is primarily used for creating models and setting the physica aspects of the Scene. The single Light in the default Scene has no effect in the 3D Viewport Editor when **in Solid Viewport Shading Mode**. The default Scene is illuminated by an arbitrary light source which is perceived to be above the mid-plane grid to the left of the default Scene displayed in User Perspective View.

The **Light** in the default Scene has effect when the 3D Viewport Editor is in **Rendered Viewport Shading Mode** which represents what will be **Rendered from Camera View**.

12.1 Scene Lighting

The default Scene in the 3D Viewport Editor is illuminated by **Studio Lighting** when in **Solid Viewport Shading Mode** (Reference Chapter 13). This Shading Mode is independent of **Light Objects**, therefore, the default Point Light in the default Blender Scene has no affect. To understand Blender Lights, change the Viewport Shading to **Material Preview Viewport Shading** and activate **Scene Lights** and **Scene World** in the **Sub Options Panel**.

Viewport Shading Options are located in the **3D View Editor Header** at the RH side of the Editor.

Figure 12.1

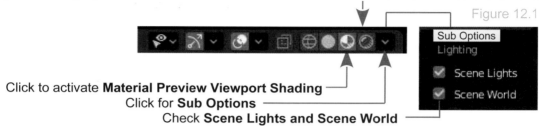

Click to activate **Material Preview Viewport Shading**
Click for **Sub Options**
Check **Scene Lights and Scene World**

12.2 Light Type

Properties Editor

The default Blender Scene contains a single **Point Light Object.**

Figure 12.2

With the **Light** selected in the 3D Viewport Editor, go to the **Properties Editor, Object Data Properties** to display the setting options (Figure 12.2). You may change the Light by selecting one of the types in the **Light Tab**.

The Properties Editor display will vary depending on the Light Type selected.

The color of light may be selected by clicking the color bar to display a color picker circle.

Object Data Properties

Note: The Sun Light is not affected by Color Change.

Lights in **Blender** are considered to be Objects and as such they may be Translated and Rotated like other Object. Each Light Type has properties which may be adjusted in the Properties Editor when the Light is selected in the 3D Viewport Editor.

The diagrammatic representation of the Light Type changes in the 3D Viewport Editor depending on the Type selected (Figure 12.3).

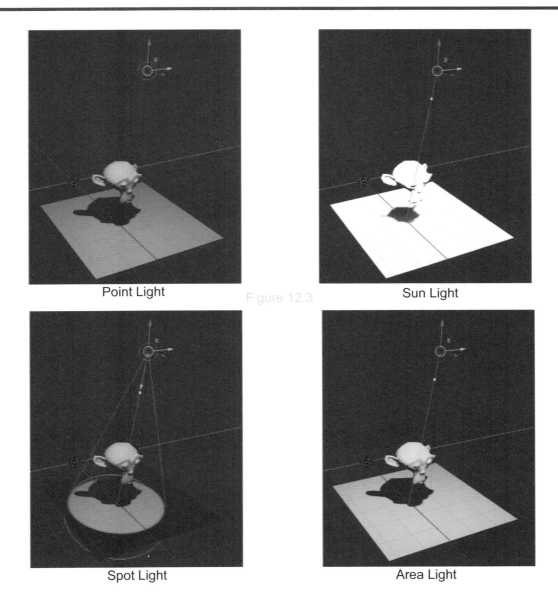

Point Light

Figure 12.3

Sun Light

Spot Light

Area Light

Remember: The 3D Viewport is in **Material Preview, Viewport Shading Mode** with Scene Lights and Scene World checked in the Options. In Figure 12.3 the different Light Types illuminate the Scene. In each example the Light Color, set in the Properties Editor, Object Data Properties, with the Light Object in the 3D Viewport Editor selected, casts the color (green) on to the Monkey and the Plane. The Monkey and the Plane do not have a Material (color) applied and, therefore, would display with the defau t gray without the Light Color being cast by the Light. In conjunction with the illumination from the Lights the World Surface Background settings in the Properties Editor, World Properties are influencing the way in which the Scene displays (Figure 12.4).

Properties Editor

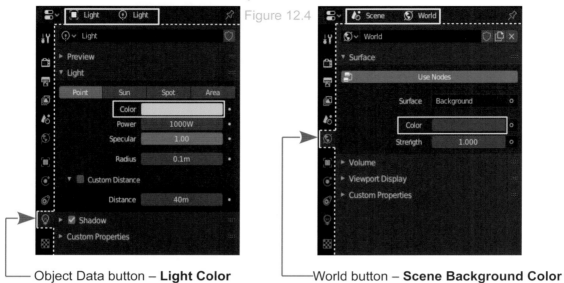

Figure 12.4

Object Data button – **Light Color**

World button – **Scene Background Color**

Adding Lights

To see the effect of the different Light Types and settings create a Scene as shown in Figure 12.5.

Scene Arrangement

Figure 12.5

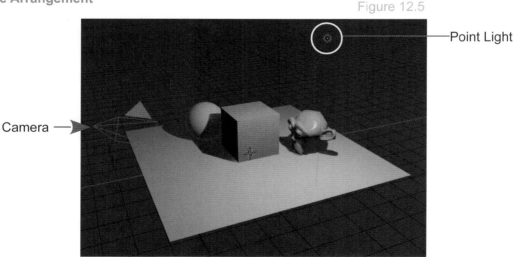

Point Light

Camera

In the Scene a Plane has been added and Scaled up five times. The Plane has been Translated (Moved) up, just above the Midplane Grid. A UV Sphere and a Monkey have been added and positioned each side of the default Cube. The Cube, UV Sphere and Monkey have been Translated up to sit just above the Plane.

Materials

Pale Magenta Material Color has been added to the Cube and Monkey with the Node System active. Material has NOT been added to the UV Sphere or the Plane.

The Camera and the default Point Light are in their default positions. The 3D Viewport Editor is in Material Preview, Viewport Shading Mode with Scene lights and Scene World checked in the Sub Options.

Lighting Effects

The default Point Light has a pale green color applied.

Make note of the different effect when you change the Light Type in the Properties Editor, Object Data Properties, Light tab (with the Lamp selected).

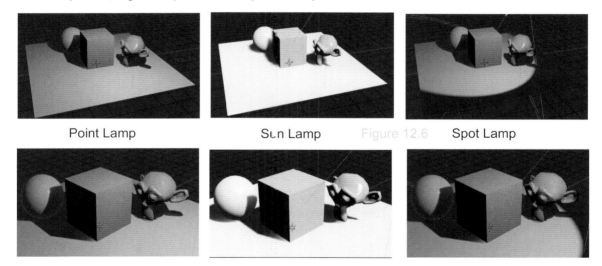

Point Lamp　　　　　　　Sun Lamp　　　Figure 12.6　　Spot Lamp

The upper row of images show part of the 3D Viewport Editor. The lower row shows Camera View. Although a Material Color has NOT been applied to the UV Sphere or the Plane they display with the pale green color cast by the Light. The Cube and Monkey show the Pale Magenta Material although it is tempered by the Light color. **Note:** Your display will vary depending on the colors that you have applied.

By leaving the default Point Light in position, then adding an additional Spot Light and directing it towards the left hand face of the Cube you remove the shadow on the Cube and the Monkey (Figure 12.7).

To add additional Lights to the Scene, position the cursor in the 3D Viewport Editor, press **Shift + A Key** and select **Light** from the menu that displays. You can choose **Point, Sun, Spot or Area**.

Figure 12.7

Top Orthographic View

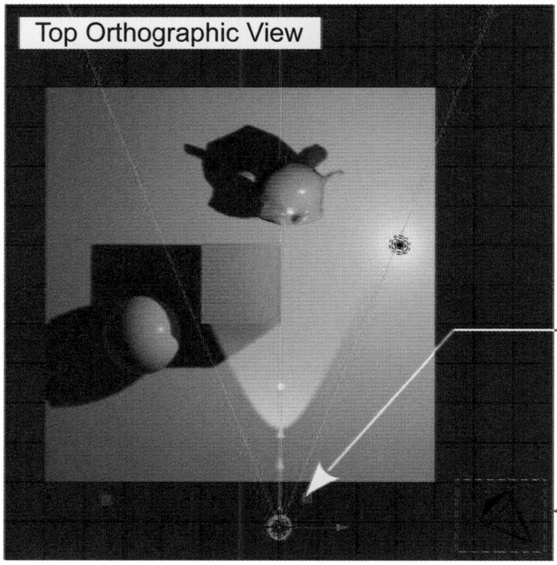

Camera View

Additional Spot Light pointing towards the Cube and the Monkey.

The Camera in its default position.

12.3 Cameras

By default the Scene has one **Camera** which is positioned to capture an image of the Cube Object. What the Camera sees and what is captured as an image is called **Camera View**. You can see Camera View in the 3D Viewport Editor by pressing **Num Pad O** on the Keyboard. To return to User Perspective View, press Num Pad 5 (User Orthographic View) then Num Pad 5 again for User Perspective View. **You have to rotate the View to reinstate the default Scene or press Num Pad 6**.

In a complex Scene you may wish to add more Cameras to capture shots from different angles. You add Cameras by pressing **Shift + A key** and selecting **Camera** from the menu or click Add in the Header and select Camera. The new Camera will be located where the 3D Viewport Cursor is positioned. If you add a Camera in the default Scene with the 3D Viewport Cursor at the center of the Scene it will coincide with the default Cube Object. Click the Move Tool in the Tool Panel and move the Camera to one side. You have to rotate the new Camera to capture the part of the Scene you require.

Depending on the Scene arrangement the Cameras may or may not be visible in the 3D Viewport. Camera View depends on which Camera is selected. If the Camera is visible LMB click to select. If it is not visible you can select it in the Outliner Editor by clicking LMB on the name (See Notes following). The original Camera is named **Camera** the new Camera is named **Camera.001**. You may rename these to something meaningful if you wish.

Note: If you select **Camera** (the original Camera) and press Num Pad 0 you will get a Camera View taken by the original Camera. To get Camera View from **Camera.001,** have Camera.001 selected then press **Ctrl + Num Pad 0**. Similarly if you have been using Camera.001 for Camera View and you select the original Camera, press **Ctrl + Num Pad 0** you get a Camera View from the original Camera.

Note: To perform Camera selection; Select Cameras in the 3D Viewport Editor or in the Outliner Editor and press Ctrl + Num Pad 0.

Outliner Editor

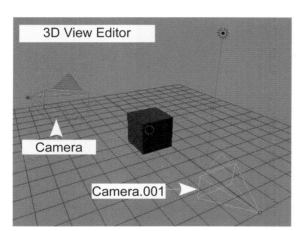

Select a Camera press Ctrl + Num Pad 0 For Camera View.

Figure 12.8

Figure 12.9

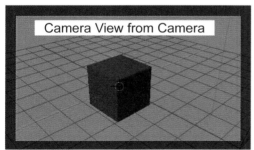

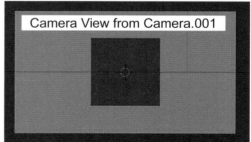

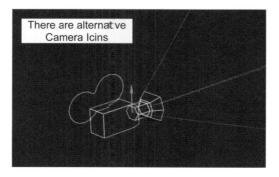

12.4 Camera Settings

Figure 12.10

Camera settings are found in the **Properties Editor, Object Data Properties** for the selected Camera (Figure 11.10).

By default the Lens Tab is displayed with six remaining Tabs closed.

The Lens Tab: By default is set to Type: **Perspective** which captures a Perspective View of the Scene as seen in the 3D Viewport Editor. Alternative Types are **Orthographic** and **Panoramic**.

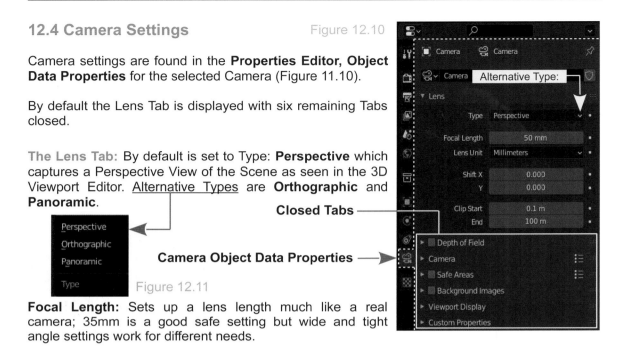

Closed Tabs

Camera Object Data Properties

Figure 12.11

Focal Length: Sets up a lens length much like a real camera; 35mm is a good safe setting but wide and tight angle settings work for different needs.

Shift: Pushes the camera's view in a direction, without changing perspective.　Figure 12.12

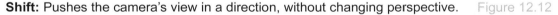

| Shift X | 0.200 | | Shift X | 0.000 | | Shift X | -0.200 |
| Y | 0.010 | | Y | 0.000 | | Y | -0.100 |

Clip Start / Clip End: How close an object can be to the camera and still be seen (Figure 12.13).
In very large Scenes, Clip End needs to be set higher or objects disappear from view.

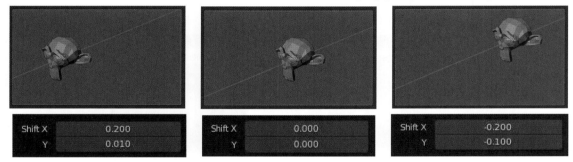

Clip End

Figure 12.13

Clip Start

To view Limits, check **Limits** in the Viewport Display Tab (Figure 17.19)

Depth of Field Tab: (Figure 12.14)

Figure 12.14

Used with **Nodes** to blur foreground and background objects (Nodes are discussed in Chapter 9).

Aperture Tab: (Figure 12.14)

Mimics f-stop settings on a real camera which control the amount of light entering the camera.

Camera Tab: (Figure 12.15)

Figure 12.15

Camera Pre-sets: Allows matching the virtual Camera in the Blender Scene with a real camera used to record video. This produces a more realistic effect when Camera Tracking (see Camera Tracking 12.6).

Safe Area Tab: (Figure 12.16)

Figure 12.16

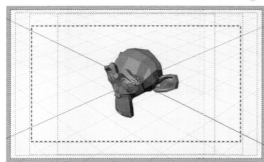

Settings define areas in Camera View for inserting Captions and Titles.

Background Image Tab (Figure 12.17)

Figure 12.17

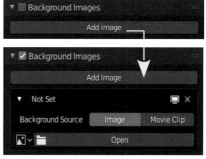

Click **Add Image** – Click **Open** Navigate to a saved image.

Inserts a reference image or movie clip in the Camera View in the 3D Viewport Editor.
The image does not render

Viewport Display Tab (Figure 12.18)

Figure 12.18

Viewport Display options determine what you see in the 3D Viewport Editor.

Size: How big to draw the Camera on the Screen; you can also control the size with scale.

Limits: Draws a line in the scene to help you visualise the Camera's range (Figure 12.19). The Limit is set by the **Clip Start** and **Clip End** values in the **Lens Tab.**

Mist: Gives you a visual display of how far the Camera sees if you are adding a mist effect.

Figure 12.19

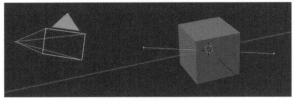

Not to be confused with the Limits, Clip Start and End for the Camera.

To create a Mist Effect See: Volumetrics 12.10

Sensor: Shows the sensor size (Film Gate) in Camera View (Figure 12.20).

Name: Displays the name of the active Camera in Camera View (Num Pad 0) (Figure 12.20).

Figure 12.20

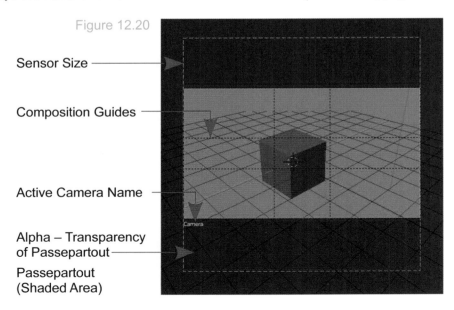

Sensor Size

Composition Guides

Active Camera Name

Alpha – Transparency of Passepartout

Passepartout (Shaded Area)

12.5 Camera Switching

In **Cameras 12.3** it was shown that you may have more than one Camera in a Scene and you can switch between Cameras by selecting one, then pressing **Ctrl + Num pad 0**. This makes the selected Camera active and opens Camera View showing what is seen by that Camera. Manual selection is fine for rendering single images of an object from different viewing perspectives but you may want to Animate the switching such that when the animation plays you switch between Cameras.

Animation is discussed in Chapter 15 but a prelude in the following demonstration will be beneficial.

Set up a Scene similar to that shown in Figure 12.21, with three **Cameras** pointed at **Suzanne** (Monkey) from different locations. You can use the default Camera and add two others. You will have to Rotate and point each Camera at Suzanne and check Camera View for each. **Remember:** With more than one Camera in a Scene you press **Ctrl + Num Pad 0** for Camera View with a camera selected.

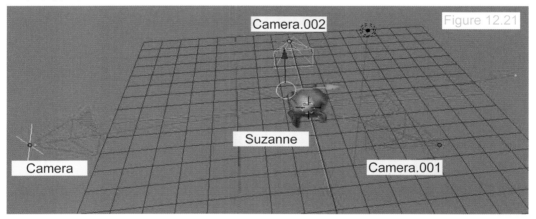

In the 3D Viewport Editor select the default Camera named **Camera**. In the **Timeline Editor** with the vertical blue cursor line at Frame 1 and the **Mouse cursor in the Timeline Editor** press the **M Key** to place a **Marker** at Frame 1. **Note:** You can only place the marker when the **Mouse Cursor** is positioned in the Timeline (Figure 12.22).

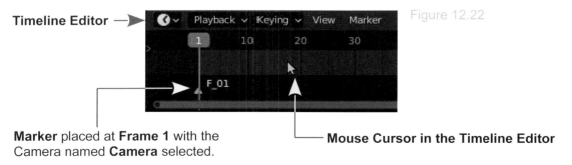

Deselect **Camera** and select **Camera.001**.

With Camera.001 selected, move the Timeline Cursor (blue line) to Frame 40. Press the M Key to insert a Marker. Repeat for Camera.002 at Frame 70. Note: It is not necessary to have Camera View for each Camera displayed when placing Markers.

At this point nothing happens in the 3D Viewport Editor when the Animation is played in the Timeline. **Each Camera has to be Bound to a Marker**.

Select **Camera** in the 3D Viewport Editor, click on **Marker F_01** in the Timeline Editor (highlights white), click **Marker** in the Timeline Header and select **Bind Camera to Marker** (alternatively Press Ctrl + B Key). The Camera is Bound and the Marker in the Timeline Editor shows as **Camera** (Figure 12.23).

Figure 12.23

Camera Bound

Click to select Marker F_40

Deselect Camera, select Camera.001, move the Timeline Cursor to Frame 40 (the position of Marker F_40), Press Ctrl+B Key to Bind Camera.001 to the Marker. Repeat for Camera.002.

Figure 12.24

When the Animation is played in the Timeline Editor, Camera View changes in the 3D Viewport Editor as the Timeline Cursor passes the Frame where a Marker is set.

Figure 12.25

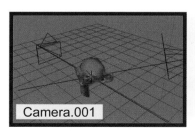
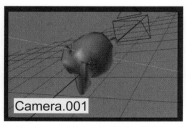
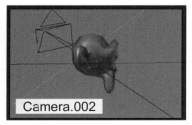

Camera View F1 to F40   Camera View F40 to F70   Camera View F80 to F250

The Animation plays from Frame 1 to Frame 250 then repeats.

12.6 Camera Tracking

Camera Tracking is a technique that imitates the real Camera motion which occurs when recording a video. This motion is applied to a 3D Camera in a Blender Scene providing a realistic effect when a 3D model is superimposed over a video background (Figure 17.26). Without this effect the Blender 3D Camera would track to a stable imaginary point or to a predetermined curve track in the Scene. This would be fine for the superimposed 3D Object but the actual video used as a background would move differently and produce an unrealistic effect. The essence of the technique is to plot the movement of multiple points in the video Scene and feed that information to the motion of the Blender 3D Camera.

At this point the technique is mentioned to make you aware of its existence and the following video tutorial is suggested: https:www.youtube.com/watch?v=O3fGc_QM3yI//w

Figure 12.26

17.7 Basic Lighting Arrangement

Scene Lighting (12.1) at the beginning of the chapter demonstrated how the illumination from Lights in the Scene influences what is captured by the Camera and ultimately Rendered.

To illuminate a Scene will usually require multiple Lights to create a mood by highlighting content and controlling shadows. To demonstrate very basic Scene Lighting the Scene arrangement created in 12.2 – Figure 12.5 will be used with the application of Material color to the Objects (Chapter 1 – 1.12 Blender Node System disabled).

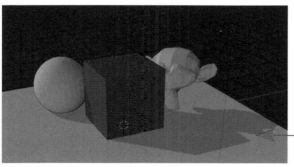

Figure 12.27

Solid Viewport Shading

Note: Direction of shadows due to the Studio Lighting

You may create the Scene with the 3D Viewport Editor in **Solid Viewport Shading Mode** (Chapter 13). The default settings in the Sub Options Panel may be left as they are, with the one exception, **check Shadows**. **Remember:** The Point Light has no effect when in Solid Viewport Shading Mode.

Note: In **Solid Viewport Shading Mode, Sub Options**, the default color setting is: **Color - Material,** meaning the Material (color) applied to the Objects will be displayed.

Add a basic Material (color) to all Objects (Chapter 9).

Figures 12.27 – 12.28 are screen captures of part of the view in the 3D Viewport Editor approximating Camera View (what the Camera sees).

With the Scene created, change to **Material Preview, Viewport Shading Mode** (Chapter 13) and check **Scene Lights** and **Scene World** in the Sub Options panel. You will immediately see a difference in the view since the effect of the single default Point Lamp is displayed.

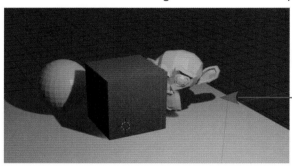

Colors brightness and the direction of shadows changed due to the single Point Light in the Scene

Figure 12.28

Make note that the Light emitted by the Point Light, by default, is white (RGB 1.000).

In the **Outliner Editor** click on **Light** to select the Point Light in Collection. Selecting in the Outliner Editor selects the Light in the 3D Viewport Editor.

In the **Properties Editor, Object Data Properties** the settings will be applicable to the Point Light in the 3D Viewport Editor (the selected Object). Change the Light setting Point to **Area**. Again you see a change to the lighting in the 3D Viewport Editor demonstrating the effect of Light settings (Figure 12.29).

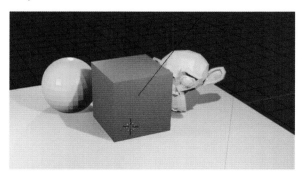

Figure 12.29

Note: What you see on your computer screen will probably differ to the Figures being shown due to differences in arrangement and settings. The objective here is to demonstrate technique.

In the 3D Viewport Editor add two more Point Lights and position as shown in Figure 12.30.

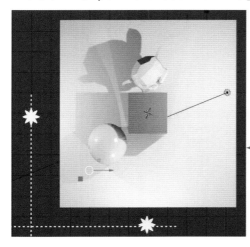

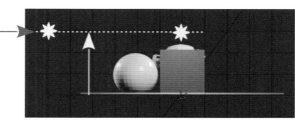

Figure 12.30   Front Orthographic View

Top Orthographic View with Sun Icons showing the approximate location of the additional (two) Lights.

With the 3D Viewport Editor in **User Perspective View** go to the **Outliner Editor** and toggle hide and display of the new Lights to see the different Lighting effects.

Note: The new Lights listed in the Outliner Editor are named **Point** and **Point.001**   Figure 12.31

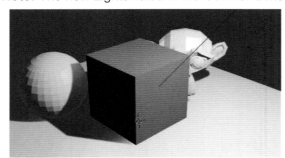

Area Light only, Point and Point.001 Hidden (off)   Area Light + Two Point Lights

12.8 Background Scene Lighting

Beside the effect of Lights in the Scene you should be aware that the Scene Background plays a part in determining how Materials display. As in the real world the ambient light surrounding Objects determines how they are seen. In Blender, the World Background light has a similar effect.

Background Color Lighting

To demonstrate this phenomena start a new Blender File and replace the Cube Object in the default Scene with a UV Sphere and set the Sphere's surface to Shade Smooth.

Have the 3D Viewport Editor in **Rendered Viewport Shading Mode** (Chapter 13). With the UV Sphere selected, In the Properties Editor, Material Properties, click **New** to add a Material. Since this is a new Object in the Scene, **Use Nodes** will be activated.

Use Nodes (highlighted blue), means that the **Blender Node System** for applying Materials is being used. An explanation describing what Nodes are and how to use them is given in Chapter 11.

For the moment, with **Nodes active**, click on the **Base Color** bar to display the Color Picker Circle and give the UV Sphere a yellow color by setting the RGB color values (R: 0.753, G: 0.531, B: 0.002). Have the intensity slider cranked all the way to the top (very bright).

Remaining in the Properties Editor, click on the **World Properties button. In the Surface Tab**, **Use Nodes** is active. By default **Surface** is set as **Background**. Click on the Color bar (the default color is gray) and change to a blue color (R: 0.011, G: 0.789, B: 0.900). Move the Intensity Slider up to about half way.

Result: Blue Background causing the Yellow Sphere to appear Green especially in the shadow.

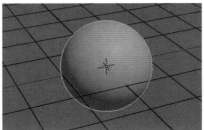

Figure 12.32

Green Shadow

12.9 Images as a Background

HDRI Maps

Colored Scene backgrounds are suitable in many cases but an image used as a background can significantly add atmosphere. Special images called **HDRI Maps** are particularly spectacular in giving a three dimensional effect when the Scene is rotated. This type of image adds lighting to the Scene thus affecting how Objects are seen.

One source of HDRI images is:　　　　https://hdrihaven.com

Figure 12.33

To demonstrate the use of HDRIs use the Scene arrangement in Figure 12.26. Deselect all the Objects in the Scene and have an **HDRI image** saved on your computer.

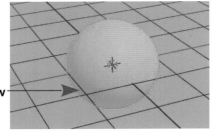

In the **Properties Editor, World Properties** click on **Use Nodes**. In the Surface tab you will see that Surface is set to **Background**.

World Properties→

Click on the dot at the end of the **Color Bar** (Figure 12.33) and select **Environmental Texture** (background displays purple). In the menu that displays (Figure 12.34). Click on **Open** and navigate to your HDRI file in the Viewer.

Figure 12.34

Select Environment Texture

Figure 12.35

Click Open

HDRI Images

Have the 3D Viewport Editor with **Material Preview Viewport Shading** and with **Scene World checked** in the Shading options. The HDRI image will display as the Background to your Scene.

Figure 12.36

Image courtyard_night_4K.hdr

At this point you manipulate the view in the 3D Viewport Editor and move the Objects to position in the Scene as shown in Figure 12.37.

In Figure 12.37 the Objects have been positioned to appear as if they are sitting on the floor just outside the open door. All the Lights in the Scene have been deleted showing that the Light from the image affects the Objects.

Figure 12.37

Images for Tracing and as Scene Backgrounds

HDRI Images will provide Scene Lighting but it may be that, simply placing an Image in the Scene to act as backdrop will do the job. Images may also be used as a template for Modeling.

Images for Tracing

To use an Image as a template for creating models you add an image file into the 3D Viewport Editor as a **Reference Image**. Be aware that in using this method the Image does **NOT Render**. Reference images are typically used for modeling. For example a front and side view of a human head (mugshot). To us an image in this way have the 3D Viewport in Front or Right Orthographic View. To enter an Image click **Add** in the Header and select, **Image** then **Reference** (Figure 12.38).

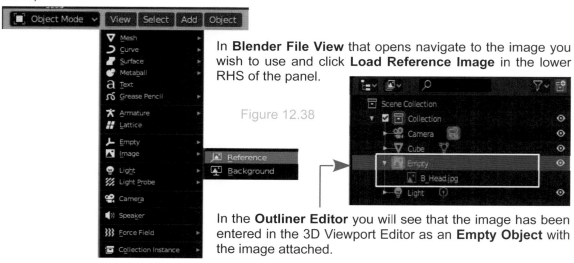

In **Blender File View** that opens navigate to the image you wish to use and click **Load Reference Image** in the lower RHS of the panel.

Figure 12.38

In the **Outliner Editor** you will see that the image has been entered in the 3D Viewport Editor as an **Empty Object** with the image attached.

On mouse over in the 3D Viewport Editor and the Empty (image) may be Translated, Rotated and Scaled but remember an Empty Object does **NOT** Render even though it displays in Rendered Viewport Shading Mode. As such, the image is suitable as a tracing template only.

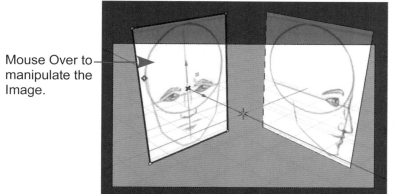

Figure 12.39

Mouse Over to manipulate the Image.

Reference Images positioned for Modeling. Camera View.

Image as a Scene Background

To introduce an image which Renders as a background to the Scene, be in Camera View and repeat the previous selection procedure, this time, selecting **Background**. Find your Background Image in Blender File View and click **Load Background Image**.

Figure 12.40

Select the Image and Scale up to fill Camera View.

Rotating the Viewport shows the Image positioned behind the default Cube (Figure 12.40).

Note: Entering the Image as Background allows you to see the Image in all Viewport Shading Modes **BUT it does NOT Render.**

To Render an Image as a background you have to Add the Image as a Plane and to do this you have to activate the **Import-Export Images as Planes** Add-on in the Preferences Editor. With the Add-on activated you will have the option to **Add Images as Planes** from the Add Menu.

Entering the Image in Camera View shows the Image (Plane) aligned along the Y Axis of the Scene at a reduced Scale (Figure 12.42). The Image (Plane) is located at the center of the Scene. You are required to Scale and Rotate the Image to fit the Camera View and move the Image back in the Scene behind any Objects. When the Image is entered as a Plane it is , in fact,

Properties Values ➞

an Object. Positioning the Image in the Scene, to be captured in Camera View, and relative to Scene Lighting has to be considered. You can have shadows being cast on the Image.

Figure 12.41

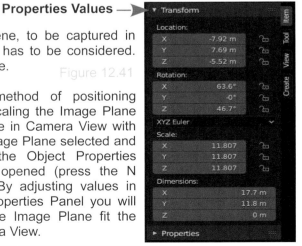

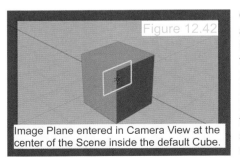

Image Plane entered in Camera View at the center of the Scene inside the default Cube.

One method of positioning and Scaling the Image Plane is to be in Camera View with the Image Plane selected and have the Object Properties Panel opened (press the N Key). By adjusting values in the Properties Panel you will see the Image Plane fit the Camera View.

Figure 12.43

Camera View (Rendered Viewport Shading) with Properties Values adjusted.

Figure 12.44

Viewport Rotated showing the Image Plane located behind the default Cube.

Figure 12.45

Rendered View

12.10 Volumetric Lighting

Using HDRI Maps as a background can give you a quick way to illuminate a Scene and combine a background but you are limited to what you can source in an image. You may want something completely unique and maybe not as complicated. Volumetric Lighting may be the answer.

Volumetric Lighting uses the light provided by Blenders Lights and scatters or diffuses the light in the Scene. A simple demonstration is to place a light source in a Scene behind an Object such that the diffuse light shines through the Object, casting shadows towards the Camera.

To produce a Volumetric Lighting effect as shown in Figure 12.46 Blender's Node System is used. How to use Nodes is explained in Chapter 9. Volumetric Lighting is explained in Chapter 12.

With the Eevee Render System Volumetric Lighting is also used to create a Mist or Fog effect.

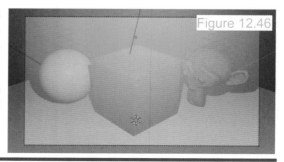

Figure 12.46

13

Viewport Shading

Viewport Shading

Definitions: **Viewport:** The View in an Editor. **Shading:** How the View in an Editor is displayed.

Blender provides a variety of shading (coloring) options which allow a Scene to be previewed during construction. Previewing, in turn, allows editing to be performed as the Scene is developed.

As Scenes are created, with Objects being added and Materials (colors) applied and lighting effects and textures introduced, it can be difficult to isolate a particular Object or even a component of an Object. By shading the **Viewport**, making the Objects display in a simplified way, allows a selection to be Edited. You may also preview how a Scene will display before adding too much detail or finally Rendering.

Rendered Viewport Shading

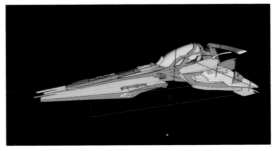

Simplified Viewport Shading

13.1 Viewport Shading Options

Options for **Viewport Shading** (How the 3D Viewport Editor displays) are found in the upper RH corner of the 3D Viewport Editor Header (Figure 13.1). Click LMB on one of the buttons to activate an option.

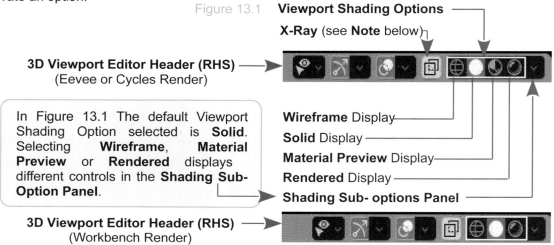

Figure 13.1 **Viewport Shading Options**

X-Ray (see **Note** below)

3D Viewport Editor Header (RHS) ➤
(Eevee or Cycles Render)

In Figure 13.1 The default Viewport Shading Option selected is **Solid**. Selecting **Wireframe**, **Material Preview** or **Rendered** displays different controls in the **Shading Sub-Option Panel**.

Wireframe Display
Solid Display
Material Preview Display
Rendered Display
Shading Sub- options Panel

3D Viewport Editor Header (RHS) ➤
(Workbench Render)

Note: Figure 13.1 shows the controls when either the **Eevee** or **Cycles** Render Engine is engaged (see Chapter 14). There is one less Shading Option with **Workbench** Render active

> **Note:** The controls in the **Shading Sub-option Panel** are applicable to the Viewport Shading Option that is selected in the 3D Viewport Editor Header.

13.2 Wireframe Viewport Shading

Wireframe Shading allow you to see Objects in the 3D Viewport Editor as a **Mesh** which is useful when one Object overlaps or hides another. In Figure 13.2 a Monkey Object is positioned inside a UV Sphere. In Solid Viewport Shading Mode you see the outline of the Monkey **when the Monkey is selected**. In **Wireframe Viewport Shading Mode** you see both Objects as a Mesh with the selected Object displayed orange (Figure 13.2)

Monkey Outline Figure 13.2

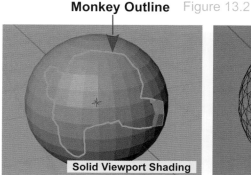

Solid Viewport Shading

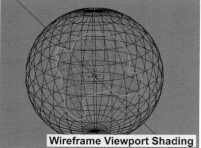

Wireframe Viewport Shading

Note: When Wireframe Display Mode is activated, **X-Ray** is also activated allowing you to see details of the Mesh behind the front surface. You may turn X-Ray off if you wish.

Wireframe Colors: The Wireframe Mesh may be set to display in different colors for each Object. This is helpful when arranging Objects in groups. The Mesh display colors are independent of the Material color applied to an Object.

A detailed study of Object Materials (colors) is explained in Chapter 9. In Chapter 1 coloring Objects was demonstrated by disabling the Blender Node System. This allowed Objects to be colored and the color viewed in Solid Viewport Shading Mode in the 3D Viewport Editor.

At this point, the UV Sphere and the Monkey Objects have been entered in the Scene but they **have not** had a Material applied. They display gray in Solid Viewport Shading Mode in the 3D Viewport Editor since they are using Blender's default Material (**a Material HAS NOT been applied**). If you select each Object in turn and look at the **Properties Editor, Material Properties** you see only the **New button**.

To have the Wireframe Mesh display in a color, obviously, be in **Wireframe Display Mode**. As an example, select the Monkey by clicking on Suzanne in the **Outliner Editor**. By default Suzanne's Mesh displays orange (Figure 13.3). In the **Properties Editor, Object Properties (NOT: Object Data Properties), Viewport Display Tab**, click on the Color bar and select a color in the Color Picker Circle.

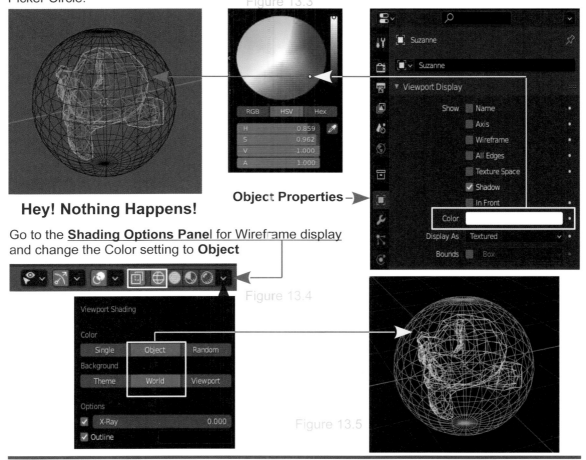

Hey! Nothing Happens!

Object Properties→

Go to the **Shading Options Panel** for Wireframe display and change the Color setting to **Object**

Figure 13.3

Figure 13.4

Figure 13.5

If you also change **Background** from **Theme** to **World.** The 3D Viewport background provides a better contrast.

Changing the Background from Theme to World means you are changing the 3D Viewport Editor background color from the default Blender Theme set in the Preferences Editor (see Chapter 2 – 2.17) to the World, Surface Color, set in the Properties Editor, World Properties, Surface Tab.

A practical application of using Wireframe Mode is to position Objects inside a Cube creating an interior Scene.

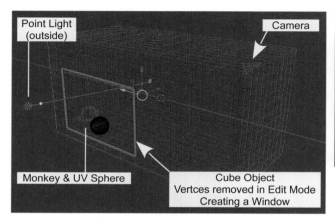

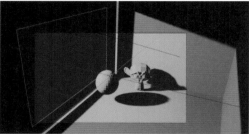

Figure 13.6   **Camera View**

Green light from Point Light

13.3 Solid Viewport Shading   Sub Options Panel ➤

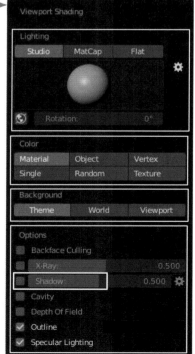

Figure 13.7

Solid Viewport Shading is the default Shading Option for the 3D Viewport Editor when Blender Opens and is the basic Viewport display for modelling.

The **Sub Options** for **Solid Viewport Shading** are categorised into four sections; **Lighting**, **Color**, **Background** and **Options** (sub, sub options).

Lighting: A Scene is illuminated by placing Lights at strategic positions or having Emitter Objects (Objects that emit light) located thorough the Scene (Chapter 12). In the course of construction complicated Scene Lighting can be a hindrance, therefore, a simplified Viewport display is preferable.

Solid Viewport Shading provides three lighting methods; **Studio, MatCap** and **Flat**. These lighting methods are all independent of any Lamps placed in the 3D Viewport Editor. While in Solid Viewport Shading Mode Lights in the 3D Viewport Editor have no effect. **Studio Lighting** is the default method.

Studio Lighting is an arbitrary lighting arrangement which is independent of the Lights in the Scene. When the Viewport is rotated mesh faces are shaded for visualisation but the shading is not influenced by light sources such as the Lights in the Scene. Rendering the Scene produces a different shading based on the lighting generated by the Lights.

To examine and understand the relationship of Object illumination, shadows can be used. To see the effect of shadows there has to be something on which the shadows will be cast. In the default Scene add a Plane Object. The Plane is positioned on the Mid Plane Grid and scaled up. Position the Cube Object just above the Plane (Figure 13.8). With Solid Viewport Shading active, in the **Sub Options Panel**, **Options** (at the bottom of the panel) **check (tick) Shadow**.

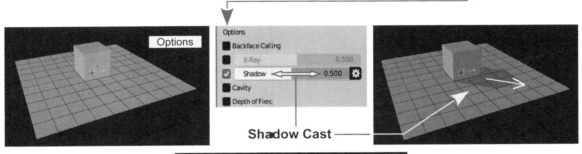

Shadow Cast

Figure 13.8

With the Scene rotated the shadow is cast relative to the Cube demonstrating that the light source is fixed relative to the Scene and is not relative to the Point Light.

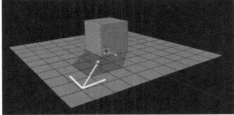

In the Figure 13.8 the Cube and the Plane do NOT have Material (color) applied. To continue with the demonstration add color (Reference Chapter 9). Figure 13.9 shows **Studio Lighting** with color added

By clicking on the sphere below **Studio**, MatCap Lighting Tones display. Clicking either of these alters the lighting tone in the 3D Viewport Editor.   **Click the sphere**

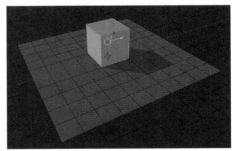

Figure 13.9

Lighting Tones

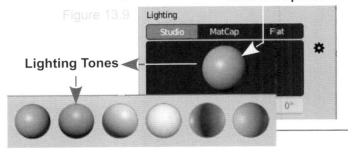

Click LMB on the sphere to preview **Lighting Tones**.

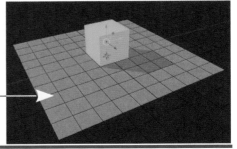

Matcap Lighting stands for **Material Capture** – it is a complete material including lighting and reflections. A Matcap is added for quick feedback, to see how an Object's shape is changing under different lighting conditions. This is a preview only, not a permanent lighting set-up.

Figure 13.10

With **MatCap** selected, clicking on the Sphere in the Sub Options Panel displays a selection of MatCap shading options which when pressed show you how Objects will display under different shading effects.

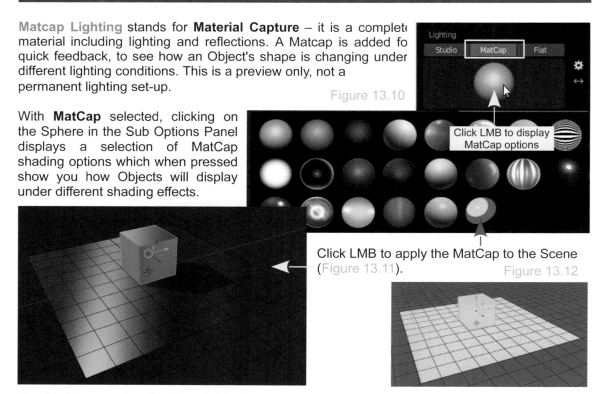

Click LMB to display MatCap options

Click LMB to apply the MatCap to the Scene (Figure 13.11).

Figure 13.12

Flat Lighting applies the Material (color) set in the Properties Editor, Material buttons as a plain flat color (Figure 13.12).

> **Note:** In the diagram, the Objects in the Scene have a Material (color) applied. The MatCap generates a lighting effect which affects the colors of the Objects giving an indication of how the Scene will appear. This effect does not render in an image.

13.4 Color Display Options (Figure 13.13)

With either **Studio Lighting, MatCap Lighting** or **Flat Lighting** there are six **Color Type** settings in the **Sub Options Panel.** The default is **Material,** which means Objects in the Scene (Viewport) are displayed with the Material color that has been assigned to the Object in the **Properties Editor, Material Properties,** when Nodes are deactivated.

Color Types ⟶

Figure 13.13

Material Color Display (Figure 13.14)

Material Color

Properties Editor

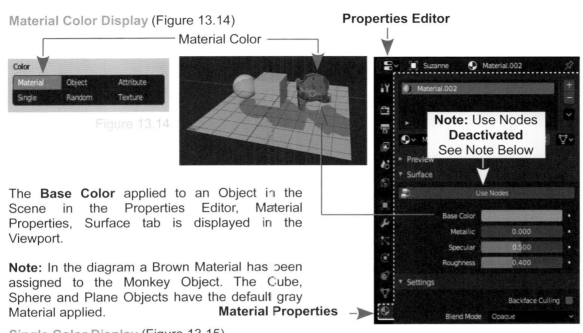

Figure 13.14

The **Base Color** applied to an Object in the Scene in the Properties Editor, Material Properties, Surface tab is displayed in the Viewport.

Note: In the diagram a Brown Material has been assigned to the Monkey Object. The Cube, Sphere and Plane Objects have the default gray Material applied. **Material Properties** →

Single Color Display (Figure 13.15)

Click to select the Single Color

Figure 13.15

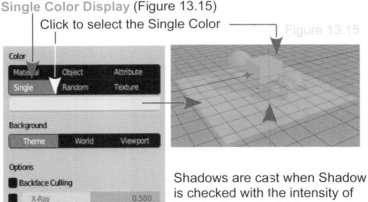

Note: Material Type - When employing the **Material Type** option, the colors only show when Nodes have been **deactivated**.

Shadows are cast when Shadow is checked with the intensity of the shadow adjustable using the slider.

Random Color Display (Figure 13.16)

Random Color

Figure 13.16

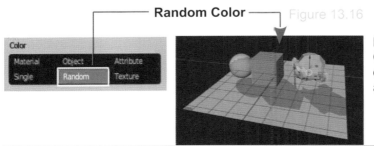

Random Color displays each Object in the Scene with a different color. The color assignment is automatic.

Texture Color Display (Figure 13.17)

┌Texture Color ─────┐

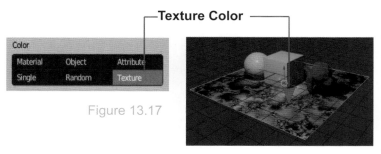

Color

Material	Object	Attribute
Single	Random	Texture

Figure 13.17

Textures are effects which give the surface of an Object characteristics. Texture Color displays Objects with a Texture that has been previously set as the Base Color in the Properties Editor, Material Properties. (Reference Chapter 10).

Note: You can only set the Base Color as a Texture in the Material buttons when the Node System is active.

Vertex Color Display

─── Shows the Active Color Attribute.

Figure 13.18

Color

Material	Object	Attribute
Single	Random	Texture

13.5 Background Displays

In **Solid Viewport Shading Mode** there are three **Background** display options.

Background

| Theme | World | Viewport |

Figure 13.19

Theme

Background option **Theme** displays the Viewport with the Theme that has been set in the **User Preferences Editor** (Reference Chapter 2).

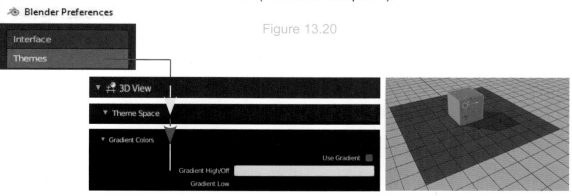

Figure 13.20

World (see 13.9 World Settings)

Background option **World** displays the Viewport with the Background that has been set in the **Properties Editor, World Properties, Surface tab when Use Nodes is deactivated (Gray).**

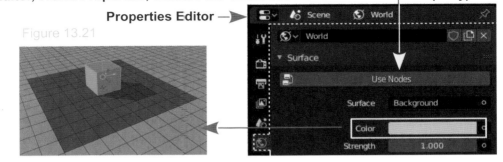

Figure 13.21

Properties Editor ➤

Viewport

A preview of the Scene Background may be set in the Shading Sub Options Panel.

Figure 13.22

Click the color bar to display the color picker circle. (**Note: The default color bar displays black on black**.)

13.6 More Solid Viewport Shading

X-Ray:

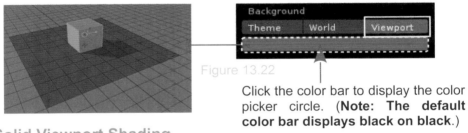

Figure 13.23

X-Ray view of the selected Object

Color bar displays Black on Black

Figure 13.24

Shadows: Previously discussed.

Outline: Object Outlines are displayed orange when selected. When **deselected** they display with a color which you choose by clicking the color bar next to **Outline** in the Sub Options panel. The colored outline may be turned off by unchecking (unticking) **Outline** in the panel.

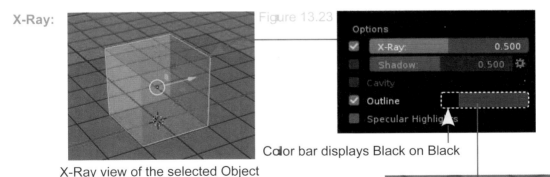

13.7 Rendered Viewport Shading

Figure 18.25

Rendered Viewport Shading gives a quick access to a preview showing exactly what you will see in a Rendered view. Clicking Rendered Viewport Shading displays the 3D Viewport Editor as a Rendered view and as such, the Lighting in the view is influenced by the Lamps and lighting arrangement set in the Scene.

Note: Textures can not be used to color Objects unless the Material **Node System** is employed.

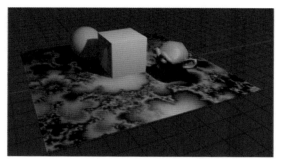

Figure 13.26

Figure 13.27

In Figures 13.26 and 13.27 the Objects have Materials (colors) applied using the Material Node System (Reference: Chapter 9) in the Properties Editor, Materials Properties (Figure 13.28). The Materials Shader Editor has NOT been used, instead, with Use Nodes active in the Properties Editor Base Colors have been selected by clicking on the Base Color bar.

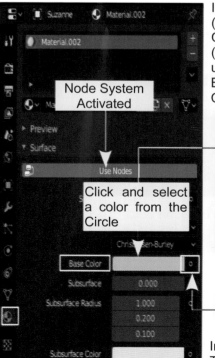

Node System Activated

Click and select a color from the Circle

Click and select Image Texture

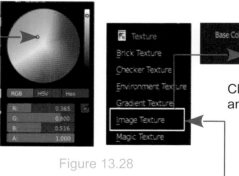

Figure 13.28

Click Open, navigate and select an Image

Click and select Image Texture

In the case of the Plane Object an Image Texture has been used for the color.

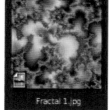

Fractal 1.jpg

13.8 Material Preview Shading

Figure 13.29

When creating or modifying a Scene using Solid Viewport Shading you may wish to quickly view the Scene as it appears with illumination provided by the Lamps instead of the illumination from the Solid Shading Mode. At times illumination is provided by special HDRI images used as a background to the Scene (Reference Chapter 12). If an HDRI image has been installed and you are in Solid Viewport Shading Mode Material Preview provides a quick preview.

Figure 13.30 shows the Scene in the 3D Viewport Editor in Solid Viewport Shading Mode with the Monkey Object selected in Edit Mode. If this were a complicated Scene where the Monkey was obscured by shadow you could clearly see the Monkey and manipulate Vertices.

Figure 13.30

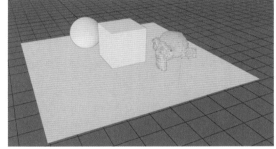

The Scene is viewed under Studio Lighting.

Figure 13.31

To quickly see how the Scene looks with the edits to the Monkey select **Material Preview Shading** (Figure 13.31).

In the Sub Options select **Scene Lighting** to view the Scene using the lighting effects in the Scene (Lamps)

You may use the **Matcap** to preview how adjustments to Lamp setting would affect the display.

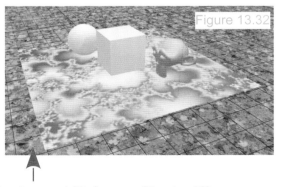

Figure 13.32

If an image has been used to illuminate the Scene select **Scene World** instead of Scene Lights to preview the Scene (Figure 13.32)

HDRI Image used as Scene background (Reference Chapter 12).

13.9 World Settings

Figure 13.33

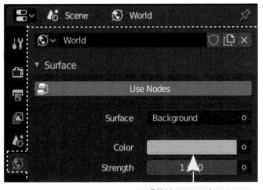

World background color settings in the Properties Editor, World Properties also influence the display in the 3D Viewport Editor (Figure 13.33).

Note: The background color set in the World Properties can be seen in the 3D Viewport Editor in Rendered Viewport Shading Mode or in Solid Viewport Shading with Background World activated or in Material Preview with Scene World checked.

Click to select a
Background Color

13.10 Simplified Viewport Shading

At the beginning of the chapter two images depicted Rendered Viewport Shading and Simplified Viewport Shading. **Simplified Shading** is a reference to a selection of Display Modes called **Render Passes**. Simply put, when a Scene is Rendered, Blender performs the operation in a series of passes which when combined produces the Rendered View. The passes may be isolated and viewed in the 3D Viewport Editor allowing adjustments to be made.

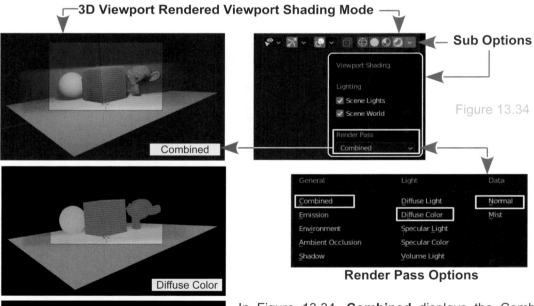

Render Pass Options

In Figure 13.34, **Combined** displays the Combined Passes, **Diffuse Color** displays the Diffuse Color of Objects in the Scene and **Normal** colors indicating the positive and negative direction of Normals (Axis at right angle to the surface).

14

Rendering

Rendering is the process of converting the Blender 3D file information into an 2D Image file or a Video Movie file. In practice this entails taking the data producing what you see in the 3D Viewport, **Camera View** in Blender and generating a photo realistic image or non-photo realistic image. The conversion may produce a single still image or a series of images which depict an Animation. There is also the ability to save storage space by generating a Movie file consolidating an Animation into a single file.

Controls for setting Rendering options are located in the **Properties Editor, Render Properties** buttons and **Output Properties**.

Render Properties   Figure 14.1   **Output Properties**

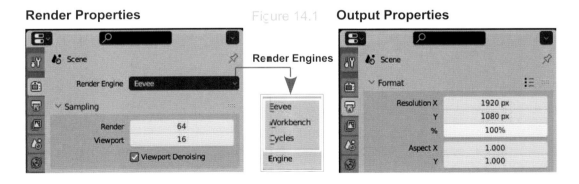

Converting the Blender data into Image files or Movie files is performed by a component of Blender called a **Render Engine**. There are three Render Engines included in Blender. The default **Eevee Render Engine** allows you to see the Render result directly, as you work, in the 3D Viewport. The **Cycles Render Engine** produces photo realistic Rendering while the **Workbench Render Engine** provides a quick preview Render allowing adjustments to be made as you work on a Scene.

14.1 Rendering with Eevee

Rendering converts what is seen in **Camera View** in the 3D Viewport Editor into a still **Image** or in the case of an animation, into a **Video Clip**.

Remember: With the default **Eevee Render Engine** engaged you see the equivalent of a Rendered View in the 3D Viewport when the Viewport is in **Rendered Viewport Shading Mode**.

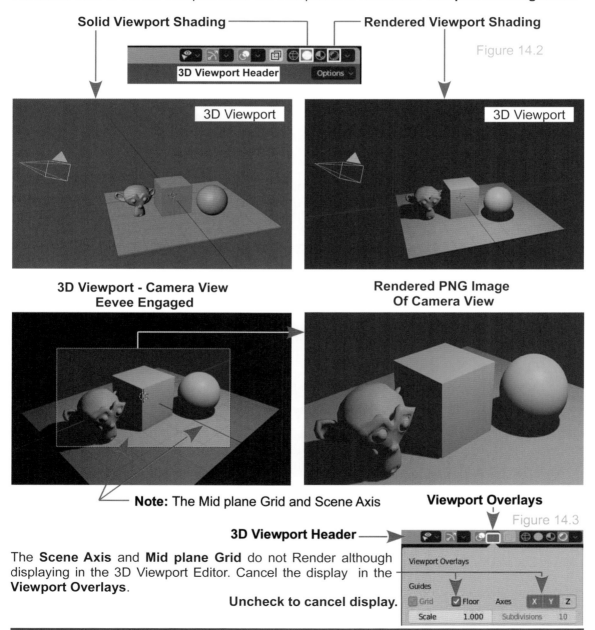

Solid Viewport Shading ───────────────── Rendered Viewport Shading

Figure 14.2

3D Viewport Header Options

3D Viewport   3D Viewport

3D Viewport - Camera View Eevee Engaged   **Rendered PNG Image Of Camera View**

Note: The Mid plane Grid and Scene Axis   **Viewport Overlays**

Figure 14.3

3D Viewport Header ─────→

Viewport Overlays

The **Scene Axis** and **Mid plane Grid** do not Render although displaying in the 3D Viewport Editor. Cancel the display in the **Viewport Overlays**.

Guides

Grid Floor Axes X Y Z

Uncheck to cancel display.   Scale 1.000 Subdivisions 10

To **Render a preview** of a still image press the **F12** button on the Keyboard. An image is Rendered and displayed in a full Screen version of the **Blender Render, Image Editor** . Press **Esc** to cancel. To Render an animation you would press **Ctrl + F12.** These Render options are also located in the Render button in the **Screen Header**. **Note:** pressing **F12** displays a **preview only**. To save the preview as an image file you perform a secondary save function.

In the **Blender Render Screen Header** click: **Image – Save.**

Figure 14.4

Rendering an animation with the default settings saves an image for each Frame in the animation and saves to the **/tmp** directory as seen in the **Properties Editor, Output Properties** (Figure 14.5). On a Windows 10 Computer this means the files are saved in Local Disk (C:)\tmp.

Note: The default Image File Format is **PNG**.

Properties Editor→

The detailed output from the Render process is controlled in the **Properties Editor, Output Properties**.

The Render controls are shown here to make you aware of their existence. The controls are arranged in Tabs. Opening a Tab displays the controls for that particular function which in some cases requires activation by checking the button preceding the function name.

When Rendering, the computer is converting the data producing the Screen display into a format for an Image display. In doing this, it processes in a series of passes, which in each pass improves on the quality of the previous pass. How many passes performed is referred to as the number of **Samples**.

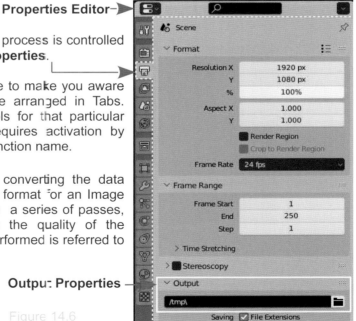

Figure 14.5

Output Properties ─

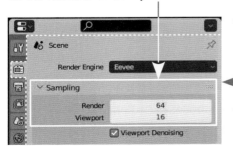

Figure 14.6

◀── Properties Editor, Render Properties

As you see in Figure 14.6 the default number of Samples is; **Viewport 16** (what you see in the Viewport) and **Render 64** (what you get when you press F12).

14.2 Output Properties

In accepting the default number of Render Samples and Render Settings, to produce an image or video, all you have to do in practice is specify the **Resolution** and where you want the file saved. This are set in the **Output Properties** (Figure 14.7)

In the Output Properties (Figure 14.7) the **Format Tab**, and **Output Tab** are expanded.

You may consider the expanded tabs as the basic controls for setting the rendering process.

14.3 The Format Tab

The **Format Tab** (Figure 14.7) is where you tell Blender how big to make your image, the shape of the image, the quality of the image (Resolution) the shape of the pixels (Aspect Ratio) and in the case of an animation where to start and stop rendering and how fast you want it to play back when finished (Frame Rate).

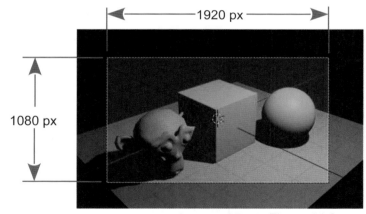

Figure 14.7

Properties Editor

Camera View Figure 14.8

Resolution

X : The number of pixels wide in the display (1920). **Y:** The number of pixels high in the display.

Pixels are the tiny little rectangles which make up the display on the computer or television screen.

> **Note:** The default **Resolution** 1920 x 1080 equates to the HDTV 1080p **Preset.**

Percentage

The percentage slider sets the quality of the render. The default is 100% which scales the resolution. If the value were 50% although the resolution is set at 1920 x 1080 the render would be a preview at 960 x 540. Since rendering takes time this is a way of seeing your image or movie as a preview prior to a final render and therefore saving time. For the final render you set the slider to 100%.

Aspect (Aspect Ratio)

The aspect ratio refers to the shape of the pixels. The default ratio X:1.000, Y:1.000 (1:1) is for computer monitors which have square pixels. TV screens have rectangular pixels so you have to set a ratio for the appropriate format i.e. HDV NTSC 1080p for America the ratio is 4:3 and HDV PAL 1080p for Europe is also 4:3 but TV PAL 16.9 the ratio is 16:11.
Aspect ratios are very confusing. Figure 14.9 is offered as a guide.

Frame Size	Aspect Ratio	Description (note these are only the most common formats)
1920x1080	16x9	1080p/i
1440x1080	16x9	1080i **(Most HDV use this format)**
1280x720	16x9	720p
852x480	16x9	480p
720x480	4:3	DV NTSC (when the pixels are square it is actually 3:2)
720x480	16:9*	DV NTSC / Anamorphic* / Wide Screen (non square pixles)
720x576	5:4	DV PAL
640x480	4:3	a ration suitable for square size pixle multimeida video.
640x360	16:9	a ration suitable for square size pixle multimeida thats widescreen.
480x360	4:3	Multimedia large (480x360 : 75%(640x480))
480x270	16:9	Multimedia Large (similar to Apple's large move trailer standard 480x272) (480x270 : 75%(640x360))
320x240	4:3	Multimedia Large
320x180	16:9	Multimedia Large / Wide Screen
240x180	4:3	Multimedia Small
160x120	4:3	Thumbnail
1600x1200	4:3	Computer Display
1280x1024	4:3	Computer Display
1152x870	4:3	Computer Display
1024x768	4:3	Computer Display
800x600	4:3	Computer Display

Figure 14.9

Frame Start – End – Step (Frame Range)

This is fairly self explanatory and shows the start frame (Frame Start) and end frame of the animation and the **Steps** which means which frames to render. **Frame Steps: 1** means render every frame, **Frame Steps: 2** would mean render every other frame **Frame Steps: 3** would mean render every third frame etc.

> **Note:** Pressing **F12** with an animation paused renders an image of the single frame in the animation where it is paused.

Frame Rate The playback speed of the animation expressed in Frames per second. The selection menu provides options for a variety of formats. 24 Frames per second is the default setting (25 FPS for PAL TV European format and 30 FPS for NTSC TV US format – These frame rates are approximate and vary with the actual **Render Preset** selected).

14.4 The Output Tab

Figure 14.10

In the **Output tab** (Figure 14.10) you set options to tell Blender where to save your render and the **File Format** required.

By default Blender will save your render to the temporary folder on your hard drive as seen by the **/tmp** notation in the output file address bar. On this computer this is C:\tmp\. You can choose a different location by clicking on the folder icon at the end of the bar and navigating in the file browser that opens.

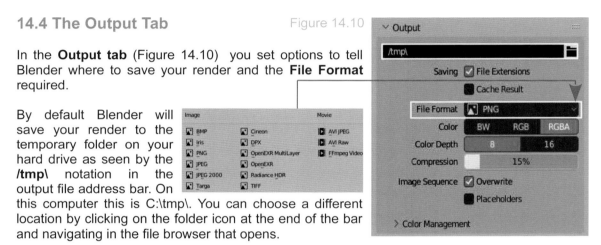

Blender will save your render in a variety of **File Formats**. The default format is **PNG** (Portable Network Graphics). Clicking the File Format bar will display a selection menu for choosing alternative formats (Figure 14.10). In the menu you will see that the options are in two categories: **Image** and **Movie**. Image types such as PNG or JPEG produce a render of a still image of Camera View. Selecting one of the Movie types produces a render of an animation in a compressed movie file such as AVI JPEG, AVI Raw or Ffmpeg Video.

> **Note:** With an **Image File Type** selected such as PNG, a render of an animation will consist of a series of images of each frame of the animation. Although this takes up a lot of room in a folder it is an acceptable method of producing a video file.
>
> **Note:** The default **Image File Type PNG** with the **RGBA** color scheme, **Color Depth 8** and **Compression** ratio of **15%**. Some formats can compress images to use less disk space.

14.5 Rendering a JPEG Image

1. When you have created a scene in the 3D Viewport Editor and decide that you wish to save an image of what you see in the **Camera View**, go to the **Properties Editor, Output Properties**. For the time being leave all the default settings just as they are. In the **Output Properties, Output Tab,** click on the selection menu where you see **PNG** and change to **JPEG**.

Note the difference in the File Format settings.

Figure 14.11

Mouse over on a setting bar for a description.

Choose BW for saving grayscale images, RGB for saving red, green and blue channels, and RGBA for saving red, green, blue and alpha channels: RGB
Images are saved with RGB (color) data

2. With your mouse cursor back in the 3D Viewport Editor, press F12 on the keyboard to render the **preview** of camera view. Alternatively; click Render in the Screen Header and select render Image. The preview displays in the **Image Editor** (Blender Render). In the Blender Render Header click **Image** and select **Save.** Enter a name for your image in the name bar at the bottom of **Blender File View** (Figure 14.12) and click **Save As Image.**

Figure 14.12

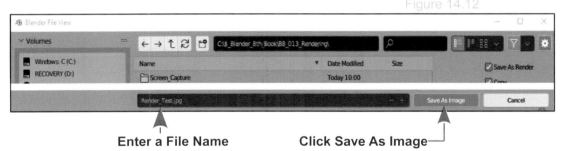

Enter a File Name   Click Save As Image

The Image will be saved as the **JPEG** File Type set in the Properties Editor, Output Properties, Output Tab (Figure 14.10).

As you see in the **Properties Editor, Output Properties, Output Tab** there is a selection of File Formats available besides JPEG in the **Image category**.

14.6 Rendering an Animation

Before rendering an Animation you obviously must have created an Animation Sequence (see Chapter 15). To keep the demonstration relatively simple have the default Cube Object travel across the 3D Viewport Editor in 5 seconds (at the default 24 Frames per Second this will be in 120 Frames) (Figure 14.13).

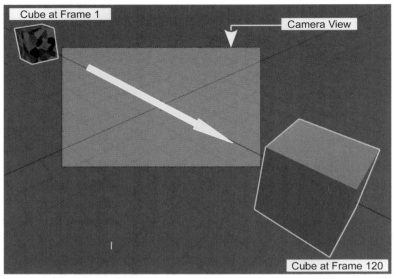

Figure 14.13

Cube at Frame 1

Camera View

Cube at Frame 120

3D Viewport – Camera View (Num Pad 0)

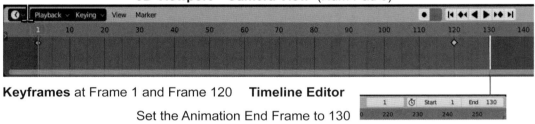

Keyframes at Frame 1 and Frame 120   **Timeline Editor**

Set the Animation End Frame to 130

With the Animation depicted in Figure 14.13 the Cube Object will travel across the Screen passing in and out of Camera View. To Render the Animation, click **Render** in the Screen Header and select **Render Animation**. Alternatively press CTRL + F12. With the default settings in the Properties Editor, Output Properties buttons, Output Tab (File Format PNG), Blender will commence Rendering, generating a PNG Image file for each Frame in the Animation (130 Frames). Each Image is saved to the **tmp** Folder.

Figure 14.14

130 Frames – 130 PNG Images in C/tmp

14.7 Rendering a Movie File

Rendering a Movie File means converting the Blender 3D Data producing an Animation into a format suitable for playing on a Video Player. In essence this is compressing the Images created for viewing into a single File. There are three options in the **Properties Editor, Output Properties, Output Tab** in the **Movie category**.

Figure 14.15

Change the default PNG File Format in the Output Tab to one of the Movie File Formats (Ffmpeg Video).

In the Screen header click **Render – Render Animation**. **Blender Render** will display showing the Animation and a single file is created in the **tmp Folder.**

Figure 14 16

14.8 Video Playback

To playback your rendered animation from within Blender you go to the **Screen Header** and click on **Render** and select **View Animation**.

Playing the animation at this stage, if you have elected to use one of the **Image File Formats** (PNG, JPEG), is simply cycling through the sequence of image files that has been created. One hundred and thirty simple image files constitute a very basic animation. Animations can run to thousands of image files which would accumulate and create a massive storage problem on your hard drive. To save space when creating a reasonable length animation you would definitely render the animation sequence to a **Movie File**.

An advantage of rendering to a Movie File is, you can export and play the file on an external video player or use a program such as VLC Media Player on your PC.

14.9 Video Codecs

In the preceding example, changing the default **PNG** file format to **AVI Raw**, elected to use the **AVI Raw Video Codec** which tells the computer how you want your animation data encoded. There are many many video codecs to chose from and simply selecting a codec type in Blender doesn't necessarily mean that you will get the result that you want. You must have the **Codec** installed on your computer.

A **Codec** is a little routine that compresses the video so that it will fit on a DVD, or be able to be streamed over the internet, or over cable, or just be a reasonable file size.

Simply put, using a codec, you encode the Blender animation data to a video file which suits a particular output media such as PAL TV or NTSC TV. When you have used the encoded data to create a video CD or DVD, the CD or DVD is played in a device (CD / DVD Player) which decodes the data for display i.e. Television Screen.

As previously stated you must have the codec installed on your computer. Codec Packs are available for download from the internet. Two examples are:

K-Lite Codec Pack 12.4.7

media.player.codec.pack.v4.4.2.setup.exe

14.10 Making a Movie

In the preceding information the procedure for rendering an image or a animation sequence has been briefly explained. In rendering the animation you first created a series of image files and then repeated the process creating a video file. The video file does not constitute a movie. In this case the video was a mere 130 frames, a Video Clip, but even if it were a thousand frames it would not be a movie. It is merely a render of one animation sequence from one Scene into a Video File. Movies are made by combining many video files and then rendering the combination to a Movie File. At the same time as this combination is compiled sound effects are added and synchronised with the video.

This combining, synchronising and editing takes place in a **Video Sequence Editor** (VSE). Blender has its own VSE.

A Video Clip (movie file) will take some time to Render (compile) depending on the length of the animation. Each Frame of the animation has to be rendered and saved. Depending on the complexity of the Scene, a Frame can take from a few seconds to several minutes to render. To begin, it is best to keep everything very basic and simple. If you get to the stage where you have created a wonderful movie, you can send the animation files to a **Render Farm** on the Internet to have them rendered—it saves you time but it costs you money.

15

Animation

Animation is the illusion of motion, of making objects depicted in a still image appear to move. In its simplest form stick figures drawn on separate pages appear to move when the pages are viewed in quick succession. Animation has advanced from that simple technique to sophisticated full length feature films with sound and voice which are experienced today. In the past Movies were produced by laboriously drawing many images, posing figures, each slightly different to the next which were photographed and transcribed to film. Each image was then said to be a Frame in an animation sequence. Today the process is accomplished by Computer Graphics which essentially mimics that same process. In Blender animation is accomplished by creating data which displays on the computer Screen. The display is programmed to change over a period of time (**The Timeline**) and then captured by a camera at intervals producing **Frames** of the animation. Each Frame is **Rendered**, which means the Blender data is correlated and turned into a series of digital images. The images are compiled into a video clip or sequence depicting an action. Finally a series of video clips are assembled, edited, combined with effects such as audio and converted to a movie file. This chapter will explore some of the techniques used for creating animation effects.

15.1 Animation in the 3D Viewport

Animation may be performed in the default Blender Screen, in the 3D Viewport Editor, in conjunction with the Timeline Editor. Alternatively Blender has a dedicated **Animation Workspace** (see section 15.33).

To demonstrate the very basics of the animation process the default **3D Viewport Editor and Timeline Editor** will be used. The Animation Workspace will be introduced at a later stage.

In the 3D Viewport Editor a **Cube Object** will be animated to move in the Scene, and change shape at the same time. Simple motion and deformation of an Object are only two of many features which may be animated.

The objective in creating an animation is to capture what you see on the Screen in the **Camera View**. This will be what is included in the final render. You may set up an animations sequence in the Blender Scene then position the Camera or position multiple Cameras to capture parts of the sequence. What is captured will be rendered to a series of still images (Frames) producing a video clip. The clip will be finally compiled (spliced together) with other clips to make a movie file.

15.2 Movement in the 3D View Editor

Moving or Translating Objects in the 3D Viewport Editor may be performed by selecting the Object, pressing the **G Key** and moving the Mouse or by using the **Manipulation Widget**. The two methods move the Object in the Scene in different ways.

Figure 15.1

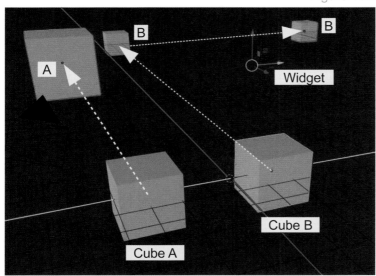

What you see in the 3D Viewport Editor when you move Objects depends on the method of Translation. In Figure 15.1 **Cube A** is Translated by pressing the G Key (Grab) and moved up and to the left. **Cube B** is translated using the **Move Tool** which activates the Manipulation **Widget** (press the T Key to see the Tool Panel).

Note: The Widget in the diagram is positioned at the center of geometry of the three B Cube Objects . This is for diagram construction only.

When **Cube A** is Translated by using the **G Key** the movement is confined to the plane of the computer Screen.

When **Cube B** is Translated by using the Move Tool Widget the movement is confined to either the X, Y or Z Axis of the 3D World (the Scene).

Cube B has been moved back along the X Axis then to the right along the Y Axis. In **User Perspective View** you see its size diminish as it recedes into the distance. In fact, all views of the Cube have the same physical size as seen in Top Orthographic View (Figure 15.2).

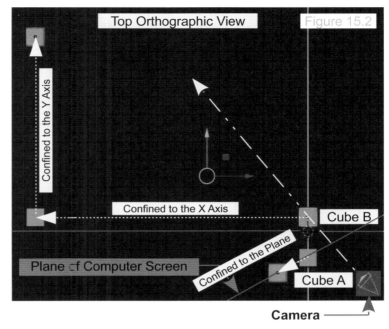

Understanding this concept of Translation on the Computer Screen and in the 3D World will assist when animating Objects to move.

15.3 Planning the Animation

Planning the animation is an important part of the process. Without having even a rudimentary idea of what you want to achieve can lead to disaster when the Scene becomes a little complicated.

In demonstrating the concept of animation, with a view to illustration, begin with a very simple sequence. The default Cube Object in the default 3D Viewport Editor will be relocated (Translated) then animated to move forward along the X Axis of the 3D World and at the same time reduced in size and Scaled along the Y Axis.

Figure 15.3

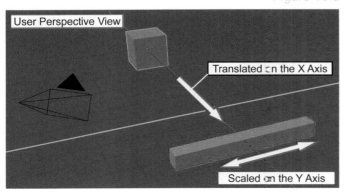

Figures 15.3 and 15.4 show the default Cube Object positioned approximately ten Blender units on the X Axis towards the back of the Scene in the 3D Viewport Editor (minus 10 Units).

The Cube will be animated to move forward along the X Axis.

At the same time the Cube will be Scaled on the X, Y and Z Axis.

Figure 15.4

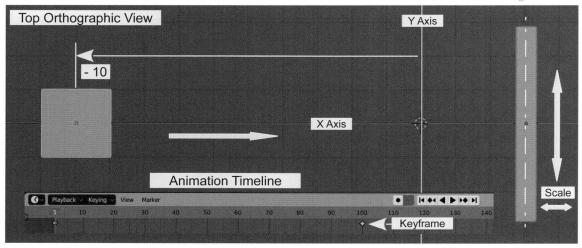

15.4 Keyframes Time and Interpolation

The first step in an animation is to decide what you want your actor to do in a given time. In this demonstration, the actor will be the Cube Object. How long it takes the actor to do something will depend on how many Frames per second the animation is run and this is determined by which format your final render will be.

The **Render Format** determines how many Frames per second the animation should run (For example when playing in a television format, **NTSC** for the US at 30 fps, **PAL** for Australia at 25 fps). When considering the animation, make the motion occur in an appropriate time. Look at the frames per second and relate it to time. If you want a movement to take 3 seconds and you are running at 25 frames per second, then the animation has to occur in 75 Frames (3 x 25 = 75).

In Blender you do not have to create every single Frame of the animation. You set up single Frames (**Keyframes**) at specific points and the program works out all the intermediate Frames.

Think of a 10-second animation that, when running at 25 Frames per second, would consist of 250 Frames. If you want your actor to go from point A to point B and then to point C in the Scene within the 250-Frame animation, you first insert a Keyframe at Frame 1 with the actor at position A. This is giving Blender data that says, at the Frame 1, locate the actor at location A. Then at another Frame, mid way in the animation, insert a second Keyframe with the actor at location B. Finally insert a third Keyframe at frame 250 with the actor at location C. These are the Keyframes for the animation. Blender will work out all the in-between Frames. The Keyframes can also include the data for other features such as scale, rotation and color.

Determining the in-between data is called **Interpolation.** There are different methods of interpolation. By default, Blender uses **Bezier Interpolation**, which for motion gives a nice acceleration and deceleration between **Keyframes**. When an object moves from point A to point B in a given time, it is said to move at a certain velocity (speed). In theory, the speed could be represented as a straight line graph, but in practice an Object at rest (motionless) has to go from being motionless to moving at a certain velocity. The rate at which it attains the velocity is called acceleration. Blender's **Bezier Interpolation** draws curves at the beginning and end of the straight line graph (acceleration and deceleration). You have the options to choose **Constant** or **Linear** type interpolation if appropriate. Selection of interpolation types will be discussed later in the chapter.

Using the term **Bezier** to describe interpolation is in fact an anomaly. Bezier actually describes a type of line (the line on a graph described in the previous paragraph). A Bezier line or curve in Blender is a line that has control points that allow the shape of the line to be altered or edited. In Blender, the control points are located at the position of the **Keyframes**. Interpolation is performed according to a mathematical formula that determines the shape of the line. When the data for the Frames in the animation is drawn as a line on a graph, the line conforms to that mathematical formula. For the moment, accept the default Bezier-Type Interpolation to demonstrate the insertion of Keyframes and the creation of a simple animation.

15.5 Animation Speed and Length   Figure 15.5

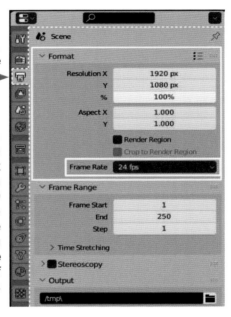

The default 24 frames per second, suitable for PAL format, as set in the **Properties Editor, Output Properties** will be used.

Note: Frame Rate 24fps in the **Format Tab**.

The **Timeline Editor** Frame range settings are, **Start: 1** and **End: 250** (Figure 20.6). This is saying the animation will begin at Frame 1 and end at Frame 250. Running at the rate of 24 Frames per second will give an animation time of approximately 10 seconds. If you think about it, 10 seconds is quite a long time for a single action to take place in a video clip. Also in the Timeline Editor, make note of the lighter grayed area beginning at Frame 1 and ending at Frame 250. Changing the **Start Frame** and **End Frame** values in the header panel will move the end positions of the lighter grayed area. The vertical blue line at Frame 1 is the **Timeline Cursor**.

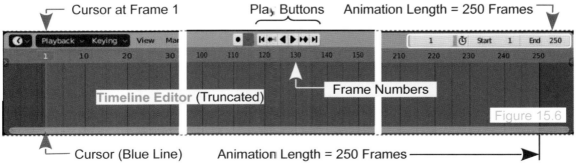

To make the process relatively simple the Cube Object will be the Actor in the Scene and will move in a straight line along the X Axis and at the same time increase in size on the Y Axis. Make sure the Cube is selected in the 3D Viewport Editor. Initially only two **Keyframes** will be inserted.

In the default Scene, the actor (the selected Object – the Cube) is located at Frame 1 in the animation. In the upper LH corner of the 3D Editor, you will see **(1) Collection I Cube** in white lettering. This indicates that you have the Cube selected at Frame 1 in the Animation Timeline. If you had ten objects in the Scene, all of which were actors with perhaps some hidden, it's nice to know which one is selected and where they are in the Timeline.

15.6 Repositioning the Timeline Cursor

In the **Timeline Editor** at the bottom of the Screen the buttons labelled **25, Start: 1 and End: 250**, show the current Frame, the Start Frame and the End frame set for default animation (25 displays as the current Frame when the Cursor is relocated at frame 25).

Clicking LMB on the scale repositions the Cursor (blue button with blue line). With the mouse cursor in the **Timeline Editor** pressing **Num Pad + or –** zooms the scale. Scrolling the Mouse Wheel zooms the scale.

Click, Hold and Drag or Click RMB in the Editor at a Frame to reposition the Cursor or Click LMB in the Scale.

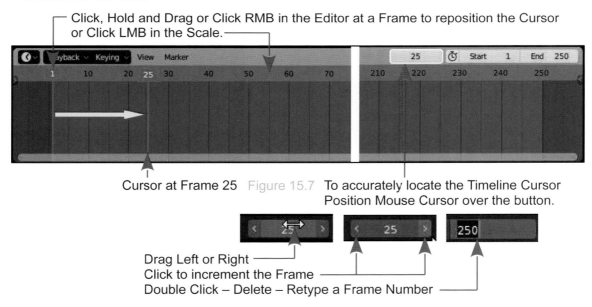

Cursor at Frame 25   Figure 15.7   To accurately locate the Timeline Cursor
Position Mouse Cursor over the button.

Drag Left or Right
Click to increment the Frame
Double Click – Delete – Retype a Frame Number

In the default view the **Timeline Cursor** (blue button with vertical blue) line is located at **Frame 1**. Click on the cursor (blue button) with the LMB, hold and drag it across to Frame 25 (Figure 15.7). Note the number in the blue button changes and also next to **Cube** at the upper LH side of the 3D Viewport Editor and in the Header bar of the **Timeline Editor**. Other ways to change the Frame are to click on the little arrows on either end of the **Frame Number** in the Timeline Editor Header, or click LMB on the button, hold and drag to change the Frame number or click on the **button**, hit delete, and retype the required frame number.

15.7 Inserting Keyframes

Keyframes are inserted in the animation at specific Frames. For example, with the Cube Object located at minus ten m (-10) units on the X Axis, position the **Timeline Cursor** at Frame 25.

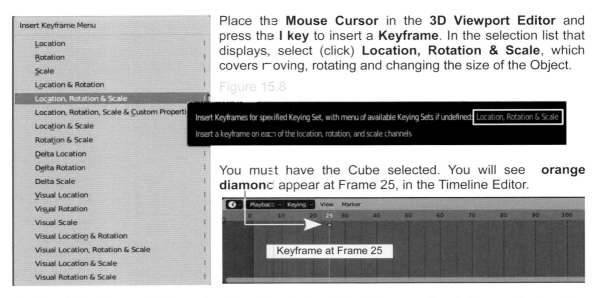

Place the **Mouse Cursor** in the **3D Viewport Editor** and press the **I key** to insert a **Keyframe**. In the selection list that displays, select (click) **Location, Rotation & Scale**, which covers moving, rotating and changing the size of the Object.

Figure 15.8

Insert Keyframes for specified Keying Set, with menu of available Keying Sets if undefined: Location, Rotation & Scale
Insert a keyframe on each of the location, rotation, and scale channels

You must have the Cube selected. You will see **orange diamond** appear at Frame 25, in the Timeline Editor.

Keyframe at Frame 25

At this point, only one Keyframe has been inserted and the Cube remains stationary at minus ten units on the X Axis of the Scene.

If you click LMB on the **Timeline Editor Cursor** (blue button) ,hold and drag the mouse from Frame 25 along the timeline the Cube (actor) remains stationary. Clicking LMB and dragging the blue line in the Editor is called **scrubbing the animation**, which is actually manually playing the animation. You can play the animation by clicking the **Play button** in the **Timeline Editor Header**.

Figure 15.9

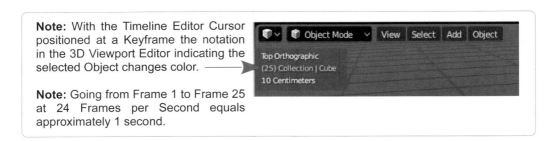

Note: With the Timeline Editor Cursor positioned at a Keyframe the notation in the 3D Viewport Editor indicating the selected Object changes color.

Note: Going from Frame 1 to Frame 25 at 24 Frames per Second equals approximately 1 second.

Remember; There is only one **Keyframe** which tells Blender that, at Frame 25 the Cube Object is positioned -10 units in the Scene. There is no other information, therefore, playing the Animation does nothing.

Continue creating the animation by moving the Cursor to Frame 100 (click on Frame 100).

In the 3D Viewport Editor, grab and position the Cube +3 Blender units on the X Axis (-10 to +3). Scale the Cube down and Scale up four on the Y Axis (Figure 15.10). With the Mouse Cursor in the 3D View Editor, press the **I key** and select **Location, Rotation & Scale** to insert a second Keyframe at Frame 100. You will see another set of orange diamonds in the Timeline at Frame 100 (Figure 15.12).

Figure 15.10

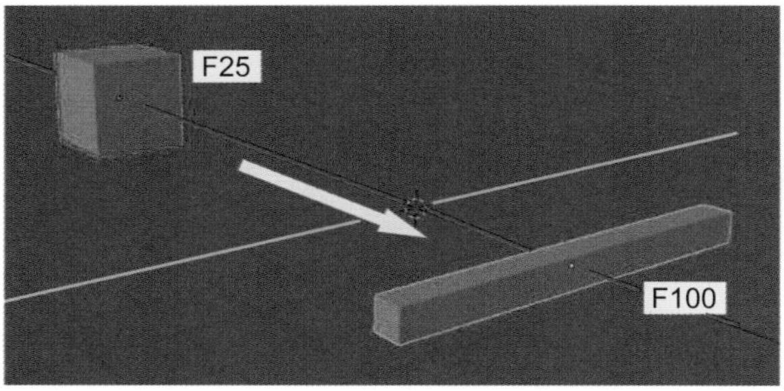

Figure 15.11

To accurately locate and scale the Cube, with the Mouse Cursor in the 3D View Editor, press the **N Key** and enter values in the **Object Properties** panel (Figure 15.11).

Values shown are for Location & Scale at Frame 100.

Figure 15.12

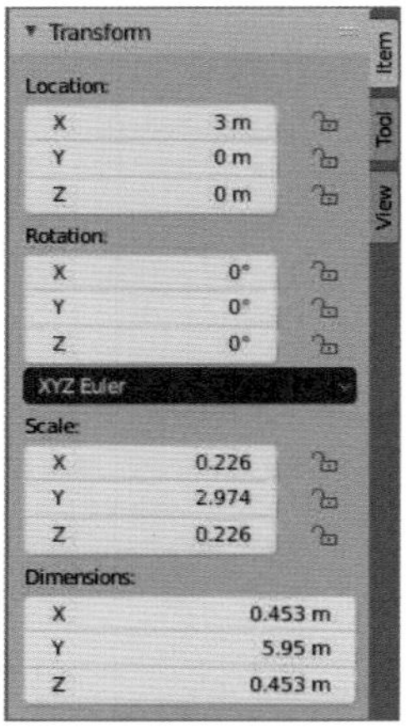

N Key to hide the panel.

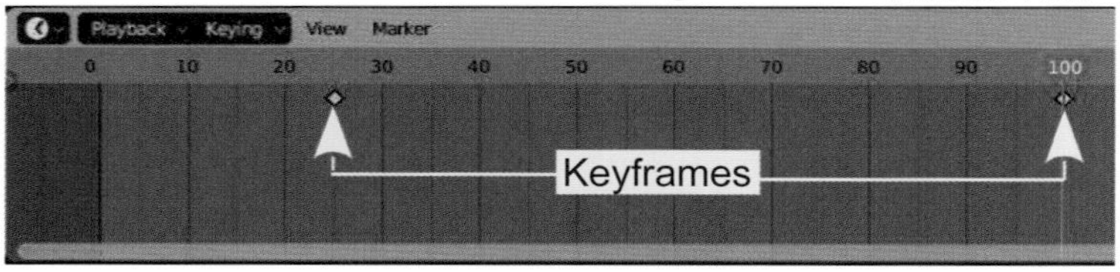

The diamonds in the Timeline Editor merely show that the Frame has been set as a Keyframe. They do not indicate the status which is required to set the Animation. The Location, Rotation and Scale properties result in the change occurring between Frame 1 and Frame 100 as displayed in Figure 15.12. To see a more comprehensive view of Keyframe status you need to expand the display Channels.

In the upper left hand corner of the **Timeline Editor** mouse over on the little arrow just below the Editor Icon.

White arrow on Mouse Over LMB Click to expand display

Click on the triangles to expand the **Keyframe Channels**.

Figure 15.13

Orange Channels indicate that no data is recorded.

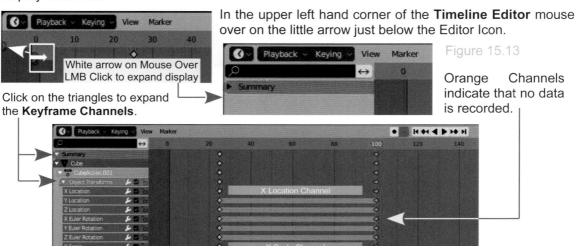

Keyframe Channels display for each dataset Animated, in this case Location, Rotation and Scale (Green Channels). **Rotation** is included since **Location, Rotation & Scale** was selected when entering the Keyframes but no data has been recorded for Y and Z Location or Rotation(Orange Channels).

15.8 Scrubbing the Animation

When you **scrub the animation** (Click, Hold and Drag the Blue Line Cursor, in the Timeline Editor or in the Dope Sheet Editor) between Frames 25 and 100, you will see the Cube move and change in size—you are manually playing the animation; **Scrubbing**. Note that the action only takes place between frames 25 and 100, which are the location of the Keyframes; no action takes place on either side of the Keyframes.

> **Note:** In moving the Cube from minus ten to plus three on the X Axis the Cube will be disappearing from Camera View. This may require addressing since Camera View is what Renders as the final animation.

15.9 Playing the Animation

To actually play a **preview of the animation**, move the Cursor in the Timeline to Frame 1 then press the **Spacebar** with the Cursor in the 3D Viewport Editor. Say "one thousand" to yourself slowly (counting one second, while the Cursor in the **Timeline** moves across to frame 25). You will see the Cube remain stationary until the Cursor reaches frame 25 then the Cube will move and change in size. At frame 100, it stops moving and changing size. The Cursor in the Timeline continues on to frame 250 then jumps back to frame 1 and the preview of the animation plays again. Press **Esc** or press the Spacebar a second time to stop playing.

Another way to play the animation is to press the **Play** buttons in the **Timeline Editor Header** (Figure 15.14). These button is much like the play button on any video or audio player.

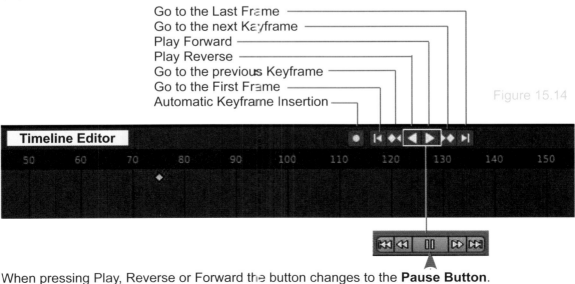

Go to the Last Frame
Go to the next Keyframe
Play Forward
Play Reverse
Go to the previous Keyframe
Go to the First Frame
Automatic Keyframe Insertion

Figure 15.14

Timeline Editor

50   60   70   80   90   100   110   120   130   140   150

When pressing Play, Reverse or Forward the button changes to the **Pause Button**.

15.10 Adding Keyframes

Keyframes may be added to the animation to translate (move), scale and rotate the actor in the Scene. For the most part, location and size Keys work flawlessly but care needs to be taken with Rotation Keys . If you try to rotate an Object too far in one set of Keys, the Object may not rotate in the direction you want it to and it may rotate oddly. Try small angular movements between Keys while rotating. There are better ways to control this and tools to simplify the process, (see 15.14). Be aware that the movement of the actor may not be exactly as planned. Blender automatically defaults to trying to create a smooth flow through the animation.

To insert additional Keyframes, position the Timeline Cursor, adjust the status of the Actor then press the I Key.

15.11 Automatic Keyframing

Keyframes have been inserted in the animation by placing the Mouse Cursor in the 3D Viewport Editor, moving to a Frame in the Timeline, changing the status of the Object and then pressing the **I Key** and selecting one of the Keyframe options.

Blender has an **Automatic Keyframe** insertion function which is activated by pressing the white button in the **Timeline Editor Header** (highlights blue when active)(Figure 15.15).

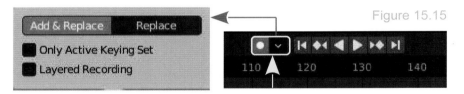

Figure 15.15

With auto on, whenever you Move, Scale, or Rotate the actor Object in the 3D Viewport Editor, a Keyframe will be inserted at whatever Frame has been selected in the Timeline.

For example; With the Cube Object in the default Scene in the 3D Viewport Editor it is located at the intersection of the X Axis and Y Axis. The Cursor in the Timeline Editor is located at Frame 1. With Auto on, Translating the Cube along the X Axis inserts a Keyframe at Frame 1 recording that this is the state of the Cube at Frame 1.

If the Timeline Cursor had been positioned at Frame 25 then the Cube Translated, a Keyframe will have been inserted at Frame 25. This will be the First Frame in the animation. If the Timeline Cursor is moved back to Frame 1 the Cube remains in its position for frame 25.

The procedure for Automatic Keyframing is, position the Timeline Cursor, Translate, Rotate or Scale the selected Object to insert Keyframes.

Remember to turn this off after you're finished using it (press the button a second time).

15.12 Controlling the Animations

When an animation has been created it may be controlled (modified / adjusted) to fine tune the action perhaps to create an interaction with other Actors which are animated in the same Scene.

Controlling the Animation can be achieved by making adjustments in the 3D Viewport Editor and or in the Timeline Editor. To demonstrate the rudimentary concept of fine tuning continue with the Animation depicted in Figure 15.10.

The Cube Object moves from minus ten Blender units on the X Axis to plus three Blender units and changes shape as it moves. An adjustment will be made to delay the Y Axis Scale extension until Frame 160 in the Timeline. This means the Cube will come to rest at Frame 100 but will continue to extend on the Y Axis until frame 160.

To achieve this delayed extension you could have the Cube selected at Frame 100, reduce the Scale on the Y Axis then Press the I Key and select Location, Rotation & Scale again which redefines the Cube's status at Frame 100. Reposition the Timeline Cursor at Frame 160, Scale the Cube up on the Y Axis and insert new Location, Rotation & Scale Keyframes.

A simpler method of making this adjustment is to relocate the Y Scale Keyframe in the Timeline Editor. With the Mouse Cursor in the Timeline, click LMB to deselect all the Keyframes. LMB click on the **Y Scale Keyframe** (orange) and drag the Mouse placing the **Keyframe at Frame 160**.

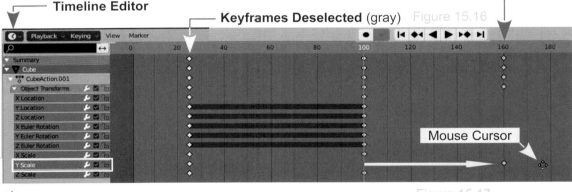

Figure 15.16

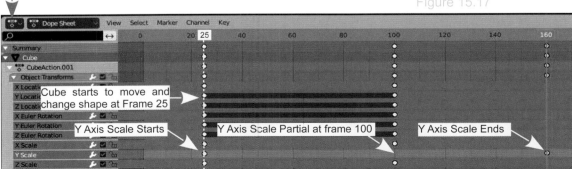

Figure 15.17

Introducing the Dope Sheet Editor (see over)

15.13 The Dope Sheet Editor

The **Dope Sheet Editor** introduces yet another means of Controlling the Animation. When comparing the Timeline Editor (Figure 15.16) to the Dope Sheet Editor (Figure 15.17) on the previous page they appear to be identical. Creating an Animation with Keyframes in the Timeline Editor then changing the Timeline to the Dope Sheet shows the same Keyframes and Channels. You will note, however, that the Dope Sheet Editor has several more option buttons included in the Header. It is not intended to describe all the options and features of either the Timeline Editor or the Dope Sheet Editor, merely to introduce each, making you aware that they exist and are in many respects similar. To demonstrate one feature of the Dope Sheet, the extension of the Cube along the Y Axis of the Scene at Frame 160 may be controlled (adjusted) in the Editor.

Clicking **View** in the Dope Sheet Editor Header reveals a selection of options (Figure 15.18). By checking **Show Sliders**, control Sliders are displayed for each Animation Channel. In the diagram the Y Scale Keyframe has been relocated to Frame 160 per the previous exercise using the Timeline Editor and remains selected. The slider is highlighted yellow. By adjusting the value in the Slider you change the elongation of the Cube in the 3D Viewport Editor with the Cube at Frame 160.

Note: the value in the Slider corresponds to the value for the Y Axis in the **3D Viewport Object Properties** (N Key to display).

Figure 15.18

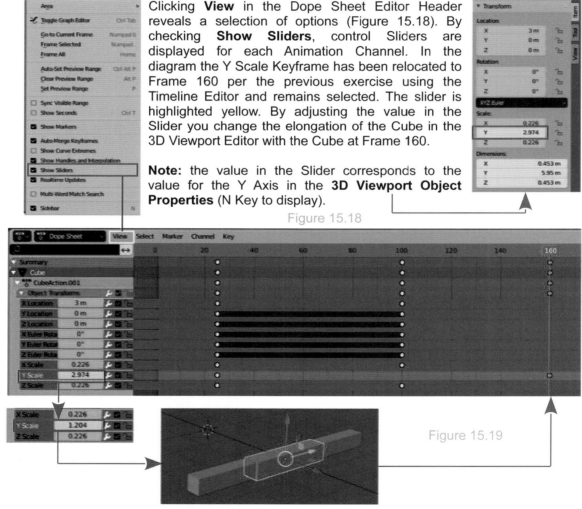

Figure 15.19

Another way to control Animation is to employ the **Graph Editor**. Each of the Animation Channels in the Timeline Editor or Dope Sheet Editor may be displayed as a Graph Line.

15.14 The Graph Editor

The Graph Editor shows a graphical display of the animation. The graphs can be edited to refine and control the animation actions. In Figure 15.20 the 3D Viewport Editor has been changed to the Graph Editor with the Dope Sheet Editor below. The Viewports have been aligned by manipulating the scales, zooming and repositioning the Viewport (details to follow).

▼—— Graph Editor

Figure 15.20

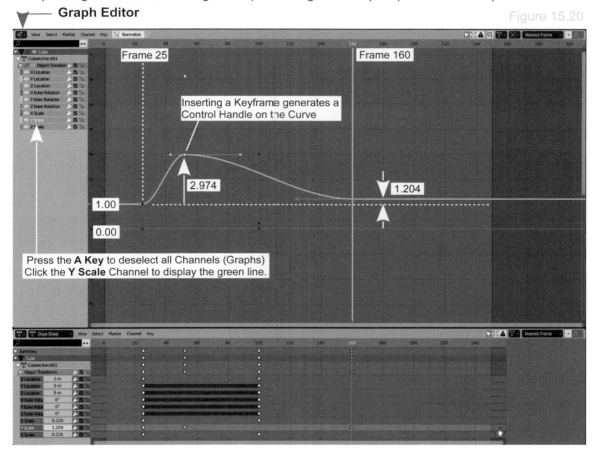

The green line in the Graph Editor represents the **Y Scale** Channel in the Dope Sheet Editor which controls the elongation of the Cube Object in the 3D Viewport Editor. Between Frame 1 and Frame 25 in the Animation the Cube is ˆ.00 X 1.00 X 1.00 (The default Cube). From Frame 25 to Frame 52 the Cube was extended along its Y Axis 2.974 Units then From Frame 52 to Frame 160 the Cube was reduced along its Y Axis to 1.204 Units.

Note: The Graph Line is a **Bezier Curve** with Control Handles located corresponding to Keyframes in the Animation Timeline. You may LMB click a Control Handle to select then G Key (Grab), drag the Mouse to reposition the Handle. This reshapes the Graph Line altering the properties of the Object, in this case, affecting the length of the Cube on the Y Axis.

Another example of control using the Graph Editor would be to reverse the direction of travel of an Object in the 3D Viewport Editor. Set up an Animation to have the default Cube Object move from the back of the Scene in the 3D Viewport Editor and travel towards the front of the Scene.

In Figure 15.21 the default Cube moves from back to front in 60 Frames.

Figure 15.21

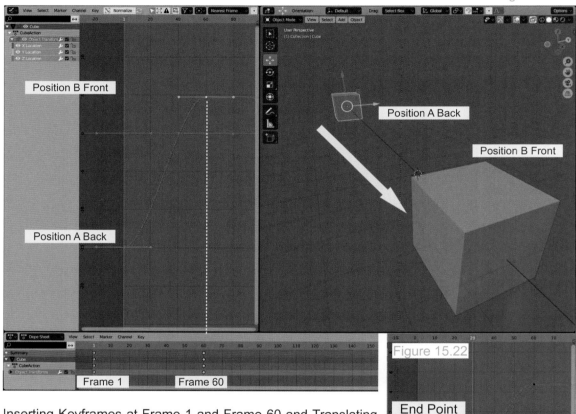

Inserting Keyframes at Frame 1 and Frame 60 and Translating the default Cube along the X Axis of the Scene produces the Bezier Curve Graph Line shown in the Graph Editor. When the Animation is played the Cube simply moves from the back of the Scene to the front.

With the X Location Channel selected move the Timeline Cursor to a mid point in the Animation and with the Mouse Cursor in the Graph Editor, RMB click and select Insert Keyframes from the menu that displays. Keyframes are inserted and a new Control Handle is placed on the Graph Line (Figure 15.22).

Select the end points of the Control Handle, G Key (Grab) and rotate to shape the Graph Line (Figure 15.23).

With the Graph Line reshaped with a pronounced S-bend the direction of travel of the Cube is reversed during the Animation when the Timeline Cursor intersects the bend.

Figure 15.23

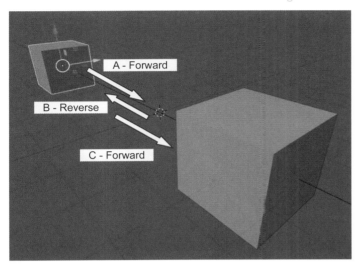

At this point the Graph Editor has been demonstrated depicting the motion of a Cube Object on the X Axis in the 3D Viewport Editor (the red line in the graph). The red line represents the X Location Channel. When inserting Keyframes in the Animation, selecting Location, Rotation & Scale you set up X, Y and Z Channels for each action (Figure 15.24).

With the default Cube in the 3D Viewport Editor Translated on the X and Y Axis, Rotated about the Z Axis and scaled down the Channels for each can be seen in the Timeline Editor Summary (Figure 15.24).

Figure 15.24

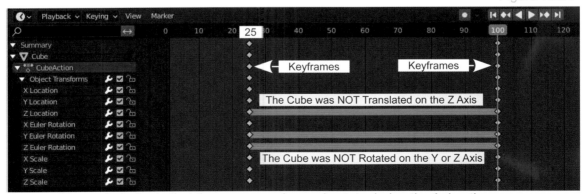

Orange Channels indicate that there was no change in state during the Animation.

The Graph Editor display for the preceding Animation is shown in Figure 20.25. Make note that the Animation Length is the default 250 Frames but the change in state of the Cube occurs between Frame 25 and Frame 100. The Dope Sheet Editor below is aligned with the Graph Editor by adjusting the Editor horizontal Scales and Panning the Views.

Figure 15.25

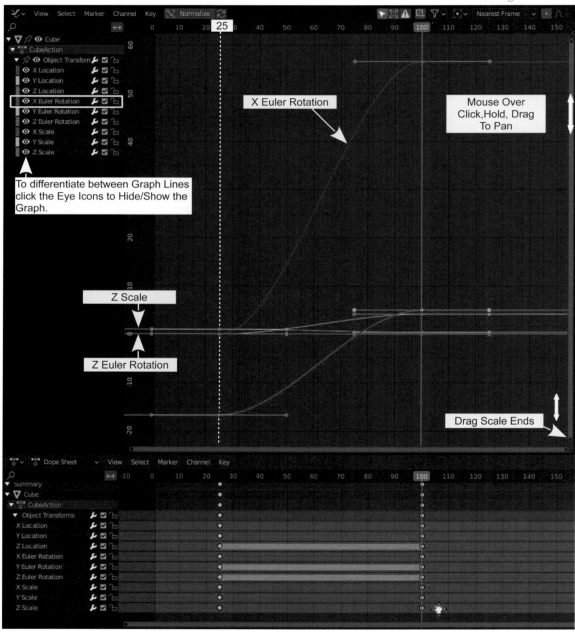

Examine the Graph Editor in more detail (Figure 15.26 over).

Note: In Figure 15.26 the Animation occurs between Frame 25 and Frame 75.   Figure 15.26

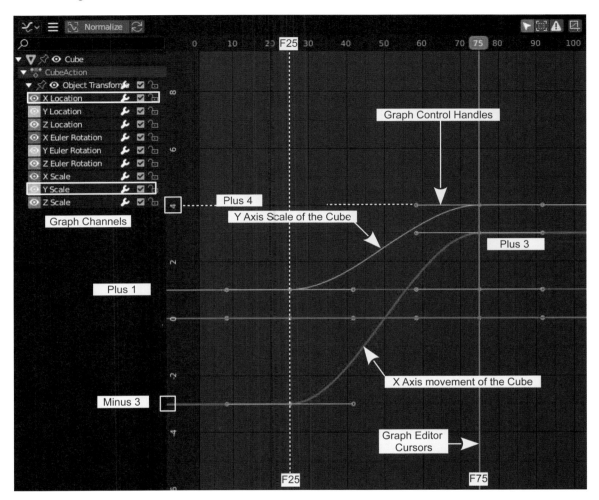

In the Graph Editor the red line represents the movement of the Cube Object on the X Axis of the 3D World. The movements initial position of minus three units changes to plus three units between Frame 25 and 75 (the position of the Keyframes). The green line represents the change in Scale of the Cube on the Y Axis (default Cube Scale = 1. Scale value entered = 4). The two horizontal blue lines represent the Z Axis Location and Scale which, being horizontal, means no change. You see Frame numbers in the scale at the top of the Editor and Blender units in the vertical scale. Note: The vertical alignment of graph lines with the scale is approximate.

The Graph Channels in the panel at the LH side of the Editor list the actions that have been entered in the animation by inserting Keyframes. When entering Keyframes, type **Location, Rotation & Scale** was selected, therefore, the Graph Channels list Location, Rotation and Scale actions. In the Cube animation only the X Location and Y Scale Channels are of significance. The remaining Channels are shown since Location, Rotation & Scale was the Keyframe Type selected.

15.15 Graph Editor Components and Commands

Figure 15.27

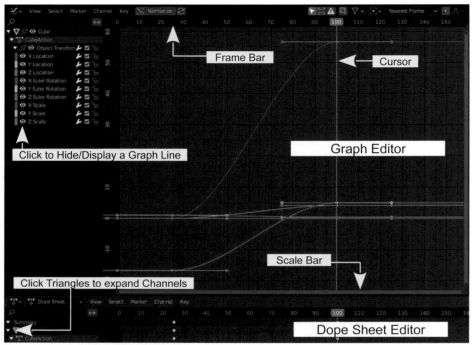

Graph Editor Cursors is the Vertical blue line – LMB click on the blue button, hold and drag in the Frame Header to position.

Scaling the Graph Editor may be done by clicking on the **Scale Bar**, holding and dragging the Mouse. Click and hold a dot at either end of a scale to shrink or extend the scale.

Scaling the Frame Bar occurs when the Scale Bar is manipulated.

The Dope Sheet Channels, Cube, CubeAction and Object Transforms may be expanded or collapsed by clicking the white triangle preceding each name. (Figure 15.27).

Hiding Graphs: Clicking the eye icons preceding each Graph Channel toggles hide and display of the graph lines in the Editor.

Collapsing Channels in the Dope Sheet and hiding graph lines in the Editor can be very useful in a complicated animation. In the demonstration only the X Axis Translation and Y Axis Scale have been animated. There are many more features of the Cube alone which may be animated, therefore, you can imagine the Graph Editor could become congested with information.

Positioning the Graphs relative to the Timeline in the Graph Editor may be accomplished by selecting Control Handles on a Graph Line, pressing the G Key and dragging the Mouse. This action moves the selection, moving the Graph Line. The movement is relative to the Timeline. Graph Lines that are not selected remain stationary, therefore, the movement of the selected line alters the action of the Object in the 3D View Editor relative to other actions.

15.16 Selecting the Curve in the Graph Editor

As previously explained, the X Location Curve in the Graph Editor is a Bezier Curve representing the X Axis movement of the Cube, therefore, the Control Handles can be selected and manipulated. The following commands execute selection procedures when the Mouse Cursor is in the Graph Editor panel:

Press **Alt + A Key** deselects the Control Handles. Press the **A Key** reselects the Control Handles.

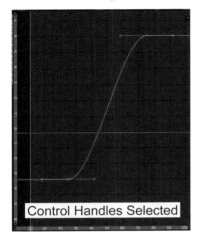
Control Handles Selected

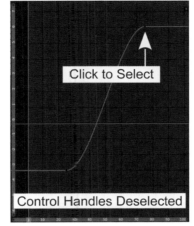
Click to Select

Control Handles Deselected

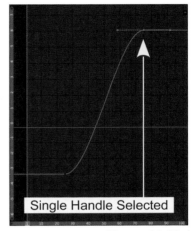
Single Handle Selected

Figure 15.28

With Control Handles deselected (click LMB in an empty space), click LMB on a Control Handle (black dot) to select. With a Control Handle selected it may be Translated, Rotated and Scaled by: **G** Key (Grab), move the Mouse, LMB click to locate.
      R Key (Rotate) move the Mouse, LMB click to set.
      S Key (Scale) move the Mouse, LMB click to set.

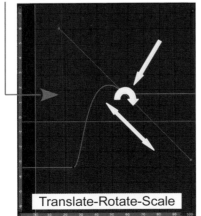
Translate-Rotate-Scale

Figure 15.29

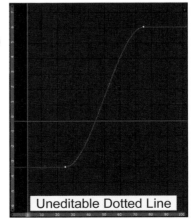
Uneditable Dotted Line

Each of the above actions reshapes the Curve affecting the X Axis movement of the Cube in the animation. With all Control handles selected or deselected, pressing the Tab Key leaves the Curve displayed as a broken line which is not editable.

15.17 Rotation – Euler Rotation.

You will have observed that Rotation values in Blender are labelled **Euler Rotation**. Simply put, **Euler**, is a method of expressing Rotation in a **Three Dimensional Environment**.

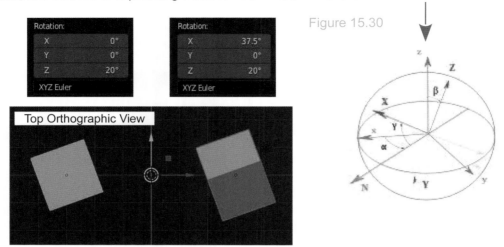

Figure 15.30

In Figure 15.29 the Cube on the left is Rotated 20 on the Z Axis of the Scene. The Cube on the right is also Rotated 20 on the Z Axis but prior to this Rotation it has been Rotated 37.5 on the X Axis of the Scene.

Rotation can be made about the **Local Axis** of the Object by selecting Local Axis in the **Transformation Orientation** options in the 3D Viewport Editor Header.

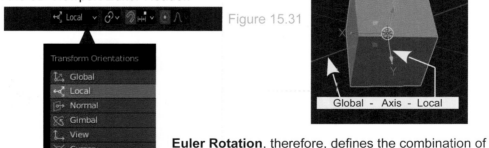

Figure 15.31

Euler Rotation, therefore, defines the combination of Global Rotation and Local Rotation.

15.18 The Graph Editor Cursor

Before proceeding, how to control the Graph Editor Cursor should be explained.

With the default Cube Object in the 3D Viewport Editor, before any animation has taken place the Graph Editor displays as shown in Figure 15.32. There is a vertical blue line Cursor at Frame 1 in the Timeline and a horizontal blue line Cursor at position 0 (zero) in the vertical Scale.

When you click LMB on a Frame in the horizontal Timeline or click, hold and drag the blue Cursor button in the Timeline, moving the vertical Cursor, the horizontal blue line Cursor disappears from view. Moving the vertical Cursor back to Frame 1 does not reinstate the horizontal Cursor.

To display the horizontal Cursor, click on the blue button in the Timeline, hold and drag down. By holding LMB and dragging both vertical and horizontal Cursors are positioned in the Graph Editor.

Default Graph Editor Display   Timeline - Frames   Figure 15.32

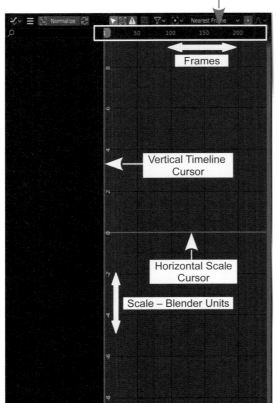

Frames

Click LMB on the blue button in the Timeline and drag Vertical Cursor to Frame 73

Vertical Timeline Cursor

Click LMB on the blue button and drag down to display the Horizontal Cursor

Horizontal Scale Cursor

Scale – Blender Units

The significance of positioning the Cursors will follow.

15.19 Editing the Curve in the Graph Editor

To edit the X Axis movement of the Cube, select the top Control Handle, press the G Key and move the handle down approximately three units and left towards the Cursor aligning with Frame 50. Click LMB to set in position (Figure 15.33).

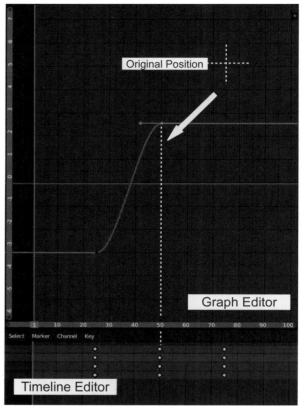

Note: When the Control Handle is moved you will see a set of Keyframes move to the Frame where you position the handle (Frame 50). This set of Keyframes is for the X Axis movement of the Cube. The Keyframes remaining at Frame 75 are for the Y Axis scale of the Cube.

Playing the animation at this point will see the Cube start to move on the X Axis at Frame 25 then stop at Frame 50. The Cube will scale on the Y Axis between Frame 25 and frame 75. Before frame 25 and after frame 75 no change in state occurs.

By scaling and rotating the top Control Handle you further edit the Curve (Figure 15.34.

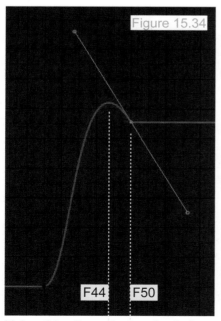

With the handle shaping the Curve as shown in Figure 15.34, when the animation is played, the Cube moves forward on the X Axis between Frame 25 and Frame 44 then reverses direction until frame 50. **Note:** With this method no additional Keyframes are added to the Timeline.

Alternatively, instead of rotating the top Control handle, press **Ctrl** and **RMB Click on the Curve** to add a new Control Handle (Figure 15.35). New Keyframes are inserted in the Timeline. With the handle selected press G Key and Translate it up and Scale approximating the Curve previously created.

Using this alternative method gives more control in editing since it provides an additional Control Handle and Keyframes.

Figure 15.35

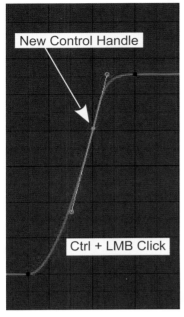

New Control Handle

Ctrl + LMB Click

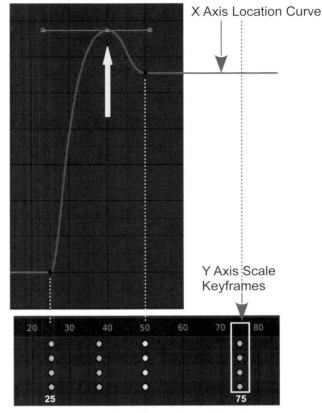

X Axis Location Curve

Y Axis Scale Keyframes

Note: The Keyframes in the Timeline.

Yellow Keyframes are selected.

White Keyframes are deselected.

Keyframes in the Dope Sheet Timeline

15.20 Editing the Curve in the Dope Sheet Timeline

Curves and, therefore, the animation may be edited, by repositioning Keyframes in the Timeline of the Dope Sheet Editor. The first operation is to select individual Keyframes.

Figure 15.36

Click **LMB** on either of the first four channels to select Keyframes

Channel

Selected   Deselected

First Keyframe   Last Keyframe

Last Keyframe Selected

Selecting Keyframes in the Dope Sheet Editor follows the basic rules for all Editors. **LMB** Click to select. Press **Alt + A Key** to deselect. Press **A Key** to select all.

With a Keyframe selected press **Delete** or the **X Key** to delete the Keyframe.

With a Keyframe selected press the **G Key**, hold **LMB** and drag to reposition the Keyframe.

With the **Object Transforms** expanded, click **LMB** on a Channel to select it (Z Location). Click LMB on a Keyframe in the Channel, Press **G Key**, hold **LMB** and reposition.

First Z Location Keyframe Repositioned ─────────────

Figure 15.37

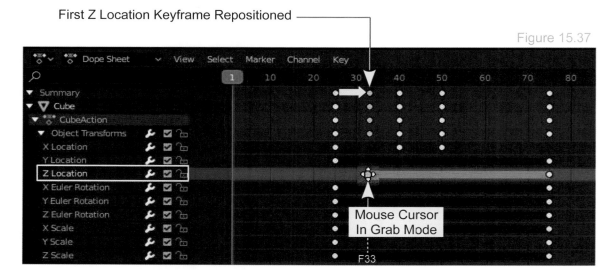

Note: Repositioning the Z Location Keyframe as shown has no effect on the Cube in the 3D View Editor. When inserting the LocRotScale Keyframe no change was made to the Z Location in the 3D View Editor, therefore, the Z Location Graph is a horizontal straight line.

─── Control Handle

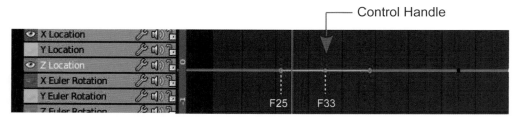

Figure 15.38

Repositioning the Keyframe in the Dope Sheet has repositioned the Control handle in the Graph Editor which, if there were a change in elevation on the Z Axis in the scene for the Cube, it would commence at this point.

To understand the correlation between the Graph Editor and the Dope Sheet align the two Editors one above the other (Figure 15.39 over).

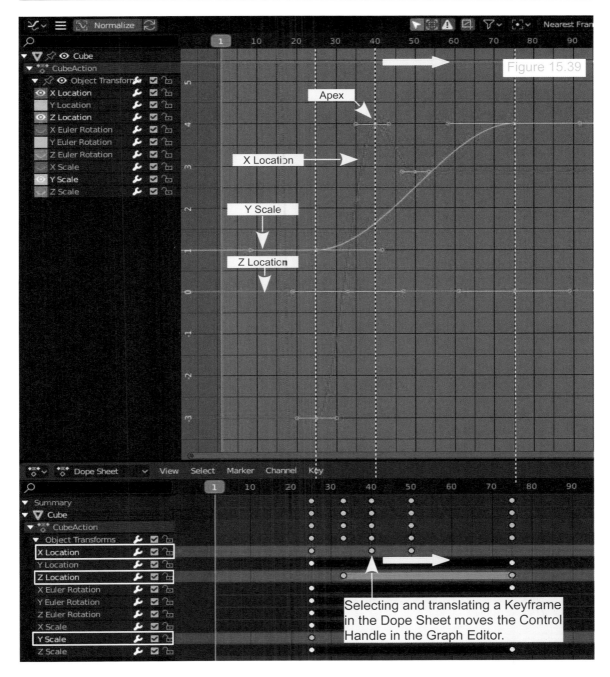

Figure 15.39

Translating a Keyframe in the Dope Sheet moves the Control Handle in the Graph Editor. Where the Keyframe/Control Handle is positioned determines where the action in the animation occurs. In Figure 15.39 the apex of the X Location Curve is the point where the forward movement of the Cube in the 3D Viewport Editor is reversed.

15.21 Scaling in the Dope Sheet

Besides moving Keyframes adjustment to when an action takes place in the animation may also be adjusted by Scaling on the Timeline in the Dope Sheet.

Note: Scaling is relative to the Dope Sheet Editor Cursor. To demonstrate consider the movement of the Cube on the X Axis between the apex of the Curve in the Graph Editor (Frame 40) and the final position (Frame 50).

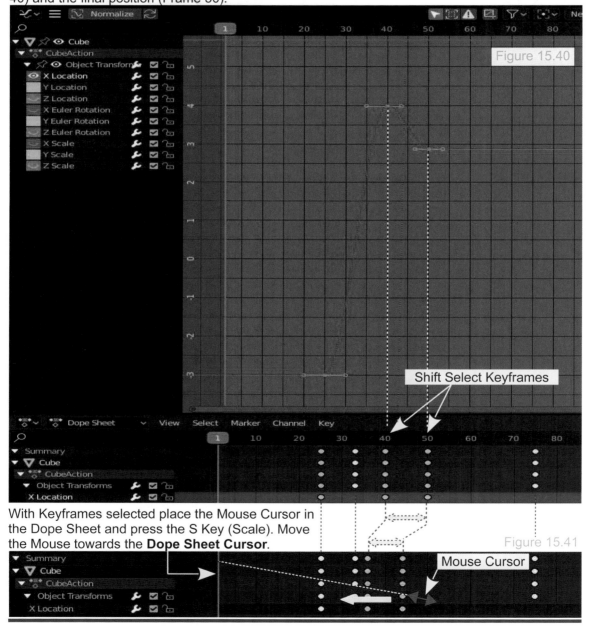

Figure 15.40

Shift Select Keyframes

With Keyframes selected place the Mouse Cursor in the Dope Sheet and press the S Key (Scale). Move the Mouse towards the **Dope Sheet Cursor**.

Figure 15.41

Mouse Cursor

The selected Keyframes are Scaled relative to the Dope Sheet Cursor (blue line). You will see the shape of the Curve in the Graph Editor modified accordingly.

Repeat the procedure, this time, positioning the Dope Sheet Cursor between the selected Keyframes. The Scaling is relative to the Cursor.

Figure 15.42

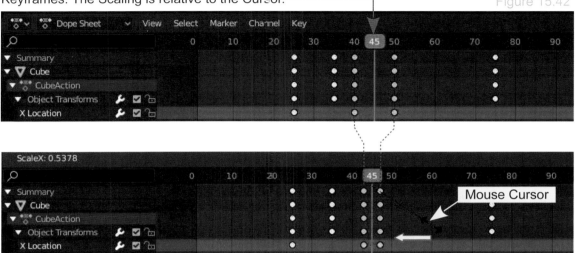

Moving Keyframes and manipulating Control Handles edits the animation Curve. The Curve has been a Bezier Type but there are alternative types to be considered which means alternative types of Interpolation between Keyframes resulting in different types of motion for the selected Object.

15.22 Other Types of Curves

By default, Blender displays **Bezier Type Curves** in the Graph Editor which means that **Bezier Type Interpolation** is used between **Keyframes**.

When considering Bezier Type Interpolation (the Curve shape) the curves at either end of the graph line represent the acceleration of the Object.

Other Types of Interpolation (Curves) are accessed in the Graph Editor or the Dope Sheet Editor. In the Dope Sheet Header click **Key** and select **Interpolation Mode** or with the Mouse Cursor in either Editor press the T Key. Either method opens the Set Keyframe Interpolation menu.

Figure 15.43

At this point only be concerned with the Constant, Linear and Bezier options.

303

With a Curve selected in the Graph Editor (the default is Type Bezier) select **Constant** or **Linear**.

Figure 15.44

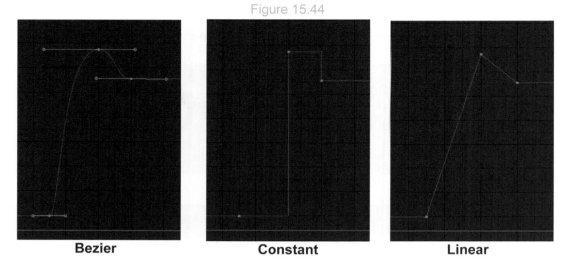

Bezier   **Constant**   **Linear**

Each Type of Interpolation (Curve) produces a different motion in the animation. **Constant Interpolation** results in a dramatic quick change from one state to the other at a given Frame while **Linear Interpolation** produces a change following a straight line graph between points . The choice of these types of graphs and motions depends on how you want your actor to behave in the animation. Both of the alternatives to Bezier give the option to grab and move points and to add additional points on the graph, but Bezier is by far the most flexible of the three.

Extrapolation

Blender interpolates to add frames between the Keyframes according to which of the previous Curve options were selected. Blender can also figure out what to do with the frames of the animation before the first Keyframe and after the last Keyframe, which is called **Extrapolation**.

With the Mouse Cursor in the Graph Editor press **Shift + E Key** to display the **Set Keyframe Extrapolation** menu.

Figure 15.45

Constant Extrapolation: Blender has inserted frames that comply with a Bezier curve. On either side of the Keyframes, you can see horizontal lines that indicate there is no further change in status. This is constant extrapolation.

Linear Extrapolation: Blender plots a straight line curve leaving and entering the curve. The action of the actor before and after first and last Keyframes follows these straight line curves.

Cyclic Extrapolation: Blender copies the graph between the first and the last Keyframes and duplicates it to infinity on either side of the graph. You **Make** the Extrapolation Cyclic or you **Clear** the Cyclic Extrapolation.

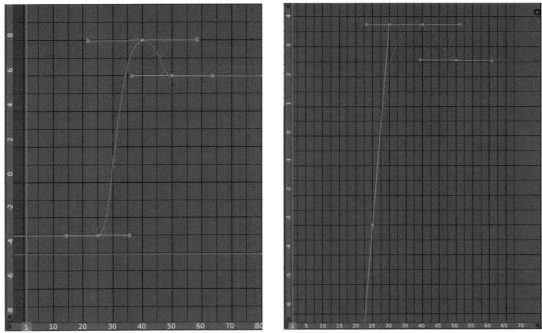

Constant Extrapolation

Figure 15.46

Linear Extrapolation

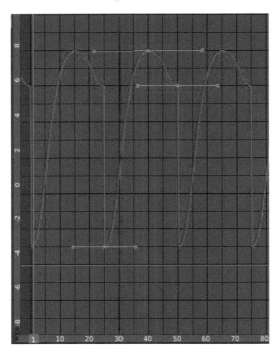

Cyclic Extrapolation

15.23 The Curve Properties Panel

The **Curve Properties panel** (Figures 15.47, 15.48) provides data and gives control to certain functions in the Graph panel. With the **Mouse Cursor** in the **Graph Editor**, press the **N key** to display the **Curve Properties panel** at the RHS of the Editor. The panel is divided into three Tabs; <u>**F-Curve**, **Modifiers** and **View** Properties.</u>

Figure 15.47

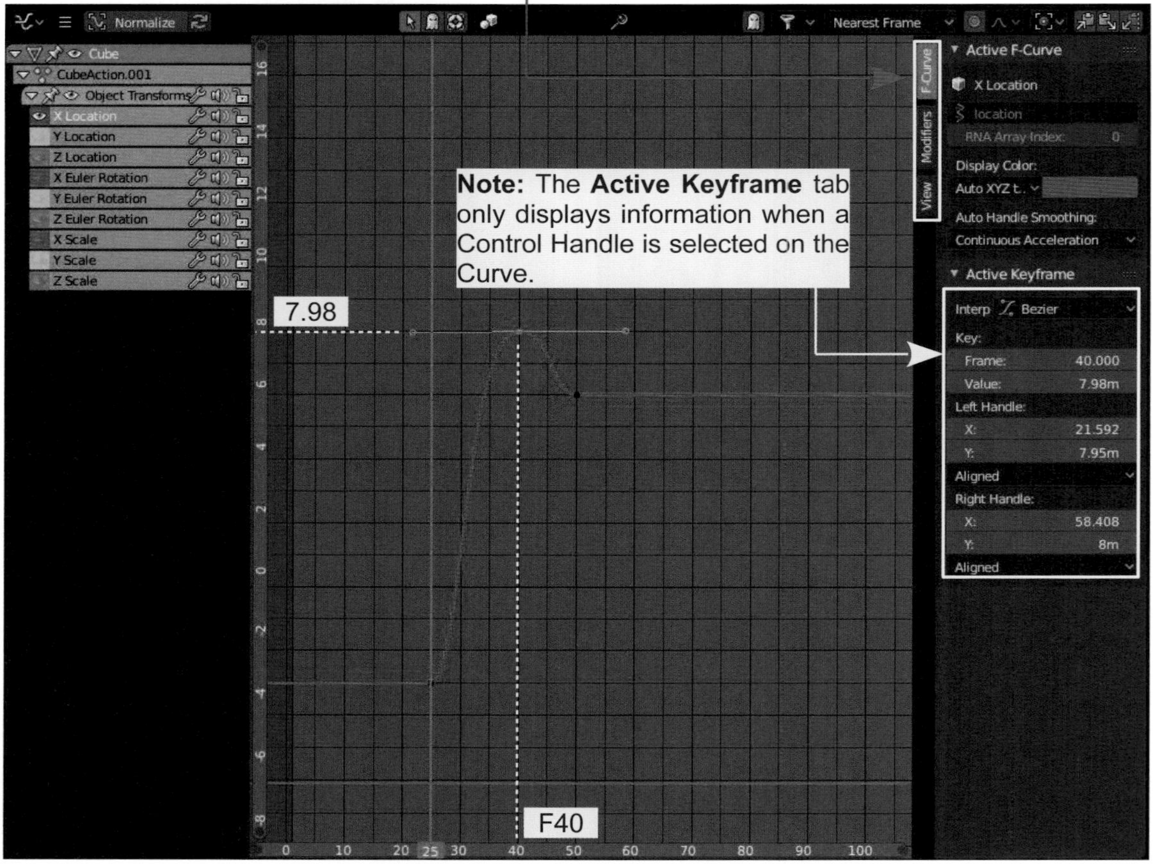

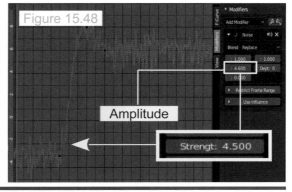

Note: The **Active Keyframe** tab only displays information when a Control Handle is selected on the Curve.

This introduction to the Curve Properties panel is presented to make you aware of its existence. Experiment with the values, especially the **Modifiers.** For example: With only the X Location Curve displayed in the Graph Editor click on the **Modifiers Tab** and then click Add Modifier. Select the **Noise Modifier** which adds a jittered effect to the Curve. Playing the animation sees the Cube shake as it moves in the 3D Viewport Editor. For a more dramatic shake increase the **Amplitude** of the **Noise.**

Figure 15.48

Amplitude

Strengt: 4.500

15.24 Animating Rotation

Animating Rotation deserves special consideration when attempting to create a continuous smooth Rotation. As an example use a **UV Sphere Object** in **Top Orthographic View** with one Vertex moved to form a pointer (Figure 15.49). In Figure 15.49 a dial has been drawn showing Rotation graduations with the intended Rotation indicated.

Divide the 3D Viewport Editor into three panels creating a **Graph Editor, 3D Viewport in Top Orthographic View** and a **Dope Sheet Editor**. The Timeline editor is retained across the bottom of the arrangement.

In the **Timeline Editor** turn on **Automatic Keyframing**.

Figure 15.49

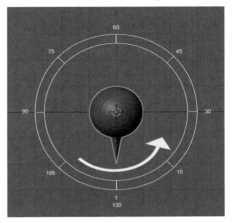

Figure 15.50

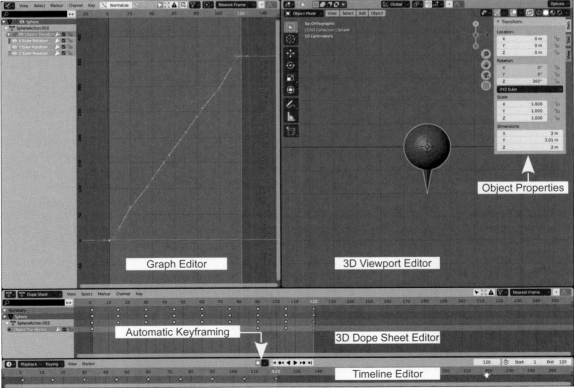

In the **3D Viewport Editor** have the modified UV Sphere selected and press the **N Key** to display the **Object Properties Panel**.

Note: In Figure 15.49 the dial graduations are expressed as **Keyframes in the Timeline**.

With the Sphere selected and the pointer directed towards Frame 1 on the dial, have the **Dope Sheet Cursor** at Frame 1 in the Timeline. With the **Mouse Cursor** in the 3D Viewport Editor press the **I Key** and select **Rotation** as the Keyframe Type. Rotation Keyframes are entered in the Dope Sheet Timeline at Frame 1. **Note:** This is manually inserting the first Keyframe.

Move the **Dope Sheet Cursor** to Frame 15. In the **Object Properties Panel,** for the Sphere, enter **Z Axis Rotation: 45°**. Keyframes are **automatically** inserted in the Timeline at Frame 15.

Move the Dope Sheet Cursor to Frame 30, enter Z Axis Rotation: 90 in the Object Properties Panel. Keyframes are automatically inserted in the Timeline at Frame 30.

Repeat the procedure all the way round to Frame 120 which coincides with frame 1 on the dial. Keyframes will have been inserted in the Dope Sheet Timeline at 15 Frame intervals from Frame 1 to Frame 120.

Figure 15.51

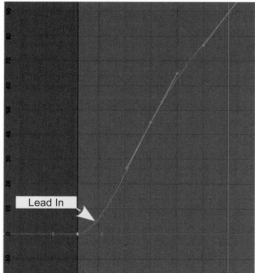

In the Graph Editor you see a graph line consisting of a series of segments punctuated by Control Handles (Figure 15.51). The Graph Line is a series of **Bezier Curves**. By zooming in on the Curve you will observe a slight lead in and lead out at each Handle. This is more pronounced at the beginning and end of the Graph. The lead in and lead out results in a hesitation in Rotation at each Handle.

With the default settings, when the Play button is pressed in the Timeline Editor the Sphere Rotates, hesitating as each Keyframe (Handle) is passed, from Frame 1 to frame 120 then stops.

The Dope Sheet and Timeline Cursors continue to move on to frame 250 then the Animation is repeated.

Figure 15.52

To produce a smooth continuous Rotation have the **Mouse Cursor** in the **Graph Editor**, then press **Shift + E Key** and select **Linear Extrapolation** in the menu that displays. Change the Animation End Frame to 120 in the Timeline Editor Header. With these changes a continuous smooth Rotation will be seen when the Animation is played.

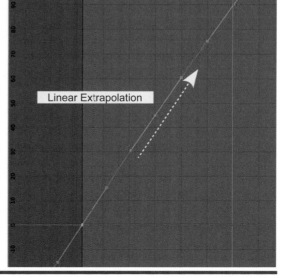

Linear Extrapolation

Entering **Liner Extrapolation** in the Graph Editor straightens out the curve and extends the curve to infinity. This has the effect of producing a smooth constant Rotation of the Object no matter what End Frame is set in the Timeline Editor.

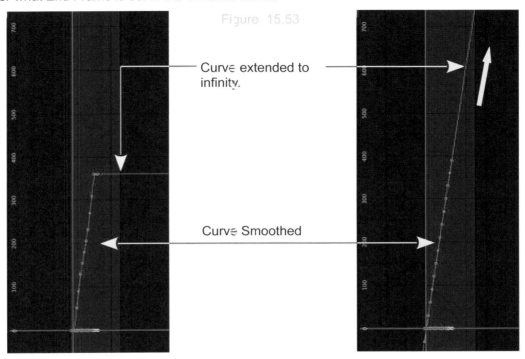

Figure 15.53

Curve extended to infinity.

Curve Smoothed

Speed of Rotation

The Speed of Rotation depends on the Frame Rate of the Animation playback set in the Properties Editor, Output Properties, Format Tab. The default Rate is 24 fps (Frames per Second). The Speed of Rotation is also determined by the number of Frames between Keyframes. For one Revolution you have 120 Frames, therefore, 120 F / 24Fps = 5 Seconds per Revolution. To alter the speed **Scale the Timeline**. With the Mouse Cursor in the Timeline Editor, press the **S Key** and drag the Mouse.

Figure 15.54

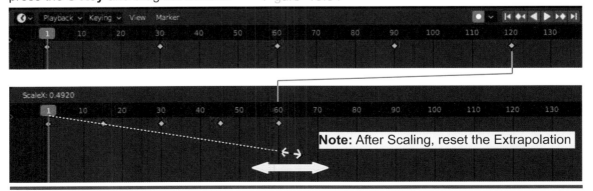

Note: After Scaling, reset the Extrapolation

15.25 Rotation Using F-Curves

The Blender Manual states, "After animating some property in Blender using Keyframes you can edit their corresponding curves. When something is "animated", it changes over time. This curve is shown as something called an **F-Curve**. Basically what an F-Curve does is an interpolation between two animated properties. In Blender, animating an object means changing one of its properties, such as the Object's Location, or its Scale.

As demonstrated, when an Object is animated a Curve is created in the Graph Editor. It, therefore, follows that this is an **F-Curve**. When considering the default Cube Object in the 3D View Editor, before it is animated, there is no Curve in the Graph Editor. The Cube may be made to Rotate by animating to create a **Location Curve** then editing the Curve using Modifiers.

Animate the Cube to move from minus 5 units on the X Axis to plus 5 units on the X Axis between Frame 1 and frame 180. An **F-Curve** is drawn in the Graph Editor.

Figure 15.55

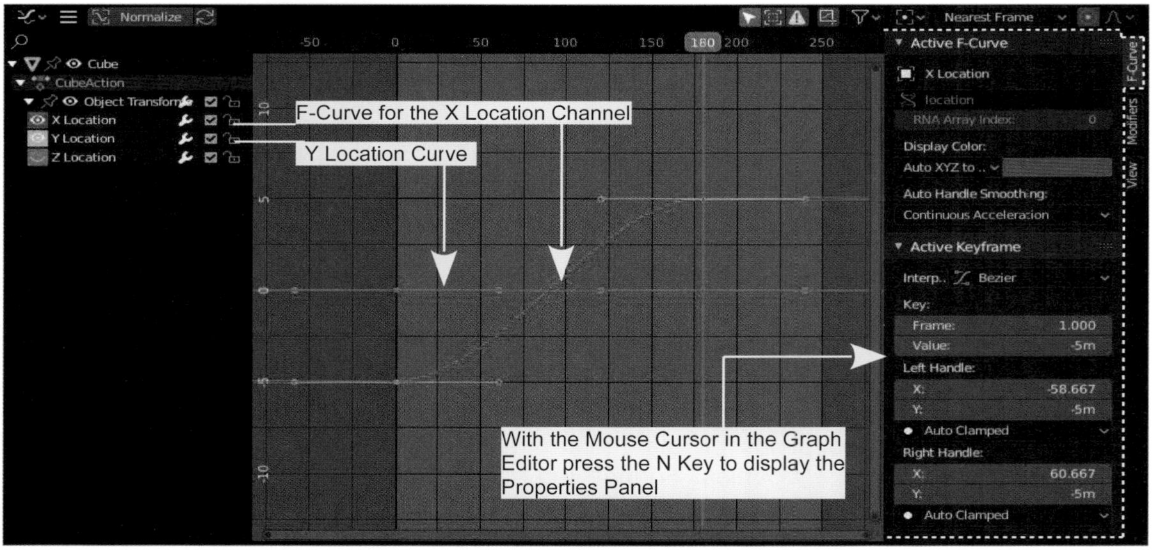

With the Curve drawn, playing the animation shows the Cube move from minus 5 to plus 5 along the X Axis in the 3D View Editor. As well as the X Location Curve a Y Location Curve has also been created (straight line).

Both Curves may be modified to produce a Rotation of the Cube.

In the **Properties Panel** click on the **Modifiers Tab**, click **Add Modifier** and select **Built in Function** (Figure 15.56). The default Built in Function is **Sine** which immediately changes the Bezier Curve in the Graph Editor to a Sine Curve or rather a Sinusoidal Curve since it repeats to infinity (Figure 15.57 over).

Figure 15.56

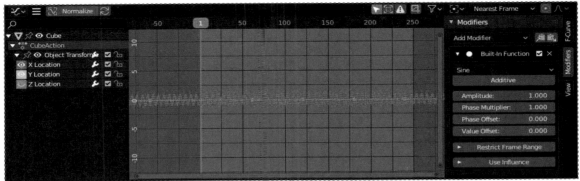

Figure 15.57

Playing the animation shows the Cube in the 3D Viewport Editor oscillate on the X Axis. The degree of oscillation is governed by the Amplitude value in the Modifier. The movement of the Cube is best seen in Top Orthographic View.

In the Modifier panel, increase the Amplitude to 2.000 and reduce the Phase Multiple to 0.100. This reduces the oscillation of the Cube to a nice smooth motion

Figure 15.58

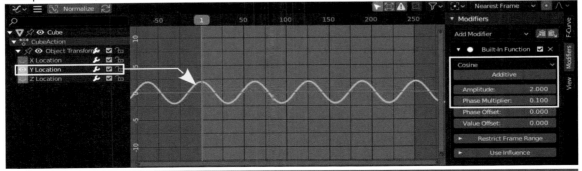

The Curve under consideration at this point has been the Curve representing the **X Axis** motion of the Cube (see the **X Location Channel** in the Graph Editor). As previously stated a **Y Axis** motion Curve is also drawn (straight line) as seen by selecting the **Y Location Channel**. By applying a Built in Function Modifier and making it **Type Cosine** with Amplitude 2.00 and Phase Multiplier 0.100, the Cube rotates around the center of the Scene.

Figure 15.59

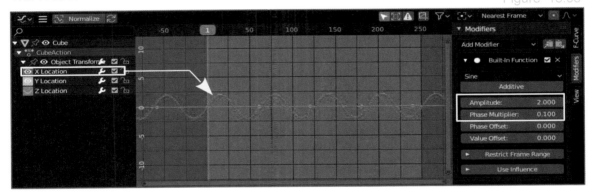

15.26 Animating Other Features

There are many features in Blender which may be animated. For example:

Material (color) Animation

Figure 15.60

As an example of animating color change perform the following using the Animation Workspace;

Add a UV Sphere in the 3D Viewport Editor and set the surface to Smooth Shading. In the Properties Editor, Material buttons, add a Material and leave Use Nodes active.

Change the 3D Viewport Editor to rendered Viewport Shading.

Figure 15.61

In the Material buttons, click on the base Color bar and select a color. **RMB click the color bar** and select **Insert Keyframe** from the menu.

This enters a Keyframe in the Dope Sheet Timeline at the location of the Cursor (the default is frame 1).

Relocate the Timeline Cursor to another Frame (Frame 50). Select a different color. RMB click the color bar and select Insert Keyframe. A Keyframe is entered at frame 50.

Repeat for Frame 100 then play the animation to see the color change in the 3D Viewport Editor.

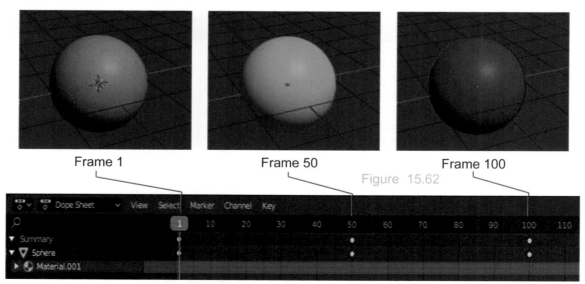

Frame 1   Frame 50   Frame 100

Figure 15.62

Timeline Cursor at Frame 1 (blue line)

Spotlight Size Animation

Properties Editor ⟶

The size of a Spotlight beam may be animated to change.

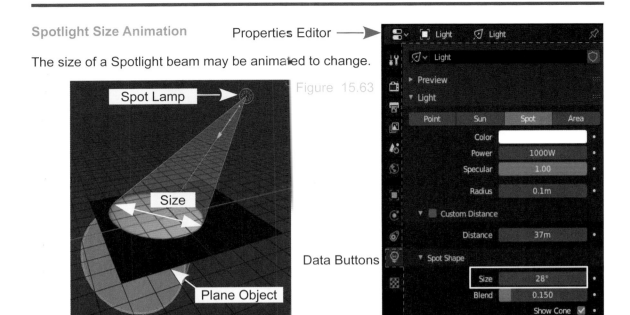

Figure 15.63

Using the 3D Animation Workspace be at Frame 1 in the Timeline . With the Spot Lamp selected in the 3D Viewport Editor, in the Properties Editor, Data buttons, Spot Shape tab, **RMB click** on Size and select **Insert Keyframe**. Change to Frame 50. Change the Size and insert a second Keyframe. Repeat at frame 100 and play the animation.

15.27 Keying Sets

In a basic capacity **Keying Sets** provide the means of assigning multiple **Animation** properties to an Object, then creating all the Keyframes in a single go.

To demonstrate have the default **Layout Workspace** with the **Timeline Editor** sized vertically, divided in two and having one half changed to the **Dope Sheet Editor**. The upper part of the Screen is the 3D Viewport Editor containing the default Cube. The Timeline and Dope Sheet Cursors will be located at Frame 1.

Keyframes will be created for the Location and Material color. Have the 3D Viewport Editor in **Material Preview Viewport Shading Mode**.

In the 3D View Editor move the Cube back along the X Axis. Note: The default Cube has the default gray Material applied.

With the Mouse Cursor in the 3D View Editor press the **N Key** to display the **Object Properties Panel**.

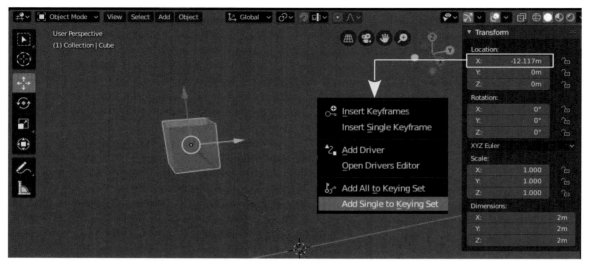

Figure 15.64

Under **Location** in the panel, RMB click on **X Location** and select Add **Single to Keyeing Set.** This is saying you wish to add a single Keyframe to the Keying Set. It does not enter a Keyframe in either Timeline Editor.

RMB click on **Y Location** and repeat the above which adds a second Keyframe request to the set. Again, Keyframes are not entered in the Timelines.

Now request a Keyframe for the Material color. In the **Properties Editor, Material buttons**, RMB click on the **Base Color** bar and select **Add to Keying Set.**

Keyframes have been requested for the X and Y Location and the Material Color of the Cube. The Timeline and Dope Sheet editor Cursors are at Frame 1. The Keyframes are, therefore, requested for Frame 1.

In the **Timeline Editor Header** click on the **Keying** button. In the menu that displays, adjacent to **Button Keying Set** click on the Key button **with the plus sign above the key icon**. This inserts the requested Keyframes in the Timelines at Frame 1. A message displays in the Header at the bottom of the Screen.

Figure 15.65

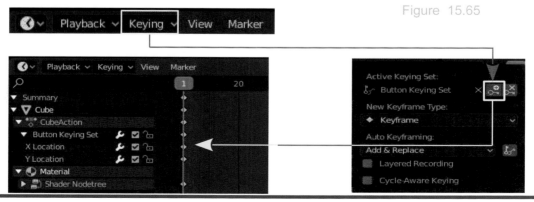

Move the Timeline Cursors to Frame 50. In the 3D Viewport Editor relocate the Cube on the XY Plane. In the Object Properties Panel, RMB click on the X and Y Location channels and request Keyframes. Change the Material base Color and request a Keyframe.

Repeat the Keying procedure, entering Keyframes in the Timelines.

Move the Timeline Cursors to a different Frame and repeat the requesting and adding Keyframes.

Scrubbing the Cursors in the Timelines shows the Cube moving and changing color.

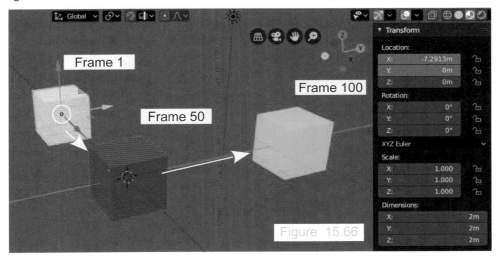

Figure 15.66

20.28 Animation Follow Path

As previously demonstrated, animating an Object to move is achieved by entering Keyframes in the Timeline with the Object located at positions in the 3D Viewport Editor. With the animation created it may be edited by modifying the Curve in the Graph Editor or relocating Keyframes in the Dope Sheet Editor Timeline.

On occasion you may wish to animate an Object to follow a pre-constructed Path. Once the Object is made to follow the Path, you reshape the Path to alter the movement of the Object in the 3D Viewport Editor.

To demonstrate the procedure for animation following a Path, open the **Animation Workspace** and change the left hand 3D Viewport Editor Camera View to the **Graph Editor**. Have the right hand 3D Viewport Editor in top Orthographic View with default Cube Object **at the center of the Scene**.

Deselect the Cube and add a **Curve Type: Bezier** to the Scene. You may use any Curve Type but the Bezier Curve has a nice profile when entered. Scale the Bezier Curve up six times (Figure 15.67).

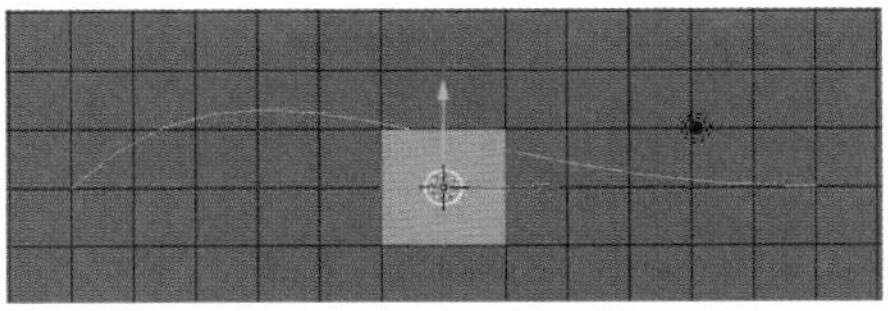

Figure 15.67

Deselect the Curve and **select the Cube**.

In the **Properties Editor, Object Constraints Properties**, click **Add Object Constraint** and select **Follow Path** in the Relationship category. The **Follow Path Tab** displays (Figure 15.68).

Properties Editor

Figure 15.68

Constraints Options Panel

In the **Follow Path Constraint** click in the bar where you see the **Target** icon and select **Bezier Curve** from the panel that displays. Also, check (tick) **Follow Curve**. **Note: Forward Y** is selected (the Object's Axis which points in the direction of movement).

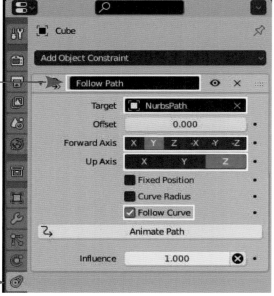

Object Constraint Properties →

Entering the Target locates the Cube in the 3D Viewport Editor at the LH end of the Curve Path. Checking **Follow Curve** aligns the Cube's Axis to the Path (Figure 15.69).

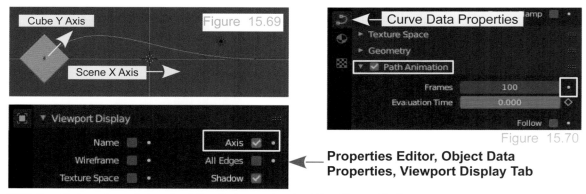

Figure 15.69

Cube Y Axis

Scene X Axis

Curve Data Properties

Figure 15.70

Properties Editor, Object Data Properties, Viewport Display Tab

With the Cube aligned deselect the Cube and select the Curve Path.

Go to the **Properties Editor, Object Data Properties** (for the Curve Path) and see the **Path Animation Tab** at the bottom of the panel. Ensure that **Path Animation** is checked (Figure 15.70). Select the Cube and go back to the Follow Path Constraint. In the Constraint panel click **Animate Path.** Press Play in the Timeline Editor Header to see the Cube traverse the length of the Path.

Note: At this point Keyframes have not been entered in the Timeline Editor.

You may select the Curve Path, Tab into Edit Mode and modify the shape of the Curve. If you Extrude the Path from either end, the Cube always locates at the start of the Path at Frame 1 in the Animation. In Edit Mode the Curve Path displays with chevrons along its length indicating the direction of travel.

How quickly the Cube appears to traverse the length of the Curve Path in the 3D View Editor depends on the physical length of the Curve and the Frame Rate of the Animation (see the Properties Editor, Output buttons, Frame Rate).

Altering the Frame Rate will change the speed of movement along the Path but the Frame Rate is set for the output required in the video format being produced. **Do not change this**. There are two alternatives; Modifying Evaluation Time and Keyframing.

15.29 Evaluation Time

Evaluation Time settings are found in the Properties Editor, Data buttons, Path Animation Tab. The setting is defined by Blender as;

Evaluation Time.
Parametric position along the length of the curve that Objects 'following' it should be at (position is evaluated by dividing by the 'Path Length' value).

In a practical sense you could consider the Evaluation Time as a percentage. At 0.000 % the Object is at the start of the Path, at 100.000 % it is at the end of the Path.

3D View Editor

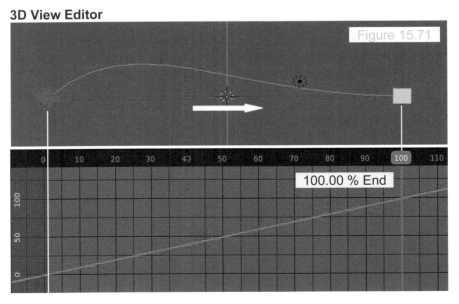

Figure 15.71

100.00 % End

Graph Editor

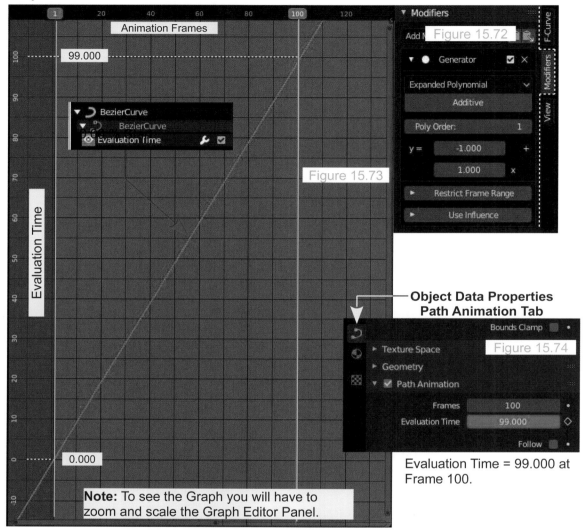

Figure 15.72

Figure 15.73

Figure 15.74

**Object Data Properties
Path Animation Tab**

Evaluation Time = 99.000 at Frame 100.

Note: To see the Graph you will have to zoom and scale the Graph Editor Panel.

Figure 15.69 shows a Cube Object scaled down 0.5 and a Bezier Curve Path scaled up 10 times. The Cube has a Follow Path Constraint applied with Target: Bezier Curve. With the Bezier Curve Path selected, the Properties Editor, Object Data Properties, Path Animation Tab (Figure 15.65) shows the value; Frames 100. This is the default value which means the Cube will traverse the Path in 100 Frames of the animation. With the Graph Editor Cursor at Frame 1 the Evaluation Time is 0.000. With Cursor at frame 100 the Evaluation Time is 99.000 (Frame 100 – Frame 1 = 99). The default Frame Rate is 24 Frames per second, therefore, actual time to traverse the Path will be approximately 4 seconds.

The Graph Editor (Figure 15.73) shows the Evaluation Time Graph (red line) indicating these values. The Bezier Curve Path must be selected in the 3D Viewport Editor to see the Graph.

With the Mouse Cursor in the Graph Editor, press the N key to display the Properties Panel (Figure 15.75) and select the Modifiers Tab at the RHS of the panel. Note the two values;

y= -1.000 and 1.000 x

Figure 15.75

Increasing or decreasing **y = -1.000** shifts the Graph Line to the right and left (the slope of the graph remains the same). Altering the **1.000 x** value changes the slope of the Graph.

Altering either value alters the position of the Cube on the Curve Path at a particular Frame thus affecting the speed of traversing.

15.30 Keyframing

Up to this point **Keyframes** have not been entered in the **Timeline.** The Graph Editor only displays the Evaluation Time (when the Curve Path is selected in the 3D Viewport Editor). Entering Keyframes in the Dope Sheet Timeline allows you to manipulate where the Cube is located along the Curve Path at a particular Frame in the animation. This also affects the speed of traversing the Path.

With the Cube path arrangement set up as shown in Figure 20.69 and with the Timeline Cursor at Frame 1, add a **Follow Path Constraint** to the Cube with **Target: BezierCurve.**

Do NOT Animate the Path.

Select the Bezier Curve Path and in the Properties Editor, Object data buttons, Path Animation Tab, click the button at the end of the Frames bar. **Keyframes** are entered in the Timeline.

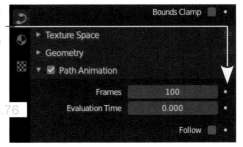

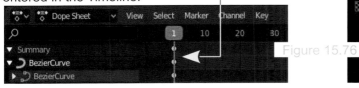

Figure 15.76

In the Path Animation Tab the Frames bar turns yellow and the button becomes a diamond shape indicating Keyframes have been added (Figure 15.77).

Figure 15.77

Move the Timeline Cursor to Frame 100, the end of the Path as indicated by Frames: 100.

Note: Frame 100 is the default value. You may reset this, bearing in mind, the default TOTAL animation length set in the Timeline is 250 Frames (Start: 1, End: 250).

Change the Evaluation Time to 100 (or to the value you have set).

Press the diamond button to enter Keyframes at Frame 100 in the Timeline (Figure 15.76 – 77).

Figure 15.78

To have the Cube traverse the Path select the Cube and in the **Follow Path Constraint** click **Animate Path**.

Pressing the Play button in the Timeline shows the Cube following the Path between Frame 1 and Frame 100. At Frame 100 the Cube stops while the Animation continues on to Frame 250 then repeats.

At this point , with the Curve Path selected in the 3D View Editor, the Graph Editor shows two Graph lines; the Evaluation Time (green) and Path Length (red) (Figure 20.80). You will have to zoom and scale the graph Editor to bring the graphs into view.

The red Path Length displays as a straight horizontal line since the motion of the Cube along the Path is constant.

With the Mouse Cursor in the Graph Editor press the N key to open the Properties panel (Figure 15.79) and note, under **Active Keyframes** that the **Interpolation Type** is **Linear**.

Figure 15.79

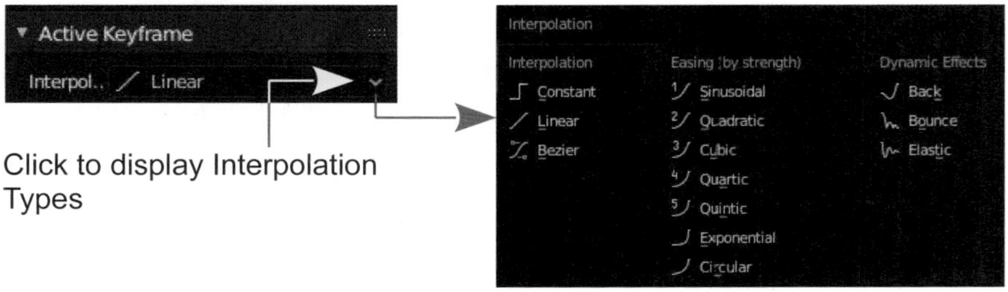

Click to display Interpolation Types

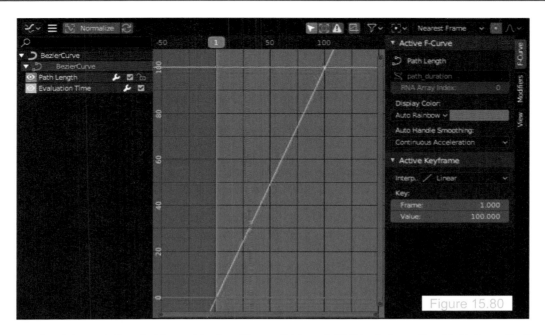

Figure 15.80

Change the Interpolation to Type: Bezier. Press Ctrl and RMB click on the Path Length Graph (red line) to add a control handle then drag down (Figure 15.81).

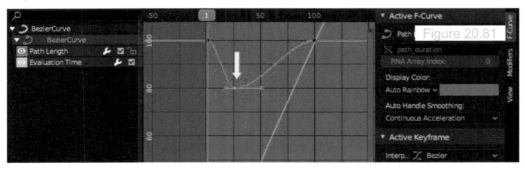

Figure 20.81

Playing the animation show a subtle variation in speed as the Cube moves along the Path, most noticeably, a deceleration as it approaches the end. Adding another control handle and arranging as shown in Figure 15.82 produces a distinct pause in motion.

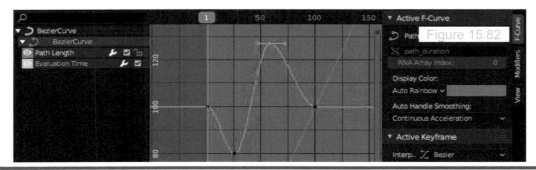

Figure 15.82

If control handles are positioned as shown in Figure 15.83 the Cube will move along the Path until it reaches Frame 85 in the animation then stop. You will observe that this is the point where the **Path Length Graph** intersects the **Evaluation Time Graph** which has become the end of the animation.

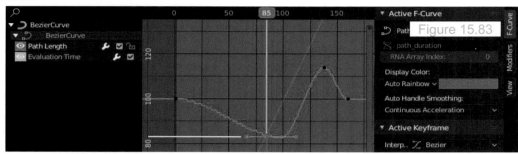

Observe that in the Properties Editor Object data buttons for the path Frames = Evaluation Time (Figure 15.84).

The foregoing has been an **introduction only** to Path Animation. With the examples shown you will be more easily placed to research and experiment to discover what can be achieved.

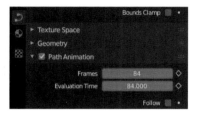

Figure 15.84

15.31 Displacement Sound Animations

A sound file (Music) can be used to affect the movement of vertices producing an interesting display effect.

For a demonstration have an image file (texture) such as that shown in Figure 15.85 and a sound file (music) saved on your hard drive. The Image Texture used in this demonstration is named Art-Fibers.jpg while the sound file is named Flex_Vector_-_Born_Ready.mp3.

Figure 15.85

Flex_Vector is a Hip Hop file with a distinct base beat. You may use any sound file (MP3).

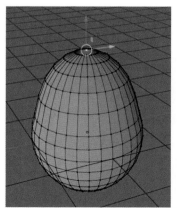

To demonstrate, set up a Sphere object (egg shaped – any shape with a reasonable number of Vertices) (Figure 20.86).

Figure 15.86

3D View Editor Header

Proportional Editing ———┐ Spherical Falloff

UV Sphere with a single Vertex selected and translated up on the Z Axis. **Proportional Editing** has been activated with **Spherical Falloff**.

With the Egg selected in the 3D View Editor, in **Object Mode** go to the **Properties Editor, Material buttons** and **Add a Material**. **Have Use Nodes active**.

Click the button at the RHS of the Base Color bar and select Image Texture. Navigate to the Texture Image file and click Open Image.

Figure 15.87

Change the 3D View Editor to Rendered Viewport Shading to see the Image applied as a Material to the Egg.

With the Egg selected in the 3D View Editor go to the Properties Editor, Texture buttons and Add a Texture, selecting the same Image as before.

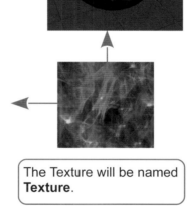

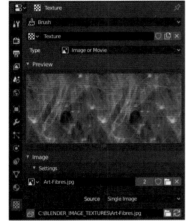

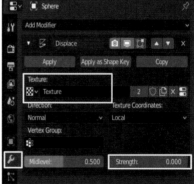

The Texture will be named **Texture**.

In the Properties Editor, Modifier buttons Add a **Displace** Modifier to the Egg selecting the Texture named **Texture**.

Modifier Buttons

With the Strength value in the Modifier: 1.000 the Egg in the 3D Viewport Editor is deformed by the Texture. Set the Strength value to 0.000.

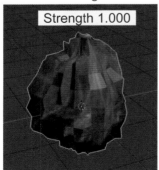

Strength 1.000

Figure 15.88

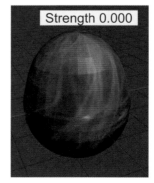

Strength 0.000

Divide the 3D Viewport Editor horizontally and make the lower part the **Video Sequence Editor.** The Timeline Editor remains at the bottom of the Screen.

With the Egg selected and the Timeline Editor Cursor at Frame 1 in the Timeline, in the Displace Modifier panel RMB click on the Strength value and select Insert Keyframe.

The Strength value slider turns yellow and a Keyframe is entered in the Timeline at frame 1.

In the Video sequence Editor Header click Add – Sound and navigate to the sound file then click Add Sound at the upper RHS, The file is entered in Channel 1 in the Video Sequence Editor.

Figure 15.89

Change the Video Sequence Editor to the **Graph Editor** and in the Header click **Key** and select **Bake Sound to F-Curve**. Navigate to and select the Sound File then click **Bake Sound to F-Curve** in upper RHS of the panel. **Note:** A Keyframe must be entered before this instruction.

Figure 15.90

A Sound Curve is drawn in the Graph Editor.

Figure 15.91

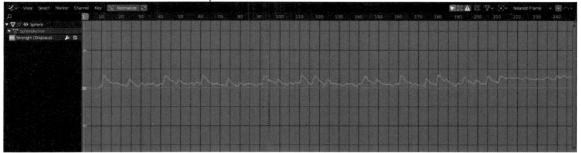

Playing the animation sees the Egg pulsate in the 3D Viewport Editor to the beat of the Sound (have the speakers turned on).

This result may be what is required but if not you can modify the Curve in the Graph Editor. With the Mouse Cursor in the Graph Editor press the N Key to display a Properties Panel and select the Modifiers tab.

Click Add Modifier and select Envelope. Click Add Point to add control points. Adjusting the Control Point values alters the Sound Curve in the Graph Editor which alters the way in which the sound affects the animation.

Figure 15.92

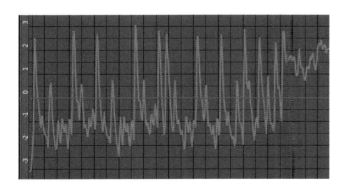

15.32 Sound Effect and Cast Modifier

Displacement Sound Animation in the previous section used a sound file to affect the **Strength value** of a **Displacement modifier.** A sound file was then **Baked** to an **F-Curve** and modified. This was to control the displacement of the Object's surface.

You may combine a sound file **F-Curve** and a **Cast modifier** with an **Empty** control object to influence an animation of the Object's surface deformation.

To demonstrate set up a Plane object with a **Cast Modifier** and an **Empty** object (Figure 15.93).

Set up the 3D View Editor

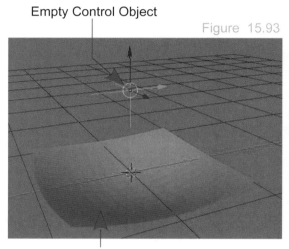

Empty Control Object

Figure 15.93

Properties Editor

Plane Object – Subdivided x 12

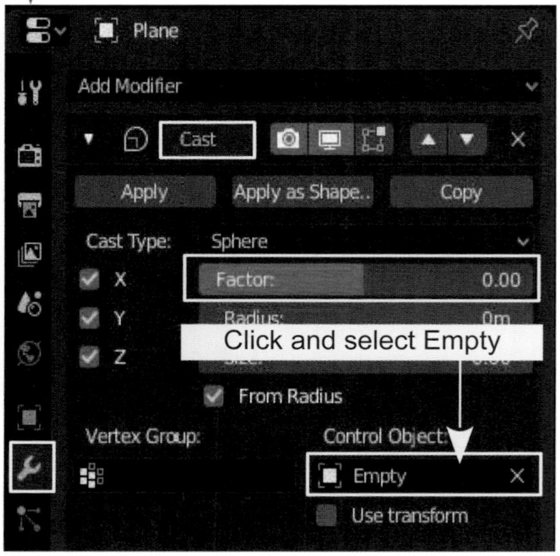

Figure 15.94

Add a Sound File to the **Video Sequence Editor**.

Create an F-Curve for the **Factor value** of the Cast modifier by selecting the Plane, then setting the **Factor value** in the **Cast modifier to 0.000.** In the **Timeline Editor** position the cursor at Frame 1. Right click on the **Factor value slider** in the Cast Modifier and select **Insert Keyframe**.

Declare the sound file to affect the Factor value by dividing the 3D Viewport Editor in two and changing one half to the **Graph Editor.** In the Header click on **Key** and select **Bake Sound to F Curves**. Navigate to the sound file, select the file and click Bake Sound to F-Curves in upper RH corner of the Editor. The bake can take a while. The sound file **F-Curve** is inserted in the **Graph Editor.**

Figure 15.95

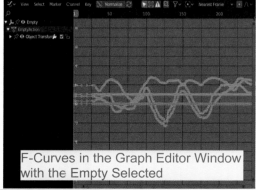

F-Curves in the Graph Editor Window with the Empty Selected

Turn on **Auto Keyframing** in the **Timeline Editor Header**. With the **Empty Object** selected in the 3D Viewport Editor play the animation and at the same time press **G Key** in the **3D Viewport Editor** and move the Empty object about. Keyframes are added to the Timeline. Stop the animation, reinstate the sound file in the Video Sequence Editor and replay to see the effect.

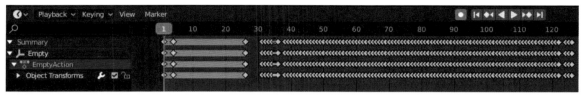

Keyframes Added in the Timeline Window   Figure 15.96

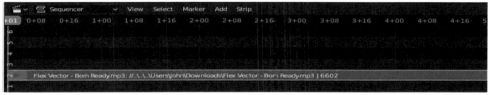

Figure 15.97

Sound file in the Video Sequence Editor

When the Animation is played the Mesh Deforms to the beat in the 3D Viewport Editor.

Figure 15.98

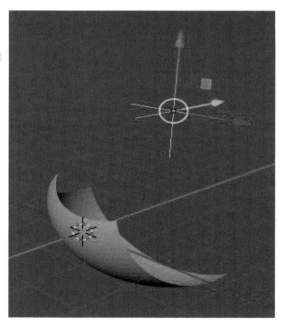

15.33 The Animation Workspace

The **Animation Workspace** is a Screen arrangement comprising, a 3D Viewport Editor in Camera View, a 3D Viewport Editor in User Perspective View, an Outliner Editor, a Properties Editor, the Dope Sheet Editor and the Timeline Editor.

All of the operations and examples described in the sections of this chapter are applicable to Editors making up the Animation Workspace.

The Animation Workspace is accessed by clicking on **Animation** in the **Blender Screen Header.**

Figure 15.99

The arrangement of Editor panels in the Workspace may or may not suit your particular way of working, therefore, the preceding explanation of working different applications in different Editors will allow you to configure your personalised Workspace.

The Animation Workspace

Figure 15.100

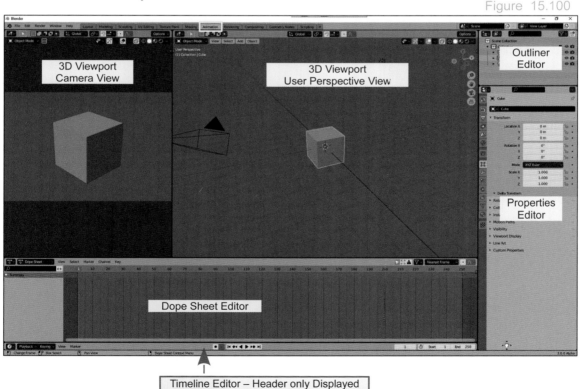

Note: The Animation Workspace is shown with **Blender Light Theme** Active.

Armatures & Character Rigging

Armatures are used to control the movement of Objects or components of an Object, in animation. In intricate assemblies, components are linked or associated with Armatures, such that, when the Armature moves the components move. Armatures themselves are made up from parts called **Bones** and may consist of a single Bone or multiple Bones linked in **Child Parent Relationships**. This means that when one Bone moves other Bones move according to the hierarchy in the relationship. Armatures do not Render, therefore, Bones can be animated controlling the animation of the components of an assembly.

A particular application for Armatures is the control and animation of Character Models. Figure 22.1 shows an **Armature** (blue bones) inside a character model. Each bone is linked to part of the surface mesh. The bones are animated to move which causes the surface mesh to move, posing the character.

The complete assembly of model, mesh, armature and controls is called a **Rig**.

Figure 16.1

16.1 Single Bone Armature

Armatures can, and usually do, comprise multiple Bones as depicted in Figure 16.1 which is said to be an **Armature Rig** since the arrangement of Bones is rigged to fit the Character Model allowing the Model to be posed for Animation.

To understand how the Armature Rig is constructed, start with the default single **Bone Armature** (Figure 16.2). The single Bone is entered in the 3D Viewport Editor by clicking the **Add** button in the Header or pressing **Alt = A Key** on the keyboard and selecting **Armature** in the menu that displays.

The default **Single Bone Armature** display is **Type: Octahedral** (due to the object having eight surfaces): The Bone appears as two four-sided pyramids conjoined at the base with spheres at the apexes. For the purpose of the demonstration, the parts of the Armature will be named **Tip, Body**, and **Root** (Figure 16.2).

Note: Type: Octahedral is one of five display **Types** (explanation to follow).

Figure 16.2

The Armature in Blender, it **is not** a Mesh Object. Its shape cannot be edited other than scaling it larger or smaller. It may be Rotated and Translated and It has a center like an Object. By default the Object Center is located at the center of the Root.

When the Manipulation Widget is used it locates at the Center.

When an Armature is entered in a Scene it displays in the 3D Viewport Editor and its name is automatically listed in the **Outliner Editor** (Figure 16.3).

Remember: Objects in a Blender Scene may be selected by clicking the Object in the 3D Viewport Editor or by clicking the Object's Name in the Outliner Editor. When dealing with Armatures and Armature Rigs comprising multiple Bones, this feature is particularly useful for selecting individual Bones.

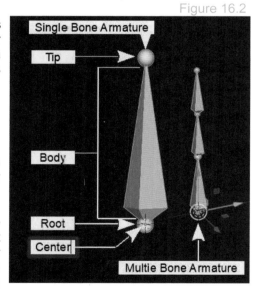

Figure 16.3

The default Single Bone Armature is listed in the Outliner Editor with the name **Armature** (white lettering). The components of the Armature are: **Armature** and **Pose**. Under the Armature Component you see **Bone** which signifies that the Armature consists of a single Bone. These entries are the names of the **Datablocks** of information generating the display in the 3D Viewport Editor. The Pose component is the Datablock specific to the orientation.

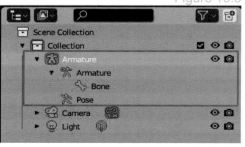

16.2 Adding Armatures

An Armature is added to the Scene from the **Add Menu** in the 3D Viewport Editor Header or by pressing **Shift + A Key.** It is located wherever you positioned the Editor Cursor, just like any other Object . You will see **Armature** listed in the **Outliner Editor** (Figure 16.4).

If you relocate the Cursor and repeat the process you add a second **Single Bone Armature** Note: The new name, **Armature.001** in the **Outliner Editor** and the sub entries, **Armature.001** and **Pose** (Figure 16.4). If you select either Armature in the 3D Viewport Editor and press **Shift + D key** (Duplicate) and Translate (drag the mouse) you create a third single Bone Armature. The name in the **Outliner Editor** for this third Armature is **Armature.002**.

Figure 16.4

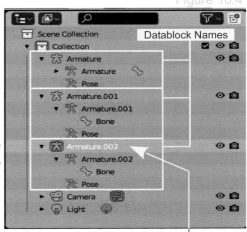

Datablock Names

Figure 16.5

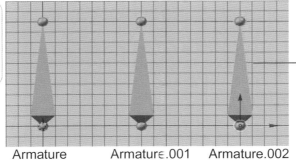

Armature   Armature.001   Armature.002

Note: All three Armatures are a single Bone and independent of each other.

Armature.002 Selected
(White Text)

Note: Datablock Names for each Armature may be independent of the Armature Name.

As you see adding Armatures quickly accumulated names in the Outliner Editor. The list can become extensive when a Rig is complicated as is a Character Rig in the 3D Viewport Editor. Selecting components of a Rig in the 3D Viewport Editor can be challenging when the Rig is Posed, therefore, understanding the way components are listed in the Outliner and the automatic naming process is beneficial.

Figure 16.6 shows a listing of Bones making up an Armature Rig for a single finger of a human hand. If the hand is posed forming a fist, selecting part of a finger for fine tuning an animation is more easily done in the Outliner Editor.

The proviso is; you have to be organised. The automatic naming process is fine but renaming components to something meaningful can be an advantage.

Figure 16.6

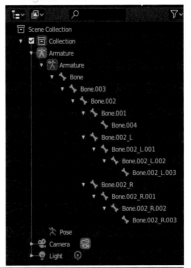

16.3 Adding Bones

Figure 16.7

Adding Bones to an Armature is akin to extruding, subdividing or duplicating the Bones in the Armature.

Adding by Extrusion (Figure 16.7)

To add a Bone by Extrusion have a single Bone Armature selected in the 3D Viewport Editor **in Edit Mode**. When you switch from Object Mode to Edit Mode, the Tip of the Armature is selected by default. Press the **E Key** and drag the Mouse, Extruding a new Bone. You may drag in any direction or confine the extrusion to an Axis.

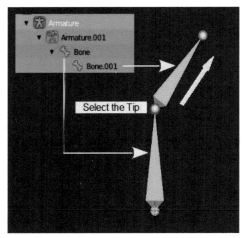

Adding by Subdivision (Figure 16.8)

Figure 16.8

Have a single Bone Armature selected **in Edit Mode** (select the Bone Body). **Click RMB** in the 3D Viewport Editor and select **Subdivide** in the Menu that displays. The single Bone becomes Bone and Bone.001.

Note: The **Last Operator** (Subdivision Panel that displays at the lower left of the Screen.

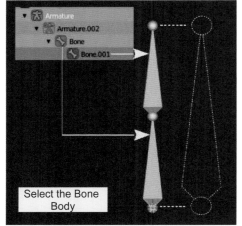

Adding by Duplication (Figure 16.9)

Figure 16.9

Have a single Bone Armature selected **in Edit Mode**. Press **Shift + D** and drag the Mouse to position the duplicated Bone (Bone.001).

Note: The new Bone (Bone.001) is a duplicate of the of the original Bone not a New Bone and although not shown, it is connected to the original.

In **Object Mode**, when the original Bone is Translated, Bone.001 follows the original.

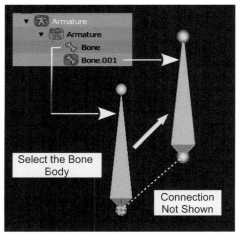

Figure 16.10

Bones may be Extruded from the Tip of any Bone, in any direction, when in Edit Mode. Any Bone may be Subdivided into any number of Bones.

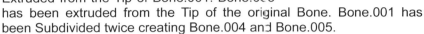

In Figure 16.10 Bone.001 has been Extruded from the Tip of Bone. Bone.002 has been Extruded from the Tip of Bone.001. Bone.003 has been extruded from the Tip of the original Bone. Bone.001 has been Subdivided twice creating Bone.004 and Bone.005.

The Bone Tree in the Outliner Editor has suddenly become a little complicated and without names being displayed in the 3D Viewport Editor it is becoming difficult to determine which Bone is which.

You may display the Bone Names (Numbers) in the 3D Viewport Editor by checking Names in the Properties Editor, Object Data Properties, Viewport Display Tab.

With the 3D Viewport Editor in Edit Mode, clicking on a Bone name (number) in the Outliner selects the Bone in the 3D Viewport Editor. This procedure is essential for Posing the Bones for animation.

16.4 The Armature Rig

In adding Bones to the Armature creating the arrangement shown in Figure 16.10 you have created an **Armature Rig**. In practice the Rig would be constructed to fit within a Model where the individual Bones are linked to parts of the Model such that when a Bone is moved the linked part of the Model follows the movement. This arrangement is being described in general terms since Armatures are used to control and animate not only characters but model you may wish to construct. For example, machine parts.

The individual Bones forming the Armature Rig are connected in a hierarchy such that when one Bone moves, others follow, depending on where they are positioned in the hierarchy.

The way in which one Bone follows another is termed a **Child Parent Relationship** (reference 16.6).

Before discovering how the individual Bones in a Rig interact in this relationship you should be aware of the three Modes in construction when considering Armatures.

The three Modes are: Object Mode, Edit Mode and Pose Mode.

Translating, Rotating and Scaling the Armature and its components (the Bones) perform differently in each Mode.

Rotating the Armature and Bones

Object Mode
Armature Selected

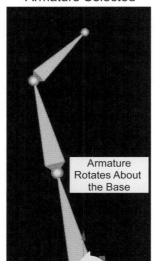

Armature Rotates About the Base

Figure 16.11

Edit Mode
Bone Selected

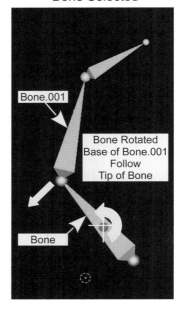

Bone.001

Bone Rotated Base of Bone.001 Follow Tip of Bone

Bone

Pose Mode
Bone Selected

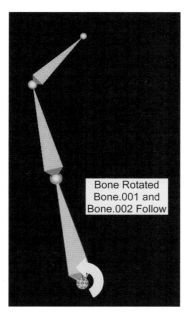

Bone Rotated Bone.001 and Bone.002 Follow

Pose Mode
Bone.001 Selected

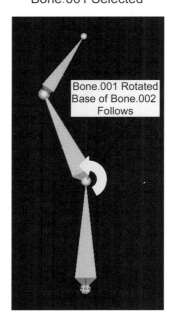

Bone.001 Rotated Base of Bone.002 Follows

16.5 Multiple Armatures

The Outliner Editor ⟶

In the preceding sections the discussion has shown how to add Bones to an Armature creating an Armature Rig. The process starts by adding a Single Bone Armature to a Scene (reference Figures 16.3 and 16.4) then adding Bones to the Armature creating a Rig. There will be occasions where you will have more than one Armature in a Scene

The Outliner Editor provides a graphical display of the Armatures and Bones in a Scene. **In Edit Mode** you can select a Bone in an Armature by clicking on its name in the Outliner Editor.

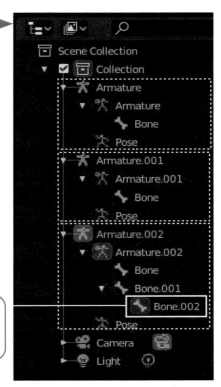

Figure 16.12

Click to select Bone.002 with the 3D Viewport Editor in Edit Mode.

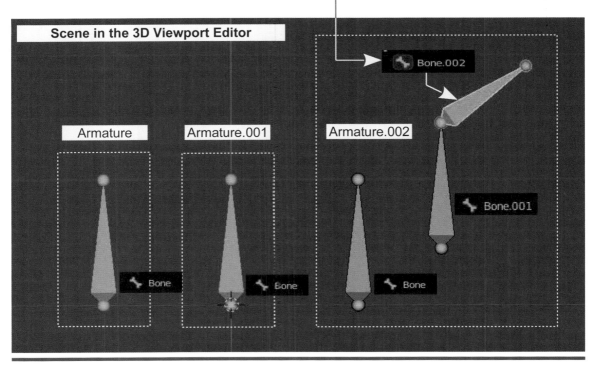

Scene in the 3D Viewport Editor

Armature   Armature.001   Armature.002

Bone.002

Bone.001

Bone   Bone   Bone

16.6 Child Parent Relationship

The Bones in an Armature are connected in a **Child Parent Relationship**. When a Bone (Bone 2) is extruded from the tip of an Armature (Bone 1) it automatically becomes the Child of Bone 1. Extruding another Bone (Bone 3) from the tip of Bone 2 makes Bone 3 the Child of Bone 2. Being a Child means that the Bone follows its parent.

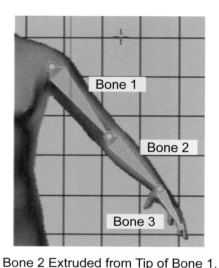

Bone 1

Bone 2

Bone 3

Bone 2 Extruded from Tip of Bone 1.
Bone 3 Extruded from Tip of Bone 2.

Figure 16.13
Pose Mode

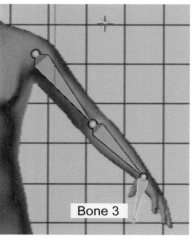

Bone 3

Bone 3 Rotates independently
but is fixed to Bone 2.

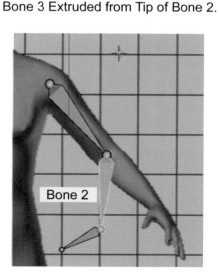

Bone 2

Bone 2 Rotated Bone 3 Follows.
Bone 3 is the Child of Bone 2.

Bone 1

Bone 1 Rotated Bones 2 and 3 Follow.
Bone 2 is the Child of Bone 1.

Note: With the Bones linked to the mesh forming the arm, the Mesh will follow the Bones.

16.7 Armature Display Types

The default Armature display type is **Octahedral.** There are four alternative display types

Figure 16.14

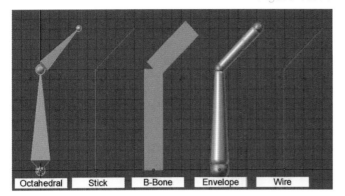

| Octahedral | Stick | B-Bone | Envelope | Wire |

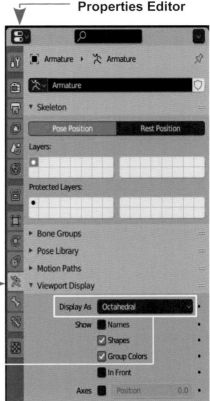

Properties Editor

With the Armature Bone selected, see the **Properties Editor, Data buttons, Viewport Display Tab.**

Which display type is used depends on what you will do with the Armature. The different uses will not be explained at this time but since the basic function of an Armature is to deform a mesh Object, you need to understand how this occurs.

Octahedral
Stick
B-Bone
Envelope
Wire
Display Type

16.8 Building an Armature Rig

In adding Bones to an Armature, as you did in Figure 16.9, you created a Multi-Bone Armature which is essentially an Armature Rig.

Adding Bones to an Armature and creating an Armature Rig is primarily for posing or animating a Character Model. In Figure 16.1 (at the beginning of this chapter) you see an Armature Rig inside a Model. There are pre-assembled Rigs which may be used but you should understand how they are created. Understanding will allow you to create Rigs for any application. Rigs are employed for many characters such as strange creatures and weird robots, not only human figures. They are also used when animating machine parts.

To demonstrate how to create a Character Rig for a model, a model of a human figure will be used which has been generated in the **Make Human** program.

Figure 16.15

http://www.makehuman.org

Make Human is a **free Open Source** human character modeling program. You can import a model from the program into a Blender file.

Figure 16.16 shows the imported model with the Multi-Bone Armature fully constructed. The Armature is shown here so you can see what you are aiming for in the exercise. Figure 16.17 shows the Armature moved to one side as a reference for construction.

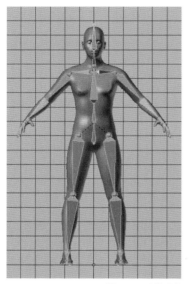

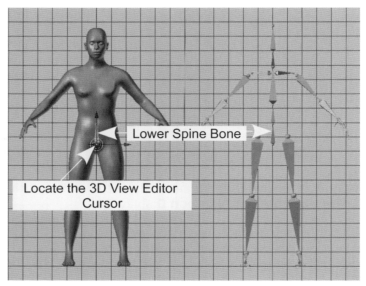

Figure 16.16

Figure 16.17

When constructing the Armature think of it as a human skeleton.

Obtaining the Model

The Model shown in Figures 16.16 - 16.17 is the default Human which displays when the Make Human Program is run. To get the Figure install Make Human and run the program. With the Model displayed click Files – Export – select Wavefront.obj as the File type. Enter a File Name in the Header, click  navigate to a folder on your PC and click Save.

Figure 16.18

In Blender, select File – Import – Wavefront (.obj). Navigate to the folder where you saved the make Human file then click **Import OBJ**.

Note: the Model will be way too big. Scale down.

To start the construction the Rig first Bone to be placed is the **Lower Spine Bone**. Locate the **3D Viewport Editor Cursor** where you want to place the Base of the Bone. Press **Shift + A key** and select **Add – Armature**. The single Bone Armature is entered in the Scene but it may be way too big or too small for the model. Scale to fit.

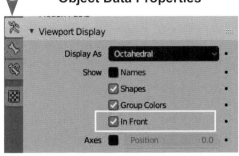

Object Data Properties

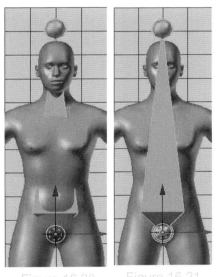

Figure 16.19

Note: When the Armature is scaled, depending on its location, it may disappear inside the model (Figure 16.20).

To see the Bone inside, check **In Front** in the **Viewport Display tab** in the **Properties Editor, Object Data Properties** (Figure 16.19). The bone must be selected in the 3D Viewport Editor.

With **In Front** checked you will see the Bone (Figure 16.21).

Figure 16.20   Figure 16.21

Creating the Spine

Figure 16.22

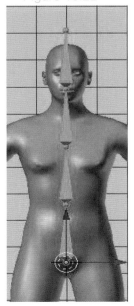

To create a **Spine** from a single Bone, have the bone selected in the 3D View Editor and in Edit Mode drag the Tip up above the top of the model's head (Figure 16.21). In Edit Mode, RMB click on the Body of the Bone then select **Subdivide**. In the **Last Operator Panel Subdivide** panel that displays, increase the **Number of Cuts** to produce multiple Bones (Figure 16.22).

Remain in Edit Mode, deselect, then select individual Tips and Bases of the bones and Translate to fit the model. You may also select individual Bone bodies and Scale and Translate.

Note: In this instance the Spine has been created by Subdivision but you may create the Spine by selecting the Tip of the first single Bone, then extruding new Bones.

Naming the Bones

At this point it is good practice to begin naming the components of your Rig. With the Bones created by Subdivision or Extrusion names are automatically applied in the Outliner Editor and may be displayed in the 3D Viewport Editor by checking **Show Names** in the Properties Editor, Object Data Properties, Viewport Display Tab. Automatic names are fine but something more meaningful will be an advantage when the Rig is developed.

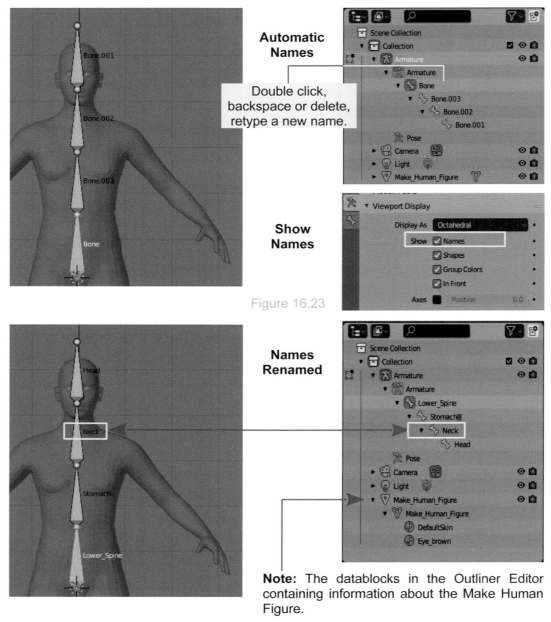

Automatic Names

Double click, backspace or delete, retype a new name.

Show Names

Figure 16.23

Names Renamed

Note: The datablocks in the Outliner Editor containing information about the Make Human Figure.

Creating Arms and Hands

To generate the Arm Bones and Hands start by selecting the Tip of the Stomach Bone (in Edit Mode), G Key (Grab) and position at the top of the chest (Figure 16.24). With the Tip selected E Key (Extrude) the Shoulder Bone.

Note: The Shoulder Bone will be Extruded on one side of the Model only. To Extrude on both sides simultaneously go back a step (Press Ctrl Z). With the Mouse Cursor in the 3D Viewport Editor press the N Key to display the Object Properties Panel and click on the Tool Tab. **Check X- Axis Mirror.**

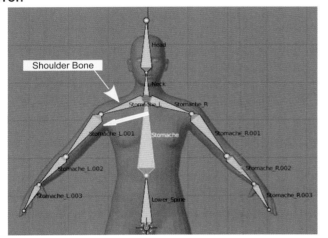

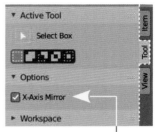

Object Properties Panel

Click on the Tool Tab. **Check X-Axis Mirror.**

Figure 16.24

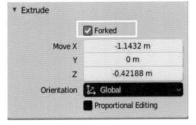

Last Operator Panel

The Extrusion will still be on one side only but you will see the Last Operator – Extrude Panel display. Check **Forked** in the Panel. Further Extrusions will take place on both sides.

Continue Extruding the Upper Arm, Lower Arm and Hand.

Note: The Automatic Names. Since the Bones have been Extruded from the Tip of the Stomach Bone they are the children of that bone. Time to rename in the Outliner Editor.

Creating Legs and Feet

Figure 16.25

Legs and Feet are Extruded from the Base of the Lower_Spine Bone using the X-Axis Mirror Function. The first Extrusion should be to generate a Pelvis/Hip Bone.

Note: The automatic naming; Lower_Spine_L, Lower_Spine_**R**.

Don't forget to incorporate the Left/Right when renaming.

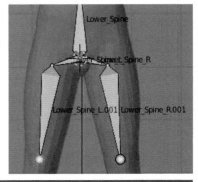

Aligning Bones

In creating the Armature Rig, the construction has been demonstrated in Front Orthographic View. In Right or Left Orthographic Views you will find the Bones are way out of position relative to the model.

They have to be inside the mesh so when the Bone is Posed the part of the Mesh associated (linked) to the Bone follows the Bone. Select individual Bone Tips/Bases and manoeuvre them into their correct locations (Figure 16.26).

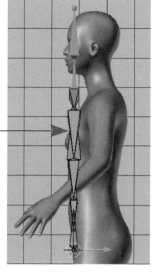

Right Orthographic View – Bones way out of position.

Figure 16.26

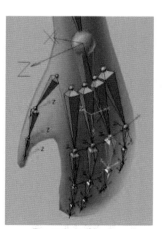

Head and Neck Bone correctly positioned

Foot and Hand Bones

Figure 16.27

The Foot Bones shown in Figure 16.27 begin to demonstrate the detail required in constructing an Armature Rig to Pose and Animate a Model. Hand Bones are even more detailed (Figure 16.8)

Figure 16.28

 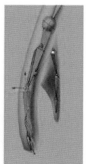

Hand Bones inside the Mesh

Bone Axis Displayed

Note: In Figure 16.8 the Finger and Thumb Bones appear to be disconnected from the Wrist. This shows that a Bone may be positioned to effect the Mesh without actually being physically connected in the view.

16.9 The Extrude Tool

An alternative to pressing the E Key to Extrude a Bone is to click the **Extrude Tool** in the Tool Panel. There are three options; Roll, Size and Extrude. Size and Extrude have sub options.

Note: When an Armature has been added to the Scene and selected in the 3D Viewport Editor, the Edit Mode Tool Panel is an abbreviated version with three Armature Tools.

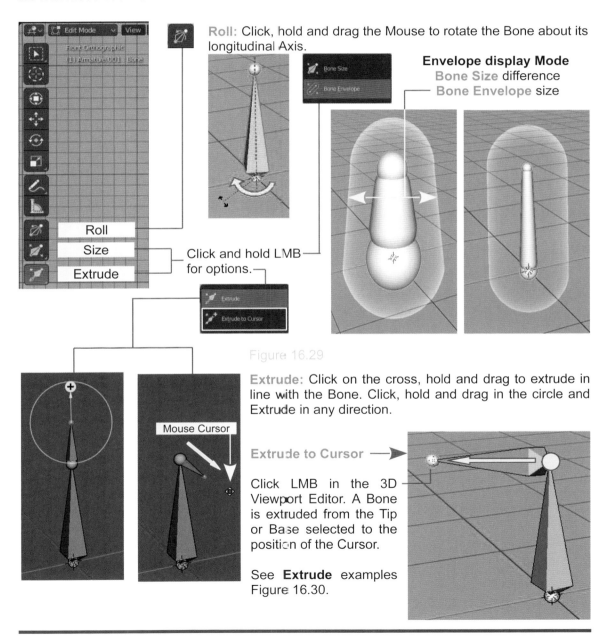

Roll: Click, hold and drag the Mouse to rotate the Bone about its longitudinal Axis.

Envelope display Mode
Bone Size difference
Bone Envelope size

Click and hold LMB for options.

Figure 16.29

Extrude: Click on the cross, hold and drag to extrude in line with the Bone. Click, hold and drag in the circle and Extrude in any direction.

Extrude to Cursor

Click LMB in the 3D Viewport Editor. A Bone is extruded from the Tip or Base selected to the position of the Cursor.

See **Extrude** examples Figure 16.30.

Mouse Cursor

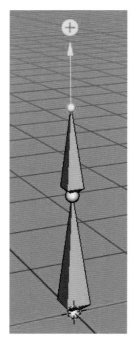
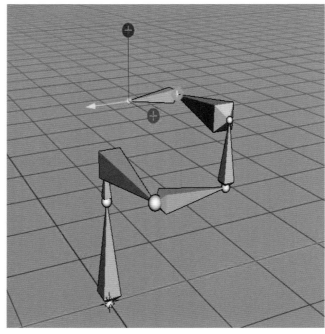

Figure 16.30

16.10 Deforming a Mesh

The basic procedure for deforming a Mesh Object with an Armature is to link or associate vertices on the mesh surface to Bones in the Armature. When the Bones are moved the Vertices in the mesh move.

Make Human models come with a considerable number of Vertices in the surface mesh. That's why they look so good. When deforming a mesh using an Armature you should consider the number of vertices that will be manipulated. A large number of vertices means the computer has to perform a large number of calculations when moving vertices about and that can slow things down considerably. That being the case, in demonstrating mesh deformation, a simple model will be used that has a minimal number of mesh vertices.

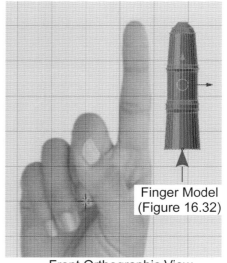

Figure 16.31

In Figures 16.31 - 32 a simple finger has been modeled by extruding a Circle. The finger is shown in Edit Mode in Figure 16.31 displaying its Vertices.

Finger Model (Figure 16.32)

Front Orthographic View

Arrange the finger model so that it is pointing up in **Front Orthographic** view with its center of rotation on the center of the Scene.

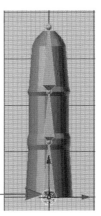

Figure 16.32

Construct a three Bone Armature as shown in Figure 16.32.

Place the Armature inside the model.

Parenting

With the Armature in place you **Parent** (associate) parts of the mesh with the Bones by using an **Armature Modifier** or using the **Set Parent To** menu.

Center of Rotation

16.11 Parenting with The Armature Modifier

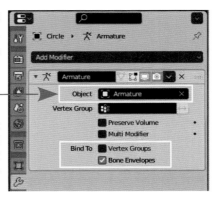

Figure 16.33

In **Object Mode** select the Mesh Model then in the **Properties Editor, Modifier Properties**, add an **Armature Modifier** (Figure 16.33).

In the Modifier panel set **Object** as **Armature**. —————

In the modifier panel, uncheck **Vertex Groups** and check **Bone Envelope** under the **Bind To** heading. This is telling Blender to associate the Armature Bones with Vertices that are enclosed by the Bone Envelopes (Field of Influence Figure 16.33).

To see what this means have the Armature selected in the 3D Viewport Editor then in the **Properties Editor, Object Data Properties, Viewport Display Tab** change **Octahedral** display to **Envelope** display (Figure 16.34). In the Viewport Display Tab check **In Front**.

Octahedral
Object Mode

Envelope
Object Mode

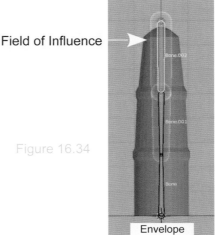

Field of Influence

Figure 16.34

Envelope
Edit Mode

Have the **Armature selected** in **Edit Mode**. In the diagram you see the upper finger Bone (Bone.002) selected in Edit Mode and with Envelope Display Mode you see the Field of Influence. This field provides a guide, approximating, which part of the Mesh will be influenced when the Armature is moved. The dimensions of the envelope are adjusted in the Envelope Distance panel, in the Properties Editor, Bone Properties buttons, Deform Tab with the Armature in Edit Mode or Pose Mode (ensure **Deform** is checked in the Tab - Figure 16.35).

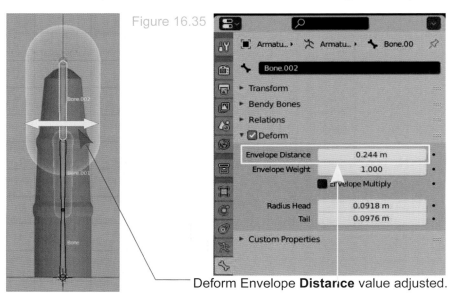

Figure 16.35

Deform Envelope **Distance** value adjusted.

With the upper Armature Bone selected in Edit Mode, change to Pose Mode in the 3D Viewport Editor Header. The Bone displays colored blue   (Figure 16.36). You may select any Bone and Rotate (R key drag mouse) to see the mesh deform (Figure 16.37).

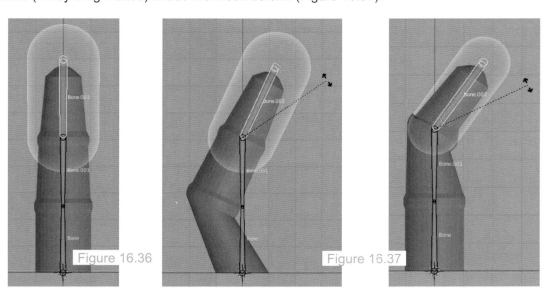

Figure 16.36

Figure 16.37

Note: The Bone Envelope Distance has an effect on how the Mesh deforms. This has to be adjusted for the each Bone section. Experiment with the Envelope Distance setting and subdivide the Mesh to achieve the desired deformation

By selecting the Mesh Model in Edit Mode, n the Properties Editor, Object Data Properties you will see that a Vertex Group has been created for each Bone in the Armature. By setting the **Bind To:** value in the Armature Modifier to **Bone Envelope** (Figure 16.33) the Vertices in the Vertex Groups are controlled by the Bone Envelopes.

16.12 Assigning Vertices – Vertex Groups

In the previous examples (20.11) **Mesh Vertices** were selected from within the **Field of Influence** of the Armature by the Armature Modifier. An alternative to this, is to manually nominate which vertices will be affected by the Armature.

Use the same Finger – Armature arrangement previously described. Select the **Armature** then in the **Properties Editor, Object Data Properties, Viewport Display Tab**, tick **Names** to show the Bones named **Bone** and **Bone.001** and **Bone.002**. Deselect the Armature.

Select the **Finger** (Mesh – Object Mode), then in **Edit Mode** deselect the Vertices. In the **Properties Editor, Object Data Properties, Vertex Groups Tab**, click the **Plus** sign to add a **Vertex Group**; a Vertex Group is added and named **Group**. By renaming **Group** to **Bone.002** (Figure 16.38), the **Vertex Group** will automatically be controlled by the Bone named **Bone.002**. Groups and Bones may be renamed to whatever you want, but for a Group to be controlled by a Bone, the names must be identical.

A second condition for control is; You must apply an Armature Modifier to the Finger with the Object set as Armature and **Bind To: Vertex Groups** checked.

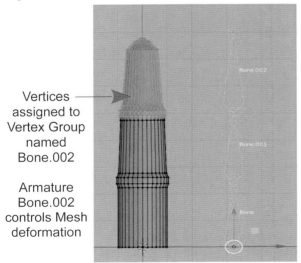

Vertices assigned to Vertex Group named Bone.002

Armature Bone.002 controls Mesh deformation

Armature shown moved to one side

Object Data Properties

Figure 16.38

In the 3D Viewport Editor, select the Vertices in the upper part of the finger (press the B key – drag a rectangle). Make sure you have the **Toggle X-Ray button turned on** in the 3D Viewport Editor Header or you will only be selecting the front Vertices of the finger.

Figure 16.39

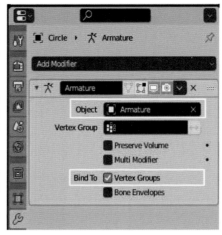

In the **Vertex Groups** tab, click **Assign** to assign the selected Vertices to the Group. Check out the assignment by alternately clicking on **Deselect** and **Select** (Figure 16.38).

Tab into **Object mode** and deselect the finger. Select the **Armature** and change to **Pose Mode**. Select **Bone.002** and press the **R Key** to rotate. **Nothing happens if you haven't applied an Armature Modifier to the finger** (Figure 16.39).

Go back and select the finger and in the **Properties Editor, Modifier buttons**, click **Add Modifier** and select **Armature**. In the **Armature Object** panel, click and select **Armature**.

Deselect the finger and select the **Armature** in **Pose Mode**. Select **Bone.002** and rotate it—the upper part of the finger will now deform as the Bone is rotated (Figure 16.40 -41).

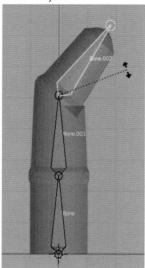

Figure 16.40

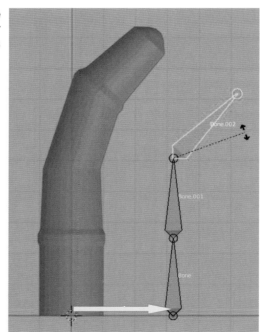

Figure 16.41

The armature may be located well away from the finger and still deform the Mesh. The Field of Influence of the Armature described in the previous exercise is not enforced, but with the Armature displaced away from the Mesh, the Mesh deformation is exaggerated (Figure 16.41).

The foregoing has outlined the manual procedure for creating a Vertex Group and employing an Armature Modifier.

Note: In the Armature Modifier, **Object: is set as Armature** and **Bind To; is set as Vertex Groups**. In the Object Data Properties for the Mesh Model the single Vertex Group is named the same as the controlling Bone (Bone.002).

As you can image, in a complicated Mesh/Armature arrangement manually creating and assigning vertices to group fore each Bone would be a tedious task. That being the case, Blender incorporates semi automatic process. This is demonstrated using the same Mesh Finger with the three Bone Armature.

Note: Be aware that when using these processes adjustments may be required to refine the control.

The automated processes are selected from the Set Parent To menu.

16.13 Assigning Vertices – Set Parent To Menu

In the Mesh Finger – Armature arrangement (Figure 16.42), in Object Mode, select the Mesh then Shift select the Armature. Press Ctrl + P key and in the **Set Parent To** menu that displays chose (click) one of the **Armature Deform** options.

Figure 16.42

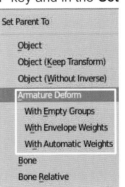
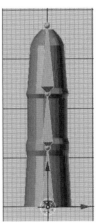

With Empty Groups creates a child parent relationship between the Mesh Object and the Armature such that when a Bone in the Armature is moved in Pose Mode part of the Mesh follows. This is accomplished by automatically creating an **Armature Modifier** for the Mesh with **Object: Armature** and **Bind To: Vertex Groups** (see the Modifier Properties). At the same time Vertex Groups are created and named in accordance with the Bones in the Armature (see the Object Data Properties). Both sets of Properties are selected in the Properties Editor with the Mesh Object selected in the 3D Viewport Editor in Object Mode.

Note: Although Vertex Groups are created and named in accordance with the Bones in the Armature, Vertices **have not** been assigned to the Vertex Groups. Hence **With Empty Groups**.

With the Mesh Object in Edit Mode, select Vertices and assign to each Vertex Group.

Moving a Bone in the Armature, in Pose Mode, will see the assigned Vertices follow the movement.

With Envelope Weights creates the same Armature Modifier and Vertex Groups but this time you change **Bind To** from **Vertex Groups** to **Bone Envelopes** in the Armature Modifier and the Envelope will control which Vertices move when the Bone is moved in Pose Mode. You may alter the Bone Envelope size to adjust the control.

With Automatic Weights, again, creates an Armature Modifier and Vertex Groups but this time Vertices are automatically assigned to the Vertex Groups. The automatic assignment may or may not create the desired effect, therefore, you manually correct the assignment of vertices to the Vertex Groups.

16.14 Assigning Vertices – Weight Paint

Blender has a painting method that selects and assigns Vertices to a group, automatically linking to an armature Bone. The Paint method allows a graduated weight to be given to vertices that dictate how much influence the armature Bone will have over the deformation of the Mesh.

Set up a new Scene as you did for the previous examples. Select the **Finger** in **Object Mode** and add an **Armature Modifier** in the Properties Editor. Don't forget to enter **Armature** in the **Object panel**. Select the Armature and enter **Pose Mode**. In the **Properties Editor, Object Data Properties**, **Viewport Display Tab**, check **Names** to display the Bone names in the 3D Viewport Editor; the names should be **Bone, Bone.001** and **Bone.002** as before.

When ticking **Names** make sure you are in the **Object Data Properties** not the **Object Properties**. If you are in the Object Properties only the name **Armature** will display.

With the Armature as the selected Object in the 3D Viewport, in Pose Mode, select **Bone.002** (the upper Bone) then change to Object Mode and left click the Finger to select it. With the finger selected, go to the 3D Viewport Header and change from Object Mode to **Weight Paint Mode**. The Finger displays dark blue, indicating that no Vertices are selected (Figure 16.44).

Figure 16.43

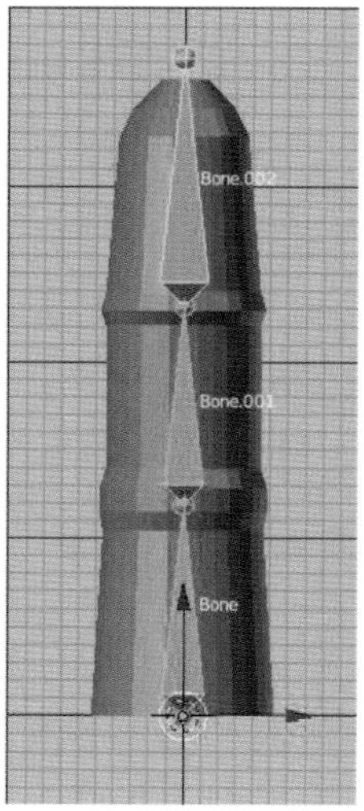

Figure 16.44

The Finger displays dark blue, which indicates that no Vertices are selected.

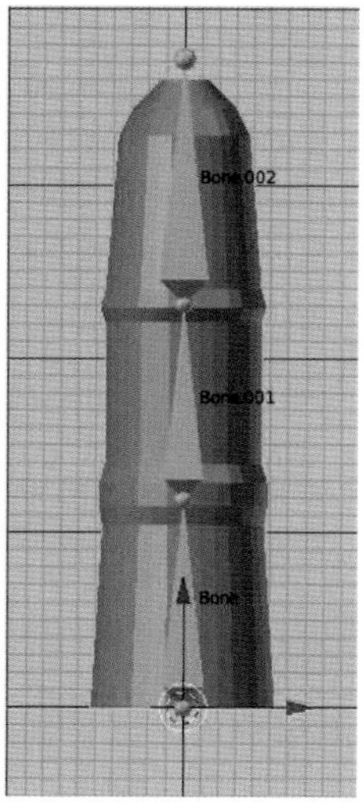

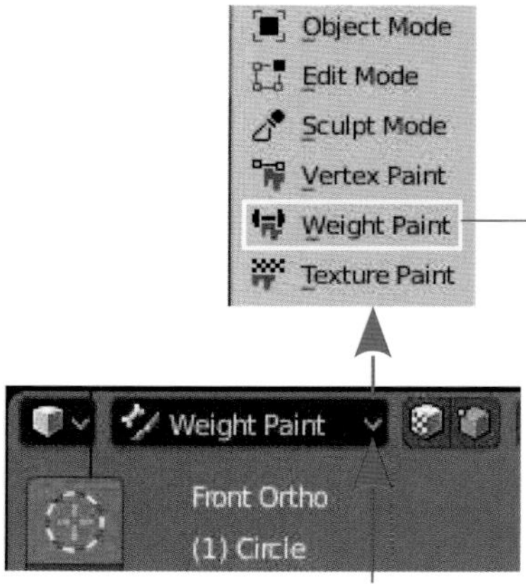

Cursor - Brush

| Armature | Finger | 3DViewport Editor Header | Finger |
| Pose Mode | Object Mode | Click to select Editor Modes | Weight Paint |

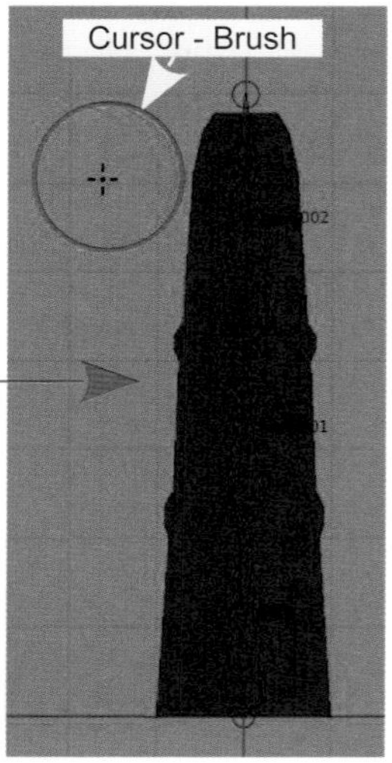

In the **Tool Panel** at the left-hand side of the 3D Viewport have the **Draw Tool** selected. In the Header click **View** and check **Tool Settings**. Make sure the **Weight** and **Strength** sliders are set to 1.000 in the Header (Figure 16.45). You are about to paint over the finger mesh to select Vertices, and by setting the strength to a high value you are telling Blender that the selected Vertices are to be rigorously controlled by Bone.002. In Weight Paint Mode, the cursor in the 3D Viewport Editor is a circle (Figure 16.45). The Radius control for the circle is in the Header. You want the upper part of the finger to be transformed by Bone.002, therefore, click, hold, and drag the Cursor circle over the upper part of the Finger. As with selecting vertices make sure **Toggle X-Ray** is turned on in the Header.

Figure 16.45

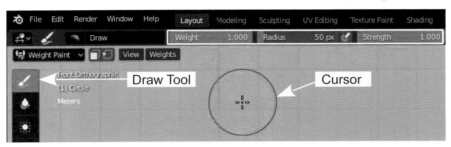

Draw Tool

Cursor

The part of the Finger painted turns red, which indicates a rigorous control (Figure 16.46). Altering the **Strength** value changes the control strength and will display a different color.

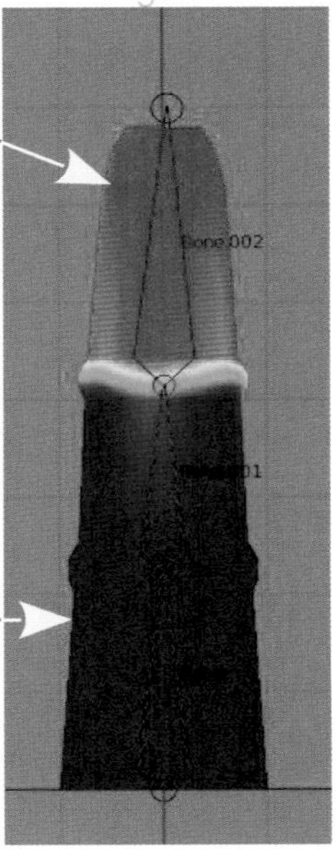

Turn the mesh around and paint the Vertices on the back side of the finger (pan the 3D Viewport around).

Figure 16.46

Vertices Assigned (Red)

Having painted the finger, note that in the **Properties Editor, Data buttons, Vertex Groups Tab** a **Vertex Group** has been created with the default name: **Group**.

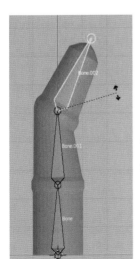

Important: Rename the Vertex Group: **Bone.002**.

Selecting **Bone.002** in **Pose Mode** and rotating it will move the upper part of the finger (Figure 16.47). Repeat the process for the remaining Bones.

Figure 16.47

Vertices Not Assigned
(Blue)

With vertices assigned to the different Bones in the Armature, when individual Bones are manipulated the Vertices follow reshaping the mesh.

There are occasions when you will want several Bones to follow a single Bone. For example; Translating Bone.002 and having Bone.001 and Bone follow the movement. In this instance you would employ the **Inverse Kinematic Constraint.**

16.15 Inverse Kinematics Constraint Figure 16.48

The **Inverse Kinematics (IK) Constraint** is used for controlling a chain of Bones (Figure 16.48).

With IK, dragging a **Control Bone** will result in the chain following the Control.

To Pose the Chain, without **Inverse Kinematics** you have to Pose individual Bones one by one; this is a tedious process but gives you full control.

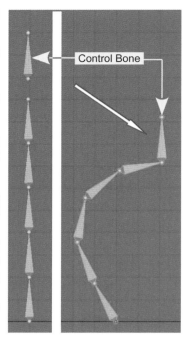

Control Bone

> Do not confuse **IK (Inverse Kinematics)** with the **Spline IK** .

An example of **Inverse Kinematics** would be to create a chain of Bones (Figure 16.48). **Note: Figure 16.49 shows two separate chains.** One chain has been created by extruding five times from the Tip of a single Bone Armature in Edit Mode. The second chain as been created by Subdividing a Scaled up single Bone Armature (in Edit Mode) five times (Number of Cuts 5).

Either method of generating the chain is acceptable **BUT,** make note of the automatic names that have been displayed. Both chains have the lower Bone named: **Bone,** while the remainder of Bones are named in reverse order. **The Bone names are important.**

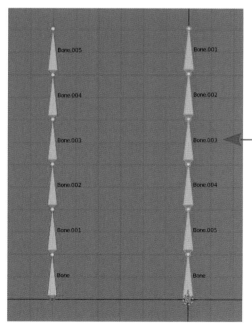

Extrusion   **Subdivision**

Properties Editor, Object Data Properties
(for the selected Armature Chain)

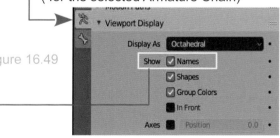

Figure 16.49

For the demonstration of the Inverse Kinematic Constraint the **Extruded Chain** will be used.

The first step in the process is to create a **Control Bone**. When the Inverse Kinematic Constraint is applied to the Armature Chain, selecting and Translating the Control Bone will see the Bones in the chain follow.

To create a **Control Bone** the uppermost Bone in the Chain (Bone.005) will be disconnected from the Chain.

In Figure 16.50 the top Bone (Bone.005) has been selected in Edit Mode and disconnected from the Armature by pressing **Alt + P Key** and selecting **Clear Parent** in the menu that displays. In Edit Mode **Control** (the top Bone) has been moved aside.

Outliner Editor

Figure 16.50

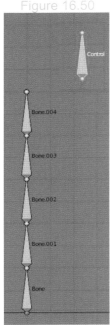

Rename Bone.005 as **Control** in the Outliner Editor. Note that it is removed from the hierarchy of the Chain. Figure 16.51

Renaming in the Outliner automatically renames the Bone in the 3D Viewport Editor.

The Bone named **Control** will be used for manipulating the Armature Chain.

The Bones in the Armature Chain are connected, therefore, at this stage, an individual Bone in Pose Mode can only be Rotated about its Base or Scaled . Bones above in the chain will also Rotate or be Scaled but that is the limit of the Posing. Grabbing the Control Bone and moving it has no affect on the Chain.

To use the Control an **Inverse Kinematic Constraint** has to be applied to **one of the Bones** in the Armature Chain.

Properties Editor

To which Bone in the Chain the Constraint is applied determines how the Control affects the Chain. This is where Bone naming becomes important. If the Chain were being used to Pose parts of a Model it would be essential that the correct Bone was selected. Figure 16.52

To demonstrate the IK Constraint select **Bone.004** in the Armature in **Pose Mode**. In the Properties Editor click the **Bone Constraints Properties** and click **Add Bone Constraint**. Select **Inverse Kinematics** in the menu that displays.

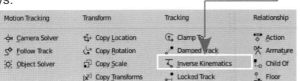

Bone Constraint Properties ➞
Object Constraint Properties ___

In the IK Bone Constraint Panel (Figure 16.52) set **Target** as **Armature** and **Bone** as **Control**.

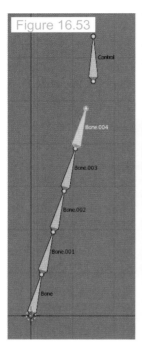

Figure 16.53

With the Constraint applied to Bone.004 you immediately see the Bone point towards the Control (Figure 16.53). Selecting **Control** and Translating sees Bone.004 being Translated with the Bone Chain following (Figure 16.54).

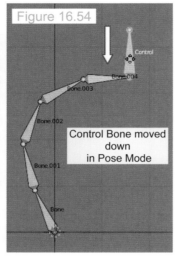

Figure 16.54

Control Bone moved down in Pose Mode

Make particular note of the **Chain Length** setting in the IK Constraint Panel. Chain Length: 0 means all the Bones in the Armature Chain are affected.

Remember: The IK Constraint is applied to Bone.004.

By selecting Bone.004 (in Pose Mode) you see a broken line connecting the Tip of Bone.004 to the base of **Bone** (Figure 16.55) **NOTE:** This is when the Chain Length is set to 5 or 0. Changing the Chain Length sees the connection change (Figures 16.56 and 16.57)

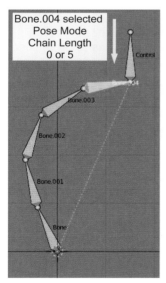

Bone.004 selected
Pose Mode
Chain Length
0 or 5

Figure 16.55

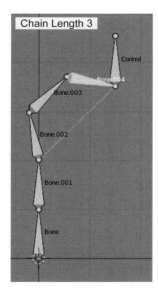

Chain Length 3

Figure 16.56

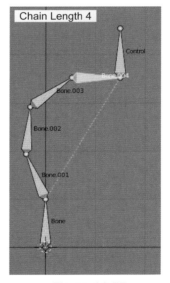

Chain Length 4

Figure 16.57

The Chain Length connection determines how the Control Bone affects the Bone Chain.

16.16 Spline IK Constraint

The **Spline IK Constraint** forces a multi Bone **Armature** to follow the shape of a Curve. With the Armature constrained to the Curve, the Curve is then manipulated to adjust the shape of the Armature and in turn any mesh assigned to the Armature.

To demonstrate, in the default 3D Viewport Editor, delete the **Cube** and add a **Bezier Curve**. Scale the Curve up. Create a multi Bone **Armature** (Figure 16.58).

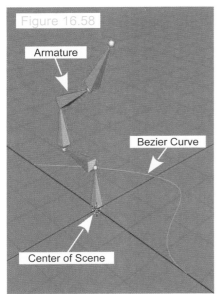

Figure 16.58

Armature

Bezier Curve

Center of Scene

Leave the 3D Viewport in **User Perspective View**.

Both the origin of the Armature and the center of the Bezier Curve are located at the center of the Scene.

Figure 16.59

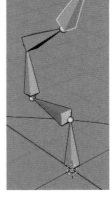

With the Armature selected, go into **Pose Mode**. **When selected,** the outline of the Armature will be displayed in blue.

Deselect the Armature then <u>select the top Bone</u> in the Armature (Figure 16.59).

In the **Properties Editor, Bone Constraints Properties** add a **Spline IK Constraint** (Figure 16.60). Change the **Spline Fittings: Chain Length** value to 5 (the number of Bones in the armature). In the **Target** panel select **Bezier Curve**.

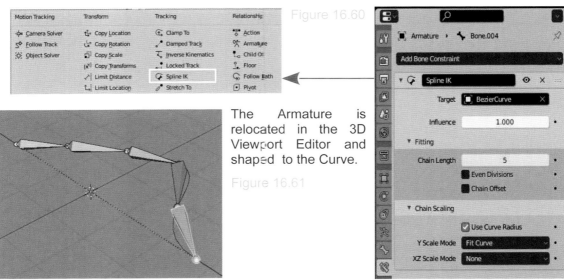

Figure 16.60

Motion Tracking	Transform	Tracking	Relationship
Camera Solver	Copy Location	Clamp To	Action
Follow Track	Copy Rotation	Damped Track	Armature
Object Solver	Copy Scale	Inverse Kinematics	Child Of
	Copy Transforms	Locked Track	Floor
	Limit Distance	Spline IK	Follow Path
	Limit Location	Stretch To	Pivot

Armature ▸ Bone.004

Add Bone Constraint

Spline IK

Target   BezierCurve

Influence   1.000

▼ Fitting

Chain Length   5

Even Divisions

Chain Offset

▼ Chain Scaling

Use Curve Radius

Y Scale Mode   Fit Curve

XZ Scale Mode   None

The Armature is relocated in the 3D Viewport Editor and shaped to the Curve.

Figure 16.61

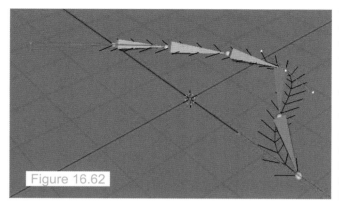

Figure 16.62

The Armature Bones are arranged with the direction of the curve. If the Curve were being used as an Animation Path, the movement along the path would be in the direction of the chevrons spaced along the Curve (Figure 16.61).

The direction may be reversed **in Edit Mode** by clicking RMB to display the **Curve Context Menu** and selecting **Switch Direction**. In doing this the chevrons are reversed and so are the Bones in the Armature.

With the Armature constrained to the curve the **Armature** may be posed by selecting the **Control Handles** on the **Bezier Curve**. The Curve may be subdivided in Edit Mode to add additional control handles and give more control over the posing. Remember the practical use of the Armature is to control the shape and movement of a mesh Object which is assigned to the Armature.

Hooks may be assigned to the control handles of the Curve giving a non renderable Object with which to translate and pose the Armature. To add a **Hook** place the Curve in **Edit Mode** and ensure everything is **deselected**. Select a Control Handle then press **Ctrl + H key** and select **Hook to New Object** in the menu that displays. A **Hook** is displayed in the form of a **3D Cross**.

Anther method of introducing an non renderable Objects to allow Curve manipulation, when you have an Armature constrained to the Curve, is to add single Bones. You then parent the Bone to the Hook.

16.17 Forward

With knowledge of Armatures and how they are constructed, manipulated and used to deform Mesh Objects you are placed to learn the intricacies of Character Rigging. This is the process of constructing an Armature to fit a Character model. The model can be anything your imagination allows but for demonstration purposes, the subject will be devoted to Character Rigging a Humanoid Figure.

A preliminary introduction to **Character Rigging** has been presented in section 16.8 **Building an Armature Rig.** Since this topic is such an important part of Modeling and Animation it is felt that a more detailed study is required. This is presented in Section 16.18 to follow.

There are pre-assembled Rigs you may download from the internet which are free to use, but using a ready made Rig for your particular application may require you to modify the download. It is therefore advisable to understand how a Rig is constructed from basics.

16.18 Character Rigging

As you have seen Character Rigging is the process of creating an Armature to suit a Model of a Character then associating the Bones in the Armature with parts of the Model. The Bones are Posed and animated and the parts of the Model follow suit. To facilitate Posing, special Control Bones are incorporated in the Armature to manipulate the Bones.

To expand and consolidate this topic an exercise in Rigging a cartoon character will be presented which demonstrates constructing an Armature for a pre-constructed Model.

To constructing an Armature and Rigging you require a Mesh Model of a Character.

Free to use models may be downloaded from the internet or you may construct your own model in Blender or use an external application such as the Make Human program.

Constructing a crude humanoid figure by extrusion in Blender was previously discussed and the basics of building a Rig for a human Model has been demonstrated in section 16.8 of this chapter.

Constructing a model of a human figure can be a lengthy process, depending on the detail employed. There are several websites where you can download pre-built models, some of which are pre-rigged. To understand the rigging process you should begin with a simple **Low Poly Mesh** model. **Low Poly** means a mesh model with a minimum number of Vertices, Edges and Faces.

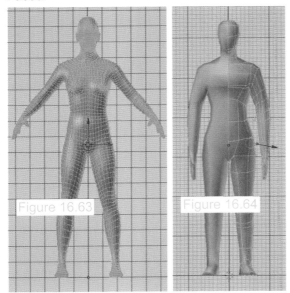

Figure 16.63 shows a model created using the **Make Human** program. As you see there is a vast difference in the number of vertices in the **Low Poly** model in Figure 16.64.

The **Low Poly** Model of a human as shown in Figure 16.65, supplied by **tweediez,** released under the Creative Commons Attribution 3.0.

In this exercise a Model named: **ChibiBase.blend** will be used

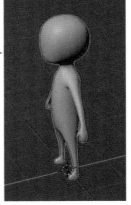

Figure 16.65

Rigging a Character Model is a reasonably intricate operation. This exercise is intended as an introduction which will allow you to understand detailed tutorials. The Rigging process, even at a basic level, requires patience, perseverance and attention to detail.

Before downloading the Model look at the following figures. They show examples of an Armature Rig and a pre-rigged Model.

Figure 16.66

Figure 16.67

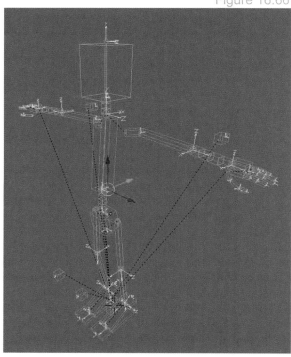

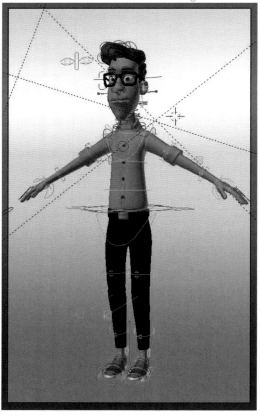

Figure 16.66 is a reasonably complex Armature Rig with the Viewport Display Type: **B-Bone**. The 3D Viewport Editor is in Solid Viewport Shading Mode with **Toggle X-Ray** engaged.

Figure 16.66 shows a fully rigged Model with Armature Controls made from various shaped Objects. This demonstrates that Armature Rigs are not limited to the Armature Display Types.

Download a Character Model

The Character Model to be used is named **Chibi**. To get this model go to the **Blend Swap** Website;

http://www.blendswap.com/

To download a model you have to register as a member. This means entering an email address and creating a user password and agreeing to the terms of use. If you don't do this you won't be able to download any of the fantastic **free models** available on the site.

Assuming that you have signed up, log in, then click on **Search** in the header at the top of the website home page. Select **Search** in **Blends** and enter **Chibi** in the Search Keywords bar. Click on **Search**.

The Model you are looking for is titled **CHIBI MODEL BASE**.

When you are logged in there will be a download link. The download is a ZIP file which you have to decompress to get the Blender file containing the model. Remember where you download to, and where you unzip to on your computer.

At this point it is assumed you have the file downloaded and unzipped.

The unzipped file is named **ChibiBase.blend** and will be located on your computer where you unzipped to.

Important: Although **ChibeBase.blend** is a Blender file with the **.blend** suffix and it will open in Blender, you may find anomalies when opening the file due to the version of Blender in which it was created. That being the case and since you are only seeking to obtain a model on which to work, it is better to Append the Mesh Model from the ChibiBase.blend file into a **new Blender file** opened in your version of Blender.

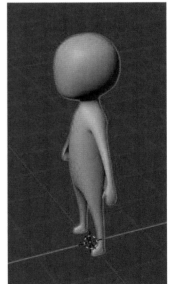

Figure 16.68

How to Append an element from one Blender file to another is described in Chapter 3 – 3.12.

To save you the frustration of reviewing that procedure, open a new Blender file. Delete the Cube Object then click on **File** in the Screen Header and click Append in the menu that displays. The File Browser Editor opens where you go find your ChibiBase.blend file.

Double Click on the file name in the File Browser to see the content of the file. Double Click on **Object** in the menu.

The Chibi model has probably been developed by modeling from the default Cube Object which appears in a new Blender file and the name hasn't been changed. In the Object folder **Chibi** is, therefore, seen as **Cube**.

Click on **Cube** in the folder menu, then click on **Append**.

Say hello to Chibi

Chibi is a humanoid character (Figure 22.68). Use your imagination to decide whether Chibi is a child or an alien or a little bow legged guy with a big head. Chibi can be whatever you decide.

With Chibi appended save the new Blender file a new name (Chibi.blend).

To proceed, it is assumed you have the new Chibi.blend file opened. Chibi displays with a red outline and there are no Object Properties in the Properties Editor. Click in the 3D Viewport Editor to deselect Chibi then click on the Chibi Model to select it. The outline will turn orange and Object Properties will display in the Properties Editor

You are good to go. **Have the 3D Viewport Editor in Front Orthographic View.**

Note: Chibi is a Mesh Model. . You may see a slight resemblance to the model created in Chapter 11–11.6. Chibi is a much nicer model.

Chibe has been created by **Magiclass** and released under the **CC Zero License**.

Note: When you Append a Mesh Model from one Blender file to another you also Append the Model's properties, such as, any Modifiers used in construction.

Prepare the Character Model

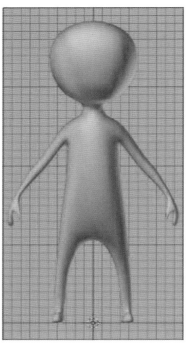

Figure 16.69

When you download a model or append from another Blender file, you should examine it before using. In examining **Chibi** you will see, in the **Properties Editor, Object Data Properties, Vertex Groups Tab**, that **Vertex Groups** have been generated. These are probably left over from a previous Blender operation. To begin with a clean slate, click on the minus button at the side of the list until **all groups** have been deleted.

Figure 16.70

Figure 16.71

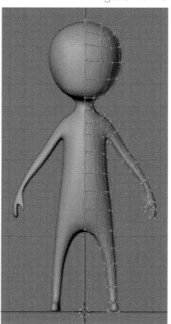

Take a closer look at Chibi. **Tab** into **Edit Mode**. You see that the model only has Vertices on the right hand side (your right, Chibie's left) (Figure 16.70). In the **Properties Editor, Modifier Properties** (Figure 16.71) you will see that a **Mirror Modifier** and a **Subserf** (Subdivision Surface) **Modifier** have been used when creating the model. The Mirror Modifier allows Vertex creation and manipulation on one side to be mirrored on the other side. Subserf makes the surface of the model appear smooth without increasing the Vertex count.

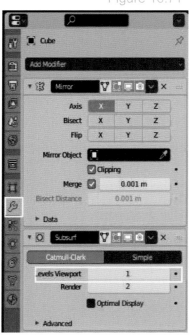

Add More Vertices

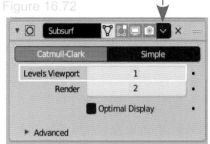

Click and select Apply

Figure 16.72

Actually, it will be better to have a few more Vertices when posing the figure so go into **Object Mode** and click **Apply** in the **Subserf Modifier** panel **(in Object Mode)**. You have to be in Object Mode to Apply a Modifier. Note: Before applying the Modifier that, in the Modifier panel, the **Levels Viewport value is 1** (Figure 16.72). This means that when the Modifier is applied, the mesh surface of the model will be subdivided once. In other words the Vertices will be doubled. In Edit Mode you will see there are more Vertices than before. You also want the model to have Vertices on both sides, so go back into **Object Mode** and apply the **Mirror Modifier** (click the Apply button) (Location Similar to Figure 16.72).

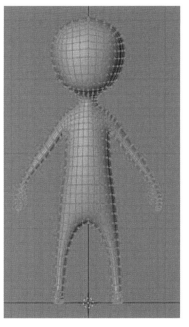

Figure 16.73

Figure 16.73 shows Chibi in Front Orthographic View with the Subserf Modifier and the Mirror Modifier applied.

Some Definitions

This chapter has been titled Character Rigging, therefore, what does Character Rigging mean?

A Character refers to a Model, in this case a model of a Humanoid Character. The model is a Mesh Model in that it is made up of a surface mesh constituting Vertices connected by Edges. There is nothing inside the mesh to begin with.

To pose the Mesh Model an Armature is constructed inside the mesh, specifically a Multi-bone Armature (single individual Bones connected together). The Armature may be considered as a skeleton for the Human Character.

Areas of the surface mesh are assigned (associated with or connected) to single Bones of the Armature or to multiple Bones.

Following the assignment of vertices to the bones the Bones will be manipulated (Translated or Rotated) to set the mesh in various poses or animated to move. When the bones move the surface mesh associated with the bones follow.

Remember: Armatures (Bones) are Non Renderable Objects, therefore, when an image or a video clip is rendered the Armature (Bones) are not included in the output.

The **Root Bone** is the starting point for creating the Armature and will act as the primary Control Bone for moving and manipulating the Model in the Scene.

With Chibi displayed as shown in Figure 16.73, **Tab to Object Mode** in **Front Orthographic View**. This presents the figure face on with the Object's center located on the center of the Scene mid way between the feet. The center of the Scene on the XZ Axis is located between the feet.

Figure 16.74

Make sure you have the 3D Viewport Editor Cursor located at the center of the Scene. Be in Object Mode with **everything deselected**. Press **Shift + S Key** to display the **Snap Pie Menu** (Figure 16.74) and select **Cursor to World Origin** .

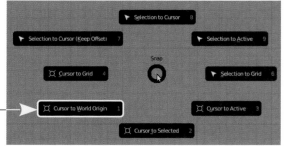

> **Tip:** Save the Blender file repeatedly at each stage of the exercise. If you get off track it will be frustrating to have to repeat the entire procedure.

With Chibi **deselected** add an **Armature** (by default a Single Bone). The Bone is entered at the location of the 3D Viewport Editor Cursor at the center of the Scene (Center of World Origin). This will be the **Root Bone**. With the Root Bone bone selected **Tab to Edit mode**. The Tip of the Bone will be selected as shown by the orange outline.

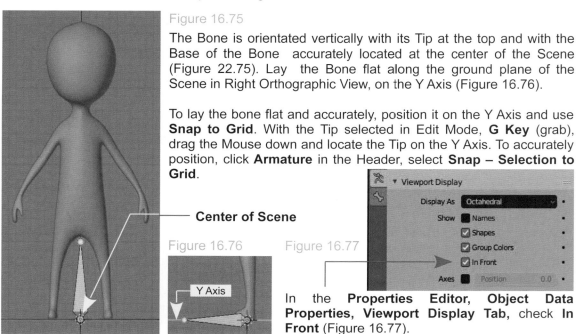

Figure 16.75

The Bone is orientated vertically with its Tip at the top and with the Base of the Bone accurately located at the center of the Scene (Figure 22.75). Lay the Bone flat along the ground plane of the Scene in Right Orthographic View, on the Y Axis (Figure 16.76).

To lay the bone flat and accurately, position it on the Y Axis and use **Snap to Grid**. With the Tip selected in Edit Mode, **G Key** (grab), drag the Mouse down and locate the Tip on the Y Axis. To accurately position, click **Armature** in the Header, select **Snap – Selection to Grid**.

Center of Scene

Figure 16.76

Y Axis

Figure 16.77

In the **Properties Editor, Object Data Properties, Viewport Display Tab,** check **In Front** (Figure 16.77).

Deselect the Tip of the Armature Bone and place the 3D View Editor in **Front Orthographic View** (Figure 16.77). Have the 3D Viewport Editor in **Edit Mode**. Additional Bones are to be added and you want them to be part of a Rig, that is, Parented to the Root Bone. The Root Bone and all additional Bones will be Parented forming a Rig assembly.

Adding More Bones
Figure 16.78

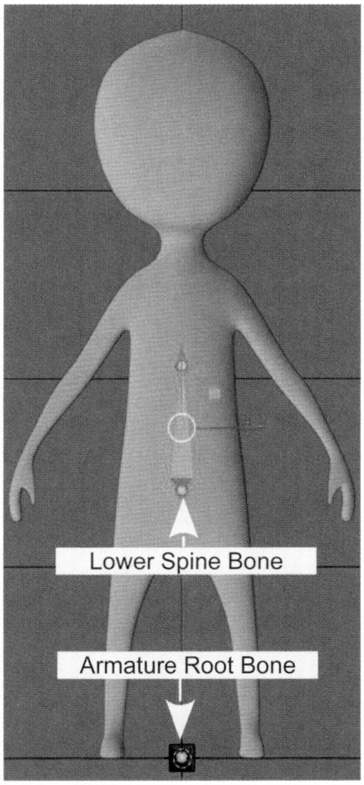

A second Bone will be added to the Rig. Select the **Body** of the **Armature_Root Bone** in **Edit mode** then press **Shift + D key (Duplicate)**. Drag the mouse and move the duplicated bone up to the pelvic area of the figure, rotate scale and position as shown in Figure 16.78 by selecting the Body of the Bone, or by selecting the Tip or the Base (in Edit Mode).

Remember: In the Properties Editor, Object Data buttons, Viewport Display tab (with the Bone selected) have **In Front** checked (ticked) so you can see the Bone inside the model.

The Base should be positioned approximately where the pelvis would be. Switch between Front Orthographic and Right Orthographic views to orientate the Bone. Consider this Bone to be the **Lower Spine Bone**.

The Armature_Root bone was **Duplicated in Edit Mode** to produce the Lower Spine because this second Bone has to be linked to the Armature_Root Bone and to be part of the Rig. **Duplicating in Object Mode would cause the new Bone to be an independent Armature not connected to the Rig.**

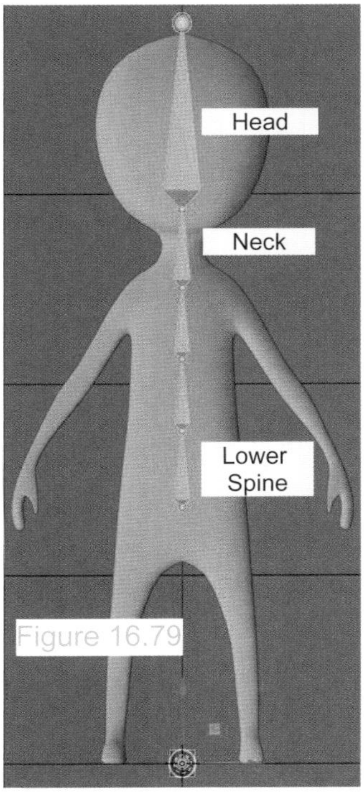

When selecting either Armature_Root or Lower Spine in Object Mode both Bones will be selected. In Object Mode you are selecting the entire Rig not individual Bones. To select individually you have to be in Edit Mode.

With the Lower Spine Bone **in Edit Mode** move the Tip down to where the belly button would be then extrude Bones to form the remainder of spine (Figure 16.79). With the Tip of Lower Spine selected, press E key then Z and drag the mouse to extrude a new Bone (E key – extrude, Z key confines the extrusion to the Z axis.).

Repeat the process for each new Bone in the spine. Right Orthographic view allows you to position Bones to shape the spine. In Front Orthographic view the Bones follow the centerline of the figure. For the Head Bone restrain the extrusion to the Z axis by pressing E key + Z key.

> **Note:** In positioning the Bones in Right Orthographic View it is not intended to replicate a human spine. Bones are placed to associate with parts of the Mesh model i.e. the Neck Bone will be linked to the Neck mesh. With Chibi, vertical Bones are fine.

Obviously there are many more Bones in a human spine than shown in the diagrams. In creating an Armature for animation it is good practice to minimise the number of Bones since this saves computer power in the animation process and simplifies the naming. The more Bones you have in a **Rig** the more flexible posing will be, therefore, you have to compromise.

Creating Arm Bones

Remember: Blender has the ability to mirror Bones to the opposite side of the model.

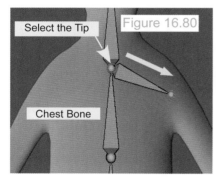

Select the Tip   Figure 16.80

Chest Bone

In **Edit Mode** select the Tip of the Chest Bone **in Front Orthographic view** and extrude a Shoulder Bone (Figure 16.80). Press the **N Key** for the **Properties Panel**, select **Tool** and check **X-Axis Mirror** in the panel.

> **Note:** There is no immediate effect in the 3D Viewport Editor.

When extruding a Bone the **Extrude Panel** displays in the lower RHS of the Screen. With X-Axis Mirror checked in Armature Properties, check **Forked** in the Extrude Panel (Figure 16.81) to duplicate the Bone on the opposite side of the Armature (Figure 16.82).

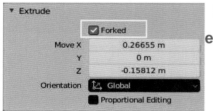

Figure 16.81

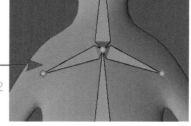

Shoulder Bone Duplicated

Figure 16.82

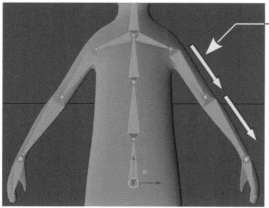

Figure 16.83   Figure 16.84

Extrude Arm Bones from the Tip of the Shoulder Bone. They will be produced on either side of the Armature (Figure 16.83).

When extruding Bones position the Tips at the appropriate joints in the Character Model, shoulder, elbow, wrist.

In Right Orthographic View select the Bone Tips and align the Bones

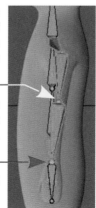

Creating Leg Bones

Figure 16.85

To add leg Bones for the figure repeat the process used for the arms, this time extruding from the Base of the Lower Spine Bone (Figure 16.85). **At the first extrusion check Forked in the Extrude Panel.**

When you come to the Ankle go to Right Orthographic View and extrude a Foot Bone and a Heel Bone (Figure 16.86).

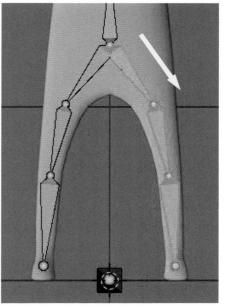

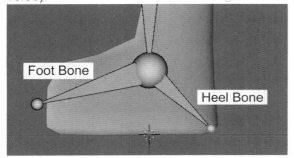

Foot – Right Orthographic View

Legs - Front Orthographic View

> **Note:** When positioning Bones, it is not intended to replicate a human skeleton. The individual Bones should be placed such that the Mesh Surface of the Model to be affected by a Bone is encapsulated in the Bone's Deform Envelope (Reference 22.11 Parenting with the Armature).

The Rig so Far

By comparing the Armature Rig so far with the introductory image (Figure 16.1) you will see where you are heading.

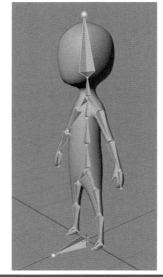

16.19 Bone Naming

In this relatively simple Armature. The individual Bones have been referred to as, Armature Root, Lower Spine, Neck, Head etc. but there is nothing in the View to specifically indicate which Bone is which. Naming Bones and giving the Bones meaningful names is very important, especially in a complicated Rig.

Figure 16.88

Blender automatically names Bones as they are extruded but the naming system provides names such as Bone, Bone.001, Bone.002 etc. and when Mirroring is involved, Bone.002_R and Bone.002_L. You see the names in the Outliner Editor.

Bone Names may be displayed in the 3D Viewport Editor by checking **Names** in the **Properties Editor, Object Data Properties, Viewport Display Tab** for the Armature (Figure 16.88). The default names are displayed adjacent to each Bone in the Armature in the **3D Viewport Editor** (Figure 16.89) and a hierarchy listing is shown in the **Outliner Editor** when in Edit Mode or Object Mode (Figures 16.90). **Note: The listing does NOT display in Pose Mode.**

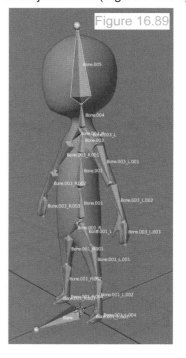

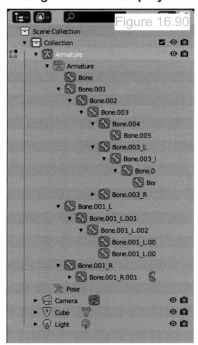

Individual Bones can be renamed by selecting a Bone in Edit Mode then editing the Bone name in the Properties Editor, Bone Properties .

Alternatively click on the name in the Outliner Editor (Figure 16.90) to select the Bone. Double click to edit the name.

16.20 Assigning the Mesh

At this point, although the **Armature Rig** is incomplete, you may assign it to the **Mesh Figure**.

This is the process of linking Vertex Groups (groups of vertices) on the figure's mesh surface to individual Bones. **Blender has an automated process for doing this**. The Bones will then control the posing (posturing) of the mesh.

Figures 16.89 and 16.90 show the Bone names in the 3D Viewport and in the Outliner Editors.

> In Figure 16.86 the 3D Viewport Editor is shown in Edit Mode. To see the full list of all the Bones in the Outliner Editor expand each entry.
>
> **Note:** Bones are named according to Chibi's Left and Right not your's.

Before engaging the automated mesh assigning process you need to exclude the **Root_Bone**. This bone is a **Control Bone** for moving the figure around in the Scene and is not a **Posing Bone**. Posing is the process of posturing the figure. In Figures 16.89 and 16.90 the Root Bone is named Bone. **Rename it to Root_Bone.**

In the 3D Viewport Editor in **Edit Mode** select **Root_Bone**. In the **Properties Editor, Bone Properties, Deform tab** click on the **Deform button** to remove the tick. This tells Blender that you do not want **Root_Bone** to be part of the deforming Rig.

In the **3D Viewport Editor** deselect the bone and change to **Object Mode**. Deselect the Armature Rig.

Assigning Mesh to Armature

Select Chibi (the Model) in Object Mode and if you haven't done so, in the Properties Editor, Modifiers buttons, click **Apply** in the Mirror and Subsef Modifiers to permanently assign the Modifiers. Both Modifiers will disappear from the Properties Editor.

Important: Before assigning the Mesh to the Armature make sure the individual Bones are positioned inside the parts of the Mesh. Check the Front and Right Orthographic Views.

With the **Mesh figure (Chibi)** selected **Shift** select the **Armature Rig** (LMB click the Figure, hold Shift, LMB click on the Armature protruding from the Head). With the mouse cursor in the 3D Viewport Editor press **Ctrl + P key** to display the **Set Parent To** menu and select the **With Automatic Weights** option.

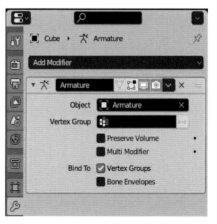

Figure 16.91

Note: In assigning Automatic Weights a new **Armature Modifier** is assigned to the Mesh Figure in the Properties Editor (Figure 16.91) (deselect and re select Chibi in Object Mode to see the Modifier).

Deselect the Mesh Figure and the Armature in the 3D Viewport Editor then select the Armature only. Go into **Pose mode** and select and rotate individual Bones to pose the figure (Figure 16.92) - Bones **Lower_Arm_L** and **Upper_Arm_L** are rotated).

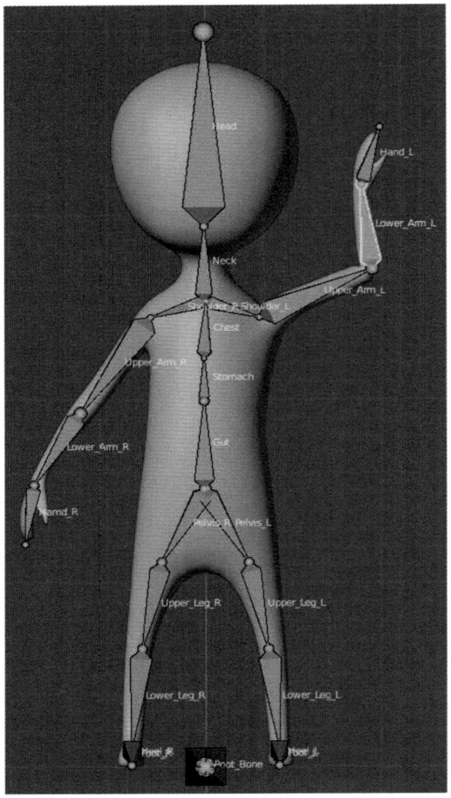

16.21 Vertex Groups

Figure 16.92

When you employ the automatic Mesh Assignment, two things occur:

An Armature Modifier is added to the Mesh (Figure 16.93) and Vertex Groups are created in the Mesh and assigned to each Bone in the Armature.

With the mesh selected in **Object Mode** go to the **Properties Editor, Object Data Properties, Vertex Groups Tab** and you will see the **Vertex Groups** (Figure 16.93) There is a scroll bar at the RHS of the Vertex Group panel or expand the panel).

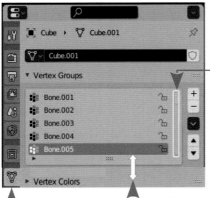

Figure 16.93

Scroll Bar

The Vertex Groups may be used for correcting incorrect Mesh Deformation. This is accomplished by selecting a **Vertex Group** and employing the **Weight Paint Tool** to clean up the connections between the Mesh and the Vertex Groups (refer to the section on Weight Painting).

Mouse over the Panel Edge and drag to expand the Panel.

Properties Editor, Object Data Properties

Note: After posing in **Pose mode,** Bones will be returned to their original positions (Reset), individually by selecting each bone or collectivly by selecting all Bones and pressing **Alt + R key** (Reset rotation) and **Alt + G key** (Reset Location - Resets Grab).

In a complicated Rig, as well as incorrect Mesh assignment, there may be Parenting issues which require addressing. Detailed tutorials provide instruction for correcting such issues but at this stage just be aware that automatic processes do not always provide perfect results.

16.22 Posing the Character Model

Posing a Model may be simply to give a character attitude when creating a still image but is mainly employed to create Keyframes in an animation sequence.

Even with a relatively simple Character Rig, posing individual Bones to create **Keyframes** can be a tedious process. There are semi automated procedures such as using an **Inverse Kinematics Constraint** (see 16.15) with a Hand or Foot such that when either is moved the Arms or Legs follow.

Figure 16.94

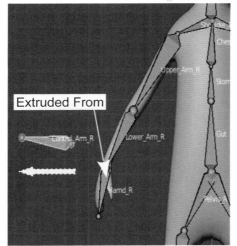

Extruded From

In Figure 16.94 a Control Bone has been extruded from the Tip of Lower_Arm_R. The Parenting has been cleared (Press ALT + P Key) and the Control Bone moved aside in Edit Mode. The Bone has been renamed **Control_Arm_R**.

Figures 16.95 shows an **Inverse Kinematic Constraint** applied to Lower_Arm_R **when in Pose Mode**. The Target in the Constraint is set as Armature with Bone set to Control_Arm_R.

Control_Arm_R has been renamed in the Outliner Editor.

The **Chain Length** in the Constraint is **2** making the Constraint effective only to Lower_Arm_R and Upper_Arm_R.

Figure 16.95

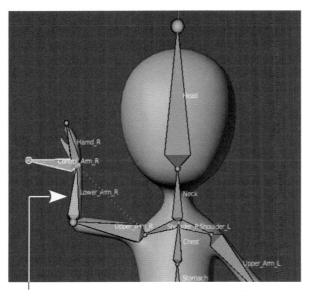

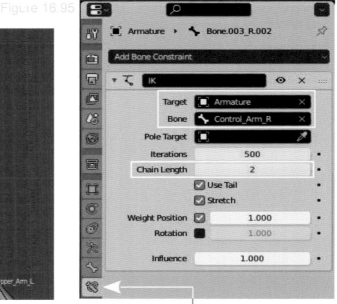

Lowe_Arm_R displays olive green indicating that a constraint has been applied.

Bone Constraints Properties
Do not confuse Bone Constraint Properties with Object Constraint Properties.

Selecting the Control Bone, **Control_Arm_R** in Pose Mode and Translating allows the left arm to be Posed. Control Bones would be generated for the right arm and the legs in the same manner and in fact for any portion of the Armature you wish to Pose.

Figure 16.96

Plane

Control Bones may be displayed as different individual shapes to distinguish from the Bones in the Armature. In the 3D Viewport Editor, create a shape from one of Blenders Primitives. Figure 16.96 shows a Plane Object reshaped. Park the Object to one side in the Scene.

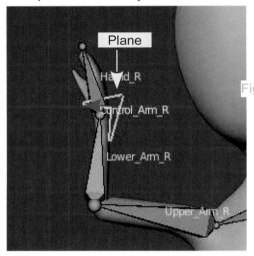

Figure 16.97

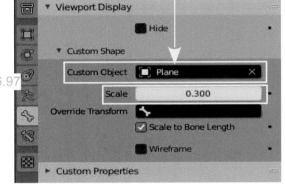

Select the Bone to be controlled then in **Pose Mode**, in the **Properties Editor, Bone Properties, Viewport Display Tab** enter the name of the new Object in the **Custom Object** panel. Adjust the Scale.

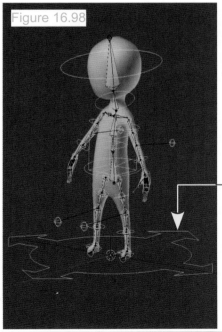

At the beginning of the chapter it was emphasised that the instructions were to be **an introduction** to Character Rigging only. The forgoing is intended to get you started and encourage you to research detailed tutorials. The following images depict how a Character Rig may be developed to provide detailed control of Posing.

Figure 16.98 shows Chibi with a myriad of Control Bones which are more precisely named Control Handles. Each handle allows Posing of separate parts of the Character Mesh.

The large Control Handle at the Base of the Character is developed from the Root_Bone and is used for moving the entire Rig in the Scene.

Using Control Handles the Character Figure is Posed at Frames in an animation creating Keyframes. This produces a Walk Cycle (Figure 16.99).

Figure 16.99

CONTACT RECOIL PASSING HIGH-POINT CONTACT RECOIL PASSING HIGH-POINT CONTACT

The Walk Cycle

With the Character Model animated to walk on the spot animating the Base Control Handle to follow a Path creates the illusion of the Character walking in the Scene.

Armatures may be generated to include intricate detail such as Chibi's hands. Control Handles can be created to manipulate fingers and thumb.

16.23 Pre-Assembled Armatures

To save you time Blender has several pre-assembled Armatures hidden in the **Preferences Editor** in the **Add-ons** Tab named **Rigging; Rigify**.

Figure 16.100

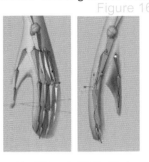

Hand Bones inside the Mesh

Bone Axis Displayed

Figure 16.101

With the **Rigging: Rigify** Add-on activated, with the 3D Cursor in the 3D Viewport Editor, Press **Shift + A Key** and select **Armature** in the **Add Menu.**

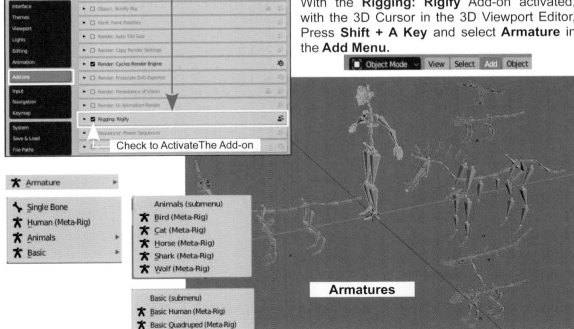

Armatures

17

3D Text

Introduction to 3D Text

3D text can be a very important element to add to a Scene. Think of all the television advertisements that contain text and how it is animated. There are two ways of adding text to a Scene in Blender. One way is to use the built-in text generator and the other is to use an external program.

Text made in Blender can be easily edited in the **Properties Editor**. Text made in an external on-line 3D text generating programs may give you additional options and different fonts.

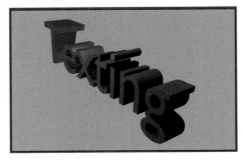

17.1 Creating 3D Text in Blender

To create Text in Blender, place the Scene in **Top Orthographic View** (Num Pad 7). Delete the Cube Object. Select the **Cursor Tool** in the Tool Panel and locate the **Editor Cursor** at the point in the Scene where you want your text to go. Press **Shift + A key** and select **Add - Text** (Figure 17.1). The word **Text** displays in the 3D Viewport Editor in **Object mode**. **Note:** Text only displays in Top Orthographic View.

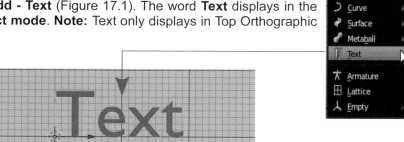

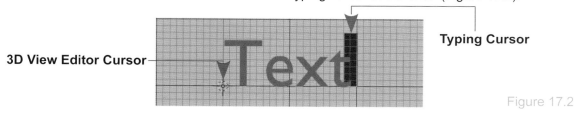

Figure 17.1

Tab into Edit mode—the word **Text** now has a Typing cursor at the end. (Figure 17.2).

Figure 17.2

Backspace to delete letters and type in your own words just like in a text editor. Don't worry about the font style or size at this stage. When you have typed in the words, tab back into Object Mode; to shape and color the text (Figure 17.3).

Figure 17.3

Edit Mode: The word Text has been modified by retyping.

Concept – Text in Blender

Typing Text in Blender is a little different to typing in a text editor program. When you Add Text in the 3D Viewport Editor, in Object Mode, the default word **Text** is an Object (a shape) similar to adding one of the Blender Primitives (Objects) such as a Cube, UV Sphere or Cone. When you entered Edit Mode, backspace and retyped a different word you modify the default Text Object. Besides modifying the letters in the text (the two dimensional shape of the characters) you can extrude thickness, bevel and round the shape. You can also add Material color, Texture and other effects. Modifying the text is done in the **Properties Editor**. Select the text in the 3D Viewport Editor, then go to the Properties Editor, Object Data Properties. Note: For Text the Data button is denoted by an a .

Text in the 3D Viewport Editor   Figure 17.4   **Properties Editor**

Note: The default Text Font (Style) is **Bfont Regular**.

Different Fonts may be used see 17.3 Fonts.

Object Data Properties
When Text is in the
3D Viewport Editor

Coloring Text   Figure 17.5

Since **Text is an Object**, you may apply **Material Color.** Remember; You will not see color in the 3D Viewport Editor when the Node System is active. Have the Properties Editor, Material Properties with Nodes deactivated.

Material Properties

17.2 The Object Data Properties "a"

The Geometry Tab has settings for shaping the text into a three dimensional Object. To see the effect of the different settings rotate the text about the X Axis of the Scene then rotate the 3D Viewport as shown below.

Figure 17.6

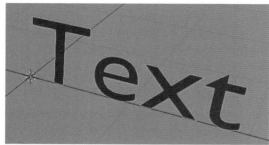

Text Rotated 90° on the X Axis.

3D Viewport Editor Rotated.
Press Num Pad 1 for Front Orthographic View,
Num Pad 6 x 2
Num Pad 8 x 2

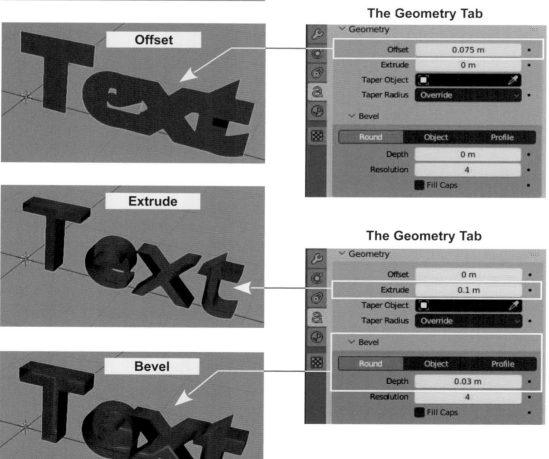

17.3 Fonts

The default **Font Style** is entered as **Bfont** as seen in the **Properties Editor, Object Data Properties, Font Tab**. **Bfont** is a **Vector Font for Text Objects** which is compiled into the Blender program and as such is not a standard font used in Windows or other operating systems. You can change the style to whatever font you have on your system. If you are using a Windows operating system, font styles can be found in **C:/Windows/Fonts.**

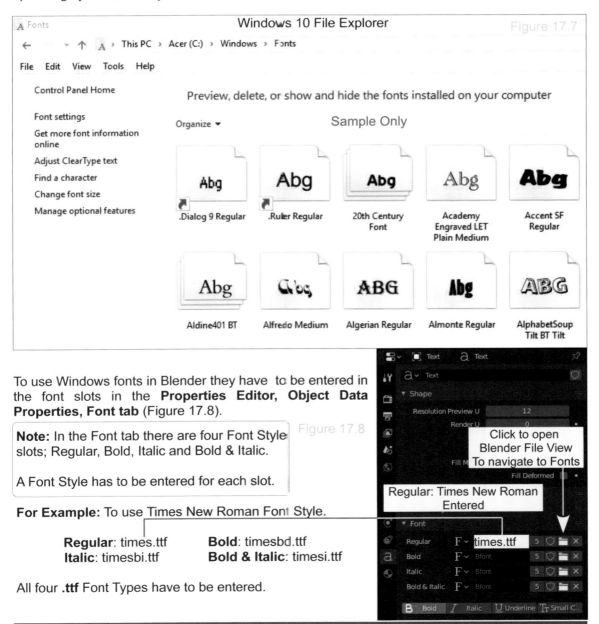

Figure 17.7

To use Windows fonts in Blender they have to be entered in the font slots in the **Properties Editor, Object Data Properties, Font tab** (Figure 17.8).

Note: In the Font tab there are four Font Style slots; Regular, Bold, Italic and Bold & Italic.

A Font Style has to be entered for each slot.

Figure 17.8

For Example: To use Times New Roman Font Style.

Regular: times.ttf   **Bold**: timesbd.ttf
Italic: timesbi.ttf   **Bold & Italic**: timesi.ttf

All four **.ttf** Font Types have to be entered.

To enter a Font Style click on the **Folder icon** (Figure 17.9).

Figure 17.9

Clicking the Folder icon opens **Blender's File Viewer** where you navigate and locate the Font style (Figure 17.10). On a Windows system go to: C:\Windows\Fonts\

Figure 17.10

Click to see Fonts as Thumbnail Images

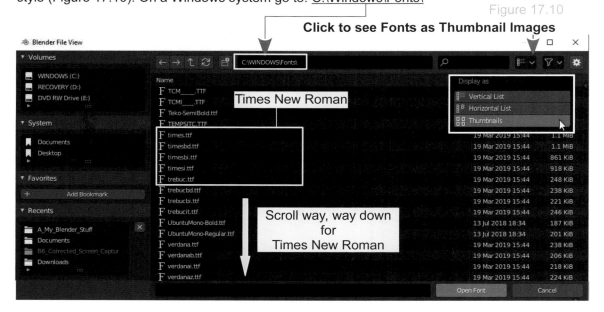

Note: Click in the Editor header to see the Fonts as Thumbnail Images.

Figure17.11

Blender will accept any of the Windows fonts, but some may be distorted when they are extruded into 3D shapes.

Having selected a font click on the **Open Font** button in the lower RH corner of the File Viewer. Do this for each font slot.

Note: you can mix and match different font styles and options. For instance you can have one font for regular text and a different font for bold or italic.

> **Note:** Entering Fonts in the Properties Editor, Fonts Object Data Properties, Font tab modifies the data for the particular Text Object you are working on in the 3D Viewport Editor (the object you have selected). It does not set the Font type for every time you add Text into the 3D Viewport Editor. When you add a new Text Object it will be the default Blender **Bfont**.

By default, typing will enter text in the 3D Viewport Editor in **Regular** text. To enter text in one of the alternative options (Bold, Italic, Underline, Small Caps) click one of the option **buttons** in the **Font Tab** (Figure 17.12). **Note: The options only display in Edit Mode.**

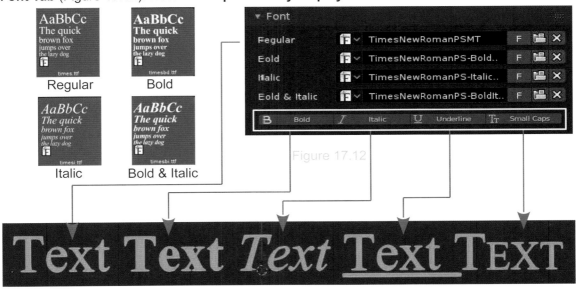

To change text that has already been entered, locate the **Text Cursor** (in Edit mode) **using the arrow keys** on the keyboard, press and hold shift while using the arrow keys to highlight text, delete the text then check one of the **Character buttons** to change the text option. Retype the text with the new option. Pressing **Ctrl + L or R arrow keys** moves the text cursor to the end of a word.

In the **Font tab**, the underline position and thickness values only operate when **Underline** is ticked under the **Character** heading. Underlining occurs as you type your text in Edit mode.

Also in the **Font Tab,** adjusting the Size and Shear value sliders increases the size of the selected Text object and shears the Text (similar to Italic – Figure 17.13).

Figure 17.13

17.4 Creating Text on a Curve

Text in Blender can be made to follow the shape of a Curved Path. Add text to your Scene as previously described then in Edit mode type something to extend the text (Figure 17.14).

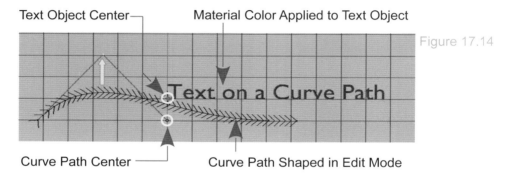

Text Object Center — Material Color Applied to Text Object

Figure 17.14

Curve Path Center — Curve Path Shaped in Edit Mode

Add a **Curve - Path** to the Scene (**Shift + A key – Curve – Path**). Note: By default the path is named **NurbsPath**.

The Curve Path is added to the Scene in Object Mode and appears as a straight line. Scale the Path to make it longer and reposition it in Object Mode.

Figure 17.15

In Edit Mode shape the Curve (Figure 6.14). With the Curve shaped tab back to Object mode and deselect it.

Select the Text Object then in the **Properties Editor, Data Properties, Font Tab**, find the **Text on Curve panel** under **Transform**. Click on the little cube icon and in the drop down menu that displays select **NurbsPath** (Figure 17.15).

The text is shaped to follow the profile of the curve (Figure 17.16).

Tip: After entering Nurbs Path in the Text on Curve panel, click on **Size** increment to activate the Text Curving.

Figure 17.16

17.5 Converting Text to a Mesh Object

There is only limited functionality in the text **Object Data Properties, Geometry tab** for modifying the text shape (see 17.1 Figure 17 4).

When you add Text to a Scene it remains a 2D Plane Object unless you have extruded the text in the Geometry tab. Entering Edit mode only allows you to retype a text change. To perform editing, which actually changes the detailed shape of the Text, you have to convert to a **Mesh Object**. To do this, select the text in **Object Mode** then in the **3D Viewport Editor Header** click **Object - Convert - Mesh**. Tab to Edit mode and you will see that the text is now a Mesh Object with vertices that can be moved, rotated, and scaled (Figure 17.17).

Object Mode with Text Extruded

Figure 17.17

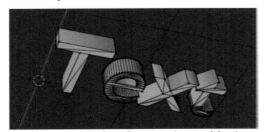

Edit Mode after Conversion to Mesh

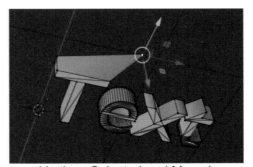

Vertices Selected and Moved

17.6 Converting Text to a Curve

If you would like to perform some fancy editing of a single letter, you can convert the letter into a Curve. The outline of the letter becomes a Curve with handles, which allows you to manipulate the shape into anything you wish.

Add **Text**, then in **Edit Mode** backspace until you are left with the single letter **T** . Tab to **Object Mode,** Scale, Rotate, and move it where you like then. In the **3D View Editor Header** click **Object**- **Convert – Curve** (Figure 17.18). In **Edit Mode** you will see the your letter with what appear to be Vertices. By placing the Mouse Cursor (White Cross) in proximity to a Vertex and clicking LMB you display Control Handles at that Vertex. Click LMB on one of the Control Points to select, G Key (Grab) and move to shape the Text profile (Figure 17.19). Note: In Edit Mode you may press A Key to select and show all the Control Handles then RMB Click and Subdivide creating additional handles.

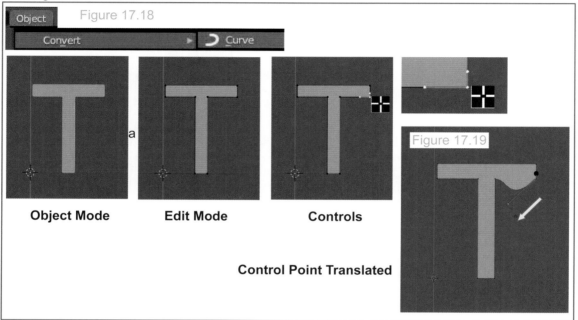

Figure 17.18

Object   Convert   ⊃ Curve

Object Mode   **Edit Mode**   **Controls**

Control Point Translated

Figure 17.19

17.7 Entering External Font

Text created in a Text Editor such as Word Pad or any editor that saves a file in .txt format may be entered into Blender.

For example a **Text File** named **Test_Text.txt** created in **Word Pad**, using **Font Style: Courier New size 36** saved in **MyDocuments** folder. The file contains the single word **Texting**.

To enter this in Blender, click **Add - Text** in the **3D Viewport Editor Header** (alternatively press **Shift + A key** and select **Text** from the menu.

Remember have the **3D Viewport in Top Orthographic** View.

Tab to **Edit mode** and backspace deleting the default word **Text**.

In the **3D View Editor Header** click on **Edit** and select **Past File** from the menu. The File Browser window opens where you navigate and find the saved .txt file (Figure 6.20 over).

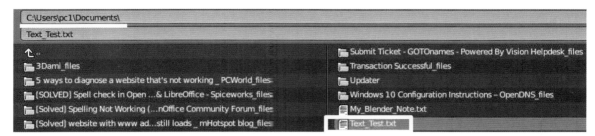

C:\Users\pc1\Documents\

Text_Test.txt

File Browser Window

Figure 17.20

Click on the file name to highlight then click on **Paste File** in the upper RH corner of the window.

The text **Texting** is entered into the 3D View Editor in Edit mode (Figure 17.21).

Figure 17.21

You may now convert the text to a **Mesh object** (see 17.5) or to a **Curve** (see 17.4).

Figure 17.22

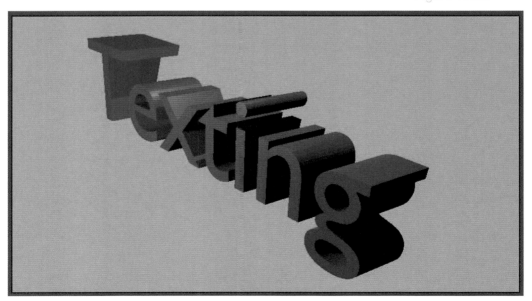

18

Making a Movie

Blender incorporates a complete Movie Making – Video Editing Workspace.

Making a Movie is performed in the **Video Sequence Editor** where you compile Video Sequences. The term **Movie** originated from Moving Pictures. Moving Pictures were originally made to entertain and tell stories and this has developed into modern Communication Systems. The basic concept however, which is, to communicate a story, remains .

Blender provides the tools which allow you to tell your story by using animated pictures (animations). You create Scenes in which actors move depicting events that you wish to communicate to an audience. The animated Scenes are recorded and **Rendered to Movie files**. The individual files are not necessarily produced in a sequence that tells the story, therefore, they need to be arranged in the correct sequence, hence the **Video Sequence Editor**.

Movies are made by piecing together short segments of video produced when you render animation sequences. Sound files and special effects are added to enhance the visual and audio presentation.

18.1 Making a Movie

Making a Movie in Blender will be demonstrated by producing a **Video Sequence** from a series of short animations which have been rendered to **Video Files** (Video Clips). The animations may have been created in separate Scenes in a single Blender file or in different Blender files. In either case the animations must be pre-rendered into **Video File Format** and be saved to a folder on your hard drive. The files should preferably be named or numbered in relation to a sequence of events which will tell your story.

18.2 Storyboard

A movie is a visual way of telling a story or communicating a message. To effectively piece together a movie you must have at least an idea of how you want to tell your story. In other words you should have a plan or sketch to use as a reference. The plan is called a **Storyboard**. It is easy to become immersed in the technical detail of the process and lose the plot.

In the this demonstration, a submarine on the surface of the ocean, dives underwater and conducts a torpedo attack. The story has been broken down into five parts. Submarine on surface, submarine dives, two underwater views and firing torpedoes. Each part has been animated in a separate Scene in the same Blender file then rendered to an **.AVI video file**.

The video files are all rendered from 250 Frame animations which when combined, equals a movie of 1250 Frames. The movie will be rendered for **PAL TV** which plays at 24 frames per second, therefore, the movie will play for approximately 52 seconds. It is a long way from being a feature film but will give you a basic idea of how a Movie is made.

To demonstrate the process of compiling a Movie work through the procedure as follows. The demonstration will combine the five video files and a sound file.

Sound file? Sound files can be background music, recorded voice, sound effects, in fact anything to enhance the video. For the purpose of the demonstration a sound file has been compiled in **.wav** format. As with video files there are many types of sound files. You are probably familiar with **MP3 and WAV** etc.

18.3 The Video Files

File Path to the Folder containing Video Files

> This PC > WINDOWS (C:) > A_Submarine_Movie > BDemo-Submarine

Figure 18.1

| 720x576 AVI | 720x576 AVI | 720x576 AVI | 720x576 AVI | 720x576 AVI |
| sub01.avi | sub02.avi | sub03.avi | sub04.avi | sub05.avi |

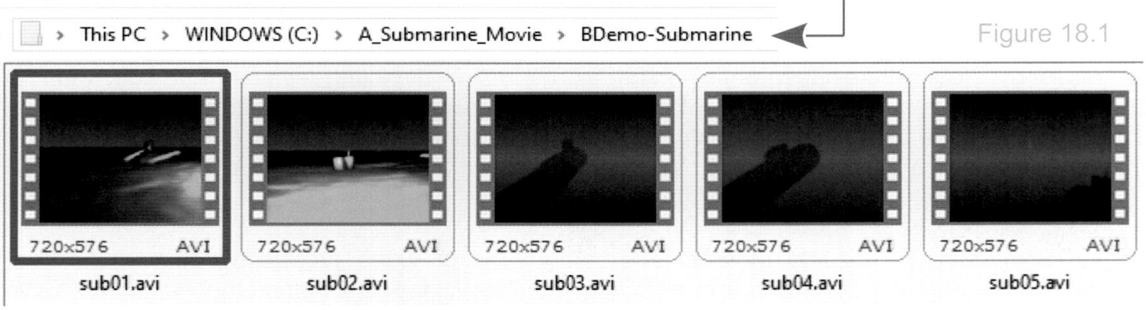

Five .avi Video Files saved in the Folder: **BDemo_Submarine**

18.4 The Sound File

For this demonstration a series of sounds, downloaded from **Free Sounds** at **www.freesound.org**, have been combined (Figure 18.2) using the free program **Audacity.**

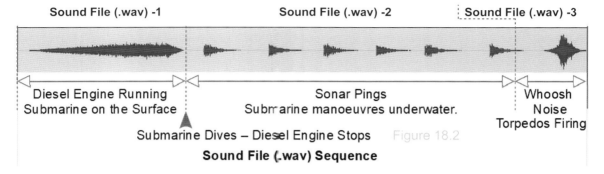

| Sound File (.wav) -1 | Sound File (.wav) -2 | Sound File (.wav) -3 |

Diesel Engine Running
Submarine on the Surface

Sonar Pings
Submarine manoeuvres underwater.

Whoosh
Noise
Torpedos Firing

Submarine Dives – Diesel Engine Stops   Figure 18.2

Sound File (.wav) Sequence

18.5 Video Editing Workspace

Video assembly is performed in the **Video Editing Workspace** hidden away. In the Screen Header. Click on **File**, then **New** and select **Video Editing** (Figure 18.3).

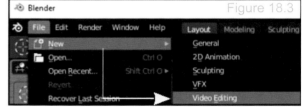

The **Video Editing Workspace** (Figure 18.4).

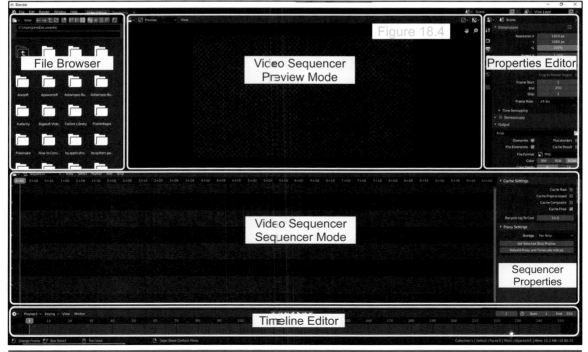

Figure 18.4

VSE Editors and Panels

File Browser Editor: Where you navigate and select files.
VSE Preview Mode: Where you see the video playback.
Properties Editor: Controls relevant to the VSE.
VSE Sequencer Mode: Where you combine Video Files (clips).
Timeline Editor: Provides control of how the video sequence plays.
Sequencer Properties: Video Channel Properties (With the Mouse Cursor in the VSE Sequencer Mode. press the **N Key** to toggle Hide and Display) .

In this basic instruction you will be concerned with the **File Browser Editor** and the **two versions of the Video Sequencer.**

Figure 18.5

File Browser
Default Folder Display

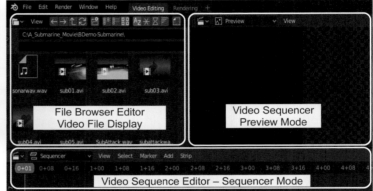

18.6 File Browser Editor

Figure 18.6

File Browser Header

The **File Browser Editor** was discussed in Chapter 3 – 3.5 but a point to remember is, the Editor will show files in a variety of ways.

The default display in the Video Editing Workspace shows thumbnail images of a series of Folders. When you navigate to the B_Demo_Submarine Folder the first Frame in each video file is displayed. You can change this to display the file names if you wish. Click on the button shown in the diagram (Figure 18.6).

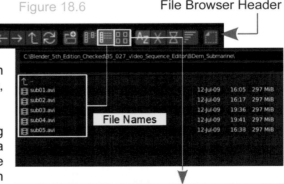

18.7 Preparation

File Definition: In this demonstration the five **.avi files** saved to the hard drive will be referred to as **Video Files**. When combined, the final output will be called, the **Movie File**.

Before attacking the **Video Sequence Editor** some preparation, which is required, must be performed. The first step in the movie making process is to set the file path to the location where you want your **Movie File** saved and to define the **Video Output Format**.

Set the File Path for Saving

By default, Blender sets the file path for saving files to the **tmp** (temporary) folder on your hard drive. This can be seen in the **Properties Editor, Output Properties, Output tab** (Figure 18.7).

You change this setting by clicking on the **Browse Folder** button (Figure 18.3) and navigating to a new folder in the **File Browser Editor**. Select the folder then click on the **Accept button** at the top right hand side. For convenience and simplicity create a new folder. In this demonstration the folder is named **A_Submarine_Movie** and the file path to the folder is: **C:\ A_Submarine_Movie** (Figure 18.8).

Note: Properties Options Curtailed

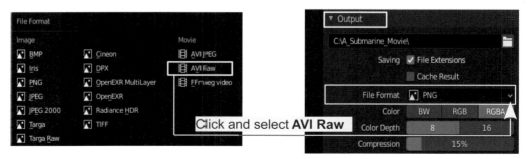

Figure 18.7

Figure 18.8

Set the Video Format

Set the Movie Video output format. To demonstrate the movie making process the **AVI Raw** codec (.avi) will be used from the **Movie** list in the **Properties Editor, Output Properties, Output Tab** selection menu (Figure 18.9).

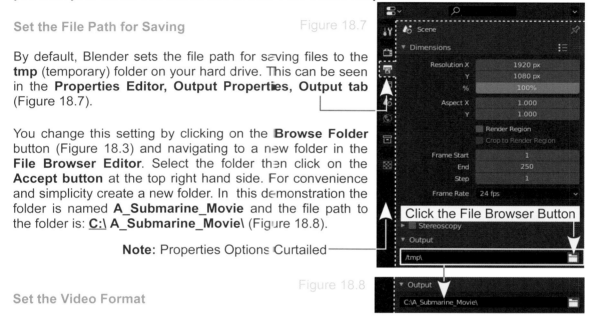

Figure 18.9

Since the **Video Files** (clips) being compiled into a **Movie File** are also **.avi file format** you are, in fact, simply assembling the files into a single file. If you select either the AVI JPEG or FFmpeg video options then the output after assembling would undergo a conversion.

18.8 Video Sequence Editor

VSE Preview superimposed in the **VSE Sequencer**

Figure 18.10

The main panel in the **Video Sequence Editor (VSE)** is divided into Channels (horizontal strips), numbered at the left hand side. In Figure 18.10 a Video File named **sub01.avi** has been entered in **Channel 1**. A preview panel has been superimposed in the diagram showing the first Frame of the animation. When a Video File is entered in the Video Sequence Editor the first Frame of the animation displays in the Video Sequencer Preview.

Placing Files in the VSE

To enter a Video File in the VSE, click the file thumbnail in the File Browser, hold and drag into the VSE. By default the first file entered is placed in **Channel 2**.   Figure 18.11

With the Video File entered in the VSE properties and controls are displayed on the VSE Properties Panel, Strip Tab, at the RHS of the VSE.

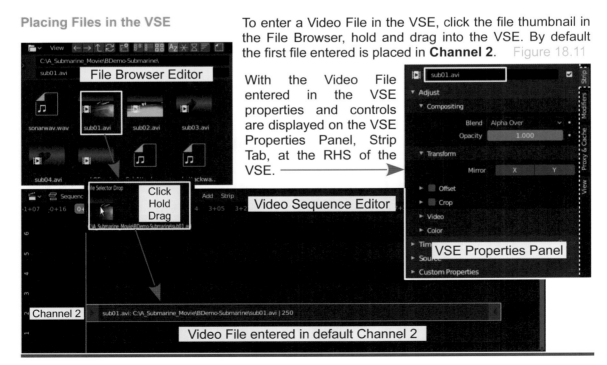

Placing Files in the VSE (Alternative Method)

Various types of files may be entered in the VSE and combined with video files. Click on **Add** in the VSE Header (Figure 18.12) and select what you wish to enter (the File Browser Editor opens). In this instance you are entering a Video File, therefore, select **Movie**. Navigate to the folder containing your Video Files and select a file. Click Add Movie Strip (upper RH corner of Screen). This is an alternative to the method previously described. By default the File is entered in **Channel 2**. Note: By default the VSE Editor Cursor is located at position 0+01 in the **Playback Timeline** along the bottom of the VSE. When Files are entered in the VSE they are located at the position of the Cursor.

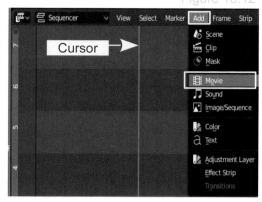

Figure 18.12

Viewing the Video File

To see Video Files in action click the Play button in the Timeline Editor at the bottom of the Screen. You may also click, hold and drag the VSE Cursor to scrub through the Video Files.

Video Files in upper Channels take precedence and play over lower Channels.

Selecting in the VSE

You select a File in a Channel by clicking LMB. Hold and drag R or L to reposition. LMB click on a file, hold and drag up or down to place the file in a different Channel.

Note: When repositioning horizontally, click LMB, hold and drag then you may release MB. When positioning horizontally you will see a Frame Number appear at the beginning and end of the Video File giving you the exact location in the Timeline.

Figure 18.13

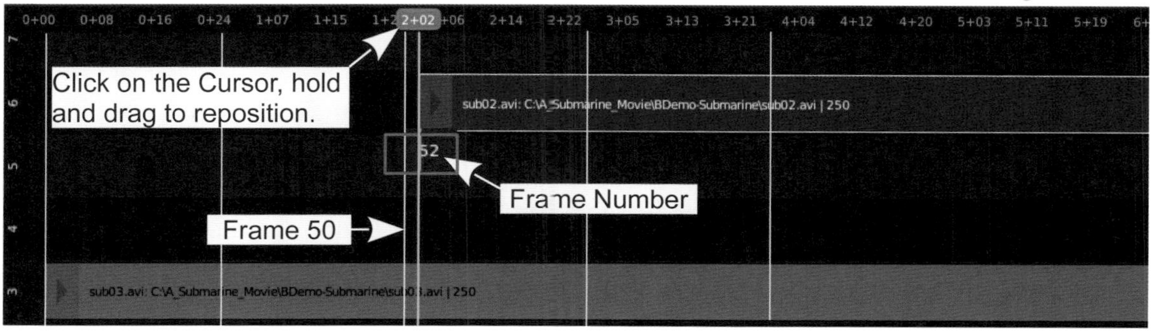

Click on the Cursor, hold and drag to reposition.

Frame Number

Frame 50

Note: The Cursor is positioned at Frame 2 + 02 (see Timeline Graduations / Positions following.

Timeline Graduations / Positions

Example: File named sub02.avi is positioned at Frame 52. In the Timeline the position is given as 2+02. The horizontal divisions (faint vertical lines) are located at:

0+00 = Frame 0.00   1+00 = Frame 25   2+00 = Frame 50

(25 Frame Divisions)

Frame 52, is therefore 2 + 02

$(2 \times 25) + 2 = 52$

Erasing (Deleting) a File

LMB click on the File in the VSE (border highlights white), press the **X Key** or press Delete or RMB click and select delete.

The Add Button   Figure 18.14

The **Add button** in the **VSE Panel** header has several options.

Scene: Adds a strip containing information about a Scene in the Blender file.

Mask: If a mask has been created it can be added to the VSE to hide or alter the appearance of parts of the video.

Image: A still image or a series of images may be inserted into the video much like adding individual frames of an animation or a slide show.

Sound: Sound files can be inserted in the VSE to enhance video.

Effects Strip: Effects to provide enhancement, background and transition

With the forgoing information you are in a position to proceed and compile the Movie File.

Adding Video Files

When adding Video Files it is helpful to scale and pan the VSE Editor. This allows you to get a bigger picture of your assembly. With the Mouse Cursor in the VSE Editor you can zoom in and out by pressing the Plus and Minus keys on the keyboard or by scrolling MMB.

At the bottom of the VSE Sequencer is a gray bar with dots at each end. Lick on the bar, hold and drag left or right to pan the display in the VSE. Click hold and drag the dots at either end to scale the VSE view horizontally. A similar vertical pan and scale bar is at the RHS of the VSE.

Figure 18.15

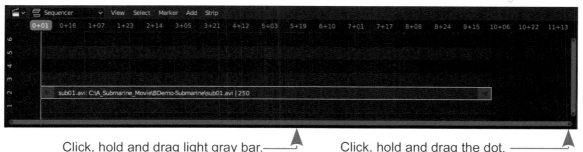

Click, hold and drag light gray bar. ⟶   Click, hold and drag the dot. ⟶

As you have seen you add Movie Files by clicking, holding and dragging from the File Browser Editor or clicking **Add** in the **VSE Editor header** (Press Add – Movie – navigate in the **File Browser window** – select etc.).

The first file is entered by default in Channe 2 with the VSE cursor located at 0+01. To add a second file, position the cursor where you want it to start and repeat the Add process. A second file is entered in Channel 3. The files can be moved to different channels as you wish and repositioned horizontally.

> **Note:** If the **VSE Cursor** is placed at the end of the first Movie File the second file will be placed in the same Channel as the first, end to end.

Each successive file addition is entered in the Channel above the preceding Channel except when the VSE Cursor is positioned at the end of the preceding file. To have two Movie Files play end to end as a continuous sequence, position the start of the second file horizontally at the end of the first file (they do not have to be in the same Channel). With the second file selected, press the **G Key** and drag the Mouse. You will see Frame Numbers display at the beginning and end of each file which makes it easy to align exact Frames. You can purposely overlap files since a file in a higher Channel will take precedence over a file in a lower Channel when playing.

Playing the Video File

No matter where the file is located you can view different Frames in the file by dragging the Cursor along the Timeline. You play the file by pressing the **Start button** in the **Timeline Editor**. Press **Esc** to quit or Pause, Fast Forward etc. by using the play controls.

To mention some more obvious information about playing consider this; the Video Files used in the demonstration are 250 Frames long. With the first located with the **Start Frame** at 0+01 it will play in its entirety then repeat until you press **Esc**. This only occurs since, in the **Timeline Editor**, **Start: 1** and **End: 250** are set. If **End: 100** was set the file would only play for 100 Frames then repeat, or if the start Frame of the file was positioned on the VSE Timeline other than at Frame 1 then only part of the file will play. (see Figure 18.16) over.

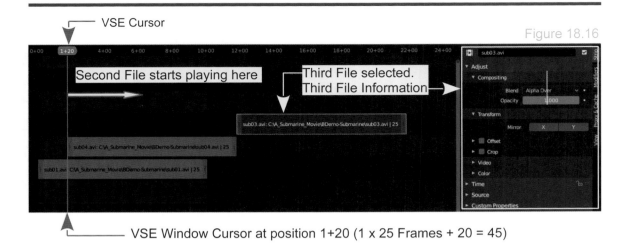

VSE Cursor

Figure 18.16

Second File starts playing here

Third File selected.
Third File Information

VSE Window Cursor at position 1+20 (1 x 25 Frames + 20 = 45)

Cutting Video Strips

A Video File in the VSE is also referred to as a **Video Strip**. Another feature of the VSE is the ability to select only part of a video strip for playback. You can cut the strip into segments. There are two ways to do this which are; a **Soft Cut** and a **Hard Cut**. In either case, position the Cursor at the Frame where you wish to make the cut. For a **Soft Cut** press the **K Key**.

For a **Hard Cut** press **Shift + K key**. In either case you finish up with two separate segments of strip which you can reposition or move to a different Channel in the VSE. The difference is, with a **Soft Cut** both segments of the strip retain the data for the other part. With a **Hard Cut** the data is not retained (Figure 18.17).

Figure 18.17

Note: When Cut, File: sub01.avi divides into sub1.ave + sub001.avi

Adding Sound Files

Sound files such as MP3 and WAVE are entered by selecting **Sound** in the **Add button menu** instead of **Movie** and then manipulating the same as a Video File.

With all your strips aligned and edited you can press the **Play button** in the **Timeline Editor** to preview the final movie.

18.9 Rendering the Movie File

When all the specifications have been set for your Movie Output File it is time to render the final movie.

Figure 18.18

In the **Screen Header** click the **Render button** and select **Render Animation**. Be prepared to wait a considerable time. Even a short movie will take awhile depending on the speed of your computer. Long movie sequences are often uploaded to websites called **Render Farms** which will perform the render process for you (at a cost). Once the render is complete you find the file in the output folder and give it a test run in a media player.

18.10 Additional Features

Additional features for enhancing and modifying video strips are accomplished by adding features from the VSE Header Add button menu or by the application of Strip Modifiers in the VSE Properties Panel.

Generally adding a feature from the Header inserts a special Feature Strip in the VSE in addition to the Video Files entered, while the application of a Modifier affects the selected Video Strip in the VSE.

Example 1: No Features Applied

Figure 18.19

Preview with Strip in VSE and default settings in the VSE Properties. **No additional features.**

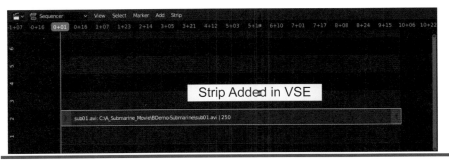

Example 2: Add Coler Feature

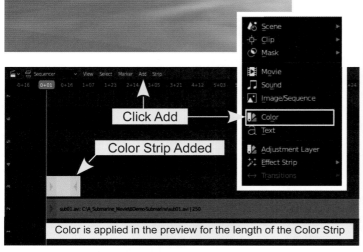

Figure 18.20

Click **Add** in the VSE Header and select **Color** in the menu. A Color Strip is added in the VSE Editor and controls display in the VSE Properties Panel in the Strip Tab.

Select a Color and reduce **Opacity**.

Example 3: Apply Color Modifier

Figure 18.21

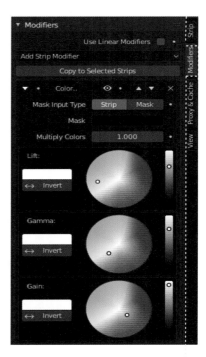

Select a Strip in the VSE. In the VSE Properties, Modifiers Tab click Add Strip Modifier. In this case select Color. Alter the values in the tri color pickers to adjust the preview display. Color is applied permanently for the whole Strip.

Note: The Strip must be selected in the VSE.

Example 4: Inserting Text Captions

Examples 2 and 3 were concerned with affecting the Preview Color Tones.

Captions may be inserted in a Strip to display a Title, credits etc.

Select a Strip in the VSE. In the VSE Sequencer Header click on **Add** and select **Text** from the menu that displays.

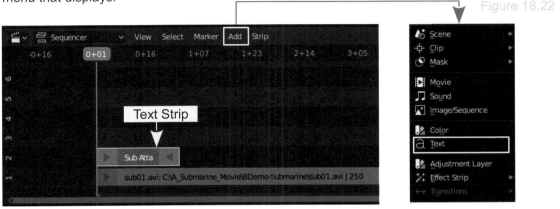

Figure 18.22

Selecting **Text** in the menu inserts the small white word **Text** at the bottom of the video display in the VSE Preview. A **Text Strip** is added in a Strip at the **position of the VSE Cursor**. In the **VSE Properties Panel** at the RHS of the VSE is the **Strip Tab** with controls for modifying the Text.

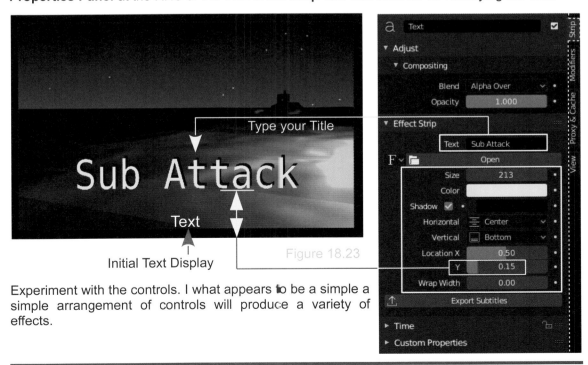

Figure 18.23

Experiment with the controls. I what appears to be a simple a simple arrangement of controls will produce a variety of effects.

19

The Outliner and Collections

The Outliner Editor

The **Outliner Editor** provides a visual display in the form of a **File Tree** showing everything in the Scene in the **3D Viewport Editor**. Each Object is listed showing its relationship to other Objects such as whether it is joined to another Object or has a Child Parent Relationship or whether it has Material or Texture applied. This information is the **Object's Data** which may be displayed in different configurations depending on the function being performed.

Collections

The File Tree in the **Outliner Editor** may be customised allowing Objects in the 3D Viewport Editor to be arranged in groups called **Collections**. Collections may be added and named and arranged in a hierarchy much the same as the folders on an operating system. Objects in the 3D Viewport Editor may be selected and deselected in the Outliner Editor or hidden from view in the 3D Viewport Editor by turning a Collection's visibility off. This assists when working on Objects in a complicated Scene.

19.1 Collections in The Outliner Editor

Outliner Editor (default display)

The **Outliner Editor** (upper RHS of the Screen) provides a visual display, in the form of a file tree, of everything in your Scene and shows how the different items are related (Figure 19.1).

Click LMB to expand the Collection File Tree.

The Scene in the default 3D Viewport Editor contains a Camera, a Cube and a Light.

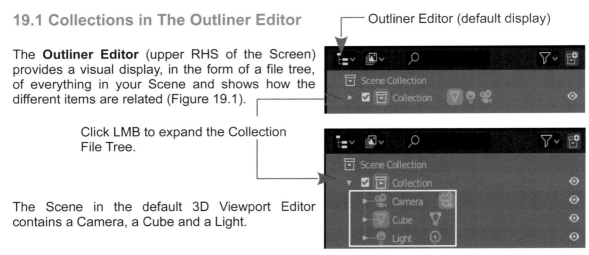

Figure 19.1

To understand how Collections operate work through the following procedure.

Start with the default Blender Screen showing the four default Editors. The **Outliner Editor** is displayed in the upper right hand corner of the Screen (Figure 19.1).

The **Outliner Editor** contains information about the current Scene in the default 3D Viewport Editor. If, under **Scene Collection,** the single entry **Collection** displays. Click on the **expansion icon** preceding Collection to expand the File Tree showing a list of Objects in the current Scene in the 3D View Editor.

Expansion Icon ▶

The 3D Viewport Editor contains three Objects: a Cube, a Camera and a Light. The three Objects are grouped together and placed in the Collection named **Collection**.

Click on the expansion icon at the beginning of the line where you see **Collection** to show the Camera, Cube and Light listed. Note that in front of each Object there is also an expansion icon. You click on each icon to display data belonging to the Objects.

Clicking the expansion icon in front of Cube reveals; **Cube** (the data creating the display of the Cube in the 3D Viewport Editor), Clicking on the next expansion icon reveals **Material** (the data producing the gray color of the Cube). Each line represents a **Datablock** (block of data) producing the display in the 3D Viewport Editor.

Figure 19.2

Blue highlight indicates that the Cube Object is selected in the 3D Viewport.

Data Displaying the Cube ─────────── ▶ Cube ⊙

▼ Cube

Data Displaying the Material (color) ─────── Material

Adding Objects

Clicking LMB on the Collection name selects the Collection (highlighted blue).

When you add a new Object to the Scene in the 3D Viewport it is automatically added to the Collection that is selected, in this case **Collection**.

Add a UV Sphere Object to the Scene followed by an Icosphere Object.

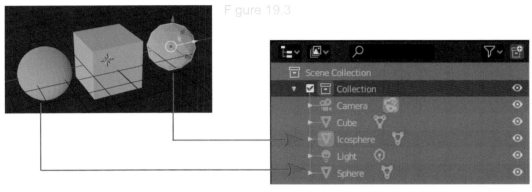

F gure 19.3

You immediately see **Icosphere** and **Sphere** added to **Collection**. Note that they are placed in the list alphabetically.

Adding Collections

As the Scene is developed, with Objects be ng added, it can be advantageous to create new Collections, grouping Objects together. You add (create) new Collections by clicking the **New Collection** button in the Outliner Editor Header.

The New Collection Button

Where Collections are added depends cn the location you select before adding. If you select **Collection** in the Outliner Editor a new Collection will be added as a sub entry under Collection . The sub entry will be named Collection 1. If you select (highlight) **Scene Collection** before adding the new Collection it will be added as a sub Co lection named Collection 2. Selecting **Collection 1** and adding a new Collection produces **Collection 1.1**

Note the Collection Names: New Collection 2 under Scene Collection and new Collection 1.1 under Collection 1.

Figure 19.4

You may rename Collection to something meaningful by double clicking on the Collection Name.

Deleting Collections

In the Outliner Editor you select the Collection name (highlights blue) and press delete to remove the Collection.

Be aware that deleting a Collection in the Outliner Editor does not delete Objects in that Collection. When you delete a Collection, Objects in the Collection are automatacially transfered to the preceding Collection in the heirachy.

Deleting Objects

You may select Objects in the Outliner Editor then RMB click and select delete in the menu to remove the Object from the 3D Viewport Editor. Deleting a Collection in the Outliner Editor transfers all Ojects in the Collection to the preceding Collection in the hierarchy.

Hiding and Restricting Object Display and Selection

Objects in the 3D Viewport can be controlled in the Outliner Editor.

Click the Eye Icon to Hide the Object from View in the 3D View Editor

Figure 19.5

By default only the Eye Icon is displayed.

Additional controls may be added to the Outliner Editor from the **Filter Menu.**

All **Restriction Toggles** Activated

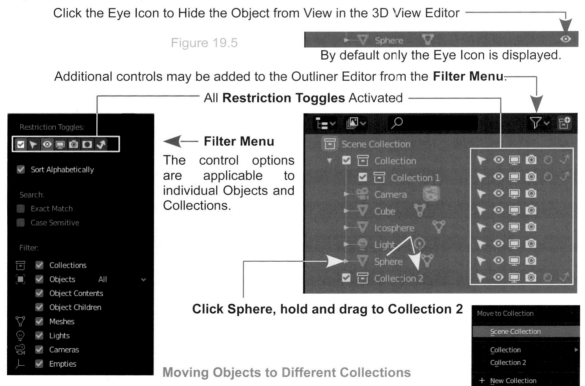

◄── Filter Menu

The control options are applicable to individual Objects and Collections.

Click Sphere, hold and drag to Collection 2

Moving Objects to Different Collections

Objects listed under a Collection in the Outliner Editor may be moved to a different Collection by simply clicking on the Object name (LMB), holding, dragging and releasing the mouse button with the Mouse Cursor positioned over the new Collection name. Alternativly press the **M Key** to display the **Move menu. Collections may be repositioned in a similar manner**.

19.2 View Options in the Outliner Editor

View Layer is the default display in the Outliner Editor which includes Collections.

Figure 19 6

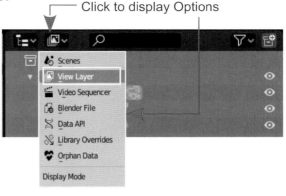

Click to display Options

Alternative options are accessed in the Editor Header. The alternatives display information about the Scene in the 3D Viewport Editor and the current Blender File.

Scenes

Sequence

Blender File

Data API   Figure 19.7

Orphan Data

As Scenes are developed the data contained in a Blender file increases accordingly. The display options in the Outliner Editor provide a record of the data and allow it to be organised.

Index